CHINA

A World Bank Country Economic Report

This report is supplemented by six annex volumes published by the World Bank:

1 China: Issues and Prospects in Education
2 China: Agriculture to the Year 2000
3 China: The Energy Sector
4 China: Economic Model and Projections
5 China: Economic Structure in International Perspective
6 China: The Transport Sector

In addition, nine background papers, numbered here as they are referred to in the text, have been prepared in connection with the report. They are available as World Bank staff working papers.

1 The Asian Experience in Rural Nonagricultural Development and Its Relevance for China (Staff Working Paper 757)
2 International Experience in Urbanization and Its Relevance for China (Staff Working Paper 758)
3 Alternative International Economic Strategies and Their Relevance for China (Staff Working Paper 759)
4 International Experience in Budgetary Trends during Economic Development and Their Relevance for China (Staff Working Paper 760)
5 Productivity Growth and Technological Change in Chinese Industry (Staff Working Paper 761)
6 Issues in the Technological Development of China's Electronics Sector (Staff Working Paper 762)
7 The Environment for Technological Change in Centrally Planned Economies (Staff Working Paper 718)
8 Managing Technological Development: Lessons from the Newly Industrializing Countries (Staff Working Paper 717)
9 Growth and Structural Change in Large Low-Income Countries (Staff Working Paper 763)

These supplementary works may be ordered, by annex or working paper number, from local distributors of World Bank publications and from the World Bank Publications Sales Unit, 1818 H Street, N.W., Washington, D.C. 20433, U.S.A.

CHINA

Long-Term Development Issues and Options

The report of a mission sent to China by The World Bank

Edwin Lim
Chief of mission

Adrian Wood
Deputy chief of mission

Contributing authors

Ian Porter
William Byrd
Timothy King
Gerhard Pohl

Robert P. Taylor
Gene Tidrick
Wouter Tims

Published for The World Bank
The Johns Hopkins University Press
Baltimore and London

The Johns Hopkins University Press
Baltimore, Maryland 21218, U.S.A.

Library of Congress Cataloging in Publication Data

Main entry under title:

China, long-term development issues and options.

  "A World Bank country economic report."
  1. China—Economic policy—1976– . 2. China—
Social policy. I. Lim, Edwin. II. International Bank
for Reconstruction and Development.
HC427.92.C46452 1985   338.51   85–22777
ISBN 0-8018-3313-2
ISBN 0-8018-3314-0 (pbk.)

Cover photograph by Curt S. Carnemark:
Family outing at Tiananmen Square, Beijing

Foreword

The idea for this study originated during my visit to China in 1983. In Beijing, I had the opportunity to meet with Chairman Deng Xiaoping and Premier Zhao Ziyang. Through discussion with them and with other distinguished Chinese leaders, I learned a great deal about the Government's perspective on development and the long-term goals for the country. We talked about the national aim to raise China's annual per capita income to US$800 by the year 2000, and we contemplated some of the exciting possibilities and complex questions that China would encounter in the process of reform and modernization. Out of these discussions in Beijing came the agreement that the World Bank would undertake a study of some of the key development issues that China might face in the next twenty years. In particular, this study would examine, in light of international experience, some of the options for addressing these issues.

This report summarizes the conclusions of that study. It is based primarily on the findings of an economic mission led by Edwin Lim and Adrian Wood, which visited China in early 1984. It was presented to the Board of Executive Directors, which represents the 148 member governments of the World Bank, in May 1985.

This report, in my view, is a good example of one of the many ways that the World Bank can assist its member countries. Indeed, China's ambitious attempt to modernize and reform its economy will shape the future of not only the Chinese people but also people throughout the world. We hope that this report will be a useful contribution to the debate in China about some of the important issues of economic and social development.

A. W. Clausen
President
The World Bank

September 6, 1985

Contents

SUMMARY AND CONCLUSIONS 1
Pattern of Growth 1
Managing the Economy 8
Social Issues and Policies 16
Overview 19

1 GROWTH AND CHANGE 21
Objectives 21
Macroeconomic Change 22
Microeconomic Change 26
Inequality 29

2 ILLUSTRATIVE PROJECTIONS 32
Description of the Model 32
Three Alternative Projections 33
Growth and Demand 36
Production and Investment 38
Employment and Income 40
Projections and Predictions 43

3 AGRICULTURAL PROSPECTS AND POLICIES 44
Production Possibilities 44
Potential Demand-Supply Imbalances 45
Changing Food Demand 50
Managing Household Agriculture 53
Agricultural Incomes Policy 55

4 ENERGY DEVELOPMENT 58
Demand and Supply: Trends and Balances 58
Coal Production, Transport, and Utilization 60
Oil and Gas 65
Electric Power 67
Rural Energy and Biomass 68
Investment, Planning, and Prices 69

5 SPATIAL ISSUES 73
Specialization and Trade 73
Transport, Commerce, and Other Services 82
Urban and Rural Development 86
Rural Poverty and Regional Inequality 91

6 INTERNATIONAL ECONOMIC STRATEGY 97
   China in the World Economy 97
   Foreign Trade Prospects and Policies 101
   External Balance and Finance 107
   Regional Issues 109

7 MANAGING INDUSTRIAL TECHNOLOGY 110
   Technology in Perspective 110
   Planning for Technological Development 112
   The Make or Buy Decision 116
   Incentives for Innovation and Diffusion 118
   Obsolescence and Scrapping 121

8 HUMAN DEVELOPMENT 123
   Education and Training Issues 123
   Employment and Productivity 127
   Allocating and Motivating Workers 130
   Population Issues beyond the Year 2000 136

9 MOBILIZING FINANCIAL RESOURCES 143
   Alternative Sources of Saving 143
   Subsidies and Transfers 148
   Revenue Needs and Sources 152
   Tax Reform 156

10 DEVELOPMENT MANAGEMENT 160
   The State and the Individual 160
   The State and Enterprises 164
   Investment and Price Reform 171
   Economic Planning 177
   Overview 181

Tables

1.1	Size Distribution of Industrial Enterprises in Selected Countries	28
1.2	Rural Income Distribution, 1979–82	29
2.1	Average Annual Growth of National Income, Alternative Projections, 1981–2000	36
2.2	Composition of Final Demand, Alternative Projections, 1981–2000	36
2.3	Average Annual Growth of Sectoral Gross Output, Alternative Projections, 1981–2000	38
2.4	Composition of Capital Stock, Alternative Projections, 1981–2000	39
2.5	Sectoral Composition of the Labor Force, Alternative Projections, 1981–2000	40
2.6	Sectoral Composition of National Income, Alternative Projections, 1981–2000	42
4.1	Energy Supply and Demand, Alternative Projections, 1981–2000	60
4.2	Share of Solid Fuels in Commercial Energy Use in Selected Countries, 1960, 1980, and 2000	62
4.3	Estimated Investment Requirements in the Energy Sector, 1986–2000	70
5.1	Dispersion of Production Activities among and within Provinces, 1982	73
5.2	Gross Output and Profits of State-Owned Industry, by Province and Subsector, 1982	74
5.3	Industrial Concentration, by Region and Key City, 1982	74
5.4	Extent and Composition of Rural Nonagricultural Activities in Selected Countries	79
5.5	Urbanization and Economic Development in Selected Countries	87
5.6	Per Capita Income in Urban and Rural Areas, 1982	87

5.7 Distribution of Employment and Population, Alternative Projections, 1981–2000 89
5.8 Average Annual Growth of Urban and Rural Income, Alternative Projections, 1981–2000 90
5.9 Urban-Rural Income Disparities, Alternative Projections, 1981–2000 90
5.10 Rural and Provincial Poverty, 1982 92
5.11 Rural Development in Dingxi County (Gansu) and Wuxi County (Jiangsu), 1983 92
5.12 Wage Levels, by Province and Type of Unit, 1982 94
5.13 State Budget Revenues and Expenditures in Wuxi and Dingxi Counties, 1983 96
6.1 Total Foreign Trade Ratios, Alternative Projections, 1981–2000 102
6.2 Share of Manufactures in Total Merchandise Exports, 1960 and 1981 103
6.3 Sectoral Foreign Trade Ratios, Alternative Projections, 1981–2000 104
6.4 Average Annual Growth of Foreign Trade, Alternative Projections, 1981–2000 104
6.5 Structure of Foreign Trade, Alternative Projections, 1981–2000 105
6.6 Foreign Trade Balance and Debt, Alternative Projections, 1981–2000 107
7.1 Index of Total Factor Productivity in State-Owned Industry, 1952–82 111
7.2 Sources of Successful Innovations in European Firms 118
8.1 Educational Attainment of the Population, by Age and Sex, in Selected Countries 124
8.2 Population Growth, Alternative Projections, 1980–2100 137
8.3 Population of Working Age, Alternative Projections, 1980–2100 139
8.4 Population Sixty-Five Years Old or More, Alternative Projections, 1980–2100 139
9.1 Gross Domestic Savings in Selected Countries, 1976–80 145
9.2 Subsidies, 1981 148
9.3 Subsidies and Transfers as Percentages of Government Revenue in Selected Countries 149
9.4 Subsidies and Transfers, Alternative Projections, 1981–2000 151
9.5 Government Expenditures, Alternative Projections, 1981–2000 153
9.6 Illustrative Projections for Figure 9.2 155
9.7 Illustrative Projections for Figure 9.3 157

Figures

1.1 Composition of Aggregate Demand in China and Other Developing Countries, 1981 22
1.2 Structure of Production in China and Other Developing Countries, 1981 23
1.3 Structure of Employment in China and Other Developing Countries, 1981 24
1.4 Enrollment Ratios in Formal Education in China, 1965–83 and Targets for 2000, and in Other
    Developing Countries, 1965–80 31
2.1 Share of Agriculture in Total Employment in China, Alternative Projections for 1981–2000,
    and in Other Selected Countries, 1960–82 41
3.1 Crop Exports and Imports, Alternative Projections, 1981–2000 48
3.2 Per Capita Food Intake in China, 1981–2000, and in Other Selected Economies, 1960–80 51
3.3 Share of Animal Products in Total Food Intake in China, 1980–2000, and in Other Selected
    Economies, 1960–80 52
5.1 Variations in Per Capita Gross Agricultural and Industrial Output, 1982 76
5.2 Distribution of Employment, Capital, and Gross Output, Alternative Projections, 1981–2000 88
6.1 Exports of Goods and Nonfactor Services in Selected Countries, 1978–82 98
6.2 Trade in Goods and Nonfactor Services, 1978–83 102
6.3 Direction of External Trade, 1983 105
6.4 External Balance, 1978–84 107
7.1 Output and Cost of Production of the JA 1-1 Sewing Machine, by Enterprise, 1980 111
8.1 Population, Alternative Projections, 1980–2100 137
9.1 Sources and Uses of Funds, 1981 144
9.2 Income Flows and Taxation, Alternative Projections, 1981–2000 154
9.3 Sources and Composition of Saving, Alternative Projections, 1981–2000 156

Boxes

1.1   Size and Growth of Enterprises in Market Economies 27
2.1   Wages, Profits, and Prices 42
3.1   World Grain Trade, Past and Future 50
4.1   Cogeneration for Industry and District Heating 63
5.1   The Spatial Distribution of Dairy Production 77
5.2   Locational Issues in the Iron and Steel Industry 80
5.3   Locational Issues in the Bicycle Industry 81
5.4   Trade, Pricing, and Transport of Cement 84
5.5   Agriculture on the Loess Plateau 93
5.6   The Benefits and Costs of Migration to Communities of Origin 94
6.1   Contrasting Types of International Economic Strategy 99
7.1   Continuous Casting of Steel 113
7.2   Strategic Options in Power Station Boiler Technology 114
7.3   A Successful Strategy in Electronics 115
8.1   The Second Health Care Revolution 140
10.1   Dispersed Social Ownership in the Federal Republic of Germany 167
10.2   Monetary Control 174

Maps

5.1   Per Capita Net Material Product, by Province, 1982 75
5.2   Provincial Budget Expenditures and Revenues, 1982 95
       Relief and Administrative Divisions 183

Preface

This report was prepared principally by members of an economic mission that visited China twice in 1984, for four weeks in February–March and for five weeks in April–May. In addition to visiting Beijing, the mission went to three provinces: one coastal and relatively high-income (Jiangsu); one inland and average-income (Hubei); and one interior and low-income (Gansu). It received a lot of information, as well as numerous valuable comments and suggestions, from officials and others in these provinces, as well as from those in many central agencies and institutions, including: the State Planning and State Economic Commissions; the Ministries of Finance, Agriculture, Coal, Communications, Education, Foreign Economic Relations and Trade, Labor and Personnel, Petroleum, Railways, Urban and Rural Construction, and Water Resources and Electric Power; the State Statistical Bureau; and various universities and research institutes of the Chinese Academy of Social Sciences. A series of seminars was organized by the Technical-Economic Research Center under the State Council. The generous and thoughtful assistance of all these people in China contributed greatly to this report.

The Bank mission was led by Edwin Lim (mission chief) and Adrian Wood (deputy mission chief) and also consisted of William Byrd (economist), Mats Hultin (senior education adviser), Erh-Cheng Hwa (senior economist), Timothy King (senior economist), Jacques Yenny (senior transport economist), Umnuay Sae-Hau (research assistant), Betty Ting (interpreter), Luc De Wulf (senior economist, International Monetary Fund), Benjamin King (consultant on statistics), Wouter Tims (consultant on planning and agriculture); and the following teams.

• *Agriculture.* J. Goering (team leader, April–May), Tom Wiens (team leader, February–March), Lang-Seng Tay (irrigation specialist), Lo-Chai Chen (fisheries consul-

tant), and Fred Bentley (consultant on arid agriculture).

• *Energy.* Roberto Bentjerodt (senior economist, coal projects), Weigong Cao (power engineer), Abdel El-Mekkawy (engineer, petroleum projects), Robert Taylor (energy economist), and Darrel Fallen-Bailey (consultant); D. C. Rao (assistant director, Energy Department) led the team in the field.

• *Industrial technology.* Gene Tidrick (team leader), Anupam Khanna (industrial economist), Reza Amin (industrial specialist), and Josephine Woo (research assistant).

• *Location and trade.* Ian Porter (team leader), Vernon Henderson (consultant on urbanization), John Sheahan (consultant on industrial location and trade), and Samuel Ho (consultant on rural nonfarm activities).

The following also contributed to the preparation of the report: Wlodzimierz Brus (consultant on socialist economies); Gerhard Pohl (energy and transport); Robert Drysdale (Annex 1); Helena Ribe and Nikhil Desai (Annex 3); Shujiro Urata (Annexes 4 and 5); and Lily Uy (Annex 6). Larry Westphal, Carl Dahlman, and Bruce Ross-Larson organized background work on technology. Behrouz Guerami-N, Tejaswi Raparla, and Kong-Yam Tan helped with the multisectoral model, the input-output table, and data for international comparisons. Ann Orr, Kenneth Hill, Moshe Syrquin, J. V. S. Sarma, Kenneth Cochran, Chang Hsin, Liu Ying, and Cai Jinyong undertook research. Linda Mitchell, Terrice Bassler, and Carol Cole Rosen edited the report; Helen Kung assisted in its processing; and Catherine Ann Kocak prepared graphics for the text.

The report also benefited from comments of a review panel consisting of Anne O. Krueger, Luis de Azcarate, Kemal Dervis, Janos Kornai (consultant), and managers of the East Asia and Pacific Regional Office.

Technical Notes

Currency equivalents. The Chinese currency is called renminbi (RMB). It is denominated in yuan (Y): 1 yuan = 10 jiao = 100 fen. In early 1984 the official exchange rate of the yuan to the U.S. dollar was around Y 2 = US$1. The internal settlement rate (ISR) of Y 2.8 = US$1, however, was used in most merchandise transactions. The official exchange rate is now about Y 2.8 = US$1. On January 1, 1985, the Government abolished the ISR.

Weights and measures. Chinese statistics are usually in metric units; in addition, mu and jin are often used: 1 mu = 0.1647 acres = 0.0667 hectares; 1 jin = 0.5 kilograms.

Fiscal year. The fiscal year is January 1 to December 31.

Transliteration. The Pinyin system is used in this report.

Terminology. With the recent reorganization of rural administration, "communes" have been replaced by "townships," and "production brigades and teams" by "villages." This report retains the former terminology in one respect, however, by referring to "commune and brigade enterprises."

The term "national income" is used in this report to encompass both the Chinese measure (net material product) and the Western measure (gross national product). Where the context makes the distinction between these two measures important, they are more precisely identified.

Tables. Individual items may not sum exactly to totals because of rounding errors. The following symbols are used: .. indicates data are not available; (.) indicates a negligible amount; n.a. indicates not applicable.

Summary and Conclusions

China's ultimate economic objective is to catch up with the developed countries, while maintaining a socialist system in which the benefits of prosperity are widely shared. Major, though uneven, progress toward this goal was made in the past three decades. During the next two decades, there could be substantial further progress. The foundations for rapid and equitable growth in the twenty-first century could also be laid. But this will require steering a difficult course, in both development strategy and system reform.

This report looks at some of the key issues for China in the next twenty years, and at some of the options for addressing them, especially in light of international experience. It covers many specific topics, including agriculture, energy, technology, transport, industrial location, internal and external trade, population, education, employment, and finance (health was addressed in another recent report[1]). The first section of this summary assembles some of its conclusions in the context of a more general discussion of the pattern of economic growth. Common themes regarding the system of economic management and planning are pulled together in the second section. A third section covers some related aspects of social policy. At the end of the summary there is a brief overview.

The most careful forecasts are often confounded. The lessons of international experience are often ambiguous and controversial. In any event, they are hard to apply to China, a country that in important respects differs from all others and is not easy for outsiders to understand. The projections of this report are thus not predictions, and its suggestions are tentative. They are no more than an attempt to contribute to the debate in China about the difficult questions that must be confronted during the country's unique socialist modernization.

Pattern of Growth

Per capita national income in the industrial countries is (in terms of purchasing power) approximately ten times higher than in China and will increase in the future by at least 2 percent and perhaps 3 percent per year. To catch up by 2050, China's per capita income would have to increase at an average rate of at least 5.5 percent and perhaps 6.5 percent per year. Such rapid progress has been rare elsewhere. In 1960–82, excluding small and oil-dominated economies, only two developing countries achieved annual per capita income growth above 5 percent: South Korea (6.6 percent) and Greece (5.2 percent). More generally, only one country—Japan—has indisputably caught up with the developed nations from a position of economic backwardness.

China's past record, on the other hand, is quite encouraging. From 1952 to 1982, despite relatively rapid population growth and periods of acute economic mismanagement, per capita national income grew at an average annual rate of 4.0 percent, with phases of significantly faster growth. Of particular relevance is China's performance during the past few years of policy and system reforms: from 1979 to 1984, per capita national income grew at 6.8 percent per year.

Although the basic objective is to improve living standards and eliminate poverty, the Government has set targets of quadrupling the gross value of industrial and agricultural output (GVIAO) between 1980 and 2000 and increasing per capita national income from about $300 to $800 (about 5 percent per year). If China's future investment efficiency were similar to the average of the past three decades, but allowing for increased investment in economic and social infrastructure, quadrupling GVIAO would require an investment rate of about 30 percent of national income. This is comparable to the rates in other fast-growing East Asian economies, as well as East European countries, and in line with China's past investment rate. With reasonable improvements in energy and mate-

---

1. Dean T. Jamison and others, *China: The Health Sector* (Washington, D.C.: World Bank, 1984).

rials use, and provided that the population in 2000 is fairly close to the official target of 1.2 billion people, quadrupling GVIAO would allow the Government's per capita income target to be attained.

The target growth rate of per capita income is far above the 2.6–3.6 percent range projected by the World Bank for middle-income countries in 1985–95. It seems feasible because China's projected population growth is unusually slow (about 1 percent per year, compared with an expected 2.2 percent in middle-income countries) and because China's investment rate has consistently been unusually high (the 1982 average for middle-income countries was 24 percent). But its attainment depends crucially on the efficiency with which resources are used. For example, if the overall efficiency of investment were similar not to China's 1952–82 average but to the 1957–77 average—roughly comparable to that of the Soviet Union in 1950–75 and India in 1960–82—the growth rate of per capita income would be about one percentage point lower.

If agricultural or energy production (discussed below) increased unexpectedly slowly, or if domestic or international misfortunes adversely affected China's efficiency or investment rate, growth could be slower still. In any event, experience in China and other socialist countries strongly suggests the desirability of cautious planning. Unrealistically high growth targets cause fluctuations, shortages, and inefficiency, while aiming too low has few adverse consequences. Indeed, continuation of China's recent practice of setting modest annual and medium-term targets could greatly facilitate reform of the system of economic management.

Sectoral Balance

Experience elsewhere also confirms the importance of striking an appropriate balance among the different broad sectors of the economy. In particular, favoring industry at the expense of other sectors does not seem to generate rapid and efficient growth. In China, incentives for agricultural production have recently been substantially increased, but additional measures to support agriculture (discussed below) will be needed. Moreover, emphasis on quadrupling GVIAO should not imply neglect of infrastructure and services, which are vital for industrial and agricultural efficiency. The adverse consequences of past underinvestment in electricity and transport are well recognized in China, but there are still difficulties in diverting sufficient funds from directly productive investment into infrastructure. And the importance of commerce and other services (including finance and enterprise support services) has only recently come to be appreciated.

The share of the service sectors—including commerce—in output and employment in China is at present strikingly small by comparison with other developing countries, despite an unusually large education and health sector. The pattern in China, however, is characteristic also of the Soviet Union and Eastern Europe. Continued emphasis on increasing the physical volume of production (for example, the target of quadrupling GVIAO) might cause this pattern to persist. But China could also shift to a different pattern of growth, with accelerated development of the service sectors.

Rapid service sector expansion and reform of the system of economic management are closely related options. Expansion of commerce would go hand in hand with expansion of market regulation and increased specialization of production units and localities. Expansion of enterprise support services, including finance, accounting, and law, would likewise be a corollary of increased enterprise autonomy and specialization. And expansion of personal services would reflect a change in the relative weights attached to planners' priorities and people's preferences. Moreover, rapid growth of services probably could not be accomplished through administrative directives and centralized resource allocation, but would have to be pulled by demand. Individual and collective enterprises may also be better suited than state enterprises to providing many types of services.

This association with system reform makes it likely that the benefits of faster service sector growth would more than offset its costs (in terms of investment, skilled labor, and—to a lesser extent—materials). In addition to the direct benefit to households from more convenient retail commerce and from more restaurants, tailors, and so on, there would be indirect contributions to the efficiency of industry and agriculture. A bigger, better-equipped, and more responsive commercial sector could reduce requirements for both circulating capital and—by permitting greater specialization and realization of economies of scale—fixed capital. Enterprise support services also make fuller use of specialized equipment and personnel, while financial institutions can contribute to better investment decisions. Larger commerce and enterprise support service sectors may also contribute to reducing material input requirements, especially by accelerating improvements in product quality, which make the cost of materials a smaller fraction of the price.

An alternative development path, involving both greater emphasis on services and more efficient resource use, is therefore analyzed in the report. With a level of investment efficiency similar to the average in Japan in 1950–80 and in all middle-income countries in 1960–82, it could attain the Government's target national income growth rate with an investment rate of only 26 percent, and hence faster growth of consumption. (The growth rate of industry would be 7 percent per year rather than 8 percent, however, and hence GVIAO would less than quadruple.) On this path, China would also have the option of maintaining the investment rate at 30 percent, which would cause national income to grow one percentage point faster than the target rate (and GVIAO to slightly more than quadruple).

Human Resources

Faster service sector expansion could also make it easier for China to absorb growth in the labor force, averaging about 10 million workers per year in 1980–2000. In the usual pattern of development—even in rapidly industrializing countries—the main intersectoral employment shift is from agriculture into services, with a more moderate increase of employment in industry, which is less labor intensive. In China, however, employment has grown faster in industry than in services. Continued emphasis on increasing the physical volume of production could perpetuate this pattern. This is especially likely because the prospective decline in the primary school age group will cause the number of teachers—now approaching a quarter of all service sector employment in China—to increase only modestly. Service sector employment in 2000 might thus remain as low as 70 percent of industrial employment (similar to the ratio in the Soviet Union in 1959).

On the alternative development path, by contrast, service sector employment in 2000 could be as much as 150 percent of industrial employment (similar to the ratio in Japan in the early 1950s). Such a change in the composition of nonagricultural employment could ease some problems in China's urban areas, which now suffer from a combination of surpluses of some sorts of labor and shortages of other sorts of labor (including competent, able-bodied workers even at relatively low skill levels). A much higher ratio of service sector to industrial employment would help to reduce this structural mismatch between labor demand and supply, since service sector jobs tend to be disproportionately filled by the categories of labor that are now in surplus in urban China—particularly women.

Perhaps more important, faster service sector expansion, by raising the overall level of nonagricultural employment, could reduce the proportion of China's labor force that must remain in agriculture, where the earnings and contribution to production of most workers are likely to remain unsatisfactorily low for the next two or three decades. On the material-production-oriented quadrupling path, the proportion of the labor force in agriculture—excluding brigade industries—might decline by 2000 to only slightly under 60 percent. On the alternative development path, though, with the same growth rate of national income, it could decline to nearer 50 percent, a difference of perhaps 40 million workers.

Even the latter percentage, which implies an absolute increase in agricultural employment of 13 million, is much higher than most Chinese projections, which envisage a decline in the agricultural employment share to under 40 percent. This would be normal for a country with a per capita income roughly double the Chinese

target for 2000. Given the growth rate of nonagricultural output implied by this target, and the present very large agricultural employment share, such a large decline in agricultural employment could be achieved only if nonagricultural labor productivity grew slowly. This might well be incompatible with efficient industrialization. In the early decades of the twenty-first century, however, agricultural employment is likely to shrink rapidly.

Especially because many of the children of today's farmers will move into nonagricultural employment at some point during their working lives, it will be important for China to continue to emphasize the wide diffusion of basic education and to improve its quality. International experience strongly suggests that this could contribute not only to faster economic growth, but also to a less unequal distribution of its benefits. In recent years, however, there have been problems in maintaining the primary school enrollment ratio (although it remains well above the developing country average); and the secondary school enrollment ratio has dropped below the developing country average. Wide variations among localities in enrollment ratios and school quality also persist. These problems are being aggravated by increased local financial self-reliance in basic education, as well as by key schools (recently modified in name, but less in substance) at primary and secondary levels. Policy changes, and greater financial support from central and provincial authorities, will be needed if the important target of making nine years of basic education universal by 2000 is to be attained.

As regards advanced education and training, the need for rapid progress to make up for the damage inflicted by the Cultural Revolution is well recognized in China, but some changes in emphasis seem advisable. University-level courses are too specialized, partly because many educational institutions are subordinate to sectoral ministries and other agencies. The Government's present policy of vocationalizing secondary education could suffer from similar problems. The case for sound general education, supplemented by subsequent, briefer training in highly specialized skills, is particularly strong in China over the next few decades. Rapid technical advance and structural change will require constant alterations in the skill composition of the labor force. The slow prospective growth of the labor force in the twenty-first century will reduce the scope for achieving such alterations through changes in the pattern of training of new labor force entrants. It will correspondingly increase the required amount of retraining, which is more difficult for people whose original education was highly specialized.

Food and Agriculture

Despite its long history of food problems, China's per capita consumption of calories and protein is currently similar to the average for middle-income countries. The

3

share of animal products in the diet, however, is that of a low-income country, and a major issue is how far and fast this share should increase. This issue is hard to address because of uncertainty about China's agricultural production potential: depending on whether the recent remarkable surge in production wanes or persists, the future trend growth rate of agricultural output could lie anywhere between 2–3 percent and 5–6 percent per year.

In addition to the successful measures already implemented in recent years, especially introduction of the production responsibility system, the Government could take a number of steps to enhance agricultural growth prospects. These include improvements in agricultural research, education, and extension services; irrigation and drainage projects; better nutrient balance in fertilizer supplies, as well as changes in the pricing and distribution system so that fertilizer is allocated among crops and localities more in accordance with its potential contribution to production; increased availability of agricultural credit; and improvements in rural transport, storage, and marketing facilities.

To permit consumption of animal products to rise from 6 percent of total caloric intake in the early 1980s to 15 percent by the end of the century, gross agricultural output would have to increase at about 4.5 percent per year, with crop production growing at 3.6 percent per year (less than the 1965–83 average) and animal husbandry at 7.5 percent per year (well above past rates). This agricultural growth rate could simultaneously satisfy the other demands of economic growth at the government's target rate, with agricultural exports and imports more or less in balance in 2000. But it is very high by international standards—well above the 3.0 percent average for middle-income countries in 1960–80 and surpassed only by Thailand and the Philippines, which started with more uncultivated land and lower yields.

To achieve such rapid growth of animal production would also not be straightforward. China's pastures are now seriously overgrazed, which makes it unlikely that present targets for beef and mutton production growth can be achieved. Much higher priority than at present would need to be given to improving techniques for the production of poultry, a potentially efficient converter of feed into animal protein. The most important issue, however, appears to be availability of grain and protein-based feeds, on which an increasing proportion of animal husbandry will have to be based. This is a matter partly of the backwardness of China's feed-processing industry, partly of achieving the required level and pattern of crop production.

With rapid growth of animal husbandry, the Government's present targets for increasing production of specific crops would tend to create a large shortage of the coarse grains needed for animal feed and a large surplus of rice, whose consumption is likely to grow only slowly.

Feedgrain imports could make up any conceivable shortage, probably without an appreciable increase in world prices, but it would be possible to export only a part of the potential rice surplus at economically attractive prices. Even if overall crop production targets can be attained, it may thus be necessary to switch some rice land either into coarse grains or into other crops that could be more easily exported.

The future pattern of agricultural production and foreign trade thus depends quite heavily on the rate of increase in consumption of animal products. The possibility of a rapid increase cannot be ruled out, but there are some significant problems and uncertainties, which could be greater in the twenty-first century. (Even with a favorable feed conversion ratio, an increase of ten percentage points in the share of animal products in the average diet is equivalent to the disappearance of 35–40 percent of China's cultivable land, or a 35–40 percent increase in population.) Particularly undesirable would be an increase in per capita consumption of animal products to a level that could not be sustained—because of a slowdown in crop production growth, poor feed-meat conversion ratios, or unwillingness or inability to sustain large feedgrain imports—and therefore had to be reduced.

Although there appears to be little danger of a decline in China's present very satisfactory food intake level, caution is accordingly needed in managing food demand. It seems especially important that consumers should pay the full economic cost of animal products, without subsidies or administrative restrictions on prices. Japanese experience suggests that high prices can bring consumer demand for animal products into line with limited supplies in a socially acceptable manner. By contrast, the experience of countries which have subsidized and rationed consumption of animal products has been extremely unfavorable.

Energy Production and Use

Because China's initially high consumption of energy per unit of output offers great scope for conservation, it would be possible to attain the Government's target of quadrupling GVIAO with a much smaller proportionate increase in energy production—though probably not as small as the originally envisaged doubling. Electricity production probably has to quadruple by 2000 to meet demand, which will require a huge amount of investment (averaging about 2 percent of national income), although it is technically feasible and in line with current plans. Crude oil production in 2000 is hard to predict, since it depends heavily on success in replacing the output of existing fields with that of new discoveries, but the 200 million ton target (twice the present level) could be more than enough to meet the likely level of domestic demand.

It is coal, however, that will bear most of the burden of bringing future energy production into line with demand.

How much coal will be needed could vary widely, depending on the rate and sectoral pattern of growth, as well as on the degree of energy conservation achieved within individual sectors. With growth of national income at the Government's target rate, the material-production-oriented quadrupling path would require 1,400 million tons of coal to be produced in 2000 on the most optimistic assumptions about progress in conservation, and more probably 1,600 million tons (as compared with 770 million tons in 1984). At the same national income growth rate, the alternative—more service-oriented and efficient—development path mentioned earlier could reduce coal demand in 2000 to 1,200 million tons on the most optimistic conservation assumptions, and 1,400 million tons on intermediate assumptions.

Especially because less optimistic, but still plausible, assumptions about progress in conservation could increase the potential demand for coal in 2000 to over 1,800 million tons, it will be vital to promote economical use of all forms of energy. The mixture of administrative controls and financial incentives applied in recent years has led to impressive energy savings. But a quota-based energy allocation system is fundamentally unsuited to achieving large and economically rational reductions in energy intensity over the longer term. It gives enterprises an incentive to exaggerate their needs and does not take enough account of the widely varying economic costs of reducing energy consumption in individual enterprises. It is very probable that more energy could be saved, with less waste of other resources, if enterprises were more strongly motivated to reduce all costs and faced with prices that better reflected the economic values of all their inputs and outputs.

It should be possible to mine the required quantities of coal, given China's ample reserves and the straightforward production technology, although this would require some advance planning, substantial investment, and continued support for small collective mines. Much more of a challenge will be to transport the coal (as discussed below) and to use it cleanly and efficiently. The share of coal in total commercial energy use is likely to remain at 70–75 percent (compared with 30–35 percent worldwide), which will require it to be put to an unusually wide range of uses, including many where backward technology and small scale in China today result in wasteful and dirty combustion.

To prevent further increases in already unacceptably high levels of urban air pollution, as well as to economize on fuel, will often require the replacement of decentralized and uncontrolled burning of coal in households and enterprises with centralized, large-scale, environmentally controlled combustion to produce cleaner forms of energy (gas, electricity, steam, hot water) for distribution to final users. This in turn will require China to import and disseminate new technology—which will also be critical

in existing large-scale uses such as steel and cement production—and to invest heavily in suitable production and distribution facilities. Careful studies will be needed to select the least costly of the various alternatives (for example, coal gasification versus cogeneration and district heating) in each case; and their implementation and operation will entail much closer cooperation than at present among a variety of agencies and organizations.

Transport Priorities

There is concern in China that economic growth over the next decade or two might be held back by transport shortages, especially given the length of time needed to construct new railways and roads. But the volume of freight transport in China is now so high (per unit of output) by international standards—though lower than in the Soviet Union—that it is hard to predict how rapidly it will need to increase in the future, given any particular trend growth rate of national income. This will depend on the sectoral pattern of growth (for example, industry is more transport-intensive than services) and on its spatial pattern (which influences average transport distance). It will also be affected by system reform, which will on the one hand tend to increase transport requirements because of increased specialization and exchange, but could on the other hand greatly reduce wasteful use of transport facilities, for example, through less cross-hauling, more preliminary processing of materials, and more rational location decisions.

If national income were to grow at the Government's target rate, with continuing strong emphasis on material production, and with agriculture and industry using transport only moderately more efficiently than in the past, freight volume could reach 3,200 billion ton-kilometers by 2000 (approaching four times its 1980 level). But with the same growth of national income achieved through faster expansion of services and slower expansion of industry, and with somewhat greater efficiency in transport use, freight volume in 2000 would be 2,400 billion ton-kilometers. Even in the latter case, China's projected freight intensity would remain high in comparison with other countries, which suggests that the possibility of even slower growth of freight volume cannot be ruled out.

Although the overall volume of transport requirements in the longer term is highly uncertain, there will certainly have to be significant changes in the composition of transport investments, as well as in organization and management. Agricultural and industrial specialization will involve much movement in fairly small lots of a great variety of goods, often perishable or fragile, over short to medium distances, to and from dispersed origins and destinations. This is generally only feasible by road. The demand for road passenger transport will also increase rapidly. However, China now has a rural road network half the size of India's and fewer trucks per rural person than the impoverished Sahelian countries of West Africa. Major intercity highways, the vehicle fleet, and vehicle fuel production and distribution are also at present strikingly backward.

That road transport should play a larger role in the future is widely recognized in China. Yet there seems to be no strategic plan to bring this about. Underutilized agricultural labor could, as in the past, be mobilized to build up an adequate rural road network. But higher levels of government (central and provincial) will need—as in other countries—to play a much more active role in planning, coordinating, and financing the road development schemes implemented at lower levels. In addition, it will be essential to produce a much larger number and wider range of more fuel-efficient trucks, to improve the utilization of vehicle fleets, to upgrade the quality of motor fuels, and to distribute and price these fuels more rationally. All this will require improved coordination among higher level government ministries and agencies.

Railways will remain the most efficient means of transporting raw materials and heavy industrial products over long distances. There will be a large increase in demand for coal transport, even with more coal washing and minemouth power generation. But there is apparently much scope for economizing on rail transport of all commodities through stronger incentives for cost reduction and less administrative intervention in materials allocation and pricing. It also seems physically and financially possible to accommodate the overall increase in rail transport demand. This could be accomplished largely by switching from steam to diesel and electric traction, although substantial double tracking and some new lines will also be necessary.

Increased use of water transport could appreciably reduce the load on the railways, expecially if future heavy industrial investments were appropriately located. And China's entire transport system could benefit from better intermodal coordination: this is partly a matter of improving technology and infrastructure (for example, containers and their handling facilities), but it also depends on rationalizing tariffs, increasing competition, and encouraging new specialized entities to provide an appropriate variety of transport, leasing, storage, and transfer services.

Specialization and Urbanization

China's size and past emphasis on local self-sufficiency offer opportunities for enormous economic gains through increased specialization and trade among localities. In recent years, agricultural specialization has proceeded rapidly. In industry, by contrast, specialization does not seem to be increasing, and indeed local planning bureaus are still promoting the development of a wide range of industrial activities, with continuing emphasis on local self-

sufficiency. This appears to result partly from transport problems, but also from shortcomings in commerce and material supply, the nature of the fiscal system, distorted prices, and insufficient competition. It could have a serious adverse effect on China's overall investment efficiency.

To prevent continued proliferation of industrial plants of suboptimal scale and product quality, there is thus an urgent need for measures to reduce the present conflict between what is rational for a particular locality and what is rational for China's whole economy. Of particular importance would be better transport, fiscal reform, and changes in the system of economic management (discussed below), regarding enterprise motivation, competition, and prices. In addition, the central government might consider legal measures to back up its existing general prohibition of barriers to interlocality trade, including possibly the establishment of a special regulatory institution, with the power to levy large fines.

Suboptimal plant size is not China's only current industrial location problem. There is also too much concentration of industry in large and medium-size cities. Research and experience in other countries suggest that economic efficiency requires weight-reducing heavy industry (for example, iron and steel production) and agroprocessing to be located near raw material sources, with other space-intensive or standardized industrial activities in specialized small cities. Industries such as petrochemicals and bicycles benefit from large-scale operation, but not from proximity to other industries—or at any rate not enough to justify the much higher economic cost of land and labor in large cities. By contrast, industries whose technology is evolving rapidly or which must respond to constantly changing demand, as well as many specialized service activities, benefit substantially from mutual proximity and clustering in large urban areas. Development of both large and small cities, as well as smaller towns providing goods and services to rural areas, could thus contribute to rapid and efficient growth in China; but planners and prices (discussed below) will need to give better guidance on what activities should go where.

How much the overall level of urbanization should increase in the decades ahead is a difficult issue, partly because the distinction between urban and rural is itself blurred in many densely populated parts of China. In any event, substantially increased rural-urban migration seems probable and desirable. Indeed, without some rural-urban migration, China's overall urbanization rate (as officially measured) would decline from 20 percent in 1981—quite normal for a low-income country—to 19 percent by 2000, simply because the natural population growth rate in existing urban areas over the next two decades is likely to be much lower than in rural areas. This could cause the general labor shortages that have already appeared in some Chinese cities to become widespread within a few years. Increasing urbanization would probably be a more economically efficient response to such shortages than accelerated automation of urban production. An urbanization rate in 2000 of 30 percent (implying that more than a third of the urban population would have come from rural areas) would still involve an unusually large amount of rural nonagricultural employment. Lower-middle-income countries today (at a similar income level) have an average of 34 percent of their population in urban areas.

Whatever the overall rate of urbanization, efficient development of towns and cities will require a very large increase in urban infrastructure and services. The administrative responsibilities for their provision, and potential financing and cost recovery mechanisms, need to be carefully reviewed. In many countries, efficient and equitable development of urban services has been seriously constrained either by fragmented and unclear allocation of responsibility among different administrative levels or by inadequate growth of urban revenue sources. In China, moreover, special attention should be given to the potential impact of economic and social reforms on the level and composition of local government revenues and expenditures.

Foreign Trade and Capital

China's recent resumption and expansion of external economic contacts have raised exports to 9–10 percent of national income, which is well within the normal range for large countries. However, inflows of foreign loans and direct investment have remained small, partly because of foreign trade surpluses. For the future, there appear to be two large and related issues. The first is how much, and in what directions, to further increase external contacts. The second is how best to manage such contacts, and in particular whether to continue the present insulation of the domestic economy from the world outside by administrative intermediation and separate price systems.

Over the next two decades, China will need to change the composition of its manufactured exports. Exports of textiles and clothing, in particular, are likely to grow fairly slowly. China will therefore need to make a major effort to expand exports of machinery and metal products. Rapid growth in such exports would permit rapid growth of intermediate and capital goods imports, as well as consumer goods imports (which can stimulate important improvements in domestic production). Exports of manufactured goods could also be used to pay for purchases of licenses and technological assistance, which in many advanced as well as developing countries have proved to be very effective ways of upgrading domestic technology.

As regards foreign borrowing, the Government's policy of cautious progress seems well founded. For a low-income country to run foreign trade surpluses, as China has done in recent years, has some obvious disadvantages, as compared with a net inflow of foreign capital to supplement domestic savings. But experience in other countries, including socialist ones, has shown how easy it is to slide into excessive or unproductive borrowing, especially when domestic enterprises and planners are not sufficiently conscious of investment costs or responsible for bad decisions.

However, China also seems wise to encourage direct foreign investment, less for the foreign capital or advanced technology it brings than for the demonstration effect of modern management techniques. The example of, and competition from, well-run foreign companies can help domestic firms identify weak links in management, product design, material supply, and so on, and spur them to make changes they might otherwise never consider. But such examples of the way modern industry operates in more advanced countries are effective only if contrasted and competing with locally managed firms. This requires foreign and joint ventures to be spread—as is increasingly the case in China—among a wide range of localities and activities, rather than confined to special zones or particular sectors.

International experience suggests that decentralization of foreign trade to the enterprise level can also make an important contribution to realizing the potential benefits of increased external economic contacts. Direct exposure of exporting firms to foreign buyers and competitors has proved elsewhere to be an extremely effective way not just of learning in the abstract about new and better products and processes, but also of learning how (and being put under pressure) to introduce them in practice. Similarly, allowing enterprises—including commercial enterprises—and consumers to choose directly between imported and domestically produced goods could greatly increase competitive pressure on Chinese producers to introduce new, better, and cheaper products.

Such decentralization of foreign trade could have some potentially serious disadvantages, too, including damage to promising but newly established industries in China, as well as greater exposure to world price instability and unpredictable fluctuations in foreign markets. But skillful use of policy instruments—including the exchange rate, tariffs, and selective administrative interventions—could minimize the costs while securing many of the benefits. China will also always be a large and diverse economy, with a relatively small foreign trade sector, which greatly reduces the possible damage that unexpectedly unfavorable external developments could inflict, even though particular industries and localities might experience quite sharp swings in prosperity.

Especially following the recent unification of foreign exchange arrangements—and given the current account surpluses of recent years, large reserves, and the ready

7

availability of external capital—China appears to be well placed to move toward a decentralized and mainly indirectly regulated foreign trade system, without the problems (of external insolvency or internal inflation or deflation) that many other countries attempting a similar move have simultaneously had to contend with. To do this immediately, or at one stroke, would probably be unwise, since most domestic enterprises do not yet have appropriate motivation or independence, and since some prior changes of domestic prices would ease the adjustments required. But it could proceed in parallel with internal economic reform.

Managing the Economy

How far China will have risen into the middle-income range by 2000 will depend crucially on how successfully the economy is managed. This is a matter partly of mobilizing financial and human resources, and of importing and developing modern technology, partly of putting these things to effective use. China's past record of economic management, for all its unevenness, is superior to that of other low-income countries, both in promoting growth and in reducing poverty. But maintaining the past pace of economic progress is likely to require greater efficiency.

Efficiency in the relevant sense means ceaseless, intense efforts by producers to reduce costs, to increase productivity, to improve product quality, to introduce new products, and to seek out and respond to changing needs and opportunities. It involves bold yet frugal investment decisions, increasing specialization, and the constant displacement of more expensive or inferior products and processes by cheaper and better ones.

These conditions for rapid, sustained growth are at present far from fully met in China, except in agriculture, where outstanding progress has been made in recent years with the introduction of the production responsibility system. Recognizing this, the Central Committee of the Chinese Communist Party in October 1984 announced a program of urban economic reforms, with invigoration of state enterprises as its central theme, to be implemented over a period of about five years. Much of the discussion in the present report is premised on the Central Committee's decision.

To be efficient, enterprises must be motivated to improve their economic performance; they must have some freedom of maneuver; they must be faced with economically rational prices; and they must be subjected to competition. None of these elements is individually easy to establish, and the absence of any one of them reduces or nullifies the benefits of the others. In addition, the state must retain the ability to direct the overall pace and pattern of development. The essence—and the difficulty—of a successful and comprehensive reform thus lies not only in bringing together the several elements of market regulation, but also in combining them with an appropriately modified system of planning.

Enterprise Motivation

The unsatisfactory results of direct administrative control of enterprises—whether by central ministries or local governments—lead irresistibly to the principle of greater enterprise independence. Yet establishing independent and appropriately motivated enterprises may be the hardest single aspect of reform in a socialist system—and perhaps also the most fundamental, since an unmotivated enterprise cannot be expected to motivate its workers, or to respond to price and tax signals, or to compete.

Appropriate enterprise motivation should include a strong desire to increase profits. Avoidance of losses is an important aspect of this, but is insufficient, since China needs enterprises that not merely pursue a passive strategy of staying out of trouble, but actively seek to increase production and sales and to cut costs of all kinds. With rational prices and competition, the best single measure of enterprise performance in this regard is usually medium-term profits (especially after deduction of the cost—depreciation and interest—of the capital employed). The active desire of peasant households to increase sales and cut costs, because their standard of living depends on it, lies at the heart of China's recent agricultural successes. Outside agriculture, the same motivation is a natural feature of individual and family enterprises, and of small enterprises owned and operated collectively by their workers. In medium-size and large enterprises, however, things are not so simple.

STATE ENTERPRISES. Some important enterprises should clearly remain subject to direct government control and should not primarily pursue profit. At a minimum, this applies to public utilities (for example, electricity, railways, and telecommunications), large-scale mineral exploitation, and many defense-related industries. Direct control of other key enterprises might also help to achieve specific development objectives, including the technological upgrading of particular sectors.

What is less clear is the best way to organize and motivate the remainder—probably the great majority—of state enterprises, which would be relatively independent. Once a suitable economic environment is created through price reform and increased competition, and provided that indirect levers such as taxes and credits are skillfully applied, pursuit of profit should lead most state enterprises in economically appropriate directions. It would thus no longer be necessary for particular individuals within enterprises to be charged specifically with representing the interests of the state. But each of the alternative possible internal management arrangements has strengths and weaknesses.

Giving direct control of state-owned enterprises to their workers is a socially attractive possibility. Japanese experience also shows the economic advantages of strong worker commitment to the enterprise. But there are also disadvantages, especially because state enterprises should operate for the benefit of the whole society and not only of those who work in them. Experience in Yugoslavia and elsewhere suggests that worker control could result in excessive wages and worker benefits, inadequate labor discipline and effort, restriction of employment, and comparative indifference to profitability.

Experience in industrial capitalist economies suggests that giving control of enterprises, instead, to their managers would increase their propensity to expand, improve, and innovate. But completely independent managers sometimes choose a quiet life or, more commonly, pursue personal power through expansion with insufficient attention to profitability. In socialist countries, moreover, managerial control tends to differ only slightly from worker control, since managers find it hard to resist worker demands for greater benefits or to insist on the often unwelcome changes in work practices that are needed for innovation and increased efficiency. This is already a problem in China: studies of experimentally reformed enterprises controlled mainly by their managers reveal large increases in worker benefits, but small increases in economic efficiency.

An alternative approach, common in nonsocialist countries (and now being tried in Hungary), is to give strategic decisionmaking authority in each enterprise to a board of directors. Such a board could contain some representatives of society at large, as well as of the workers. But to impart the necessary motivation, the board would mainly have to represent institutions with a strong interest in the enterprise's profits. It could insist that the enterprise managers behaved accordingly, partly by appointing and dismissing them, partly by linking their remuneration to profitability. The managers might in practice make most decisions, but would be greatly influenced by their ultimate accountability to the directors.

Such boards should be free from direct government intervention. But, precisely because these are state enterprises, this may be difficult to achieve. In China, for instance, even if the boards were to consist of representatives of the Ministry of Finance or a new Ministry of State Property, rather than of sectoral ministries or the governments of the localities in which the enterprises are situated, informal connections and pressures for direct administrative control could persist. A possible solution might be to spread the ownership of each state enterprise among several different institutions, each in some way representing the whole people, but with an interest mainly in the enterprise's profits rather than directly in its output, purchases, or employment. (Examples of such institutions, in addition to central and local governments,

are banks, pension funds, and insurance companies.) Such a system of socialist joint stock ownership could perhaps be created initially by suitable dispersion of the ownership capital of existing state enterprises. Over time, it could be reinforced by a more diversified pattern of investment finance (discussed below), with a variety of state institutions acquiring financial interests in existing and new enterprises.

COLLECTIVE AND INDIVIDUAL ENTERPRISES. China's policy is to encourage the coexistence of state and other sorts of enterprises. In small-scale economic activities, whose importance will increase with economic development and reform, individual and collective enterprises are already making a valuable contribution. They could be even more productive if given better access to materials, credit, skilled labor, and technology. Their potential role in medium- and large-scale activities, however, remains to be determined.

Experience elsewhere suggests that genuine collectives flourish only in certain lines of activity and rarely above a certain size. Many of the most successful examples elsewhere are in commerce and are marketing or purchasing cooperatives. There are far fewer examples of medium-size genuine worker collectives or of any sort of collectives in manufacturing. China's numerous township and village enterprises may appear an exception; however, these are not collectives in the ordinary sense, but community enterprises. They have been successful partly because of restrictions on personal mobility among communities, which has given local residents a strong common interest in their establishment and profitability.

Collectives and community enterprises could in the future constitute a significant proportion of China's medium-size enterprises. Many individual enterprises could also grow rapidly to medium size, if allowed to do so, and could be an important dynamic force in the economy. As an alternative to the present restrictions on the size of individual enterprises, these enterprises might be obliged to sell (at a fair price) majority ownership to one or more state institutions once they reached a certain size. The then minority owners could continue as managers, supervised by a board of directors representing all the owners.

ACCOUNTING AND LAW. The best way of motivating independent state enterprises, and the best balance among state, collective, individual, and mixed enterprises, can only emerge from experience and experiment over a protracted period. But certain necessary conditions for success can already be identified.

One is improvement of enterprise accounting and auditing, which at present leave much to be desired. Without accurate accounts, subject to thorough, compulsory, and independent audits, with severe penalties for noncompliance, it is hard to see how any system of independent enterprises—state or nonstate—could function properly.

Moreover, a decentralized economy cannot function properly without a comprehensive system of commercial and contract law and institutions and personnel to implement it. Laws are also needed to regulate the economic activities of independent enterprises. Among other things, laws or decrees should prohibit specified types of monopolistic, anticompetitive, or exploitative behavior, with legal institutions to interpret and implement these prohibitions. At present in China, the situation is unsatisfactorily vague, with enterprises and local officials free to place their own interpretations on general guidelines from the center.

Competition

As the Central Committee's 1984 decision clearly states, competition among enterprises is crucial to efficient growth—without it, customer requirements are neglected, innovations diffuse slowly, and market-regulated prices are distorted for monopolistic gain. One key ingredient of competition is allowing purchasers to buy from the best and cheapest source. China has already taken some significant steps in this direction, but further progress is needed. It could probably be assisted by dismantling the annual production planning and allocation system, either in one step (as in Hungary) or more gradually, by reducing each year in each enterprise the proportion of material requirements covered by the state allocation and, in parallel, the obligatory state production and procurement quota.

It would also be assisted by dismantling administrative barriers to internal trade, which would be easier if fewer enterprises were directly controlled by government organs anxious to avoid competition within their "families" of enterprises. Consolidation of enterprises into large sectoral corporations, by contrast, would normally tend to reduce competition, although this could be offset by increased exposure to foreign competition. Equally important would be measures to enlarge, diversify, and strengthen commerce and related services. Individual and collective enterprises might be given a greater role in wholesaling and material supply and better access to transport facilities.

Another key ingredient of competition is free entry of new producers into particular markets. One step in this direction for China could be to allow larger enterprises to diversify more freely out of their existing lines of business. Provided that prices are rational, such diversification can transfer profits earned in one line of activity into other lines where the economic returns to investment are greater. And it can permit enterprises to transfer workers who can no longer be profitably employed in one line to other lines, without having either to discharge them or to keep them idle.

Another important step toward free entry could be to allow individual and collective enterprises to operate in more lines of activity, including technologically dynamic sectors. Studies in other countries have shown that small enterprises are just as innovative as large ones. (Chinese visitors to foreign countries are often given a misleading impression in this regard, because they are usually taken only to well-known, large enterprises.) Particularly because of the strong incentive that small enterprises have to innovate, the overall pace of technological advance could very probably be accelerated by letting them compete for some of China's skilled manpower, technology imports, and research support.

Lastly, effective competition has to involve the elimination of obsolete or unwanted products and processes. Subsidies or protection for backward technology and inefficient enterprises—other than on a temporary basis to permit reorganization—hold back the growth of efficient enterprises and remove a powerful negative stimulus to innovation and improved efficiency. At the same time, this aspect of competition can obviously cause hardship, especially for displaced workers. Social policies and institutions (discussed below), and government retraining schemes, can alleviate this hardship. But the conflict between the gains of the majority from greater competition (and faster technological change) and the losses of particular individuals and groups cannot be completely eliminated.

Prices

The Government is well aware of the need to establish economically rational prices, without which the decisions of independent, profit-oriented enterprises would often be inefficient for the whole economy. The Government also recognizes that this must be accomplished by changing the price-setting system to give market supply and demand forces a greater role, and not only by administered changes in prices set by the state, which tend to lack the flexibility, complexity, and precision needed in a modern economy. The prices of many minor items, and of some transactions in more major items, have already been successfully decontrolled.

Further progress in this direction is impeded by chronic shortages of many goods. It is feared that these shortages, if prices were no longer subject to direct state control, would cause general price inflation, as well as obstructing the allocation of materials to key projects. For this reason, it is often argued in China that further price decontrol should be postponed until rising production has eliminated most of the shortages.

Soviet and East European experience suggests, however, that chronic shortages are not the temporary result of inadequate production capacity, but an enduring feature of administrative economic management, which can be eliminated only by systemic reforms, including price decontrol. This view is supported by China's experience in the past few years, especially in agriculture, where relaxation of direct controls has turned long-standing shortages into abundance. The same could happen in industry. Increases in specific prices could eliminate specific shortages by stimulating supply and reducing demand. These price increases, moreover, would tend to reduce purchasing power over (and hence the prices of) other goods, provided that the government kept strict control of the budget balance and credit.

Nonetheless, there is substance to the fear of immediate and general decontrol of prices in China. The downward inflexibility of some prices, and of wages, could obstruct the smooth adjustment outlined above. The full response of demand and supply to price changes may take years. China lacks experience in indirect fiscal and monetary regulation of the general price level, and other countries with much greater experience still suffer from rising prices. The elimination of shortages, moreover, would also require increased competition and stronger enterprise motivation to hold down costs, including investment costs, which cannot be brought about overnight. For these reasons, price decontrol probably has to be gradual though steady—perhaps in conjunction with the gradual dismantling of annual production planning and allocation mentioned earlier.

Some steps, however, could be taken more quickly. Large increases, either administratively imposed or market-determined, in the prices of most forms of energy—and some other materials—are a case in point. Without them, there would be little chance of achieving the essential reductions in energy use discussed earlier. There is concern in China that large energy price increases would have ripple effects, since energy-intensive industries and enterprises could not absorb all the increased cost through conservation and profit reduction and would therefore have to raise their prices. But most such ripple effects should in fact be welcomed (and cushioning through reduction of taxes and profit remittances avoided): experience elsewhere suggests that increases in the prices of energy-intensive products, by discouraging their use, can make a vital contribution to raising the economy's overall energy efficiency.

Agricultural prices are another instance. With the new system of household agriculture, if production is to be efficient and surpluses and shortages of particular commodities avoided, prices must be allowed to respond flexibly to supply and demand trends. At the same time, it would be desirable to avoid the large short-term price fluctuations—often because of weather—that characterize unregulated markets for agricultural commodities. The Government's present strategy is to decontrol completely the prices of minor items and, for major items, to have two-tier pricing (flexible prices for amounts in excess of official, fixed-price procurement contracts). A possible al-

ternative would be to have wholly market-determined prices, but with a price stabilization scheme—Government intervention to keep fluctuations at any given time within a predetermined range by purchasing for addition to stocks at the lower end and selling from stocks at the upper end.

A third instance concerns the relationship between producer and retail prices, which needs to be altered not only to reduce the presently high level of subsidies, but also to encourage consumers to buy less of things (such as energy or animal products) in short supply or whose production costs are increasing and more of things in abundant supply and whose production costs are falling. This could be achieved by establishing relatively rigid margins between producer and retail prices, sufficient to cover the costs and normal profits of commerce as well as indirect taxes (whose rates could vary from commodity to commodity).

In the near term, what is mainly needed are some substantial increases in the retail prices of staple food and coal and in rents. These should be as fully and accurately compensated as possible, by wage increases and income supplements to households with high dependency ratios (discussed later). Special supplementary interest payments on saving deposits which would otherwise lose part of their real value might also be needed (financed perhaps by a corresponding special levy on borrowers, whose loan repayment burden would otherwise decrease in real terms). A large-scale program of selling state- and enterprise-owned housing to its present tenants, who would otherwise face increased rents, could soak up a large fraction of existing saving deposits and hence reduce the possible scale of panic buying in anticipation of price increases.

There is room for disagreement as to whether such a major realignment of retail prices, incomes, and assets should be done in one step, or more gradually. The social problems that have sometimes followed large retail price increases in other countries seem to have occurred mainly because of the absence of compensation—often deliberate, because of the need to reduce real consumption in the face of economic difficulties. In China, however, there is no need for a cut in household consumption, and full compensation could be provided (although this would mean no net improvement in the state budget balance). A carefully prepared and well-explained one-step adjustment could thus be quite acceptable and would avoid the protracted uncertainty and delays to other necessary reforms associated with gradual adjustment. But it would also obviously increase the cost of errors in preparation (especially calculating the required changes in prices, wages, and other forms of compensation) or implementation.

Following this initial phase of adjustment, subsequent rises and falls in producer prices could be reflected in retail prices. Experience in other countries suggests, however, that it would be inadvisable to provide continuing automatic compensation for retail price increases in the form of general wage or income indexation, since this tends to aggravate inflation. Even selective indexation (of state income supplements to poor households, for example, or for pensions) should be approached cautiously.

A fourth instance concerns prices that influence the spatial location of economic activities. One is transport: prices for each mode should more accurately reflect long-run marginal economic costs, without cross-subsidies among different length hauls, to provide incentives to reduce the present waste of rail facilities, to encourage greater use of roads, and to enable proper assessment of the costs and benefits of locating particular activities in particular places. The other is urban land: for social as well as economic reasons, enterprises and planners should be made to feel the dramatically varying economic usefulness (or opportunity cost) of different sites—higher in coastal cities than in more remote regions, higher in large than in small cities, higher near the center than in the outskirts (in a city the size of Shanghai, experience in other countries suggests that a central site is worth approximately 150 times as much as one in the suburbs).

A differentiated urban land tax reflecting these variations could be introduced. Alternatively, a competitive rental market might be established—which would in principle be more efficient and quite consistent with public ownership of all land. (Either or both could provide a useful supplement to municipal revenues.) This would encourage better use of existing sites and more economically efficient location decisions. The presently huge incentives for rural-urban migration would likewise be reduced to more economically rational proportions, especially if differing land values were reflected in house rents and wages, and hence in the costs of living and employing workers in large urban areas.

Finally, further strengthening of the linkages between internal and world prices could be beneficial, though there would need to be some exceptions—for example, rice, where an increase to the present world price could aggravate incipient overproduction. For most goods, especially manufactures, enterprises should eventually directly feel the relationship between their value (for exports) or cost (for imports) to China in world markets and their domestic prices. Such linkages (which are now standard in Hungary and have begun to be introduced in China) are essential for the efficient functioning of a decentralized foreign trade system. They would also contribute to a much-needed widening of price differentials between low- and high-quality products, without which enterprise incentives to innovate and improve quality will remain small.

Labor and Wages

To reduce the risk of shortages of highly skilled workers

constraining China's growth in the next two decades, measures to improve their allocation and motivation seem worth considering. Among the more important possibilities would be freedom of job choice, for both new graduates and experienced staff, allowing employers to recruit and release freely and competitively, and higher and more flexible salaries. Provided that they were accompanied by reform of enterprise motivation, competition, and prices, these measures could help move highly skilled labor to where its economic contribution was greatest, speed the diffusion of new technology, improve motivation (with better matching of jobs to personal preferences and skills just as important as more money), and send much clearer signals of needs and priorities to education and training institutions.

More generally, it will be essential to make better use of all categories of labor. This is because long-term growth of average per capita income will be almost entirely determined by growth of labor productivity, most of which must come not from movement of labor out of agriculture into other sectors, but from higher productivity within each sector. Unskilled labor is currently in surplus, but this will change in the twenty-first century; experience elsewhere shows how hard it is at a late stage to break out of an established pattern of low productivity and indifference to labor costs.

It might therefore be desirable to give enterprises progressively more discretion in deciding how many, and which, less-skilled workers to employ. This should in principle encompass not only the right to dismiss idle or negligent workers, but also to release or reject workers who are simply not needed for production. Lifetime employment would not necessarily disappear (Japanese experience confirms its potential advantages in training and motivation), but would be likely to be limited to larger enterprises, which would be highly selective recruiters.

Some open unemployment would be an inevitable consequence of these changes. In addition to its adverse human consequences (which could be mitigated by changes in social policies and institutions, discussed below), this would involve waste of human resources. The waste of unemployment, however, has to be weighed against the waste of human resources associated with the present employment system, which transfers unemployment from the streets into the factories and discourages managers from realizing the full productive potential of their workers. It is also important to bear in mind the tremendous potential for creation of new jobs in the service and small enterprise sectors. Nonetheless, movement should be gradual, perhaps with an early end to the obligation of enterprises to accept unwanted new workers (usually as part of a package also containing some useful recruits), and subsequent release of unneeded workers each year up to a specified percentage of an enterprise's labor force.

Greater flexibility of less-skilled wages might smooth

this transition, as might stronger linkages between individual pay and performance. But these changes, too, could be only gradually introduced, to avoid a sharp drop in unskilled wages. It will also be necessary for some time to retain administrative control of total and average wages (and other benefits) in state enterprises, to prevent excessive increases in response to pressure from workers. In this regard, the Government is contemplating formal linkages between the remuneration of workers and the performance of their enterprises. But experience elsewhere suggests that this could generate inequities and misrepresentations that might undermine aggregate wage control. It might be preferable to have wage guidelines that were more uniform across enterprises, coupled with greater managerial discretion in the distribution of wages among workers within particular enterprises.

Gradual wage adjustments could also help remote and backward localities. At present, nationally uniform state sector wages, and unofficial pressure to tie collective sector wages to state wages, make it harder for enterprises in these localities to compete effectively against enterprises in more advanced regions or in international trade. Nonagricultural employment in backward areas might therefore increase faster if unskilled wages in these areas declined in relative terms. At the same time, though, these areas probably need to offer skilled workers higher wages than elsewhere.

Investment Decisions and Finance

In energy, transport, education, health, and defense, the Government will undoubtedly retain direct control over most investment decisions, mobilizing the necessary finance through the budget. The same will apply to major land and water development projects. Budgetary saving to finance other sorts of investment may also have to remain substantial, if the high aggregate saving rate necessary for rapid growth is to be attained. But households and enterprises could contribute a much larger share of aggregate saving than in the past and could make an increasing proportion of investment decisions. This pattern is already established in agriculture and other small-scale activities. In larger-scale industry and services, however, the degree to which investment decisions should be devolved to enterprises remains an important issue.

Such devolution could have a number of advantages. It would give greater meaning to enterprise independence, especially since the economic performance of an enterprise at any given time depends heavily on previous investment decisions. It would increase the medium and long-term responsiveness of production to evolving needs and demands. It would make fuller use of the detailed knowledge of enterprise managers. It might also provide a way of strengthening incentives for sound investment decisions, in whose outcome enterprise managers could be given a substantial direct personal financial interest.

Experience suggests that this would encourage bold and innovative thinking combined with thorough analysis, hard-headed calculation, and the avoidance of waste.

Delegating more responsibility for investment decisions to independent enterprises might also help in striking a better overall balance between infrastructural and other investment. China's local governments have proved dedicated and resourceful investors, but are probably unduly biased in favor of directly productive industrial investment. Making enterprises independent, with more investment responsibility, could thus give local governments a stronger incentive—as in other countries—to improve infrastructure in order to attract industrial investment.

China's recent mixed experience with devolution of investment decisions to enterprises, however, confirms that without other systemic changes such an arrangement can have undesirable results. Inappropriate managerial incentives, irrational prices, lack of competition, and shortcomings in commerce and material supply can lead enterprises to undertake investments of little economic merit, while neglecting other investments of much greater use to the economy.

Reforms in enterprise motivation, competition, and prices could eventually overcome many of these problems, making it possible to consider devolving a much greater proportion of investment decisions to enterprises and, relatedly, allowing state enterprises to retain a much larger proportion of their profits. More mobility of investment funds, through more varied channels, could also increase the efficiency of decentralized investment decisions.

Investment flows in China in the past have been largely vertical, with most savings being mobilized upward through the budget and dispensed downward through sectoral ministries and state banks. In addition, there has been some compartmentalized reinvestment of savings generated within particular sectors and localities. In the future, although vertical flows and compartmentalized reinvestment will remain important, they could advantageously be supplemented and replaced to an increasing extent by horizontal investment fund flows of three main types. The first, mentioned earlier, would be allowing existing enterprises to diversify into new lines of activity. The second, which overlaps with the first, is direct investment linkages among economic units: enterprises could increasingly be permitted to invest in other enterprises, establish new enterprises, or participate in various sorts of joint ventures. The third sort of horizontal flow is through socially owned financial institutions, acting as intermediaries between the suppliers and users of resources.

Such financial institutions, offering interest rates that reflected the scarcity of capital, could mobilize funds from households and institutions, including enterprises with limited internal investment opportunities. They could make these funds available to potential investors, especially enterprises of all kinds, perhaps mainly in the form of loans, but also in the form of ownership capital—partly because many worthwhile projects are too risky to be largely loan-financed, partly because directly sharing in the risks and benefits would motivate financial institutions to provide more assistance in project design and implementation, including information on markets and technology. These institutions could in effect create a socialist market for investment funds.

For such a market to function well, the financial institutions should be numerous and diverse, acting in most respects as independent state or collective enterprises. Nonetheless, government regulation of their activities would be essential. At a minimum, as in all other countries, rules to protect depositors would need to be designed and enforced, with other rules and central bank intervention in the financial market to regulate the overall supply of money and credit. In addition, the government could—as for many years in Japan and South Korea—influence the allocation of funds in accordance with strategic economic objectives. This could be done in various ways, including channeling some budgetary savings through these institutions and subsidizing or taxing loans for particular purposes, as well as by selective direct controls on interest rates and loan allocation.

For China, continued experimentation and exploration in the area of investment decisionmaking and financing will be necessary, especially since the experience of other countries provides no precedent for a socialist financial market. The relative shares and importance of the various possible elements discussed above—vertical and compartmentalized, as well as horizontal—should be allowed to evolve with experience and the development of institutions. In general terms, however, it seems likely and desirable that diversified investment arrangements will emerge as both consequence and cause of a diversified pattern of enterprise ownership.

Planning

Reform of the system of economic management along the lines of the Central Committee's 1984 decision will reduce the Government's direct involvement in production, commerce, prices, employment, and so on, but should not diminish its responsibility or capacity to promote and steer China's development. The preceding discussion has touched repeatedly on areas in which continued, and often enlarged, direct government involvement is needed, especially in establishing the physical, educational, scientific, institutional, and legal infrastructure essential for rapid and efficient growth. The Government will also continue to intervene directly in some other key sectors and enterprises, though more in investment decisions than in current operations.

INDIRECT CONTROL. In the remaining areas of the economy, where decisions will increasingly be made by households, farmers, and independent enterprises, there will be a shift from direct to indirect control. This, however, need not diminish—and indeed might well increase—the Government's ability to manage the economy. For up to now in China, what has not been directly controlled has often not been properly planned. The broader reach of indirect controls, which shape the environment in which all economic units operate, could more than compensate for the associated loss of direct control over particular economic units.

Instruments of indirect control fall into two main categories—those connected with credit and those connected with taxes or subsidies. A third category is prices. But indirect control through administrative determination of prices has the drawback of being able for any particular commodity to govern either demand or supply, but not in general both, and hence having to be supplemented with administrative quotas either on demand (in the case of shortages caused by a low price) or on supply (in the case of surpluses caused by a high price). Moreover, reduction in the scope of administrative price determination will gradually change prices—apart from their tax or subsidy element—from instruments of government control into independent indicators of value, cost, and scarcity. These both influence and are influenced by the actions of producers and consumers, usually in economically appropriate directions. Government intervention, however, may still be needed in some cases to dampen fluctuations, as well as to set one very basic price, namely the exchange rate, which strongly affects exports and imports in a decentralized economy.

Control of the overall level and growth of credit, which depends not only on caution in financing budget deficits by note issue or borrowing from banks, but also on regulating the whole banking system (according to well-established rules), is a fundamental element of indirect macroeconomic management. And, as mentioned earlier, preferential interest rates and repayment terms in certain sectors or regions, as well as direct government intervention in the allocation of credit, are feasible and effective ways of influencing the composition of investment. But experience elsewhere suggests that they should be used cautiously, to avoid undesired side effects. Low interest rates on rural credit, for example, can lead to uneconomic mechanization in areas with surplus agricultural labor.

Personal income taxation, including progressive rates and selective relief, can influence the proportion of household income saved and the composition of consumer demand. Above-average indirect taxes on particular goods (for example, luxuries) can reduce the amounts purchased and supplied by driving a larger wedge between the price paid by the customer and that received by the producer; the reverse is true for below-average indirect taxes or subsidies (as on food, children's clothing, books and the arts in many countries). Taxes on enterprise profits, including selective concessions by product or locality, can be designed to regulate the total amount of funds available to enterprises, the proportion of profits reinvested, and the amount of external finance used and can stimulate investment in certain activities or regions while discouraging it in others. Similarly, import tariffs can be used to promote increased production in particular sectors through import substitution (although without complementary export incentives they produce an inefficient bias toward the domestic market), and in certain cases it is rational to tax exports.

This range of instruments can enable planning and markets to coexist reasonably harmoniously, though it involves greater emphasis than hitherto in China on managing demand rather than supply. Direct control of supply will, as mentioned earlier, continue in some important sectors. But in most cases, rather than dictating what should be produced, the Government could use taxes and credits to guide the changing composition of demand and to influence the relative profitability of different sorts of production and investment, allowing supply to respond through the decentralized decisions of enterprises and farmers.

Experience in other countries suggests that this indirect approach can be as effective as direct controls in shaping the pattern of development and often can be more economically efficient. But the relationship between objectives and indirect instruments is much less precise and predictable, especially in the absence (as in China) of much systematic study of the behavior and responses of economic units. This element of unpredictability can be reduced by research and by flexible and responsive implementation, with adjustment of policies to achieve desired objectives over the medium term. But it can never be eliminated, and many countries (including Hungary in recent years) have experienced practical difficulties in indirectly regulating their economies. The increased uncertainty associated with greater reliance on indirect controls thus has to be weighed against the inefficiency of direct controls.

SCOPE OF PLANS. To the extent that direct control of production and allocation was reduced as part of the reforms, annual plans would become less significant in themselves, although they (and the budget, with which they should be linked) would remain important as a means of monitoring and adjusting medium-term plans. The medium-term plan, by contrast, would become the core of the entire planning process. Although the instruments for its implementation could be different, the general form of the plan document might be much the same as at present. Its preparation could serve even more than now as a focus for the exchange of views among different government agencies and between the center and local governments (who would still have their own, complementary, medium-term plans, at least at the provincial level). Other sorts of planning could also play an important role.

One is what is called in other countries "policy planning." This is the design of packages of policies to achieve specified medium-term objectives—for example, improving road transport, or increasing machinery exports, or raising primary school enrollment. It is of particular value when indirect policy instruments are used, or when several different government organizations are involved, or when different objectives and policy instruments are interrelated. For this reason, policy planning is generally the responsibility of a high-level government agency, with strong analytical capabilities, which can evaluate alternative approaches to an objective, make recommendations to the political leadership, and monitor implementation.

Another is location planning. Even with more economically rational pricing of transport and urban land, most countries have found that zoning plans and regulations are necessary to preserve urban amenities. Moreover, in industries where a single optimal-size plant would supply a high proportion of the national market (for example, automobiles or electronic chips), but many alternative sites would be equally attractive in economic terms, the Government needs to arbitrate among competing localities to prevent wasteful duplication. In other industries (cement and fertilizer, for example), government intervention is required because the location and scale of all the enterprises need to be simultaneously determined to minimize transport plus production costs.

In addition, Japanese experience suggests the potential usefulness of long-term sector planning, especially where major technological changes are expected or desired. (In China, such plans would provide a particularly useful framework for establishing industry-specific priorities for modernization—a very difficult task because of the comprehensiveness as well as the backwardness of the whole industrial sector.) However, Japanese experience also suggests that such plans should not be designed and imposed from above and must have competitiveness in international markets as their not-too-distant objective. Through close contact with the enterprises in an industry, sectoral planners need to create a consensual "vision" of future development, which increases the consistency (and reduces the risks) of investment decisions. This vision has to be backed up by, for example, government financial participation in—or loans to—key investments, including pilot plants, or by temporary restrictions on imports and assistance to exports. But enterprises that wish to pursue a different strategy should often be allowed to do so: though this may seem wasteful, the flexibility it provides has proved valuable, since neither planners nor enterprises can pick technological winners consistently.

Long-term (ten- to twenty-year) plans in individual sectors need not, and probably cannot, be coordinated in detail. But they could benefit from a projected long-term framework for the whole economy—a broad and fairly aggregated "vision" of future growth and structural change, worked out and regularly revised by central government planners. Such a plan could also provide guidance to enterprises in industries without specific sectoral plans, as well as for the planning of direct state investment in infrastructure and natural resource development, and as a context for the medium-term plans.

In all these areas, although the common sense and good judgment of planners will remain fundamental, China could make some significant technical advances in planning methods, including greater use of quantitative models of various kinds. This could be assisted by improvements in economic training (for both planners and other relevant people). Increased use of computers could permit better and more flexible use of the large amounts of data now collected at lower levels. These, and other sorts of economywide and sectoral information, should increasingly be disseminated to lower-level decision-makers, including enterprises—who at present receive far less information from the Government than in many other countries.

Social Issues and Policies

China has been outstandingly successful in reducing extreme poverty. Although there is substantial income inequality between urban and rural areas and among different rural localities, the hunger, disease, high birth and infant death rates, general illiteracy, and constant fear of destitution and starvation that haunt very poor people in other countries have been more or less banished. It will be of the utmost importance in the future to preserve and build on this achievement. But will the policies and institutions that have worked so well in the past meet the social objectives of a middle-income China? And are they compatible with changes in the system of economic management?

To a large extent, the answer to both questions is "yes." Social ownership of land and other productive assets, widely dispersed access to basic education and health care, and a guaranteed minimum food intake should all contribute to maintaining much less inequality and poverty than in other developing countries. Continued encouragement of agriculture and of other small-scale and labor-intensive activities should also—in light of experience both in China and elsewhere—play a vital role.

However, economic reforms and greater technological dynamism could increase income disparities, while economically desirable changes in the price, wage, and employment systems could make it more difficult to use these things as instruments of social policy. Demographic trends, and major changes in the pattern of disease, will also pose new problems. Some changes and innovations in social policies and institutions may thus be necessary.

Income Disparities

Improving the allocation and motivation of skilled labor could involve some substantial increases in relative wages. Even higher incomes could be earned—and in some instances already are being earned—through entrepreneurship. Although perhaps not yet fully accepted in China, entrepreneurship can make an important economic contribution. Entrepreneurs perceive and supply hitherto unmet needs, initially at a high profit, thus luring others into the same activities, which increases supply and drives profits down. If allowed to, entrepreneurs in China could also—as in other countries—play a major role in technological innovation, whose risks may require the stimulus of high rewards.

In such cases, there is unavoidably some conflict between considerations of economic efficiency and the desire for minimal income inequality. But this conflict can be eased by progressive income taxation (tax rates that rise with income level) and by high indirect taxes on luxury goods. China already has a progressive personal income tax, aimed mainly at resident foreigners, which could be extended to cover, say, the top quarter of personal incomes. Although this would have administrative costs, it would probably make it easier for the central government to prevent the informal income redistribution that is now reportedly occurring in some localities.

International experience also suggests the desirability of not attempting to conceal economically necessary income disparities. In some countries, for example, bribery has been aggravated by keeping the wages of public officials low for political reasons. In other countries, formal incomes are fairly equal, but for important people there is access to shops providing goods not available elsewhere, and sometimes even unrecorded but regular supplements to official salaries. Since these and similar practices quickly become well known, their social benefits are temporary, while they seem to have a high long-term cost in terms of corruption and the evolution of a society based on special privileges.

Social Security

At the other end of the income spectrum, a social security system consistent with a reformed economy is urgently needed. It will be increasingly difficult to reconcile the need for greater enterprise independence and efficiency with the present role of enterprises as providers of social welfare benefits and lifetime employment. Prices and wages will be increasingly governed by economic considerations, which will make it much harder to use them to guarantee minimum urban living standards. Faster structural change will involve contraction and closure of some enterprises. Some skills will become obsolete, and some workers—often through no fault of their own—may become at least temporarily unemployed.

In devising new institutions and policies to tackle these problems, China might draw on the experience of the developed Western countries, all of which over the past few decades have established social security systems aimed at providing an adequate income for all citizens and at eliminating poverty due to old age, illness, disability, and unemployment. These systems have not been free of problems, but have effectively attained their main objectives. All but a few developing countries, however, have been deterred from introducing such comprehensive social security systems by their financial cost and administrative complexity. The challenge for China will thus be to devise a social security system that is effective, affordable, and workable for a lower-middle-income country.

In industrial countries, the social security system consists mainly of a state-run insurance scheme, financed primarily by compulsory wage-related contributions from workers and their employers, which provides old-age pensions, unemployment benefits, sickness and maternity benefits, and so on to those who have contributed. In addition, some noncontributory income supplements are usually provided to households whose per capita income (including social insurance benefits) would otherwise fall below some minimum level. This would be one possible approach for China, which could be implemented by consolidation and extension of the present enterprise-based labor insurance and welfare arrangements.

An alternative approach might be for the state in China to concentrate its resources on noncontributory income supplements to low-income households. These could perhaps advantageously be financed partly from the taxes on high incomes mentioned above, although some additional contribution from general revenues might well be required. The total fiscal cost of these supplements could be substantial, but, because they would be targeted on the poor, would be a fraction of the cost of equivalent price subsidies, which benefit rich and poor alike. Their administrative cost could be minimized, and their effectiveness maximized, by making use of existing institutions. In urban areas, there is the household registration system used to administer grain rations. This might be a particularly useful basis for providing income supplements to households with high dependency ratios that would otherwise on balance lose from the upward adjustment of retail prices and wages mentioned earlier. In rural areas, the scheme could be implemented by the administrative successors to communes, brigades, and teams.

In administering either state-run social insurance or an income supplement scheme, China, like other countries, would face some difficult choices concerning coverage and benefits. There might be a uniform urban scheme, including the self-employed as well as state and collective employees. It could be hard, however, to extend the same scheme to rural areas, because incomes are much lower and vary widely among localities. A compromise also always has to be struck among the desire to alleviate existing poverty, the need to give people an incentive to avoid poverty, and the wish to minimize budgetary and administrative costs. For example, setting unemployment benefits high, though it reduces hardship, also reduces the incentive to seek (or remain at) work, particularly if the alternative to unemployment is a monotonous or arduous job at a low wage.

Especially if noncontributory income supplements were chosen in preference to state-run social insurance, the state should encourage collective and local development of contributory pension and insurance schemes. Some of these pension and insurance schemes might, as in other countries, be organized by enterprises and other employers. But they should be financially independent (or "funded"), so that, for example, a scheme would be able to continue paying pensions even if the enterprise that had originally organized it were closed. Such pension and insurance schemes, which would have substantial funds to invest, might play an important role in a socialist financial market.

Because many complex issues are involved, and because improved social security arrangements could be essential to a successful reform of the economic system, a commission could perhaps be established soon to formulate proposals. These might be implemented in stages, and should probably initially be of a modest kind. But the long-term objective should be to maintain China's social achievements, as in the past, well above those of other countries at comparable income levels.

Housing and Social Services

China's large and medium-size enterprises are now unique in the degree to which they provide housing and education and health services to workers and their families. As with social security arrangements, it would be much easier for enterprises to function as independent, efficient economic units if these obligations were removed from them. This would enable managers to concentrate on economic activities, facilitate labor mobility, reduce the social problems caused by the release of unneeded workers and closure of inefficient enterprises, and diminish the present reluctance of many workers to consider employment in small urban enterprises.

The social services now provided by enterprises could be taken over by local governments. So might some of the housing. But experience in China and elsewhere (including Eastern Europe) suggests the advantages of giving households as much responsibility as possible for their own homes, through individual ownership or housing cooperatives. This can provide a powerful stimulus to personal saving, release government resources for other purposes, and produce a higher quality and better maintained housing stock. The Government could usefully assist this, as mentioned earlier, by selling more existing urban housing to tenants, as well as by "sites and services" projects (planning and providing basic utilities for new individually constructed housing), coupled with technical assistance and limited subsidies or tax concessions to housing cooperatives. At the same time, universal entitlement to a minimum standard of accommodation could be maintained, through both income supplements and direct provision.

Increased central and provincial government support of rural social services seems to be needed, especially in poor and backward localities. The introduction of the production responsibility system adversely affected social services in such places, with a sharp decline in cooperative health programs, as well as in primary and secondary school enrollment rates, especially among girls. This is unfortunate, especially since powerful evidence from other countries confirms that improvement of basic education and health is one of the most effective ways of helping poor people, as well as contributing to economic growth. Thus although self-reliance may remain an appropriate policy in more prosperous rural areas, the state should consider financing a larger proportion of the costs of social services in poor areas, for example, through matching grants.

Population

A further reason for taking financial and other steps to maintain and improve basic social services is that studies in other countries have shown that both education—especially of females—and health are major contributors to voluntary fertility reduction. As noted earlier, the expected slow rate of population increase, due also to successful birth planning policies, is an important ingredient of China's relatively favorable economic growth prospects. Given, in addition, the limited amount of cultivable land in China, the achievement of replacement level fertility (2.1 children per woman) is clearly desirable.

It might not be so desirable, however, to hold fertility well below the replacement level for a long time (which would be necessary, for example, to attain the ultimate population of 700 million suggested by some Chinese demographers). This is because the gains from having a smaller population in the late twenty-first century could be more than offset by the costs of transitional changes in the population's age structure. Of particular concern would be the long-term impact of very low fertility on the labor force, which could decline rather rapidly in the middle decades of the twenty-first century. Negative labor force growth might have some economic advantages, but would inevitably cause problems of adjustment. There would also be a rise in the average age of the labor force, with shortages especially of younger, more recently trained, more adaptable workers. In addition, maintaining very low fertility could cause the proportion of elderly dependents (those age sixty-five or more) to bulge temporarily above its ultimate long-term level.

The increase in the proportion of elderly people will be a serious social issue in the twenty-first century even with a more moderate reduction in fertility. It will increase from about 5 percent today eventually to about 20 percent. Though there will be an offsetting decline in the proportion of young dependents, providing financial support to elderly people is more costly and more difficult to organize. China's existing institutions, including the family, for supporting elderly people are unlikely to be able to cope with their increased numbers. This strengthens the arguments mentioned above for starting now to plan long-term reform of the social security system. The early establishment of wider and better pension schemes in rural areas would, among other things, make it easier to reduce fertility.

Health

The aging of the population will also contribute to the fundamental changes that are occurring in the nature of China's health problems. These have already moved from the pattern typical of low-income countries to one where the leading causes of death are heart disease, strokes, and cancer, as they are in high-income countries. These chronic diseases constitute a fundamental challenge for China, which other countries have had difficulty in meeting despite vast financial outlays.

One essential ingredient of the required "second health care revolution" will be prevention. Some steps—particularly control of salt intake and tobacco consumption—could be taken straightaway. But much additional research is needed to identify and field test appropriate preventive strategies, which are much less straightforward than with communicable diseases. Another essential ingredient will be strategies for dealing with the large number of cases of chronic disease that will, inevitably, occur. These strategies should include capacity for treatment where treatment holds promise of results and can be afforded; they should pay careful attention to affordable plans for rehabilitation of incapacitated individuals; and they should be concerned with humane care for the terminally ill (an area in which there have been major and quite affordable advances in Western medical practice).

A third ingredient of the second health care revolution will be designing an insurance and financing structure that encourages prevention and discourages current tendencies toward overuse of facilities and introduction of high-cost procedures. Assembling these three ingredients will, inevitably, be difficult. But, to the extent that success is achieved, China could become a world leader in the effective and humane handling of the burden of chronic disease without succumbing, as other countries have, to endlessly costly investments in medical technologies of limited efficacy.

Rural Poverty

Increases in agricultural labor productivity should permit agricultural incomes to grow quite rapidly over the next two decades. It is not easy, however, to find a plausible set of assumptions under which agricultural productivity would grow fast enough to narrow the large agriculture-nonagriculture earnings gap (even in proportionate terms) until the twenty-first century. Because members of farm families will increasingly be engaged in nonagricultural activities, their total incomes will rise faster than their earnings from agriculture, but could still remain unsatisfactorily low. Additional measures to raise them are worth considering.

Higher agricultural product prices and lower prices for agricultural inputs could conflict with other objectives of agricultural pricing policy, including avoidance of surplus production and encouragement of efficient input use. The present two-tier pricing system, though, would in principle make it possible to boost the incomes of farmers by increasing offical procurement prices, while allowing market-determined above-contract prices to balance supply and demand for the various agricultural commodities. But this would be quite complicated, especially if unacceptable inequities among farmers in different places and situations were to be avoided. Direct income supplements to broad categories of farm households might pose fewer administrative problems.

Increased government expenditure on things that mainly benefit the agricultural population, financed by taxation of other sectors, could provide another means of transferring nonagricultural productivity gains to those who must remain farmers. Development of agricultural and other rural infrastructure, improvements in agricultural research and extension services, and support to rural social services are obvious examples. Another possibility is subsidies to rural participants in social security schemes.

Though generally low agricultural incomes are an important problem, the most serious rural poverty in China is concentrated in specific localities, where incomes are far below the average. (For example, in Dongye township, in Dingxi county, per capita income in 1983—the township's best-ever year for agricultural production—was about one-sixth of the national rural average.) Many such localities will benefit absolutely, and some relatively, from reform of the economic system—this appears to be the reason why the production responsibility system has not yet generated the anticipated increase in overall rural income inequality. But others will tend to remain very poor and could even become worse off, especially if they are remote or have meager land and water resources.

To solve the problems of poor localities would gener-

ally require packages of complementary measures, whose composition would vary according to the particular circumstances of the locality and other government priorities. Improved education and health services, in addition to meeting immediate social needs, build up capacity to work and innovate. Focused research and extension services can release untapped agricultural potential. Agricultural specialization and industrial development can be made possible by better roads and other infrastructure, and assisted by temporary subsidies for local industry. Allowing part of the population to move elsewhere, thus increasing per capita land and water availability, can also be an effective and economical way of reducing poverty.

Overview

To sustain rapid growth for several more decades will be a hard and complicated task for China. Better access to advanced foreign technology than in the past will make it easier, but will not be sufficient: the cumulative economic effect of individually inconspicuous improvements in processes and products has been shown to be larger than that of radical innovations, and the size of the technological gap between the best and the average enterprise in an industry to be as important as the technological level of the best enterprise. Nor will availability of energy, land, and other natural resources—despite their importance—be the deciding factor. China's economic prospects will depend, rather, on success in mobilizing and effectively using all available resources—especially people.

This in turn will depend largely on success in reforming the system of economic management, including coordinated progress on three fronts. First is greater use of market regulation to stimulate innovation and efficiency. Second is stronger planning, combining indirect with direct economic control. Third is modification and extension of social institutions and policies to maintain the fairness in distribution that is fundamental to socialism, despite the greater inequality and instability that market regulation and indirect controls would tend to cause.

On each of these fronts, there are promising ways forward, but also problems and hard choices to be faced. In addition, it is hard to overstate the importance and difficulty of striking a correct balance among the three. Very few countries have combined state and market regulation in such a way as to produce rapid and efficient growth, and fewer still have also managed to avoid intolerable poverty among substantial segments of their populations. On the contrary, there are far more countries in which unhappy combinations of plan, market, and social institutions have produced neither rapid growth nor efficiency nor poverty reduction.

There is thus a vital need to guard against losing the strengths of the existing system—its capacity to mobilize resources, as well as to help the poor—in the course of overcoming its weaknesses. This will surely not deter China—a successful pioneer in many areas—from moving ahead. But it argues for a gradual advance, with experimentation and evaluation at each step, even though a one-stroke change would in principle involve fewer internal inconsistencies. Experience in Eastern Europe also suggests the importance of moving steadily and of trying to avoid ill-judged steps in the direction of market regulation that subsequently have to be reversed or administratively tampered with, thus creating needless uncertainty.

Not all the steps need be small, though. In some cases, despite the greater risk of error, it may be best to introduce substantial packages of simultaneous reforms. Nor need progress be slow. What has been accomplished in China's rural areas in the past few years has provided not only an example, but also an excellent opportunity and indeed a vital need for complementary and similarly rapid progress in the urban economy. Though in many ways more complicated and troublesome than rural reform, urban economic reform probably has the advantage of not needing to be so uniform. Other countries have successfully applied different management methods in different sectors and enterprises, and China should be able to do the same, while constantly seeking to refine and improve the mixture.

In system reform, and in the many other areas covered by this report, both the potential for progress and the problems involved are so large, and there is so much that is without historical precedent, that an even-handed and credible conclusion may be impossible. At a minimum, though, China's long-term development objectives seem attainable in principle, and if recent experience is any guide, there is a good chance that they will be attained in practice.

Growth and Change

1

Over the next two decades, China—now a low-income country—will become a middle-income country. This chapter explores possible implications for China's development strategy of international experience during the low- to middle-income transition. Its three main sections deal with macroeconomic change, microeconomic change, and inequality. But first are some objectives—both for China and for this report.

Objectives

China's ultimate economic objective is to catch up with the developed countries, and as quickly as possible. The impressive progress of the first three decades of the People's Republic, described in an earlier World Bank report (*China: Socialist Economic Development*, 1983) represents the first step toward that goal. The next step envisaged by Chinese leaders is to give most Chinese people a relatively comfortable living standard and eliminate the worst manifestations of poverty.[1] Toward this objective, quadrupling of agricultural and industrial output between 1980 and 2000 has been set as a target, with per capita GNP to increase from about $300 to $800 (in 1980 dollars). Beyond this, the path is as yet uncharted. But the direction of development during the next two decades will powerfully and perhaps irreversibly influence China's economic prospects in the twenty-first century.

The magnitude of the task ahead is readily illustrated. In real (purchasing power) terms, GNP per capita in the industrial countries is approximately ten times greater than in China[2] and will increase in the future by at least 2 percent and perhaps 3 percent per year. To catch up by 2050, China's GNP per capita would have to increase at an average rate of at least 5.5 percent and perhaps 6.5 percent per year (the Government's 2000 target implies a rate of 5.0 percent). Such rapid progress has been rare elsewhere. In 1960–82, excluding small countries and economies dominated by oil, only two developing countries achieved annual per capita income growth above 5

percent: South Korea (6.6 percent) and Greece (5.2 percent).

More generally, only one country—Japan—has indisputably caught up with the developed nations from a position of economic backwardness. Several Latin American countries, including Brazil and Chile, entered the modern growth phase at least as early as Japan and have subsequently experienced periods of rapid growth, but still remain far behind.[3] Even the Soviet Union, with an exceptionally high rate of investment in physical and human resources over many decades, has raised its per capita GNP in real terms to only about half the U.S. (and two-thirds of the West European) level.[4]

China's past record, nonetheless, is quite encouraging. From 1952 to 1982, despite relatively rapid population

---

1. "A relatively comfortable living standard" is a rough translation of the Chinese term *xiaokang*, which originated from a Chinese classic *Li Ji*. In that context the term was contrasted with *datong*, which refers to a very rich society. Some people in China now classify the various stages of development in terms of improvement in living standards, as follows: *jihan* (poverty), *wenbao* (basic needs satisfied, which is considered applicable to the present situation in China), *xiaokang* (which is to be achieved by the end of this century), and *fuyu* (rich). See Liu Guoguang, ed., *Zhongguo Jingji Fazhan Zhanlue Wenti Yanjiu* (Issues of China's economic development strategy) (Shanghai: Shanghai Renmin Chubanshe, 1984), p. 98.

2. At actual prices and exchange rates, the gap is much larger—a factor of thirty rather than ten. But the huge nominal income gap between rich and poor countries is apparently due more to differences in prices than to differences in purchasing power, large though the latter are. See I. B. Kravis and others, *World Product and Income* (Washington, D.C.: World Bank, 1982), and *China: Socialist Economic Development* (Washington, D.C.: World Bank, 1983), Main Report, para. 3.32.

3. See, for example, Lloyd G. Reynolds, "The Spread of Economic Growth to the Third World: 1850–1980," *Journal of Economic Literature*, vol. 21 (September 1983), pp. 941–80.

4. This is the conclusion of several Western studies. Soviet calculations suggest smaller gaps.

Figure 1.1 Composition of Aggregate Demand in China and Other Developing Countries, 1981
(share of GDP)

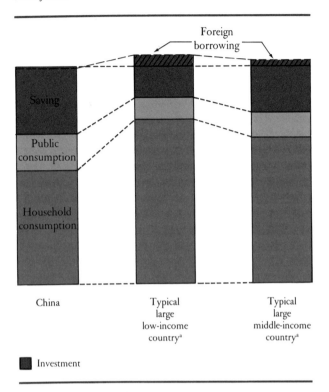

a. Data are from the period 1980–81.
Source: Annex 5, Table 3.1.

growth and periods of acute economic mismanagement, per capita national income grew at an average annual rate of 4.0 percent, with phases of significantly faster growth.[5] Of particular relevance is China's performance during the period of policy and system reforms that began in 1979 (described in more detail in World Bank Report 4072-CHA, March 1983). From 1979 to 1984, largely as a result of much accelerated agricultural growth, per capita national income grew at 6.8 percent per year.

The objectives of the present report are to identify some of the key issues and problems that China may face in the next twenty years and to review, in light of international experience, some of the options for addressing them, with particular emphasis on decisions that might need to be made soon. As well as considering issues within specific sectors, such as agriculture and energy, and intersectoral linkages—the ways in which prospects and problems in each sector depend on circumstances and decisions in other sectors—the report gives special attention to cross-sectoral or economywide issues, including human and financial resources, spatial location of economic activity, and reform of the system of economic management.

The future is inherently unpredictable, and the most careful forecasts are often confounded. The lessons of international experience are commonly either obvious (though frequently ignored) or ambiguous and controversial and in any event are hard to apply to China, a country that in important respects differs from all others and is not easy for outsiders to understand. Thus, although this report is about planning in the broadest sense, its projections and calculations are not predictions, and its suggestions are no more than an attempt to contribute to the debate in China about the difficult questions and problems that must be confronted during the country's unique socialist modernization.

Macroeconomic Change

China's future economic growth will require and cause changes in economic structure. At the macroeconomic level, the pattern of structural change associated with rising income has been broadly similar in most countries, and many of its features are likely to recur in China. But because individual countries have deviated significantly from the average pattern, it is also important to consider China's particular starting point and circumstances.

Figures 1.1 to 1.3 summarize some essential results of available research.[6] Each figure juxtaposes three things: China in 1981; a typical large low-income country; and a typical large middle-income country. The first figure deals with the sectoral composition of domestic demand, the second with the sectoral composition of production, and the third with the sectoral composition of employment.

China's Present Economic Structure in International Perspective

The figures show that China is in essence a low-income country with an unusual pattern of domestic demand and production. Output per agricultural worker is small and agriculture's share of total employment is large—similar to the typical low-income country. Output per worker in manufacturing is higher than in the typical low-income country, because of massive investment in heavy industry; with nonagricultural employment only 30 percent of

---

5. State Statistical Bureau, *Statistical Yearbook of China, 1983* (Hong Kong: Economic Information and Agency, 1983), p. 6.

6. The discussion in this section is based on Annex 5, which compares the present structure of China's economy with those of other countries, and on Background Paper 9, which presents the results of empirical research on the structural changes normally associated with the low- to middle-income transition in large countries. Figures 1.1–1.3 are derived from Tables 3.1, 3.6, 3.8, and 3.9 of Annex 5. In the figures, per capita GNP is taken to be $300 and $1,500 (1981 dollars) for the typical low-income and middle-income country, respectively. In the Annex tables, the predicted values for large lower-middle- and upper-middle-income countries are presented separately.

the total, however, the higher output raises China's per capita income only modestly.[7]

The most unusual aspect of demand in China (Figure 1.1) is the high share of saving—unique among low-income countries, well above the average for middle-income countries, and matched only by Japan and the East European socialist countries. However, although household consumption composes only half of China's low per capita income, basic living standards—as measured for example by calorie intake, literacy, and life expectancy—are similar to those of middle-income countries. This has been achieved partly through a share of public spending (particularly on education and health) well above—and better focused on basic needs than—that of the typical low-income country, partly through imposing an austere but cost-effective pattern of household consumption. Although the share of food in household consumption expenditure is quite normal for a low-income country, staples such as grain constitute an unusually high proportion of food consumption.

Especially because exports and imports are small in relation to total output (though not unusually so for a very large country) and almost balance in both agriculture and manufacturing, China's unusual pattern of demand contributes to an unusual pattern of production (Figure 1.2). The high saving share has its counterpart, because of the need to produce a large volume of investment goods, in a manufacturing share far larger than that of the typical low-income country and similar to that of the typical middle-income country. The share of agriculture in total production, by contrast, resembles that of the typical low-income country, simply because of the need to allocate a substantial proportion of limited resources to feeding the population. The share of infrastructure (electricity, transport, and construction) is also similar to that of other low-income countries, despite China's large manufacturing share.

The share of services in output is thus much smaller (about 17 percent of GDP) than in the typical low-income country (35 percent) or middle-income country (40 percent). The share of education and health services is (as already mentioned) significantly above average. The low overall service share thus mainly reflects the small shares of commerce (including restaurants), banking and finance, and miscellaneous business and personal services. This in turn reflects the small share of household consumption in national income and the high proportion of food consumed directly by its producers, which tend to reduce trade (especially retail), as well as past official neglect of personal services. In addition, China's present system of economic management, and the high degree of enterprise and local self-sufficiency, reduce the provision of (especially wholesale) trade, and financial and other business services.

Although the share of agriculture in total employment

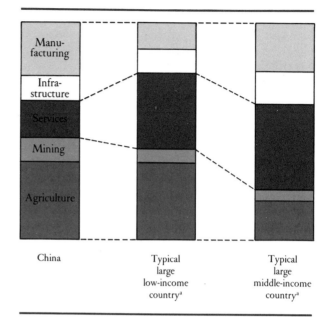

Figure 1.2. Structure of Production in China and Other Developing Countries, 1981
(share of GDP)

China

Typical large low-income country[a]

Typical large middle-income country[a]

Note: Infrastructure includes electricity, transport, and construction; services includes housing.
a. Data are from the period 1980–81.
Source: Annex 5, Tables 3.8 and 3.9; World Bank, *World Tables,* 3d ed. (Washington, D.C., 1984), vol. 2.

in China is similar to that of the typical low-income country, the composition of nonagricultural employment is rather different (Figure 1.3). The share of manufacturing in employment is significantly higher than in the typical low-income country, but by less than its share in output, since output per worker in manufacturing in China is unusually high (which in turn mainly reflects the unusually low share of labor-intensive consumer goods within the manufacturing sector). The share of services in employment in China is correspondingly lower than in the typical low-income country.

International comparisons of economic efficiency are difficult. But the available evidence (reviewed in Annex 5) gives considerable support to the view that China's economy is relatively inefficient. Usage of intermediate material inputs—most conspicuously energy, but also other industrial and agricultural products—seems high. (Indeed, inefficient use of industrial intermediate inputs appears just as important as the high saving rate in ex-

7. As explained in Annex 5, China's per capita GNP in 1981 is $300 at Chinese prices and official exchange rates and is tentatively estimated to be $350 at prices comparable to those in other developing countries.

23

Figure 1.3 Structure of Employment in China and Other Developing Countries, 1981
(share of the labor force)

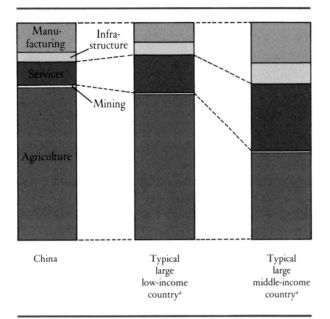

China

Typical
large
low-income
country[a]

Typical
large
middle-income
country[a]

Note: Infrastructure includes electricity, transport, and construction; services includes housing.
a. Data are from the period 1980–81.
Source: Annex 5, Table 3.6.

plaining the large share of industry in China's total production.) The data do not permit a firm conclusion regarding efficiency in the use of fixed capital, but the amount of circulating capital used appears unusually high.

Possible Implications for China's Future Development

Partly because China now differs in important respects from any other developing country, low or middle income, the macroeconomic structural changes that occur during the typical low- to middle-income transition (summarized in Figures 1.1–1.3) are of only limited relevance to China's future development. Nonetheless, some implications—explored further in subsequent chapters—can be drawn from individual elements of this transition, the experiences of some other atypical countries, and China's unusual starting point.

SAVING. China's saving rate is already so high—about 30 percent of national income—by international standards that the usual low- to middle-income trend of a rising saving rate (Figure 1.1) is unlikely to apply. In principle, indeed, China could reduce saving to a level—perhaps 20 percent of national income—similar to other developing countries. But this would be incompatible with China's long-term growth targets. Middle-income

country levels of output per worker require about five times as much capital per worker as in a low-income country; to accumulate this capital rapidly requires a high investment rate, as for example in other fast-growing East Asian economies.

China has, though, the option of supplementing domestic savings with external finance. In recent years, as Figure 1.1 makes clear, China's balance of payments surplus has added to the need for domestic savings—reducing consumption below the already low level required to finance domestic investment. By contrast, the typical large developing country (low or middle income) runs an external deficit, with domestic investment exceeding domestic savings, thus easing the conflict between consumption and growth. Recent international experience, however, has underscored the need—discussed further in Chapter 6—for caution and good judgment in external borrowing, and the essential role of matching increases in export earnings.

EFFICIENCY. A high rate of investment (in education and training, as well as physical capital), though necessary, will not be sufficient to attain China's growth targets. It must be accompanied by increased efficiency and improved technology, which Western economists call growth of total factor productivity (TFP)—the difference between the rate of growth of aggregate output and that of some aggregate of inputs.

Though different studies have often yielded significantly different estimates for particular countries and time periods, most studies suggest that TFP growth has typically contributed about one-third of aggregate net output growth in middle-income developing countries, and nearly one-half in industrial market economies. In the Soviet Union, TFP growth has apparently been slower than in most industrial market economies and has contributed a smaller proportion of output growth. Rough calculations for China suggest that TFP growth during 1952–82 was on average low by comparison with other developing countries, though better in some sectors and subperiods than in others.[8]

Research on the causes of variations in TFP growth across countries and sectors and over time has had limited success, partly because of difficulty in quantifying potential explanatory variables (such as improved technology and knowledge, increased division of labor, and incentives to economize on materials and capital and to use workers more effectively). However, differences in TFP growth among sectors are apparently less systematic and pronounced than differences among countries: in a fast-growing country, TFP growth in all sectors tends to be higher than in other countries. This—like China's experi-

_____
8. Annex 5, Table 3.16; Table 7.1 herein.

ence since 1978—confirms that the general orientation of policies and the system of economic management are crucial determinants of the pace of economic advance.

The same finding—and much other evidence, including China's own experience—confirms the need for a balanced allocation of resources among sectors. In particular, favoring industry at the expense of other sectors does not seem to generate rapid and efficient growth, even though industry is usually the fastest-growing sector and the shift of employment from agriculture to industry contributes significantly to overall productivity growth. Countries that have stimulated agricultural production and incomes have generally experienced faster, rather than slower, industrial growth. Similarly, even in countries where manufacturing production has grown very rapidly, infrastructure and services—which are vital for industrial (and agricultural) efficiency—have absorbed a much larger share of resources. For example, in South Korea in 1965–74, manufacturing accounted for only 27 percent of total annual fixed investment, excluding housing, and in Japan in 1951–65, 30 percent. In China, the corresponding share in the period 1950–80 seems to have been close to 40 percent (Annex 5, Table 3.11).

CONSUMPTION. Like the domestic saving rate, the share of public consumption in national income in China is already above the normal level for a middle-income country and will thus not necessarily follow the rising trend observed in other countries (Figure 1.1). Indeed, it could even fall, given the large weight of education in government expenditure, because of the large and highly atypical prospective decline in primary school enrollment in China over the next two decades, as a result of low birth rates (see Annex 1). Increases in enrollment at higher levels, improvements in educational quality, and pressure for greater public expenditure on health, administration, defense, and other public services will, on the other hand, tend to increase public consumption. Clearly, the Government has many options, whose budgetary implications can only be assessed in relation to possible trends in subsidies, transfer payments, and public investment—discussed in Chapter 9. But public consumption (much of which is in fact essential investment in human skills and knowledge) in the narrow sense of current purchases of goods and services seems unlikely to rise faster than national income in the next twenty years.

Since household consumption in China is probably more concentrated on basic necessities than in the typical low-income country, it will almost certainly change, as per capita income rises, in the same directions as it has changed in other countries. These include a decline in the share of expenditure on food, with an increase in the relative weight of nonstaple foods, especially meat; a slight rise in the share of expenditure on clothing; and a sharp rise in expenditure on other items, most notably those connected with housing, travel, and recreation, and with a disproportionate increase in expenditure on relevant services (as distinct from goods).

However, with any given level and distribution of income, the composition of household consumption varies significantly among countries. This appears to be caused by variations not so much in national tastes (which influence only the details) as in the relative prices and availabilities of different items, which in turn vary partly because of natural resource endowments, partly because of government policies. For example, people in Japan, as compared with those in the United States, eat less meat and dairy products and are less well housed, mainly because land is scarcer, but also because imports of agricultural products are restricted to protect Japanese farmers. In the Soviet Union and Eastern Europe, retail trade and other services are a much smaller share of household consumption than in Western countries, mainly because planners have allocated few resources to these activities.

China's future pattern of household consumption, though following certain universal trends, will thus to some degree accommodate itself to physical constraints, as well as to government policies affecting the supply and prices of particular goods and services. Some of the Government's policy options (especially as regards consumption of food, energy, and services) are examined in later chapters. Naturally, at a given level of aggregate real consumption, if Chinese people are induced—by high prices or restricted quantities—to consume less of one thing, they must also be induced or allowed to consume more of something else. But planners often find it difficult to identify items (other than basic necessities) whose consumption should be disproportionately increased. In most market economies, by contrast, profit-seeking enterprises seek continuously to produce consumer goods and services whose consumption can be expected to increase unusually rapidly (sometimes with the assistance of advertising). Changes in China's system of economic management (Chapter 10) may thus be needed, among other reasons, to enable household consumption to grow at the same high rate as national income.

FOREIGN TRADE. Choices connected with the level and pattern of foreign trade are less significant for large countries than for small ones, since the former generally have more balanced resource endowments, higher internal transport costs, and domestic markets large enough to realize economies of scale in basic industrial activities. China appears to be an exception to this generalization only in respect of resource endowment: its 0.1 hectares of cultivable land per person is one of the lowest ratios in the world. The long-term possibility of net agricultural imports paid for with manufactured exports—the pattern observed in South Korea and Japan—thus requires careful investigation.

But China's foreign trade options (Chapter 6) are significant mainly because of the relationship elsewhere between foreign trade and economic performance. Developing countries—including Japan—that have become sucessful exporters, especially of manufactures, have generally also experienced faster growth. The causation runs in both directions, but exposure to trade seems to be a necessary ingredient of rapid and efficient growth. Thus, although the ratio of exports (and imports) to national product is typically no higher in large middle-income countries than in large low-income countries, the possibility of raising China's foreign trade ratio seems worth considering.

SERVICE SECTORS. A decline in agriculture's share of production and employment is the most universal feature of economic development, and one that will undoubtedly continue in China. The two issues are, rather, how fast this decline will occur and what the relative sizes of the various nonagricultural sectors will be. Especially as regards employment, the two issues are intimately related, since, in the usual pattern of development, the main shift is from agriculture into services, with a more moderate increase in employment in industry, which is less labor intensive. The conspicuous smallness of the service sectors in China at present raises questions about their future contribution: will they continue to be unusually small, or will they—as in the past few years—expand unusually fast?

China's small commerce, finance, personal and enterprise support service sectors, partly offset by a large education and health sector, constitute a pattern that also emerges when the Soviet Union is compared with Western countries at comparable income levels. Neither in the Soviet Union nor in China can this pattern be explained by the "concealment" of service activities within other sectors.[9] As in other countries, the share of employment in services in the Soviet Union has risen with income, but has always been at an unusually low level, with a correspondingly above-normal share of employment in agriculture. There are variations also among developing countries. But the striking contrast between the Soviet Union (and Eastern Europe) and virtually all other countries (including Japan, which has always had a large service sector) is more indicative of the range of options China has.

This contrast also strongly suggests that rapid service sector expansion (discussed further in Chapter 2) and reform of China's system of economic management are closely interrelated options. Expansion of commerce would go hand in hand with expansion of the role of market regulation and increased specialization of production units and localities. Expansion of enterprise support services, including finance, accounting, and law, would likewise be a corollary of increased enterprise independence and specialization. And expansion of personal services would reflect a shift in the balance between planners' priorities and people's preferences as criteria for allocating resources. More generally, rapid and efficient expansion of the service sectors probably could not be accomplished through administrative directives and centralized resource allocation. International experience strongly suggests that growth of services should be pulled by demand, with government in a permissive rather than an active role. Individual and collective enterprises may also be better suited than state enterprises to providing high-quality, flexible, and customer-oriented services.

Microeconomic Change

The changes in macroeconomic structure illustrated in Figures 1.1–1.3, and discussed in the preceding section, are slow—at most, a few percentage points per decade. Moreover, these broad structural shifts are more a consequence than a cause of growth. By contrast, microeconomic structural change (affecting individual products, processes, enterprises, and workers) is typically much faster, and its speed is a crucial determinant of the aggregate growth rate.

Microeconomic change contributes to growth mainly by enabling cheaper and better products and processes—in agriculture and services, as well as in industry—to displace more expensive or inferior ones (Chapter 7). This involves introducing new technology—better seeds, faster machine tools, computerized inventory control—and abandoning obsolete products and equipment. It involves increasing specialization, which realizes technical economies of scale and allows people to become expert in particular sorts of work. It involves responding to needs and opportunities created by alterations in economic circumstances—energy and materials prices, the pattern of demand, transport facilities, and so on. It involves innumerable small modifications to existing products, processes and practices—in procurement and marketing, as well as production—which cumulatively can reduce costs and improve the quality of products and services by striking amounts.

Much microeconomic change takes place within existing production units—farms and enterprises—sometimes involving radical transformation of the product mix. But

---

9. Gur Ofer, *The Service Sector in Soviet Economic Growth* (Cambridge, Mass.: Harvard University Press, 1973). See also Annex 5 of this report. Nor can this pattern be explained by the classification in China and the Soviet Union of many services as not materially productive (and hence excluded from national income): the shortfall is in fact more conspicuous for material services (commerce and enterprise support services) than for nonmaterial services (where the gaps in finance and personal services are offset by education and health).

The seemingly disorderly process of enterprise births and deaths and widely differing enterprise growth rates in most market economies has a strong underlying element of evolutionary natural selection: enterprises that provide cheaper and better products or services, and market them more effectively, expand at the expense of their less efficient rivals, which are forced to improve or to disappear.[1] Studies—mainly of U.S. and British enterprises—have also established that this process exhibits certain statistical regularities.[2] Small enterprises are a large and stable proportion of the total (whose overall size distribution is approximately lognormal). On average, small enterprises grow just as fast, and are just as profitable, as large enterprises, but small enterprises display much more diversity of growth and profitability, which means that the most profitable and fastest growing enterprises, as well as the least profitable and slowest growing (or contracting) enterprises, are mainly the smaller ones. As a result, a significant proportion of initially very small enterprises are rapidly propelled into the large enterprise category, while an equally significant number collapse altogether.

There is also a strong association, independent of size, between profitability and growth; enterprises that are more profitable also grow faster. This is largely because they depend mainly on retained profits to finance investment needed for expansion, but also because higher profits make it easier to borrow and issue new shares. Since greater profitability generally reflects greater efficiency, this financial linkage between profitability and growth plays a crucial role in enabling efficient enterprises to expand at the expense of less efficient ones. Success and failure, moreover, are persistent: enterprises with above-average growth and profitability in one (say, five-year) period are likely also to have above-average performance in the next period. But the evolutionary process takes time: in every sector, there is always a wide spectrum of enterprise profit and loss rates.

1. Several relevant studies are surveyed in Richard R. Nelson, "Research on Productivity Growth and Productivity Differences," *Journal of Economic Literature*, vol. 19 (September 1981), pp. 1029–64.

2. Many studies are surveyed in Robin Marris and Adrian Wood, eds., *The Corporate Economy* (London, 1971), Appendixes A–C.

microeconomic change is also associated with the birth of new enterprises, marked changes in the relative sizes of existing enterprises, and the disappearance—through closure or merger—of particular production units (Box 1.1). For individual workers, change may be less rapid, partly because workers with obsolete skills retire and are replaced by new entrants with new skills, partly because processes change less than products, and partly because changes in enterprise product mix reduce the need for workers to move among enterprises. But microeconomic change inevitably entails considerable relearning of skills and movement of workers among jobs and—in most countries—enterprises (Chapter 8). It may also affect the relative prosperity of different localities—sometimes in a persistent and even cumulative way—and thus create pressure for geographical movement of people and capital (Chapter 5).

The ingredients of microeconomic change described above can be discerned, in some form or to some degree, in China over the past three decades. Many new products and new processes have been introduced. New enterprises have been born at high rates, especially since 1970 with the expansion of commune and brigade enterprises and (more recently) individual enterprises. Largely as a result, the proportion of small enterprises in China is quite similar to that in a typical developing or industrial country, and far higher than in Eastern Europe (Table

1.1). Individual enterprises have expanded at widely varying rates; some have merged, diversified, and changed their product mix, such as one Shanghai engineering enterprise, whose expansion from a repair shop to a manufacturer—first of gear lathes, then of welding equipment, then of electrical cable equipment, then of pumps—resembles the history of many engineering firms in other countries. Some enterprises, including many small cigarette and machinery manufacturers, have been closed down, especially in recent years.

But there have also been some basic differences between China and most other countries in the area of microeconomic change. Product and process innovations by existing enterprises appear to have been less frequent; the trend of increasing specialization has been much more muted; and producers have rarely sought new customers and markets (for example, smelters in China, unlike those in the United States, normally produce only pure metals, with users having to make their own alloys). Changes of product mix, diversification, merger, and spinoff of new enterprises seem to have been less common. Enterprise closure rates have been low. Workers have generally remained employed by the same enterprise throughout their career.

The competitive process by which better and cheaper products drive out worse and more expensive products likewise seems to have been slow in China. Especially in

Table 1.1 Size Distribution of Industrial Enterprises in Selected Countries
(percent)

Size of enterprise	China, 1982	United Kingdom, 1979	United States, 1977	South Korea, 1981	Japan, 1972	India, 1976–77	Yugoslavia, 1981	Hungary, 1981
5–33 employees	59.2	65.2	56.4	70.6	80.2	51.7	6.6	2.2
33–75 employees	19.5	15.7	20.3	14.4	10.7	35.3	15.8	4.8
75–189 employees	12.2	10.8	12.4	9.2	6.1	7.8	32.1	18.7
189–243 employees	8.5	1.4	3.8	1.5	0.8	0.8	12.0	9.2
More than 243 employees	0.6	6.9	7.1	4.3	2.2	4.4	33.5	65.1

Note: Data are percentages of the number of enterprises with five or more employees in the country.
Source: For China, estimates based on data in the State Statistical Bureau, *Statistical Yearbook of China, 1983* (Hong Kong: Economic Information and Agency, 1983); for other countries, various national sources.

the state sector, backward enterprises have been protected, and progressive enterprises held back—sometimes deliberately in order to maintain profits, capacity utilization and employment in less efficient enterprises. In recent years, for example, despite general agreement that there are too many bicycle producers, the output of enterprises producing good-quality bicycles has been restricted by the Ministry of Light Industry in order to protect the producers of inferior bicycles. Similarly, a cotton mill in one province was recently obliged by the provincial authorities to stop sending its cloth elsewhere for dyeing and printing, because the province's own substandard printing and dyeing enterprise was underutilized. Subsidies to keep inefficient plants and old equipment in operation are common, partly because enterprises play a key role in providing housing and social services.

Chronic shortages, strong emphasis on production targets, small price differentials between high- and low-quality products, and inadequate incentives have made product quality improvement, innovation, and cost reduction occasional, rather than everyday, concerns of Chinese enterprises. The former policy of local self-sufficiency and deficiencies in the material supply system have led local governments to construct many plants of suboptimal scale and inferior product quality to supply local needs for commodities such as steel. (This may explain why, by comparison with all the other countries in Table 1.1, China has so few enterprises in the largest size category.)

Deliberate and incidental obstacles to microeconomic change of course exist in other countries. Declining industrial sectors are protected by trade barriers; large firms in difficulty are helped out with loan guarantees and subsidies. Monopolistic practices, distorted prices, corrupt or incompetent bureaucracies, and inadequate retraining facilities, too, retard the speed and efficiency of development elsewhere. Nonetheless, the obstacles to microeconomic change in China seem to have been unusually substantial and comprehensive and could—if allowed to persist—prove incompatible with China's objective of sustained rapid growth.

In all countries, the potential for "extensive growth" through duplication of existing production is limited, no matter how much capital is accumulated, by shortages of natural resources and (ultimately) of labor and by the unwillingness of consumers to buy ever-increasing amounts of the same goods. To attain a high level of economic development thus requires "intensive growth" based on innovation, cost reduction, and product improvement; this in turn requires much faster microeconomic change. With close to 70 percent of the labor force still employed in agriculture, extensive growth alone could probably carry China up into the middle-income range over the next two decades or so, albeit at rather high cost. But, over the longer term, intensive growth will be essential to China's catching up with the industrial nations, and the experience of other countries such as the Soviet Union has shown the difficulty of switching to intensive growth at a late stage of development.

Faster microeconomic change in China will require—above all—changes in the system of economic management, many of which have already been implemented or proposed.[10] System reform is thus a pervasive theme of this report: the general treatment in Chapter 10 builds on the discussion of specific aspects of system reform in other chapters, especially those on technology, spatial issues, and human and financial resources. In all chapters, the need for difficult choices will emerge; this is partly because, beyond a certain point, the objective of faster growth, with which this chapter has so far been solely concerned, conflicts with the objective of equity in income distribution.

---

10. In addition to the major reforms already carried out in rural areas, and numerous experiments in urban areas, a general strategy for reform of the urban economy is contained in the Communique of the Third Plenary Session of the Twelfth Central Committee of the Chinese Communist Party, October 20, 1984.

Inequality

The distribution of income—and of living standards more generally—is of critical importance for a socialist country such as China, whose central economic objective is not merely rapid growth, but growth whose benefits are widely spread. Considerations of equity will inevitably play a central role in shaping China's future development strategy and system reform.

Inequality in China in International Perspective

China's past strategy and present system have created, on the whole, an extraordinarily equal society. The first World Bank economic report on China dealt with this at length (Main Report, paras 3.46–3.102); its conclusions, which are essentially unaffected by more recent information and developments (to be described subsequently), merit summary recapitulation.

Inequality of urban incomes is uniquely low in China, with virtually no extreme poverty in urban areas. There is, however, a large gap—comparable to that in other developing countries—between average urban and rural incomes, which in terms of living standards is magnified, as in some other countries, by concentration of social services on urban residents. In addition, there is substantial inequality of rural incomes in China, largely because of wide differences in the quantity and quality of agricultural land per person, coupled with tight restrictions on geographical mobility.

Thus, because China is a low-income country, and because of substantial rural income inequality, a large minority of the population have extremely low incomes. These people, however, have a much higher standard of living than their counterparts in most other developing countries. Agricultural collectivization has prevented the emergence of a class of impoverished landless laborers; the state guarantees a minimum food supply; primary school enrollment is high; and basic medical care and family planning services are available to most people. As a result, the hunger, disease, high birth and infant death rates, general illiteracy, and constant fear of destitution and starvation that haunt very poor people in other countries have been more or less banished from China. Life expectancy, whose dependence on many other economic and social variables makes it probably the best single indicator of the extent of real poverty, is on average in China outstandingly high (sixty-seven years in 1980[11]) for a low-income country; even in the poorest province, life expectancy is not far below the average for middle-income countries.

NEW INFORMATION. Since the first World Bank economic report on China was written, substantial additional information has become available and further studies made. The preliminary results (from a 10 percent sample) of the 1982 census have been published, as have more household survey results. Health, nutrition, and population issues were examined by the World Bank in *China: The Health Sector* (1984). In general, this material has reinforced the conclusions of the first report. But a few changes of emphasis are required.

The distribution of income in rural areas is less unequal than the World Bank's first estimate (based on fragmentary data) had suggested. Rural household survey data, summarized in Table 1.2, show the Gini coefficient in 1979 to have been 0.26, rather than 0.31. This means that rural income inequality in China is significantly less than in other South Asian countries (with Gini coefficients of 0.30–0.35), rather than in the same range.

The same data, however, underscore the importance of geographical differences in rural incomes. Table 1.2 al-

---

11. World Bank estimate based on the 1982 census and other recently released demographic data: see Kenneth Hill, "China: An Evaluation of Demographic Trends—1950–82," Technical Note DEM 4 (Washington, D.C.: World Bank, Population, Health, and Nutrition Department, 1984), which is Supplementary Paper 1 of Dean T. Jamison and others, *China: The Health Sector* (Washington, D.C.: World Bank, 1984). The estimate for 1979 in the first economic report (sixty-four years) was too low.

Table 1.2 Rural Income Distribution, 1979–82
(percentage of population)

Income per capita	National average				Gansu, 1982	Jiangsu, 1982
	1979	1980	1981	1982		
Less than Y 100	19.6	10.1	4.9	2.9	21.1	16.8
Y 100–200	54.0	53.2	39.5	25.6	45.2	
Y 200–300	20.7	26.0	36.2	39.3	22.5	36.2
Y 300–400	4.2	7.7	13.5	20.2	8.2	27.6
Y 400–500	1.1	2.2	4.0	7.4	2.3	11.4
More than Y 500	0.3	0.9	1.9	4.6	0.7	8.0
Gini coefficient	0.257	0.237	0.231	0.225	..	..

Source: Estimates based on household survey data (Annex 5, Appendix I).

lows comparison of the rural income distribution for the whole of China with the distributions in a relatively rich province (Jiangsu) and in a poor province (Gansu); the differences are extremely striking, with four-fifths of the people in Jiangsu in the Y 200–500 or more range, and two-thirds of the people in Gansu in the range below Y 200. Moreover, because Chinese provinces are large and internally diverse, these provincial statistics do not adequately convey the range of incomes among localities. For example, Gansu's average rural per capita income in 1983 was Y 228 (as compared with the national average of Y 310); but in Gansu's poorest county, Dingxi, the average was only Y 108; and in one of Dingxi's poorest townships, Dongye, it was only Y 55—and this was the township's best-ever year for agricultural production.

Census data on educational attainment by sex and age group (Table 8.1) confirm that China's performance in basic education surpasses that of most low-income countries. Moreover, they clearly reveal the adverse effect of the Cultural Revolution on the proportion of younger people with postsecondary education. The same data also show a persistent (though narrowing) gap between male and female educational attainment. This, together with the census data on occupation by sex, suggests that the World Bank's first report may have overstated the degree to which China has reduced inequality between men and women, though it is still less than in most developing countries.

RECENT DEVELOPMENTS. The data recently released also allow an examination of trends over the past five years—a period of important policy and systemic changes, including above all the replacement of collective agriculture by household farming. This, in conjunction with major increases in procurement prices and rapid development of rural nonagricultural activities, has caused an astounding surge in agricultural production (more than 7 percent per year since 1978) and rural incomes—up in real per capita terms between 1979 and 1983 by about 70 percent (Annex 2, para. 1.33). Urban wages and employment have also increased and urban staple food prices have been held constant, which has raised real urban per capita incomes by about 40 percent over the same period, but the urban-rural income gap has still narrowed significantly. Rising agricultural production has also caused a sharp increase in food consumption, which, at about 2,700 kilocalories per person per day in 1982 (Annex 2, para. 2.03), compares favorably with levels in most middle-income countries. Nonetheless, food consumption in many localities still falls far short of the average, and the composition of the Chinese diet is still that of a low-income country.

It was generally anticipated that the rural reforms, by making the incomes of individual households more dependent on their effort, skill, and luck, would increase income inequality in rural areas. The statistics in Table 1.2, although they may have various biases (Annex 2, para. 1.34), suggest that so far this has not happened and that if anything rural inequality has declined. This could be due to increases in inequality within localities having initially been more than offset by reductions in income differentials among localities: the reforms spread fastest in poor and backward areas, some of which had also been especially disadvantaged by the former policy of concentrating on grain production even when other activities would have been more economic. In any event, the lack of deterioration in the distribution of rural incomes has meant that the sharp rise in average rural incomes has greatly reduced the number of households with very low incomes. On the basis of the data in Table 1.2, and a poverty line based on food intake requirements of 2,185 kilocalories per day, it is estimated that the proportion of the rural population in poverty declined from 31 percent in 1979 to 13 percent in 1982 (Annex 5, Table I.7). Though the latter figure still means 100 million people, and though people in places like Dongye township have gained little, the speed and scale of the improvement is probably unprecedented in human history.

In other respects, however, the rural reforms have had some unfortunate consequences for inequality. One has been a sharp decline in rural cooperative medical insurance, financed from collective welfare funds, to which individual households are reluctant to contribute. This has been particularly pronounced in poor and backward areas (in richer provinces, the swelling profits of commune and brigade enterprises have by contrast led to improvements in collective medical and other social services). The drop in the proportion of production brigades covered by cooperative health insurance from 85 percent in 1975 to 58 percent in 1981 (with further declines since then) thus represents a considerable step backward, although the Government is making efforts to upgrade the quality of primary medical care by, for example, giving barefoot doctors more training.

Similar problems have arisen in basic education, mainly because the household responsibility system has induced more rural parents—as in many other countries—to keep their children out of school to work on the family farm. As shown in Figure 1.4, the proportion of primary school age children enrolled (the net enrollment ratio) dropped in 1980–82, although subsequent government efforts seem to have reversed the decline; the gross enrollment ratio at the secondary level has dropped from about 46 percent to about 30 percent, below the developing-country average of 39 percent (Annex 1, paras. 2.04–2.11). The declines have been particularly marked in poorer areas, where enrollment ratios were already unsatisfactorily low (and actual attendance rates lower still); in richer areas, such as Jiangsu, rural parents see clearly that their children will not be able to join the rapid exodus into nonagricultural employment without a good education. The declines in enrollment have also been particularly marked among girls.

Possible Future Trends in Inequality

China may not in the future be able to achieve such a low degree of inequality as in the past—and indeed, the Government's position is that past strategy was excessively egalitarian. The rural responsibility system, though thus far it has increased inequality only through its impact on education and health care, will probably also start to increase income inequality before too long. Systemic changes in urban areas could also increase inequality, by

making diligent workers and successful individual business proprietors richer, and the idle or unlucky poorer. Increased interlocality specialization and trade will surely benefit some localities more than others.

In addition, China may be affected by the forces that have tended to increase inequality during the low- to middle-income transition in other countries. The incomes of the poorest 40 percent of the population have usually increased more slowly than the average; the gap between agricultural and nonagricultural earnings has widened; and interregional income disparities have increased.[12] At higher income levels, though, all these trends have usually been reversed, as the modern sectors have come to dominate the economy and people have moved in search of higher incomes. And even in middle-income countries with an unusually high degree of inequality, most people have a much higher standard of living than in a low-income country.

China will also have to deal with the losses that microeconomic change may inflict on certain families, occupations, enterprises, and localities—even though these may not be visible in aggregate measures of inequality and even though the gains of other groups may hugely outweigh these losses. An example would be a backward enterprise suffering from competition from cheaper or better goods. Governments in all countries, especially socialist ones, feel impelled to reduce the social and political costs involved. Yet protecting potential losers, or routinely compensating them, also has a high cost, because protection and compensation can slow microeconomic change and reduce growth. Ways of easing this dilemma will be discussed in subsequent chapters, but some compromise between conflicting objectives is unavoidable.

Despite all this, if appropriate policies are followed (experience in other countries suggests the importance of support for agriculture, labor-intensive industry and services, and small-scale economic activities) and if important features of the past system are preserved (including social ownership of land, widely dispersed access to basic education and health care, and a guaranteed minimum food intake), China should be able to maintain a much lower degree of inequality than in the typical developing country. In addition, the new dynamism of the rural sector could further narrow the urban-rural income gap. And in the longer term, regardless of the precise pattern of distribution, the great majority of China's people will unquestionably gain substantially from rapid growth—although special attention will have to be given to people and localities excluded by isolation or inadequate resources from the general process of development.

Figure 1.4 Enrollment Ratios in Formal Education in China, 1965–83 and Targets for 2000, and in Other Developing Countries, 1965–80

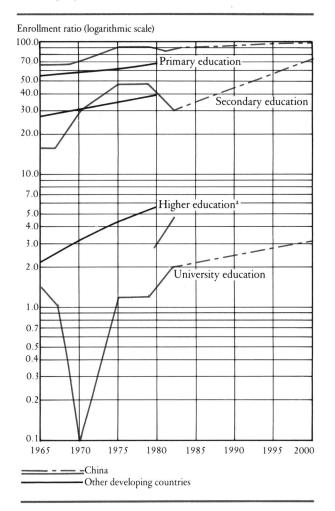

Enrollment ratio (logarithmic scale)

Primary education

Secondary education

Higher education[a]

University education

========--=China

————————Other developing countries

Note: The enrollment ratio expresses the number of students in a level of education as a percentage of the relevant age group.
a. Targets for nonuniversity higher education in 2000 are not available.
Source: Unesco, *Statistical Year Book*; World Bank data.

12. See, for example, World Bank, *World Development Report 1980* (New York: Oxford University Press, 1980), Chapter 4; and Background Paper 3.

2
Illustrative Projections

To explore further China's long-term prospects for growth and structural change, discussed in the previous chapter, and to provide a consistent numerical framework for the discussion of other topics in subsequent chapters, projections to the year 2000 have been made with an economic model. This chapter provides a simple description of the model, explains the main assumptions underlying three alternative projections, and summarizes their results. (A fuller, technical account of the model and projections is in Annex 4. The underlying data, including an estimated input-output table, are in Annex 5.)

Description of the Model

The model is a simplified representation of China's whole economy, broken down into twenty sectors. There are two agricultural sectors (crops—including forestry—and animal husbandry—including fishing), four energy sectors (electricity, coal, oil extraction, and oil refining) and seven other industrial sectors (metallurgy, chemicals, machinery, building materials, food processing, textiles, and other manufacturing), as well as construction, transport, commerce, education and health, public administration and defense, miscellaneous services, and housing. The last four sectors are not regarded as "materially productive" in China; they are included partly to permit calculation of Western-style national accounts, but mainly to make it easier to handle some important components of investment, public expenditure, and household consumption. Chinese-style national accounts are also generated by the model, however, and in most respects the sectoral classification corresponds with that used in Chinese statistics.[1]

For each of the twenty sectors, the model has production, use of materials, employment, investment, and prices. And for each sector, several sources of demand are distinguished: intermediate purchases by other sectors, household consumption, public consumption, exports (less imports), and use for investment. The model projects all these variables—about 600 in total—into the future,

simultaneously and in an internally consistent way, with allowance for the many accounting linkages among them.

To make a projection requires many assumptions, both about the future path of the numerous variables that are in the model, but not determined by it (examples of such "exogenous" variables being population and energy conservation rates in particular sectors), and about the numerous causal—as distinct from accounting—linkages governing the variables that are determined by the model. By comparison with some recent models, the assumed causal linkages in this model are simple and mechanical and not based on any particular theory of household, farmer, or enterprise behavior. This makes them less precise and complete, but also easier to grasp and less controversial.

Growth

Growth of national income in the model depends mainly on the level and efficiency of investment. The level of investment is determined by the proportion of national income saved and (to a much lesser extent) the amount of foreign borrowing, both of which are treated as government policy decisions. Investment is added to the existing capital stock, which increases production capacity in accordance with assumed linkages in each sector between capital stock and gross output (sectoral capital-output ratios). Because these ratios are not the same in every sector (a unit of capital adds more, for example, to the gross output of textiles than of metallurgy), the impact of investment on growth depends partly on its allocation among sectors. It also depends on the ratio of net output (that is, contribution to national income) to gross output in each sector, which in turn depends on efficiency in the use of materials, energy, and other intermediate inputs.

---

1. Except that brigade enterprises are included in the relevant industrial sectors rather than in agriculture and that transport includes both passenger and freight.

Increased production in the model requires not only more capital and more materials, but also more labor. Sectoral labor requirements, and hence employment levels, are governed by assumed growth rates of labor productivity. But the overall growth rate of the economy is not constrained by availability of labor. This is partly because skilled labor is not distinguished from unskilled labor, partly because there is assumed to be (over the next two or three decades) a pool of surplus labor in agriculture, which can be drawn into employment in other sectors with no reduction in agricultural output.

The determinants of growth in the model are a great simplification of reality. In particular, the sectoral capital-output and net-gross output ratios summarize and conceal a host of important underlying factors—product and process innovations, the quality of investment decisions, the training and effective use of skilled labor, and pressures on enterprises to improve product quality and to use less materials, labor, and fixed and circulating capital. Growth in the model is also smooth. In particular, it is never held back by bottlenecks or shortages in individual sectors (such as metallurgy or transport), partly because imports and increased use of existing capacity are assumed to provide short-term flexibility, partly because capacity shortfalls in specific sectors are assumed to be remedied through increased investment within a year or two. These assumptions, though technically convenient, and reasonable for analyzing growth over a twenty-year period, make the model unsuitable for analyzing medium-term (say, five- to seven-year) growth prospects.

Structure

Except for agriculture and energy, where natural resource constraints are important, the structure of production— the relative sizes of the different sectors and the way in which these change as the economy grows—is determined in the model by the structure of demand. This is because the allocation of investment among sectors in the model is governed by the expected growth of demand for their output: in any given year, demand and production capacity in particular sectors may not balance,[2] but sectors where there are shortages, and where the trend growth of demand is more rapid, receive larger shares of total investment, and hence experience faster growth of production.

The model's basic assumption that the long-term structure of production is determined mainly by the structure of demand means only that the Government's production policies will be based mainly on assessment of needs. These production policies may be implemented directly, by quotas and administrative decisions, or indirectly, by using economic levers to regulate the pattern of demand and allowing farmers and enterprises to respond. The model is compatible with both methods of implementation.

As regards final demand, the division of national income between saving (the main determinant of demand for investment goods), public consumption, and household consumption is treated in the model as a direct government policy decision, as is the composition of public consumption (mainly for education, health, public administration, and defense). Household consumption is spread among sectors by assumed "income elasticities" that cause the share of food to decline and the shares of other goods and services—including housing—to increase at varying rates as income rises. The Government can, of course, influence these elasticities by taxes and subsidies or by rationing or other administrative means, but these policy instruments are not included in the model.

Exports (less imports) are also a significant component of final demand in several sectors. They are determined over the longer term in the model mainly by assumptions regarding the openness of each sector (the ratio of exports or imports to sectoral production), the degree of self-sufficiency in each sector (the sectoral trade deficit), and the composition of manufactured exports—all of which are treated as government policy decisions, although the instruments necessary to implement these decisions are not explicitly included. Sectoral exports and imports are also influenced in the model by the need to equate the overall outflow and inflow of foreign exchange, given the Government's chosen amount of foreign borrowing.

About half of total demand is not final, but intermediate. For any given sector, growth of intermediate demand depends partly on growth of production in the other sectors that use its output as an input (for example, intermediate demand in metallurgy is governed largely by machinery production), partly on changes in the pattern of intermediate use within those sectors (for example, reductions in the amount of metal per machine). The composition of intermediate demand in the model thus depends on all the factors that govern the structure of final demand, plus the assumed pattern of constancy or change in input-output coefficients, which may be influenced in various ways (not explicitly modeled) by government policies.

Three Alternative Projections

Since a large number of assumptions, both about the future values of exogenous variables and about specific

---

2. In sectors where there is foreign trade, temporary demand-production imbalances are accommodated in the model by adjustment of exports or imports, in other sectors by temporary changes in capacity utilization (reflected in temporary deviations of sectoral capital-output ratios from their assumed long-term values). Demand-production imbalances do not affect prices. These assumptions are made more for simplicity than for accuracy, since the model is not intended for short-term analysis.

causal linkages among variables, are required to make a projection, there is a colossal number of possible alternative sets of assumptions (and hence different projections), even if each individual assumption is varied only within a limited, plausible range. After many experiments, three have been selected for discussion (some variants will also be mentioned).

These three projections—named QUADRUPLE, MODERATE, and BALANCE—have no monopoly of merit, but are useful for illustrative purposes. Although all of them lie within the range of international (including Chinese) experience, they span a fairly wide range of possibilities, both for policy and for factors beyond government control. They also reveal a number of specific questions and problems, which are addressed later in this report. The present section outlines the assumptions of each of the three projections. The rest of the chapter describes their results.

QUADRUPLE

The QUADRUPLE projection attains the Government's target of quadrupling the gross value of industrial and agricultural output (GVIAO) between 1980 and 2000. Specifically, given a reasonable set of assumptions—described below—about the efficiency of investment and the forces shaping the structure of the economy, the aggregate saving rate was varied until the rate that quadrupled GVIAO was found.

As regards the efficiency of investment, sectoral capital-output ratios in agriculture and energy were direct (though approximate) estimates of the likely investment cost of increasing gross output in these sectors, drawing on World Bank project experience in China and elsewhere. In other industrial sectors and in construction, it was assumed that capital-output ratios would be equal to the average of the past thirty years in China (based on estimates of sectoral capital stocks in 1981), with reforms checking their past upward tendency. In transport, the capital-output ratio for new investment was set about 25 percent above its past level to correct for past underinvestment. In commerce, it was assumed that greater discretion in purchasing would cut circulating capital requirements by 20 percent, and hence that the sector's future capital-output ratio would be lower than in the past.

Energy conservation rates in individual sectors in QUADRUPLE (and also in MODERATE and BALANCE) are those regarded as most likely—the consequences of more optimistic and more pessimistic assumptions are discussed in Chapter 4. Intermediate use of other materials and goods was assumed to change in accordance with average international experience. Specifically, the assumed pattern of change in input-output coefficients includes some substitution of manufactured for agricultural materials, increased use of chemicals (especially plastics), and re-

duced use of metals (especially in machine building). Total nonenergy intermediate requirements per unit of gross output in individual sectors (other than agriculture) were assumed to remain approximately constant, as in most other countries.

The division of consumption between public and household consumption was assumed in QUADRUPLE to stay the same as in 1981, as was the proportionate allocation of public consumption among sectors. The share of household consumption allotted to food declines, despite a steep increase in expenditure on animal products (see Chapter 3 and Annex 2). The share of clothing in household consumption was assumed to rise slightly, and the shares of other manufactured goods, electricity, transport, miscellaneous services, and housing to increase significantly—broadly in line with average international experience. Household consumption of fuel, though, was assumed to increase more slowly than income, because of improvements in thermal efficiency (see Annex 3).

Other assumptions of QUADRUPLE include growth of crop production at an average annual rate of 3.6 percent, doubling of crude oil production (in accordance with the official target), attainment of the Government's targets for hydro and nuclear power, and coal production in 2000 of 1,400 million tons. The present orientation of foreign trade policy is assumed to be broadly maintained, but the composition of manufactured exports shifts away from textiles toward machinery and other manufactures, and there is somewhat greater dependence (to save energy) on imports of metals and chemicals. Foreign borrowing increases gradually toward a level consistent with a 15 percent ratio of debt service (interest and repayment) to exports.

MODERATE

The MODERATE projection maintains most of the assumptions made in QUADRUPLE, including the same aggregate saving rate, but takes a less optimistic view of the future efficiency of China's economy. Sectoral capital-output ratios in (nonenergy) industry and construction are assumed to increase gradually, as in the Soviet Union and less efficient developing countries. Specifically, the amount of investment required per additional unit of industrial output is assumed to be 40 percent greater than in QUADRUPLE. In addition, crop production is assumed to grow more slowly (an average annual rate of 2.9 percent), because of smaller increases in the efficiency with which investment and industrial inputs are used in agriculture. Lower efficiency in converting animal feed into meat is also assumed. Coal production in 2000 is 1,200 million tons.

Lower efficiency was also assumed to be associated with slower growth of labor productivity in nonagricultural sectors. In QUADRUPLE, on the basis of past experience in China and other countries, gross output per worker was assumed to increase at an annual rate of 5 percent in heavy industry (3 percent in coal mining), 4 percent in light industry, 3 percent in construction, transport and commerce, and 2 percent in miscellaneous services. In MODERATE all these rates were reduced by one percentage point.

BALANCE

The BALANCE projection represents an alternative way of attaining the same growth rate of per capita national income as in QUADRUPLE, giving greater weight to the service sectors—specifically, to commerce and miscellaneous business and personal services. This shifts the future structure of China's economy away from the Soviet pattern and toward the pattern of Japan and most other countries at comparable stages of development (Chapter 1).

In the model, the shift is accomplished partly by changing the pattern of household consumption. Relative to household income, consumption of miscellaneous services and of commerce (retail trade is treated as part of consumption in the accounting framework used) grows faster in BALANCE than in QUADRUPLE. To compensate, the share of household income spent on food declines somewhat faster—although this is partly offset by increased food consumption in restaurants, which are also part of commerce—and the share spent on manufactured goods increases somewhat more slowly. There is also faster growth of intermediate demand for services. Relative to gross output, the volume of intermediate commerce and material supply activities is assumed in BALANCE to increase by 3 percent per year (it remains constant in QUADRUPLE); expenditure on miscellaneous business services is assumed to increase gradually in every sector from virtually nothing in 1981 to about 3 percent of gross output in 2000—comparable to other countries.

Faster expansion of the service sectors involves costs—investment and use of energy, materials, and labor in those sectors. In BALANCE, these costs are deliberately augmented by making the fixed capital required per unit of gross output in commerce three times its QUADRUPLE level, to reflect improvements in the size and quality of warehouses, shops, vehicles, and other equipment, which at present in China lag far behind those in other countries. In addition, to allow for improved staffing of large-scale commercial facilities, a larger share of more labor-intensive smaller facilities, and a shift in the composition of miscellaneous services toward more labor-intensive activities, the growth rates of labor productivity in commerce and miscellaneous services are reduced in BALANCE (to 1 percent per year in both sectors).

Faster expansion of commerce and miscellaneous services would also have economic benefits—in addition to the gains that consumers would realize directly—especially in association with comprehensive reform of China's system of economic management (Chapter 1). For these sectors are indispensable to reducing costs and improving quality in material production through increased reliance on markets, more specialization and competition, and greater orientation of production toward customer requirements.

CAPITAL. In this broader context, faster expansion of the service sectors could reduce investment requirements in several ways. A larger, better-equipped, and more responsive commercial system could require—in light of experience elsewhere—smaller amounts of circulating capital, especially within the sector, but also in other sectors, which would be less likely to produce unsalable goods and would have less need to stockpile materials and semifinished goods (of which it is now difficult for Chinese enterprises to get regular supplies of suitable quality and specifications). A larger and better commercial system would also permit greater specialization in production, and hence larger-scale enterprises with lower capital costs, and a greater payoff to agricultural investment.

Business service enterprises can also make fuller use of specialized equipment (and personnel). This is obviously true of equipment leasing and rental enterprises. But it also applies to professional and technical services—such as advertising and market research, law, accounting, design, engineering, repair and maintenance, and data processing—which can often be provided at lower cost and at a higher standard by specialized entities than by an enterprise's own staff. Even mundane business services such as catering, cleaning, and trash removal can sometimes be undertaken at lower cost by specialized enterprises. Finally, banks and other financial institutions can contribute to better investment decisions (Chapter 10).

The potential for reducing investment requirements in these ways cannot be accurately calculated or apportioned between fixed and circulating capital. However, on the basis of rough international comparisons, it was assumed for illustrative purposes in BALANCE that faster expansion of the service sectors would enable circulating capital requirements to be reduced (below their QUADRUPLE levels) by 30 percent in nonenergy industry, construction, and miscellaneous services and by about 70 percent in commerce.

MATERIALS. It was also assumed in BALANCE that the increased intermediate purchases of commerce and business services would be offset by reduced purchases of manufactured intermediate goods (and hence indirectly of agricultural materials and energy, as well as other industrial materials). This is the pattern observed in the few studies that have been made in other countries—increasing service-intensity of production in individual sectors, but declining materials-intensity, with little systematic change (outside agriculture) in total intermediate purchases per unit of gross output. Part of the explanation apparently lies in the transfer of particular activities from manufacturing enterprises to more specialized service enterprises. But a more important factor appears to be constant improvements in product quality, with the cost of materials becoming a smaller part of the product price, and the value added by processing (including indirect processing, design, packaging, and marketing) a greater part.

Of course, many materials-saving improvements in product quality are unrelated to service sector expansion. Independent technological advances, including methods of weight reduction and miniaturization, as well as general enterprise incentives to reduce waste and improve products, are crucial. But the service sectors stimulate and facilitate these improvements. Design agencies and technical consultants provide essential information, while a good commercial sector, supplemented by advertising and market research enterprises, increases the flow of information between customers and producers and sharpens competition, making it both easier and more necessary for enterprises to improve their products.

Growth and Demand

For each of the three projections, using both Western and Chinese measures, Table 2.1 presents aggregate growth rates over the period 1981–2000, while Table 2.2 shows the composition of both total final demand and household consumption. (More detailed breakdowns are available in Annex 4. The projections start in 1981 because this is the latest year for which all the necessary data exist; the projected values for 1982–84 do not conform closely to actual developments in those years.)

In QUADRUPLE, as mentioned earlier, the saving rate was deliberately chosen so as to attain the target of quadrupling GVIAO in 1980–2000 (annual average growth of 7.2 percent). The required domestic saving rate is 29

Table 2.1 Average Annual Growth of National Income, Alternative Projections, 1981–2000
(percent, at 1981 prices)

Measure	Quadruple	Moderate	Balance
National income			
GDP	6.6	5.4	6.6
NMP	6.3	5.1	6.2
National income per capita			
GDP	5.5	4.3	5.5
NMP	5.2	4.1	5.1
Gross value of industrial and agricultural output	7.2	6.0	6.4

Note: A Western measure of national income, GDP (gross domestic product) is the net output of all sectors, including all services, plus depreciation. The Chinese measure, NMP (net material product) is the net output of the materially productive sectors.
Source: World Bank projections (Annex 4).

Table 2.2 Composition of Final Demand, Alternative Projections, 1981–2000
(percent)

Component	1981	2000 Quadruple	Moderate	Balance
Shares of national income (expenditure)[a]				
Investment	28 (29)	29 (29)	29 (28)	26 (26)
Public consumption	15 (10)	15 (9)	15 (10)	16 (10)
Household consumption	56 (61)	56 (62)	56 (62)	59 (64)
Shares of household consumption[b]				
Food (including processed food)	55	48	49	44
Manufactures	24	29	28	25
Services (including commerce)	18	20	20	27
Fuel, electricity, and transport	3	4	4	4

a. Figures without parentheses are Western measures; those within parentheses are Chinese measures. The Western measures may not sum to 100 because of external trade imbalances.
b. Calculated on a Western basis, at 1981 producer prices, with all commercial margins included in services.
Source: World Bank projections (Annex 4).

percent, although the investment rate is closer to 30 percent for most of the period because of foreign borrowing. This is higher than China's average investment rate in 1952–82 (28 percent), but lower than the 1970–82 average (32 percent). It is also quite close to Chinese projections of the investment rate needed to quadruple GVIAO in 1980–2000 (26–29 percent), though somewhat higher, perhaps because QUADRUPLE assumes more of an increase—over China's past levels—in capital requirements in agriculture, energy, and transport.[3]

National income—as a result of the many other specific assumptions made, rather than by deliberate choice—also grows in QUADRUPLE at a rate consistent with the Government's targets. Per capita GDP (which in China differs only trivially from GNP) grows at 5.5 percent per year—from $300 in 1981 to $830 in 2000—which is the minimum rate that China would need to sustain to catch up with the industrial countries by the middle of the twenty-first century (Chapter 1). The Chinese measure of per capita national income grows slightly more slowly—5.2 percent—because the relative size of the nonmaterial service sectors increases.

In MODERATE, with the same investment rate, the assumption of lower efficiency causes significantly slower

---

3. The Chinese projections are from Liu Guoguang, ed., *Zhongguo Jingji Fazhan Zhanlue Wenti Yanjiu*, (Issues of China's economic development strategy), (Shanghai: Shanghai Renmin Chubanshe, 1983), pp. 405–406.

growth. The growth rates of national income and of GVIAO are reduced by rather more than one percentage point, and per capita GDP rises to only $670 by 2000. To attain the same aggregate growth rates as in QUADRUPLE, the investment rate would have to be increased to about 36 percent. (All three projections, incidentally, assume that the Government's target of a population of 1.2 billion by 2000 is attained. A higher population would cause a commensurately lower level of per capita income.)

In BALANCE, with greater weight given to the service sectors, the saving rate was deliberately chosen to attain the same growth rate of per capita GDP as in QUADRUPLE, in line with the Government's long-term objectives. The Chinese measure of national income in BALANCE grows only slightly more slowly than in QUADRUPLE, because most of the increase is in materially productive services (commerce and business services). GVIAO, however, grows significantly more slowly, because the greater share of services means smaller shares for agriculture and—especially—industry. Partly as a result, but also because of the assumed reductions in use of circulating capital and materials within individual sectors, the same growth rate of national income as in QUADRUPLE is attained in BALANCE with less investment—26 percent of national income. The increase in consumption that this makes possible is divided proportionately between public consumption and household consumption (which in real per capita terms in 2000 is 9 percent higher than in QUADRUPLE).

By most international standards, the growth rates projected for China are quite high. Even in MODERATE, per capita GDP growth is slightly above the 4.1 percent 1960–82 average for upper-middle-income developing countries (3.2 percent for lower-middle-income countries), and similar to Western estimates of Soviet growth in 1950–75. It is well above the 2.6–3.6 percent range projected by the World Bank for middle-income countries in 1985–95.[4] Nonetheless, the projected MODERATE growth rate of national income per capita is almost exactly what China achieved in 1952–82 (4.0 percent by the Chinese measure), and the rates in QUADRUPLE and BALANCE are no higher than those attained by China in periods of good economic management. These rates in turn have been surpassed by a few other countries, including Japan in 1953–73 (8.5 percent).

China's unusually rapid projected per capita income growth, as compared with most other developing countries, is due mainly to an unusually high investment rate (the 1982 average for middle-income countries was 24 percent) and unusually slow population growth (1 percent per year, as compared with a projected 2.2 percent in middle-income countries), rather than to unusually efficient investment. This can be seen by looking at the aggregate ICOR (incremental capital-output ratio), which

is the average amount of investment required to produce an additional unit of output. It can be calculated by dividing the average share of investment in national income in a given period by the growth rate of national income.

The projected ICOR in MODERATE (calculated using Western national income measures) is about 5.5, much as in China in the two decades before 1978, and comparable also to the Soviet Union in 1950–75 and India in 1960–82. In QUADRUPLE, the projected ICOR is substantially lower—about 4.5, which is similar to the 1952–82 average in China. In BALANCE, it is lower still—about 4.0, which is comparable to the average in Japan during 1950–80, but also to the average for all middle-income developing countries in 1960–82. The assumptions on investment efficiency underlying the three projections thus seem to span a plausible range of international experience.[5]

It should be emphasized, though, that China's experience in the next two or three decades—in terms of growth rate and investment requirements—will not necessarily lie within this range. The possibility of faster growth cannot be ruled out. To illustrate this, a variant of BALANCE was constructed, with the saving rate increased to the same level as in QUADRUPLE. Per capita GDP in this projection increases at an annual average rate of 6.5 percent (one percentage point higher than in QUADRUPLE and BALANCE, though still slightly below the 6.8 percent of 1979–84) and reaches $990 by the year 2000. GVIAO in this variant of BALANCE more than quadruples (growth of 7.4 percent per year), with a commensurate increase also in energy and materials use.

Equally, if internal or external misfortunes were adversely to affect China's saving rate or investment efficiency, growth could be slower than in MODERATE. In addition, it is possible that all three projections may have underestimated the backlog of past investment needs—especially in transport and in housing (the estimates for electricity are more reliable)—in which case their saving and investment rates would be too low, or their growth rates too high, or some combination of the two. In any

---

4. World Bank, *World Development Report 1984* (New York: Oxford University Press, 1984), Table 3.2. Most other developing country statistics in this chapter are from the Indicators at the back of this *World Development Report*.

5. Total factor productivity (TFP) for the whole economy grows at 1.6 percent per year in QUADRUPLE (contributing 24 percent of output growth), 0.8 percent in MODERATE (14 percent), and 1.9 percent in BALANCE (29 percent). The average TFP growth rate in a sample of mainly middle-income developing countries between 1950 and 1980 was 2 percent and contributed 31 percent of output growth (Annex 5, Table 3.16). In these TFP calculations, output is measured by GDP; for China, labor force and capital stock growth are given equal weight.

event, experience in China and elsewhere (including Eastern Europe) strongly suggests the need for cautious planning: the fluctuations and inefficiency caused by setting unrealistically high growth targets are usually much more serious than the problems caused by unrealistically low growth targets, which can be gradually adjusted upward.

The projected changes in the composition of household consumption (Table 2.2) are broadly consistent with experience elsewhere. In all three projections the share of food declines: in QUADRUPLE and MODERATE the reduction is unusually small, mainly because of rapidly increasing consumption of animal products; BALANCE is more normal by international standards (Chapter 3). In QUADRUPLE and MODERATE, most additional nonfood consumption is manufactures, although expenditure on housing and miscellaneous personal services also grows quite rapidly. In BALANCE, consumption of services (including retail commerce) grows abnormally fast, to bring China more into line with the usual pattern. The share of household income spent on manufactures thus increases slowly, but because—as mentioned earlier—aggregate consumption increases faster, real per capita consumption of manufactures in BALANCE in 2000 is only 5 percent less than in QUADRUPLE.

Production and Investment

Table 2.3 shows gross output growth in the three projections, broken down among five broad sectors (the twenty-sector breakdown is in Annex 4). In all three cases, agriculture—discussed further in Chapter 3—is the slowest growing sector, although its growth rate in QUADRUPLE and BALANCE is very high by international standards, partly because animal husbandry production is assumed to keep up with rapidly increasing consumer demand. Slower agricultural growth in MODERATE thus

reflects both lower efficiency in crop production and slower overall growth, which reduces the demand for meat. (In these projections, the output of nonagricultural brigade enterprises is included in other sectors, rather than—as in present Chinese statistics—in agriculture.)

The projected growth rate of total industrial output in QUADRUPLE (about 8 percent) is in line with most Chinese projections, as is the slightly faster growth of heavy than of light industry.[6] Within heavy industry, the fastest-growing sector (9.1 percent) is machinery, pulled along mainly by investment demand and by household and public consumption, but also by foreign demand (the share of machinery output exported rises over the period from 4 percent to 11 percent). Chemicals production—pulled mainly by intermediate demand—grows almost as fast (8.8 percent), but metallurgy production grows more slowly (7.0 percent), partly because of increased efficiency of metal use in the machinery sector, partly because of increased net imports. Coal and petroleum are the slowest-growing heavy industrial sectors (on average, 4.8 percent). Within light industry, the fastest-growing sector is food processing (8.7 percent), followed by wood, paper, and miscellaneous manufacturing (8.4 percent). Textiles and clothing, the biggest light industrial sector, grows more slowly (7.1 percent), partly because consumer demand grows only slightly faster than income, partly because textile exports grow relatively slowly (but still by 6.0 percent per year in real terms).

In MODERATE, both heavy and light industry grow more slowly than in QUADRUPLE (because the whole economy grows less fast), but the difference between their growth rates is somewhat more pronounced, largely because, by assumption, coal production is not much lower and petroleum production remains the same. Gross output in other industrial sectors in 2000 in MODERATE is about 80 percent of its level in QUADRUPLE—the range is from 84 percent in chemicals to 77 percent in food processing.

In BALANCE, the assumed greater efficiency of investment and materials use—and the consequently lower investment rate—enables heavy industry to grow slightly more slowly than light industry and significantly more so than in QUADRUPLE (even though national income grows just as fast). Machinery production in 2000 in BALANCE is only 80 percent of the QUADRUPLE level; metallurgy, 74 percent; building materials, 85 percent; and chemicals, 82 percent. Light industry in BALANCE also grows more slowly than in QUADRUPLE, partly because some consumer demand is shifted from manufactures to services,

Table 2.3 Average Annual Growth of Sectoral Gross Output, Alternative Projections, 1981–2000
(percent, at 1981 prices)

Sector	Quadruple	Moderate	Balance
Agriculture	4.5	3.7	4.6
Heavy industry[a]	8.1	6.9	7.0
Light industry[b]	7.9	6.5	7.1
Infrastructure[c]	7.3	6.1	7.0
Services[d]	7.2	6.0	10.5

Note: These broad sectoral definitions correspond only approximately to those used in China.
a. Metallurgy, coal and petroleum (including extraction), chemicals, and building materials and machinery; excludes electricity.
b. Food processing, textiles and clothing, wood, paper, and other manufacturing.
c. Electricity, construction, and transport (freight and passenger).
d. Commerce, miscellaneous services, and housing; excludes education, health, public administration, and defense.
Source: World Bank projections (Annex 4).

---

6. Most Chinese projections envisage this relationship for the whole period 1980–2000, but with faster growth of light than of heavy industry in the 1980s (see, for example, Liu, *Zhongguo Jingji Fazhan Zhanlue Wenti Yanjiu*, pp. 146–49).

but mainly because of smaller stock building, more efficient intermediate use, and smaller net exports (because of less need to generate foreign exchange to pay for imports of energy, chemicals, and metals).

The infrastructure sectors (electricity, transport, and construction) in all three projections grow nearly as fast as industry, the main user of their outputs and supplier of their inputs. The link between infrastructure and industry is particularly clear in QUADRUPLE and MODERATE—with slower industrial growth in the latter projection causing an equiproportionate reduction in infrastructure growth. In BALANCE, relative to QUADRUPLE, the reduction in infrastructure growth is much less pronounced than the reduction in industrial growth, because of increased use of infrastructure by the service sectors. Electricity projections are discussed further in Chapter 4 (and Annex 3), transport projections in Chapter 5 (and Annex 6); in both sectors, the plausible range of outcomes in the year 2000 in each of the three projections is quite wide (depending largely on the degree of success in reducing wasteful use of electricity and transport). The construction industry's output growth is determined mainly by investment demand: it therefore grows more slowly in MODERATE (6.1 percent) than in QUADRUPLE (7.2 percent), because of slower overall growth; it also grows somewhat more slowly in BALANCE (7.0 percent), because the investment rate is lower.

Excluding education and health and public administration and defense, where gross output is a particularly elusive concept (employment in these sectors is discussed below), the service sectors in QUADRUPLE and MODERATE grow at about the same rate as the infrastructure sectors and somewhat more slowly than industry. Commerce grows at almost the same speed as GVIAO, while miscellaneous services and housing (both of which are propelled by above-average growth of consumer demand) grow rather faster. In BALANCE, commerce grows faster (9.1 percent) than GVIAO (6.4 percent), with an increased amount of trade relative to production, while consumer and business demand for miscellaneous services grows rapidly (15.3 percent). The service sectors thus grow faster than industry.

Table 2.4 shows broad sectoral shares of the economy's total capital stock (fixed and circulating) in the three projections. These depend, of course, on the sectoral allocation of investment, which in turn is related both to sectoral gross output growth and to sectoral capital-output ratios (investment requirements per unit of output). In all three projections, agriculture's share of the capital stock does not change much over time, since the sector's below-average output growth is largely offset—as in other countries—by a rising capital-output ratio. Its share in BALANCE is higher than in QUADRUPLE simply because the total capital stock is 10 percent smaller, because of the lower aggregate investment rate permitted by greater effi-

Table 2.4 Composition of Capital Stock, Alternative Projections, 1981–2000
(percent)

Sector and type	1981	2000		
		Quadruple	Moderate	Balance
Sector				
Agriculture	9.6	8.8	8.4	9.8
Heavy industry[a]	29.5	33.4	37.3	28.4
Light Industry[a]	7.9	7.7	8.5	6.4
Infrastructure[a]	14.1	18.1	16.4	18.4
Services[b]	38.9	32.0	29.4	37.0
Type of capital stock				
Fixed (net of depreciation)	65.3	67.5	66.9	74.8
Circulating	34.7	32.5	33.1	25.2

a. For sectoral definitions, see notes to Table 2.3.
b. Includes education, health, public administration, and defense, as well as commerce, housing, and miscellaneous services.
Source: World Bank projections (Annex 4).

ciency—reflected in the table in the lower ratio of circulating to fixed capital.

In QUADRUPLE, industry's share of the capital stock increases over the period—implying that its share of total investment (about 42 percent) is greater than in the past (about 37 percent).[7] This is the result of rapid output growth in sectors such as machinery and chemicals (which between them absorb around 20 percent of annual investment), coupled with rising capital-output ratios in slower-growing coal and petroleum. Light industry's small share of the capital stock does not change much. In MODERATE, lower industrial investment efficiency causes the capital stock shares of both heavy and light industry to be even higher than in QUADRUPLE. In BALANCE, these shares decline slightly, because of slower industrial output growth and greater industrial investment efficiency.[8] Industry's share of total investment (36 percent) in BALANCE is still large, however—excluding mining and extraction, it is about the same as in Japan in 1951–65.

In all three projections, the infrastructure sectors increase their shares of the economy's capital stock. In QUADRUPLE, transport absorbs about 10 percent of an-

---

7. These percentages include all mining (including oil extraction), but exclude electricity (included with infrastructure). The past estimate is based on the 1981 capital stock data in Annex 5, which, as with the projected estimate, covers all investment in fixed and circulating capital, including nonstate and nonproductive investment.

8. The share of light industry declines more than that of heavy industry partly because coal and petroleum capital requirements are not reduced, partly because greater investment efficiency is assumed to be reflected in lower circulating capital requirements (which are more important in light than in heavy industry).

Table 2.5   Sectoral Composition of the Labor Force, Alternative Projections, 1981–2000
(percent, unless otherwise noted)

Sector	1981	Quadruple	Moderate	Balance
Agriculture	70	59	61	52
Heavy industry	9	11	11	9
Light industry	6	9	8	7
Infrastructure	5	7	7	7
Services	10	14	13	25
Labor force (millions)	452	631	631	631
Population (millions)	990	1,196	1,196	1,196

Note: For sectoral definitions, see notes to Table 2.4.
Source: World Bank projections (Annex 4).

nual investment (excluding purchases of vehicles by farmers, households, and nontransport enterprises). Transport and electricity together account for a higher proportion (19 percent) of total investment than in the past (12 percent), but about the same proportion as in Japan in 1951–65. In MODERATE, these sectors' shares of the capital stock increase less, mainly because of greater absorption of investment by industry. In BALANCE, their capital stock shares are much the same as in QUADRUPLE, although in absolute terms somewhat lower (because demand for the output of these sectors grows more slowly).

At the outset, the service sectors have a large share (39 percent) of the economy's capital stock—of which about one-half is commerce (mainly circulating capital), one-third housing, and one-sixth education, health, public administration, and defense. In QUADRUPLE, this share declines, partly because circulating capital requirements in commerce are assumed to be somewhat lower than in the past, partly because capital-output ratios in other sectors are rising (they rise faster in MODERATE, which causes the service sectors' capital stock share to decline even more). Nonetheless, these sectors absorb substantial amounts of investment. In QUADRUPLE, about 12 percent of annual investment goes into housing and 11 percent into commerce (still mainly circulating capital), while education, health, public administration, and defense between them absorb about 5 percent (the underlying assumption is a doubling of capital per worker over the period in these social sectors). Miscellaneous services absorb only 0.5 percent of investment.

In BALANCE, the capital stock share of the service sectors also declines slightly, but is significantly higher than in QUADRUPLE, partly because the total capital stock is smaller. In commerce, faster output growth and higher fixed capital requirements are offset by lower circulating capital requirements, and the sector's capital stock in 2000 is 5 percent smaller than in QUADRUPLE (its share of annual investment is virtually the same). The social sectors and housing absorb slightly more investment be-

cause of faster growth of public and household consumption. Miscellaneous services absorb three times as much investment as in QUADRUPLE, but still less than 2 percent of the total.

Employment and Income

Table 2.5 shows projected sectoral employment shares (the twenty-sector breakdown is in Annex 4). These depend in the model on sectoral output growth rates and assumptions about sectoral labor productivity growth (mentioned earlier)—except in agriculture, where employment is a residual, and in education, health, public administration, and defense, where it is determined by public consumption.

In QUADRUPLE, nonagricultural employment increases at 3.5 percent per year. This is somewhat slower than over the past thirty years in China—in 1952–82, the rate was 4.5 percent—because of slower gross nonagricultural output growth (7.8 percent in QUADRUPLE, excluding nonmaterial services, versus 8.9 percent in 1952–82). Average nonagricultural labor productivity in QUADRUPLE grows at the same rate as in 1952–82 (about 4 percent), though significantly faster than in 1957–77 (about 3 percent). Labor productivity is assumed to grow fastest in heavy industry, with the result that this sector's employment share increases only modestly, despite rapid output growth. Conversely, the share of employment in services increases more, despite slower output growth, because labor productivity does not rise so much.

Although faster growth of productivity in industry than in services is the normal international pattern, the share of employment in services in QUADRUPLE not only remains unusually low, but also increases more slowly than normal (even by comparison with the low service share countries such as the Soviet Union). This is because of the prospective decline in the primary school age group, which will cause the number of teachers—now approaching a quarter of all service sector employment in China—to increase only modestly, even given higher enrollment rates (Annex 1). Faster growth of employment in health, research, culture, and so on will to some extent offset this. But the projected increase of 15 million, or 80 percent, in education and health employment during 1981–2000 in QUADRUPLE—MODERATE and BALANCE are similar—may in fact be an overestimate, as may the projected increase of 5 million, or 50 percent, in employment in public administration and defense (which is currently approaching a quarter of total service sector employment).

Nonagricultural employment in QUADRUPLE increases between 1981 and 2000 by rather more than 120 million. The total labor force—assuming a slight decline in the participation rate of the adult population—increases by nearly 180 million. Employment in agriculture thus increases by 56 million, even though agriculture's share of employment drops from 70 percent to 59 percent. This pattern is typical of the low- to middle-income transition elsewhere, with an absolute decline in the agricultural labor force occurring only at a later stage of development. But the projected decline in the agricultural employment share in QUADRUPLE is rather small by international standards (Figure 2.1).

It is also much smaller than in most Chinese projections, which envisage a decline in the agricultural employment share by 2000 to less than 40 percent.[9] This would be normal for a country with a per capita income roughly double that projected for China in 2000 (Annex 5, Table 3.8). Given the rates of gross output growth in QUADRUPLE, it could be achieved in China only if nonagricultural labor productivity increased at less than 2 percent per year—half the past rate and probably incompatible with efficient industrialization. In 1960–82, industrial labor productivity increased on average in all middle-income countries at rather more than 2 percent per year; but in the faster-growing upper-middle-income group, at 3 percent; in South Korea, at 6 percent; and in Japan in the 1950s and 1960s, at more than 8 percent. (Productivity and surplus rural labor are discussed in Chapter 8.)

Sectoral employment shares in MODERATE are similar to those in QUADRUPLE. This is because the assumed lower efficiency that causes slower output growth is also associated with slower growth of nonagricultural labor productivity (on average about 3 percent). But the nonagricultural labor force grows slightly less than in QUADRUPLE, and hence the share of employment in agriculture does not decline quite so much.

In BALANCE, employment in services grows much faster than in QUADRUPLE—partly because the demand for commerce and miscellaneous services expands faster, partly because improved quality and the changing composition of activities within these sectors are assumed to entail slower labor productivity growth. By 2000, the service sectors, which employ 14 percent of the labor force in QUADRUPLE, employ 25 percent in BALANCE—almost exactly the 1980 average for lower-middle-income developing countries, with an average per capita income very similar to that projected for China in 2000. Because industrial output grows more slowly in BALANCE, and industrial labor productivity grows just as fast, industrial employment does not increase so much as in QUADRUPLE—and indeed increases very little as a proportion of the total labor force (although in absolute terms it rises by 35 million workers). Employment in the infrastructure sectors, however, increases only slightly less than in QUADRUPLE.

The greater increase in service sector employment in BALANCE much more than offsets the smaller increase in industrial employment, so that nonagricultural employment increases by over 40 million more than in QUADRUPLE (the annual growth rate of nonagricultural employ-

Figure 2.1 Share of Agriculture in Total Employment in China, Alternative Projections for 1981–2000, and in Other Selected Countries, 1960–82

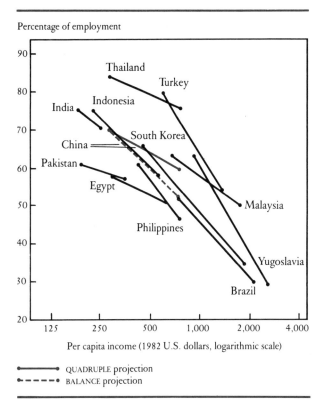

Percentage of employment

————— QUADRUPLE projection
– – – – – BALANCE projection

Source: World Bank, *World Development Report 1984* (New York: Oxford University Press, 1984), table 21; World Bank, *World Tables*, 3d ed. (Washington, D.C., 1984), vol. 2.

ment is 4.3 percent). Agricultural employment in BALANCE thus increases between 1981 and 2000 by only 13 million, and declines to 52 percent of the labor force. This would be quite normal for a large lower-middle-income country (Figure 2.1 and Annex 5, Table 3.8).

Sectoral employment shares largely determine sectoral shares of national income, although these also depend on the amount of capital per worker, on wage rates, and on prices—especially in relation to costs. The projections of sectoral national income shares in Table 2.6 (both Western and Chinese measures are presented) assume that sectoral prices change in parallel with sectoral costs, which means that the relative profitability of different sectors remains constant (Box 2.1). Different assumptions about prices—for example, that they do not change or that there is movement toward equalization of sectoral

9. The most commonly quoted Chinese projection of agricultural employment in 2000 is 225 million—50 percent of a rural labor force of 450 million. The projection cited in Annex 2, Table 5.1, is somewhat higher—250 million, or 39.6 percent of the World Bank's total labor force projection of 631 million.

Table 2.6 Sectoral Composition of National Income, Alternative Projections, 1981–2000

(percent)

Sector	1981	2000 Quadruple	2000 Moderate	2000 Balance
Agriculture	35 (40)	26 (30)	27 (32)	23 (29)
Heavy industry	24 (26)	28 (30)	29 (31)	23 (28)
Light industry	15 (17)	15 (18)	15 (18)	12 (17)
Infrastructure	11 (10)	14 (14)	13 (13)	13 (14)
Services	16 (7)	17 (7)	16 (7)	28 (13)

Note: Figures without parentheses are Western measures (shares of GDP); those within parentheses are Chinese measures (shares of NMP). In the latter case, infrastructure excludes passenger transport and only commerce is in services; the contribution of business services to material production is included in the net output of other sectors. Other sectoral definitions are as given in Table 2.4. Figure 1.2 differs from the present table mainly because of price adjustments (see Annex 5).
Source: World Bank projections (Annex 4).

profit rates—would somewhat alter the projected shares of national income.

In QUADRUPLE, the share of agriculture in national income drops by ten percentage points between 1981 and 2000, with increases in the shares of other sectors, especially heavy industry and infrastructure. In MODERATE, the movements are similar, although the share of agriculture declines less. In BALANCE, there is a much greater increase in the share of services, especially using the Western measure (partly because some of the increase is in nonmaterial services, partly because the material contribution of miscellaneous services is in the Chinese measure included in the output of the material production sectors rather than of services). The share of industry in national income in BALANCE increases less by the Chinese measure and declines significantly by the Western measure (the difference is again due mainly to the treatment of business services). Agriculture's share of national income declines more in BALANCE than in QUADRUPLE,

---

Box 2.1 Wages, Profits, and Prices

Sectoral relative prices—which are producer (ex factory or farmgate) prices—are determined in the model by sectoral costs, including intermediate input costs, wage costs, and capital costs. Intermediate input costs depend on usage rates—input-output coefficients—and on input prices. Wage costs in each sector depend on labor productivity and on wage rates, which in turn depend on the rate at which wages in general are rising and on the relationships among wage rates in different sectors. In the model, general wage increases are tied to household consumption increases; in these projections, sectoral relative wage rates (agricultural earnings are included in wages) are assumed to remain constant in proportionate terms—except in education and health, where the initially low wage rises gradually to the same level as in public administration.

Capital costs in each sector are governed in the model by the capital-output ratio and the sectoral profit rate (gross of depreciation), which in turn depends on the economy-wide average profit rate and on the relationships among profit rates in different sectors. The average rate of profit (including tax) is determined in the model by the need to generate a large enough surplus to finance the planned level of saving (net of household saving) and government consumption. In these projections, it was assumed that relative sectoral profit rates would remain constant in proportionate terms.

In short, prices in these projections adjust over time so as to maintain constant the relative wages of the workers in each sector and the relative rate of profit on capital in each sector. As a result, in sectors with increasing use of intermediate inputs (such as agriculture), or where labor productivity is rising more slowly than average (such as services), or where the capital-output ratio is rising faster than average (such as energy), relative prices rise.

Conversely, in sectors where intermediate—including energy—use is reduced, or with above-average labor productivity growth or below-average capital-output ratio increases (many industrial sectors), relative prices fall. Some sectors are subject to conflicting cost pressures, which, moreover, may vary among projections—for example, agricultural prices rise less in BALANCE then in QUADRUPLE because agricultural labor productivity rises more, as a result of greater absorption of labor by other sectors.

The assumptions of the present trio of projections thus allow in a simplified way for the most important long-run tendencies in sectoral relative prices, but not for any modification of the present relationships in China among wages in different sectors or among sectoral profit rates. Such modifications could easily be incorporated (for example, to approximate the results of specified types of wage and price reform), although they would make it harder to interpret the projected structural trends with which this chapter is mainly concerned. It would also be possible—if complicated—to extend the model to distinguish retail prices from producer prices, enterprises from government, and urban households from rural households. The determinants of the absolute price level and the rate of inflation, however, probably could not be handled satisfactorily in this model.

although the difference is more pronounced by the Western measure.

The share of agriculture in national income in 2000 in BALANCE would be normal for a large lower-middle-income country (Annex 5, Table 3.6). The share of services, however, is almost ten percentage points lower, notwithstanding the similarity of the service sector employment share, and the projected income share of industry and infrastructure is correspondingly higher than in these countries—indeed, it exceeds that of almost all other countries, including Japan. These discrepancies between employment and income shares partly reflect real differences in the composition of industry (more heavy industry in China) and services (a lower proportion of social services elsewhere). But they also reflect the currently unusual structure of prices and wages in China, most features of which in these projections are assumed—perhaps incorrectly—to persist (Box 2.1). The differences between the projected sectoral income shares for China in 2000 and the normal shares in large lower-middle-income countries are of course even greater in QUADRUPLE and MODERATE than in BALANCE.

Projections and Predictions

Subsequent chapters will further discuss the implications of these three (and some additional) projections for agriculture, energy, transport, urbanization, foreign trade, and public finance. It is important, however, to interpret all these projections appropriately. They are not predictions, but simply complicated calculations based on many assumptions, whose results could be altered considerably by different, but still defensible, assumptions. As such, they should be taken seriously—as an indication of some future possibilities—but not literally.

The choice of terminal year (2000) is also quite arbitrary; the purpose of the projections is to illustrate possible long-term trends, most of which would continue into the twenty-first century, rather than to assess China's position in any particular year. And for planning purposes, the process of making projections is often as helpful as the particular model and numbers selected for presentation. Cumulatively, the innumerable ''unsuccessful'' experiments with different assumptions and model specifications are very illuminating, especially in practical judgment of particular plans and policies.

For these reasons, and because there is much scope for improvement of the model and the underlying data (especially the input-output table and sectoral capital requirements), the projections presented in this report should be viewed as no more than a preliminary contribution. Further work, and better statistics, would be needed to turn them into a reliable basis for planning.

3 Agricultural Prospects and Policies

During the next two or three decades, agriculture will remain one of the largest and most important sectors of China's economy.[1] Even in 2000, food will account for about half of household consumption, and about half the labor force will be engaged in agricultural activities. The economic linkages between agriculture and other sectors will become ever closer. The pace of agricultural progress will depend increasingly on growth of nonagricultural demand for food, materials, and labor and on the availability of nonagricultural goods and services. And the pace of nonagricultural progress will continue to depend on growth of agricultural purchasing power and on agriculture's capacity to supply the right amount and mixture of produce for industrial processing and nonagricultural consumption. System reform and government policies, moreover, will greatly influence these mutually reinforcing interactions between agriculture and other sectors.

This chapter, which draws heavily on Annex 2, first reviews China's long-term agricultural production potential. It then examines the long-term balance between the demand for and supply of agricultural products, with special emphasis on China's future options regarding the level and pattern of food consumption. Finally, the chapter discusses the choice of policy instruments for managing agricultural production under the recently implemented responsibility system, and possible ways of narrowing the large gap between agricultural and nonagricultural incomes. (Rural nonagricultural activities, interregional agricultural specialization and trade, and the problems of poor localities are discussed in Chapter 5.)

Production Possibilities

The rural reforms of 1979–80 have stimulated exceptionally rapid growth of agricultural production, and of rural incomes and food consumption (Chapter 1), based on rapidly rising yields. In grain production, for example, average yields—which were already high by most international standards—increased by 22 percent between 1979

and 1983. Giving adequate incentives to individual farmers—the essence of the reforms—will continue to be a vital ingredient in expansion of agricultural production over the longer term. But their effectiveness will depend on the availability of key inputs such as agricultural land and irrigation, fertilizer, and improved seed. Also important, though less tangible, will be improvements in support services, such as research and extension, and transport and marketing.

Future availability of land will depend heavily on the extent to which reclamation can compensate for land lost to nonagricultural uses. Taking account of land quality and use by herdsmen, perhaps another 3 million to 5 million hectares of "wasteland" are suitable for development in the medium term for sustained production of annual crops. Losses of land to nonagricultural uses in 1959–78 were about 1 million hectares annually; the current surge of rural housing construction suggests that these losses will continue to be substantial and are unlikely to be fully offset by increases in the amount of land irrigated, which has not increased significantly in recent years.

Although organic fertilizer will remain an important source of nutrients (particularly phosphorus, potassium, and some trace elements), it is unlikely to meet the Government's target of half of total nutrient offtake by 2000, if China's fertilizer use patterns follow those of other countries. However, China now has the capacity to design and construct efficient, large-scale plants to produce nitrogenous chemical fertilizers; if raw materials are made available, the rather modest future production targets for nitrogen seem realizable. But achieving the 2000 targets for both phosphorus and potassium would require an early commitment of substantial resources to develop local raw materials and introduce new production technol-

---

1. "Agriculture" is defined throughout to exclude brigade and team industry.

ogies. Even so, sizable amounts of phosphorus and potassium would still need to be imported. Equally important will be improvements in the fertilizer distribution system, to ensure the timely availability of supplies in economically optimal quantities (discussed later). For seed, however, the basic mechanisms for production and distribution are already in place, but processing facilities and quality assurance procedures need to be improved.

Experience in other countries suggests that building an effective national agricultural research capability requires an annual investment of up to 2 percent of the value of agricultural output—considerably higher than current expenditure in China. Despite some very notable achievements, work at many research institutes is hampered by poor facilities and inadequately qualified staff. Good progress has, however, been made in reorganizing the extension service in accordance with the rural reforms, so that it can deliver technical advice to many small producers. Close links need to be maintained between research and extension. Moreover, agricultural education needs to be strengthened to support these programs: recent studies indicate shortages of appropriately trained personnel (at both professional and technical levels), as well as a need to upgrade the qualifications of those already employed.

It will be essential to improve rural transport, processing, storage, and distribution, whose limited capacity is already an important constraint on the restructuring of China's agricultural sector and increased specialization. Efforts are needed to both expand the rural marketing system and increase its efficiency, with simplification of procedures and reduction of administrative barriers to internal trade. The Government is currently taking further important steps in this direction, by switching from procurement quotas for major crops to contracts, by increasing price flexibility, and by allowing collective and individual enterprises a greater role in marketing. In the provision of support services, as in agriculture itself, the economic environment will thus need to be conducive to individual and collective investment. Especially because state investment in agriculture is not expected to increase significantly, it will be critical to put much of the growing volume of rural savings to productive use.

Prospects for Major Crops

The Government's long-term growth target for grain production is about 2 percent per year—to be achieved by raising yields, with the cropped area declining. Rice production is projected to grow at 1.8 percent per year—a target that appears readily attainable. The projected 2.6 percent annual growth in wheat yields would require continued attention to wheat diseases, good water control in irrigated areas, and improved nutrient balance in fertilizer use. Similarly, the projected growth in corn yields (2.8 percent per year) would require attention to

the problems of poor seed quality, low fertilizer application rates, and less advanced cultural practices than those applied to wheat and rice.

Among the industrial crops, prospects seem good for further yield and production gains in cotton. Increased production of soybeans is essential for meeting livestock product targets; there is also a need to improve processing of oilseeds to increase supplies of protein meals suitable for livestock feeding. For industrial crops such as sugar cane and beets, emphasis should be on increasing productive efficiency through better cultural practices, improved planting materials, and careful choice of planting location. Development of the state forestry sector is hampered by limited investment and low administered prices, although price and marketing restrictions have recently been abolished for individual and collective forestry.

Prospects for Livestock

The Government expects rapid growth of the livestock sector (tentatively projected to increase its share of gross agricultural output—excluding brigade industry—from about 18 percent in 1982 to over 30 percent in 2000). But achievement of the livestock growth targets could be constrained by the supplies of grass and feed, the weaknesses of the systems of transport, processing, and distribution, and the availability of investment funds. Many of China's grasslands are overgrazed and probably cannot provide additional meat and wool in the short to medium term without further degradation. An urgent requirement is therefore to match livestock numbers with the land's carrying capacity, through herd reduction and improved range management. The prospects for pigs and poultry are more favorable, but depend on increased supplies of high-quality energy and protein feeds, as well as on the price relationship between feed concentrates and meat products. Because poultry provide Chinese consumers with a preferred meat and are, moreover, efficient converters of feed to high-quality protein, China's poultry industry should be a priority development area.

The prospects for dairy development over the long term will depend largely on the availability of low-cost, high-quality forage and feed protein and on the establishment of efficient milk processing and distribution systems. Milk supplies for some urban consumers might also be increased at lower economic cost by importing powdered milk. Aquatic production will continue to be a valuable supplementary source of high-quality protein, and good potential exists for increasing the output of fresh and marine fish.

Potential Demand-Supply Imbalances

Projecting China's long-term agricultural demand-supply balance is peculiarly difficult. This is partly because of the dramatic difference between the sector's performance in the past five years (gross output up by over 7 percent per year) and in the preceding twenty years (average under 2.5 percent). Depending on what past period is regarded as representative, and what other countries as relevant comparators, the future trend growth rate could be predicted at anything between 2–3 percent and 5–6 percent per year—which, over twenty years, is the difference between less than doubling and tripling. Moreover, even given a particular view of potential production growth, most projected imbalances between agricultural demand and supply will not actually materialize—or at least not to the extent indicated—simply because producers or consumers or the Government will automatically react in ways that reduce them. The following analysis (which is based partly on the economywide model and projections presented in the previous chapter, partly on the more detailed agricultural projections in Annex 2) is thus not an exercise in prediction, but an exploration of possible tendencies and problems—some of which could be avoided if anticipated sufficiently early.[2]

A starting point for the analysis was the assumption—based partly on Chinese planning targets—that over the next two decades there would be a rapid increase in the share of meat, poultry, fish, eggs, and dairy products in the average Chinese diet, with a corresponding decrease in the share of direct grain consumption. Specifically, it was assumed that, if the Government's targets for national income and population growth were attained, per capita consumption of animal products would approximately quadruple (by weight), raising their share of a slightly increased total caloric intake from 6 percent in the early 1980s to about 15 percent by the end of the century. (In the next section, some possible alternative food consumption patterns are considered.)

The economywide model also assumes that investment will be allocated—and hence production will respond to demand—in such a way as to maintain approximate national self-sufficiency in animal products and processed food. Agricultural demand-supply imbalances thus show up mainly in projected net crop exports or imports (though these are powerfully influenced by the rate of growth of animal husbandry production, since animal feed is an important component of crop demand). The potential size of these imbalances, given the overall pace and pattern of economic growth, can accordingly be investigated by varying the assumed future rate of growth of crop production (which, as already mentioned, cannot be predicted with any accuracy).

The QUADRUPLE projection introduced in the previous chapter is a convenient point of reference. It incorporates the assumption of a rapidly changing diet, as well as attaining the government's other main long-term targets, but allows for some substitution of industrial for agricultural raw materials in manufacturing. Crop production is assumed to grow in 1981–2000 at an average annual rate of 3.6 percent. This particular growth rate was chosen because it approximately balances agricultural demand and production in 2000—net crop imports equal to 0.5 percent of crop production. Though well above the long-term trend increase in China prior to 1979, this projected crop production growth rate is close to the 1965–83 average (3.7 percent per year).

Given the underlying assumptions about agricultural efficiency, this crop production growth rate requires use of chemical and other industrial inputs to increase at about 6 percent per year, and investment in fixed and circulating capital averaging about Y 6 billion (or 2–3 percent of total investment) per year. Production of animal products—responding to the assumed steep increase in consumer demand—grows at 7.5 percent per year, which requires, in addition to rapid growth of animal feed consumption, investment averaging about Y 15 billion (or 5–6 percent of total investment) per year. In total, gross agricultural output grows at an average annual rate of 4.5 percent, and the sector absorbs 8 percent of total annual investment.

This agricultural growth rate lies within the fairly wide range (under 4 percent to over 5 percent) contemplated by most Chinese economists.[3] Though well below the growth rate of the past five years, it is higher than any past long-term trend rate in China (in 1965–83, the average was 4.1 percent). This is because of the high projected growth rate of animal husbandry production (in 1965–83, growth of livestock and fishery production averaged 5.4 percent and 3.6 percent per year, respectively). By international standards, it is a very high long-term growth rate—double the 2.3 percent average for low-income countries in 1960–80, well above the 3.0

---

2. The strength of the economywide model lies in relating agricultural production, input use, and employment, as well as demand for food and agricultural materials and agricultural exports and imports, to corresponding developments in other sectors (including food processing) and in macroeconomic aggregates. Its weakness is that—to avoid unmanageable complexity—it distinguishes only two agricultural subsectors, crops (including forestry and sidelines) and animal husbandry (including fishing). Annex 2, conversely, contains projections for more detailed subsectors and some specific agricultural commodities, but without full consideration of all the linkages with other sectors. These two sets of projections, though they cannot be precisely reconciled, were made in a coordinated way and are fundamentally consistent in their assumptions and implications.

3. Some Chinese estimates of future agricultural growth appear significantly higher because they include rapidly expanding brigade and team industries. For agriculture proper, the Ministry of Agriculture's preliminary targets imply a growth rate of 3.8 percent (Annex 2, Table 5.3). Higher estimates are given in Liu Guoguang, ed., *Zhongguo Jingji Fazhan Zhanlue Wenti Yanjiu* (Issues of China's economic development strategy), (Shanghai: Shanghai Renmin Chubanshe, 1983), p. 155 (4.7–5.7 percent) and p. 404 (4.4–4.5 percent, perhaps 5 percent).

percent average for middle-income countries, and surpassed only by Thailand and the Philippines, which started with more uncultivated land and lower yields.

Alternative Outcomes in 2000

China's strict birth planning policies are motivated partly by concern about food availability. A projection was thus made with the economywide model that maintained the assumptions of QUADRUPLE, except that the population rises to 1.3 billion in 2000 (rather than 1.2 billion). This causes a larger foreign trade deficit in crops. But the projected deficit is surprisingly small—about 2 percent of total crop production in 2000, which is similar to that in the early 1980s. This is because the higher population causes per capita income to be lower, which, given the assumptions linking consumer demand to income, causes lower per capita consumption of crops and of commodities whose production directly and indirectly requires crops.[4] If per capita food consumption were unchanged, the impact of a larger population would be much greater—an increase in direct and indirect grain requirements in 2000 of about 40 million tons, or 8 percent of projected requirements (Annex 2, Table 2.3). Moreover, the possible range of alternative population sizes for China becomes far wider in the twenty-first century (see Chapter 8).

Projections were also made under somewhat more pessimistic assumptions about agricultural efficiency, both in crop production (given the same resource inputs, gross output was assumed to grow about 0.7 percent per year more slowly) and in animal husbandry (feed requirements per unit of product in 2000 up by about 15 percent).[5] Retaining all the other assumptions of QUADRUPLE, lower agricultural efficiency pulls down the aggregate growth rate (GDP grows at about 6.4 percent per year, rather than 6.6 percent). Its impact on the agricultural demand-supply balance depends, however, on whether it is assumed to cause more resources to flow into agriculture (to maintain production) or to cause slower agricultural production growth.

In the former case, with growth of crop production maintained at 3.6 percent per year, exports and imports of crops are almost unaffected. This is because lower efficiency in converting feed to livestock products, which would tend to increase the crop deficit, is almost exactly cancelled out by slower growth of total and per capita income, which reduces crop consumption both directly and indirectly (through lower consumption of meat and other commodities). In the latter case, with growth in crop production reduced to 2.9 percent per year, lower agricultural efficiency causes a substantial crop deficit by 2000—net imports equal to nearly 9 percent of domestic demand for crops (and nearly 20 percent of total imports). Were it not for the slower overall growth of income and demand, the deficit would be even larger.

If aggregate income growth were slower still, the projected crop deficit could disappear, even with crop production growth at 2.9 percent. This is so in the MODERATE projection (introduced in the previous chapter), in which lower efficiency in industrial investment causes the whole economy to grow at an annual rate about one percentage point lower than in QUADRUPLE, while lower agricultural efficiency manifests itself in slower growth of crop production. Though crop production in 2000 in MODERATE is 12 percent lower than in QUADRUPLE, there is a significant trade surplus in crops (about 2 percent of domestic crop demand), because slower growth of incomes reduces demand by even more. Direct human consumption of crops is only 6 percent less, mainly because grain remains a larger proportion of the diet at the lower per capita income level (indeed, direct grain consumption might be higher in absolute terms if incomes were lower; see Annex 2, Table 2.1). But indirect consumption—mainly animal feed—and other uses of crops together are 17 percent lower.

Changing Imbalances over Time

In considering the long-term agricultural demand-supply balance, it may be misleading to look simply at projected values for 2000. Although the present model is not designed to analyze medium-term movements, the projections suggest some changes in the pattern of imbalances during 1981–2000, with possible implications for policy in the rest of this century and beyond.

Figure 3.1a illustrates this for the QUADRUPLE projection, by showing what happens to crop exports and imports. Up to the mid-1990s, domestic demand for crops falls short of production, causing a projected foreign trade surplus and—not shown in the figure—abnormally high accumulation of stocks because of an assumed upper limit on crop exports imposed by world market conditions (discussed further below). This represents a continuation of the actual situation of abundance in the early 1980s as a result of the surge in production induced by the rural reforms. This initial surge is assumed eventually to diminish, with somewhat slower growth of crop production in the 1990s (3.4 percent per year) than in the 1980s (3.8 percent per year). In consequence, and despite an assumed reduction also in the rate of increase of food consumption, the demand-supply balance begins to change in

---

4. In the model, faster population growth has almost no effect on total national income in 2000, partly because it would not significantly alter the size of the labor force until later, partly because of the assumption of surplus agricultural labor.

5. The assumed increase in animal feed requirments is substantial. But the difference between low and high efficiency in conversion of animal feed to meat could in fact add as much as 50 percent, or 60 million tons, to feedgrain requirments in 2000 (Annex 2, Table 2.2).

Figure 3.1 Crop Exports and Imports, Alternative Projections, 1981–2000

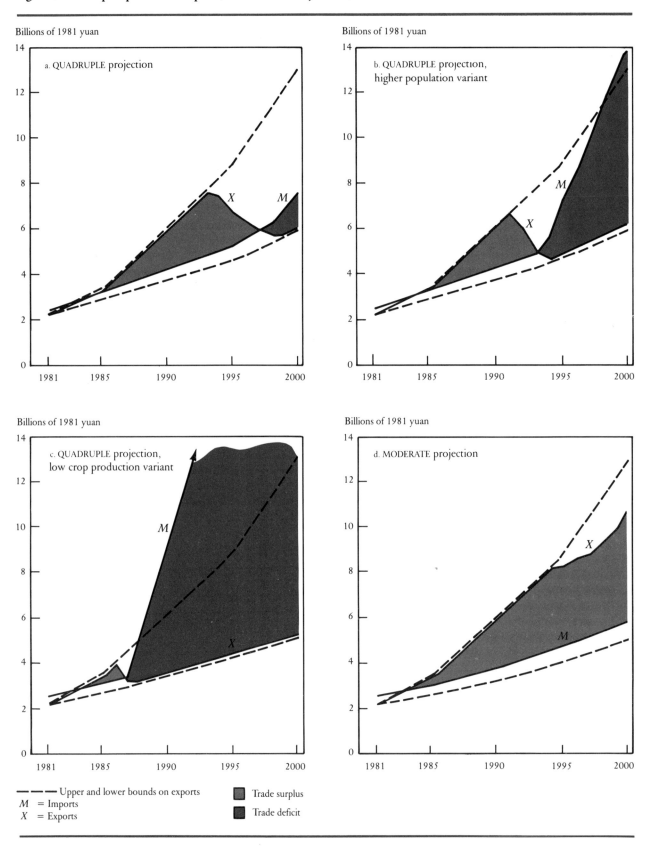

Billions of 1981 yuan

a. QUADRUPLE projection

X

M

Billions of 1981 yuan

b. QUADRUPLE projection, higher population variant

M

X

Billions of 1981 yuan

c. QUADRUPLE projection, low crop production variant

M

X

Billions of 1981 yuan

d. MODERATE projection

X

M

— — — Upper and lower bounds on exports

M = Imports

X = Exports

Trade surplus

Trade deficit

Source: World Bank projections.

the early 1990s, with an absolute decline in crop exports and, in the last years of the century, the emergence of a crop trade deficit. Though the deficit in 2000 is very small, it is growing: if the projected demand and production trends of the late 1990s were to continue, it would increase to 5 percent of domestic demand by 2020.

Most of the other projections discussed above follow a similar time path, with crop surpluses in the earlier part of the period diminishing or disappearing in the later part, although the speed of the transition varies (Figures 3.1b and 3.1c). In the variant on QUADRUPLE with slower crop production growth, for example, the surplus becomes a deficit before 1990 and thus becomes large by 2000. MODERATE, however, is an exception (Figure 3.1d): despite slower crop production growth, the slow overall growth of the economy causes projected crop exports to exceed imports throughout the period (though abnormal stock accumulation ceases in the 1990s); even in the last few years of the century, there is no tendency for a deficit to emerge.

Product Mix within Agriculture

Expansion of animal husbandry at the high rate (7.5 percent per year) entailed by demand growth in the QUADRUPLE projection might be technically feasible, but would require attention to some curent problems and weaknesses in the livestock sector (as discussed earlier and in Annex 2, paras. 4.41–4.88 and 5.28–5.38). It would also require substantial diversion of crop output to animal feed, which could cause problems of demand-supply imbalance within the crop sector.

Even with an overall crop balance, as in QUADRUPLE and in a more detailed alternative projection with lower animal husbandry production (see Annex 2, Table 5.2), the Government's present targets for increasing production of specific crops could well lead to sizable surpluses of rice (possibly 30 million tons, unprocessed, by 2000), and of tubers and pulses, with a large shortage of feedgrains (perhaps 60 million tons, or 12 percent of total grain production, by 2000). Though the magnitudes vary, a broadly similar pattern of imbalances arises in all the other projections described above. It occurs partly because direct consumption of fine grains by humans is unlikely to increase on a per capita basis if income growth and dietary change proceed according to Government targets (the projected surplus of rice would be even greater if China were assumed to experience the shift of consumption from rice to wheat that has occurred in other Asian countries in response to higher incomes— Annex 2, para. 2.11 and Table 2.3). These imbalances arise also because of the projected rapid growth of demand and production in animal husbandry and the need for such production to be increasingly based on grain and protein-based feeds, rather than pasture or forage.

Taking the projected pattern of food demand as given,

the substantial projected imbalances within the crop sector would have to be resolved through international trade or by altering production patterns, both of which would be feasible up to a point, but not without problems.

INTERNATIONAL TRADE. It would generally be more economic to import feedgrains rather than an equivalent amount of animal products, simply because wages in China's agriculture are likely to remain far below those of the main animal product–exporting countries. It also appears that China could purchase a large amount of feedgrains on the world market without much effect on prices, mainly because of the large unexploited production potential in grain-supplying countries. World trade in coarse grains, on the basis of past trends, could increase by 7 million to 8 million tons per year, and prices could continue to decline in real terms (Box 3.1, and Annex 2, paras. 5.17–5.19). Even if the whole of the large feedgrain shortfall identified above were to be met through imports, these would not exceed 15–20 percent of world market growth, and by the end of the century China's imports would be unlikely to exceed 10 percent of world trade in grain. Diversification of suppliers in recent years has also reduced the ability of any single large supplier to use grain embargoes or restrictions for political ends. Nonetheless, it might be unacceptably risky for a country of China's vast size to become heavily import-dependent (60 million tons would be about a third of China's projected feedgrain requirements in 2000).

There is also the necessity of earning sufficient foreign exchange to pay for these imports. This need not be earned by agricultural exports: indeed, in some of the projections mentioned above, in which there is an overall agricultural deficit, some of it would have to be covered by exports of manufactures and services (conversely, an overall agricultural surplus could be a net source of finance for nonagricultural imports). But the projected coexistence of shortages of feedgrains and surpluses of other crops obviously suggests the possibility of exporting the latter.

Here a major question arises. The surpluses are mainly in rice, and world trade in rice is comparatively small. Indeed, the potential rice surplus for 2000 mentioned above (some 20 million tons on a milled basis) is about as large as most estimates of total world rice trade at that time (the total is now about 12 million tons and is expected to grow at about 2.5 percent per year), which would imply a doubling of total trade and an increase in China's share from the present 10 percent to around 50 percent. It is unlikely that world trade in rice could be doubled without depressing the world market price of rice to uneconomic levels. However, the present relative level of the world rice price—2.5–3.0 times that of wheat—has little foundation in nutritional content. And in China, the cost of rice production is probably lower than that of wheat production (Annex 2, Table 1.3). It could therefore be in China's economic interests to expand rice exports substantially—but gradually, for smooth adjustment—and to reduce the world rice price to a level much nearer that of wheat.[6]

PRODUCTION PATTERN. In addition, or as an alternative, to using international trade to match demand and supply for particular crops, there is scope for altering the domestic production mix. This would involve switching rice land either into coarse grain production or into the production of other crops that could be more easily exported to pay for coarse grain imports. The extent to which either of these switches would be economic, let alone the economically optimal combination, cannot be determined on the basis of presently available information on China's soil and water resources. Much of the presently irrigated rice land would not be as well suited to other crops, but in rainfed upland, rice yields are much lower in relation to those of corn and oilseeds. Major expansion of some of China's traditional export crops (tea and mushrooms, for example) would be as difficult as expanding rice exports; major expansion of alternative—and potentially promising—export crops would require tremendous improvements in storage, transport, and packaging facilities.

Since these changes in the production pattern would require certain areas to become more specialized in production of animal feed or export commodities, the Government would have to further relax local food self-sufficiency requirements (see Chapter 5). In addition, the present regional pattern of production is such that most

feedgrains are grown in the North, while most pork and poultry are produced and consumed in the South. In the future, there will therefore have to be either more North-South movement of feedgrains or an increase in livestock production in the North for transportation to the South (which would involve a smaller volume of transport, but more expensive refrigerated equipment).

Changing Food Demand

The preceding discussion of potential agricultural demand-supply imbalances has assumed a rapid increase in the share of animal products in a gradually rising total food intake. Because animal products are relatively expensive, this implies an income elasticity of demand for food (0.85) that is rather high by international standards (0.70 would be normal for a country at about China's income level).[7] Clearly, however, adjustment of the level

---

6. To maximize China's economic gains, the price should be reduced to the point where the increase in foreign exchange earnings from additional rice exports—taking account of the loss of revenue on existing exports caused by the price reduction, as well as the increase in volume at the new price—is approximately equal to the cost of additional rice production, measured in foreign exchange. The price level in question could be roughly identified in advance on the basis of information on the price elasticity of world demand, but its attainment would require gradual adjustment and careful monitoring of demand and cost development.

7. The income elasticity of demand for food is defined as the growth rate of real per capita expenditure on food divided by the growth rate of real per capita household income. The figure of 0.85, for example, implies that each 10 percent increase in income leads to an 8.5 percent increase in food expenditure.

and pattern of food consumption is an additional possible response to these imbalances.

The present food situation in China is very unusual, in two senses. First, by comparison with other countries: total food intake, in terms of protein as well as calories, is above the average for middle-income countries; yet the proportion of animal products in the Chinese diet is similar to the low-income country average. This limits the relevance of international experience, since a "normal" diet at the Government's target income level for 2000 would involve significantly less food (though more animal products) consumption than at present. Second, by comparison with the past: for much of China's history, feeding the population at a level—at best—just above subsistence has been a major problem; yet in just five years a remarkable surge of agricultural production has transformed the situation. Even looking a long way ahead, agricultural production seems likely to grow at least twice as fast as population, which implies that there should be no difficulty in maintaining or improving on China's present satisfactory average per capita calorie and protein intake.

The projections discussed above also allow the possibility of an increase in animal product consumption over the next two decades as rapid as present targets imply. But this would require crop production to grow at a high rate, international trade or changes in production patterns to balance supply and demand for particular crops, and feed-meat conversion ratios to improve substantially. There is no guarantee that any or all of these conditions will be fulfilled, especially over the longer term. There are some difficult technical and economic obstacles to overcome, as well as the possible risks of dependence on feedgrain imports. The meager scale of China's cultivable land resources and the possibility of substantial population growth in the twenty-first century are also reasons for caution. Even with a favorable feed conversion ratio, an increase of ten percentage points in the share of animal products in the average diet is equivalent (other things being equal) to the disappearance of 35–40 percent of China's cultivable land, or a 35–40 percent increase in China's population.[8]

One possibility of particular concern would be an increase in per capita consumption of animal products to a level that could not be sustained, because of a future slowdown in crop production growth, inefficient meat production, or inability or unwillingness to import feedgrains on a sufficient scale. International experience suggests that the cutback in meat consumption that would then be required could cause acute social problems.

Alternative Food Consumption Patterns

China's target increase in total food intake is modest by international standards (Figure 3.2). If the 1981–2000 trend were continued to a much higher income level, the

Figure 3.2 Per Capita Food Intake in China, 1981–2000, and in Other Selected Economies, 1960–80

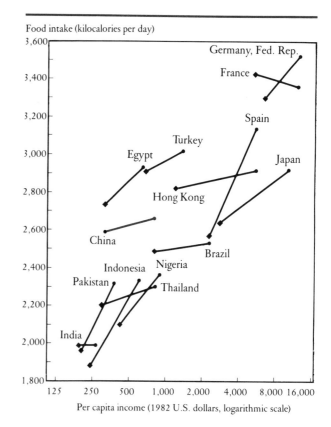

Food intake (kilocalories per day)

Per capita income (1982 U.S. dollars, logarithmic scale)

◆ Relationship in about 1960[a]
● Relationship in about 1980[b]
● QUADRUPLE projection, 2000

a. Based on 1960 per capita income and the 1961–65 average for food intake.
b. Based on 1982 per capita income and the 1978–80 average for food intake.
Source: World Bank data.

figure shows that it would lead to roughly the food consumption level of Japan (under 3,000 kilocalories), rather than to the substantially higher levels (around 3,500 kilocalories) of Western Europe and the United States. (In the U.S.S.R., the corresponding figure is 3,300 kilocalories; in Eastern Europe, it ranges from 3,200 to 3,800 kilocalories.)

By contrast, China's target increase in consumption of animal products, relative to the target increase in per capita income, is high by international standards (Figure

---

8. This is because more than four kilograms of grain are required to produce a kilogram of meat, which contains only three-quarters as many calories as one kilogram of grain consumed directly.

3.3). Over similar low- to lower-middle-income ranges, the share of animal products in the diet in most other countries either increased only slightly (Egypt and Nigeria) or declined (Indonesia, Pakistan, Thailand, and Turkey). Moreover, if this Chinese trend were continued, it would lead to West European levels, rather than to the much lower level of Japan. Indeed, China at an income level of $800 would have a share of animal products in food consumption similar to Brazil at a comparable income level, but 50 percent higher than Japan had at an income level of $2,500, and only 25 percent lower than at Japan's present income level of $10,000.

Figure 3.3 **Share of Animal Products in Total Food Intake in China, 1980–2000, and in Other Selected Economies, 1960–80**

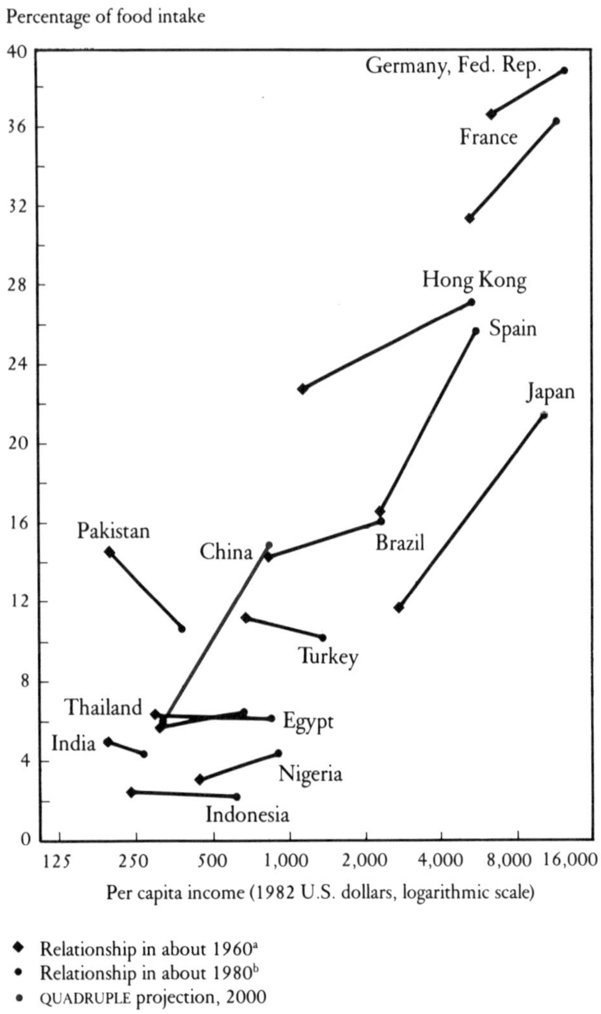

Percentage of food intake

Per capita income (1982 U.S. dollars, logarithmic scale)

♦ Relationship in about 1960[a]
• Relationship in about 1980[b]
• QUADRUPLE projection, 2000

a. Based on 1960 per capita income and the 1961–65 average for food intake.
b. Based on 1982 per capita income and the 1978–80 average for food intake.
Source: World Bank data.

Japan's food consumption pattern is of special relevance to China's future development, largely because the two countries have in common a very small amount of cultivable land per person (although China's is more than double Japan's). Japan's pattern differs from that of other industrial market economies not only in its substantially lower caloric intake and far lower animal products intake (although the latter increased from 300 kilocalories per day in 1961–65 to 550 in 1977), but also in the composition of the animal products intake, with an unusually high share of aquatic products and unusually low shares of meat—especially beef—and dairy products. This dietary pattern, moreover, has been achieved through relatively high food prices, with the result that expenditure on food is actually a higher proportion of consumer expenditure in Japan (around 30 percent) than in Western Europe and the United States (around 20 percent). Prices for Japanese farmers that are well above world market levels—enforced by restrictions on most agricultural imports—have been passed on to consumers.

Variants on the QUADRUPLE projection were constructed to illustrate the impact that changes in the food consumption pattern in 2000 could have on agricultural demand-supply imbalances. For example, reducing consumption of animal products by about 6 percent, but increasing direct crop consumption by a roughly equivalent number of calories, transforms the slight overall crop deficit into a small surplus. The impact of this change is greater for individual crop subsectors: the potential rice surplus is reduced from about 20 million tons to 15 million tons, and the coarse grain deficit from about 60 million tons to 40 million tons.

Another variant assumed a lower income elasticity of demand for food (0.70, as mentioned earlier), with significant reductions in both meat consumption (about 12 percent in 2000) and direct crop consumption (about 8 percent). This transforms a projected crop deficit of 0.5 percent of production into a 2 percent crop surplus. The change would be larger, except that the reduction in consumer expenditure on food is matched by an increase in expenditure on other things, especially light manufactures, whose production requires considerable amounts of cotton and other industrial crops. The BALANCE projection introduced in the previous chapter also assumes an income elasticity of demand for food (0.80) lower than in QUADRUPLE, but attains almost the same level of food consumption in 2000 because of faster growth of total household income and consumption. However, domestic demand for crops in 2000 is 2 percent lower because of the increase in the weight of services in the economy relative to that of industry.

Managing Food Demand

As the preceding discussion suggests, the long-term capacity of China's agriculture to provide its people with, in particular, a higher level of consumption of animal products cannot be accurately predicted. The uncertainties are especially great in the twenty-first century—although past long-term predictions of food production potential (in other countries and worldwide) have almost always been unduly pessimistic, because they have underestimated technological progress in agriculture.

These uncertainties, and the adverse social consequences of possible future reductions in per capita consumption of animal products (or food in general), suggest the need for caution in managing food demand in China. One essential policy objective will be to continue to guarantee a minimum supply of food to everyone, and especially to people in poor rural areas. Indeed, some of the present grain surpluses could be used to increase the guaranteed minimum. This would not only reduce the gap between the minimum and the average level of food intake, which has probably increased in the past five years, but it could also help to eliminate the stunting due to mild chronic malnutrition that persists among a significant proportion of China's rural children (Annex 2, para. 2.05).

At the other end of the social spectrum, considerations of efficiency and equity suggest that consumers should pay the full economic cost of animal products (including the opportunity cost of diverting scarce agricultural resources and foreign exchange from other uses). A long-term food trade strategy, especially with regard to tariffs or quotas on imports of animal products and feedgrains, has to be established in advance. Given this, it would probably be inadvisable to subsidize or administratively restrict either the retail prices of animal products or the prices of inputs into animal husbandry and aquaculture, particularly feedgrain. The experience of Japan suggests that high prices can bring consumer demand for animal products into line with limited supplies in a socially acceptable manner. By contrast, the experience of other countries with subsidized and rationed consumption of animal products has been extremely unfavorable, both economically and politically, notwithstanding its short-term social appeal.

Managing Household Agriculture

The production responsibility system has been extraordinarily successful. Yet there may be substantial scope for further improvement of agricultural management, in light of China's own experience with the new system, as well as experience in the many other developing countries where households are the basic agricultural production units. The major issues include: how best to stimulate growth of household agricultural production; how to improve its economic efficiency, which is essential to increases in both national and rural incomes; and how to ensure that the composition of agricultural production

adjusts to the changing pattern of demand, thus minimizing the costs of the potential imbalances discussed earlier. These issues all raise the question of how prices and other economic levers should be used in managing household agriculture and of the appropriate roles of the state and the collective in the new system.

Recent changes in government policies will substantially increase the regulatory role of the market. From 1985, compulsory procurement and production quotas for grain and cotton have been abolished. This is to be extended gradually to all agricultural products, with an accompanying loosening of price controls. However, the state will continue to fix the price at which it procures agricultural products under contracts that will account for a large proportion of the total marketed by farmers. Important inputs to agriculture are still administratively allocated. The state also remains significantly involved in agricultural production—including the state farm system—and directly productive investment, and it is apparently envisaged that large-scale state-owned units will play an important role in the rapid growth of meat and dairy production.

Output Pricing and Marketing

The discussion of imbalances in earlier sections, and additional analysis in Annex 2 (paras. 3.30–3.39), suggest some general directions in which agricultural producer prices may need to move during the next few years. Potential shortages of animal feed and surpluses of rice could be alleviated by increases in the price of coarse grains (and possibly soybeans, the most useful source of animal feed protein—Annex 2, para. 4.75) relative to the price of rice. Pork and fish prices will need to be higher than in the past to make it financially attractive for producers to invest in the more feed-intensive systems necessary for rapid output expansion—and of course the required animal product price increases will be made greater by the increases in animal feed prices. Higher timber prices also seem necessary to stimulate production, although some other tree crop products (such as tea and rubber) at present appear overpriced.

More important than these possible specific price changes, however, is the issue of whether necessary price adjustments should be administratively imposed or generated by the market. With the new system of household agriculture, and with increasing reform of the nonagricultural economy, it will not be possible, let alone efficient, to have an administered structure of agricultural prices that ignores or fundamentally contradicts the forces of demand and supply. Yet it would also be impossible to calculate and apply an economically efficient set of administered agricultural prices, especially because they would constantly be altering. Even at a very aggregated level, the projections discussed earlier suggest the possibility of changes in agricultural imbalances over time. The point is strengthened when specific categories and quality subdivisions of agricultural products are considered: the detailed pattern of demand is bound to change in innumerable ways, with the added complication that demand for particular products is affected by the prices and availability of other products; the detailed pattern of production costs will also change, again with the complication that the willingness of farmers to supply particular crops at particular prices is affected by the prices and production potential of the alternative crops they might grow.

Nonetheless, experience in other countries and international markets suggests that market forces alone may produce undesirably unstable agricultural prices. Actual or anticipated changes in production—often weather-related—and demand can cause large short-term price fluctuations that inflict needless hardship on producers or consumers, increase the cost of adjustment to fundamental changes in economic circumstances, and create risks that can discourage farmers from specialized production for the market rather than subsistence. For these reasons, there are few countries in which governments do not in some way intervene in agricultural price formation. Similarly, the Chinese government intends to limit the influence of market forces on agricultural prices: although the prices of minor products will be allowed to float freely, for major products market-determined prices will apply only to above-contract sales (that is, sales in excess of contracted state procurement) and even then will be subject to a state-set floor price.

A possible alternative approach for major agricultural products would be for the Government to let prices be determined by demand and supply, but to intervene in the market to prevent excessive fluctuations. At any given time, prices would be allowed to move only within a range established by the Government's willingness to purchase for addition to its stocks at the lower end and to sell from its stocks at the upper end. The range could be narrow, which would require frequent interventions at both ends and comparatively large stocks. Alternatively, as in most schemes of this sort elsewhere, the range could be wider, with price volatility reduced by starting intervention on a modest scale before prices reach the established limits. Over time, if a price persistently remains at its upper or lower limit, with the Government's stocks becoming very small or very large, the Government gradually alters the two limits, shifting the whole range in the direction required by demand and supply trends.

To operate such a price stabilization scheme would not be simple. It would be technically quite complicated, especially given the likely need for coordination with export and import policies and for interregional price variations within China. It would involve financial costs, especially because it is possible to be wrong about market trends (and hence to adjust price limits too soon or too late); and the political and social repercussions of altering the price limits could be as significant as those of altering purely administered prices. Nonetheless, it could have certain advantages over the two-tier (contract and above-contract) pricing system now being implemented in China, especially in terms of administrative simplicity and responsiveness to changing circumstances.

Though a price stabilization scheme could not be used directly to redistribute income, as is possible with two-tier pricing (discussed later), it could contribute indirectly to raising rural incomes by enabling the state to reduce its present heavy direct involvement in agricultural commerce. Indeed, the Government would need to purchase and sell agricultural products only as required for stabilization purposes and to secure emergency stocks and supplies for poor areas. Scarce state resources could thus be released from commerce for other, more vital, agricultural support activities. And allowing collective and individual enterprises a large share of (at least) the increment in agricultural commerce over the next two decades could make an important contribution to boosting rural nonfarm incomes—as experience in other countries confirms. The same applies to food processing, whose volume is projected to increase nearly fivefold between 1981 and 2000, and to the processing of other agricultural products.

Input Pricing and Allocation

Under the production responsibility system, farmers have a strong incentive to make more efficient use of industrial and other inputs to agricultural production, applying them just up to the point where their contribution to increased output value is balanced by their cost. However, to ensure that farmers use inputs in a way that is optimal for the economy as a whole, it is necessary that output prices and input prices be economically rational, and that farmers be able to obtain sufficient quantities of inputs at these prices. At present in China these conditions are not always fulfilled.

Chemical fertilizer is a good example (Annex 2, paras. 3.17–3.25, 3.35–3.36). Although its price seems quite rational by international standards, especially in relation to the price of wheat, it is allocated to farmers through a cumbersome administrative procedure. The allocation criteria are not at all clear and are not always followed, although they appear to include priority for food crops over feedgrains and compensation for state procurement at low prices. In any event, the present system does not allocate fertilizer among farmers or localities in a way that maximizes its contribution to production (which would involve equalizing the marginal output response to a kilogram of fertilizer in all uses).

Nor, more importantly, could any administrative system of fertilizer allocation in practice achieve this desirable result: the yield response to fertilizer varies not only among crops and localities, but also among individual plots of land within a given locality. Individual farmers are usually better informed about such variations than government officials and could use their knowledge in deciding how much fertilizer to purchase in a competitive market. China should thus consider moving toward market allocation of fertilizer, although this would make it even more necessary to maintain economically rational agricultural product prices. The immediate impact of market regulation on the general level of fertilizer prices cannot be predicted, but could be cushioned by suitable changes in imports. The level of imports, in conjunction with economic calculations of the relative cost of imports and domestic production, would then provide a guide to investment needs in the domestic fertilizer industry.

Similar arguments for moving, in the context of a system of household agriculture, away from administrative measures and toward market allocation of inputs (with market-regulated prices) can be made for pesticides, animal feed, farm machinery, fuel, and so on. They also apply to credit, which, together with the farmer's own saving, is in household agriculture the main source of finance for fixed investment and of circulating capital. Extensive experience with rural credit in other developing countries has made clear the disadvantages of subsidizing interest rates and of the administrative rationing consequently required by excess demand for available funds. China's farmers, including the poorer farmers, will probably be able to get more credit, and hence to increase their production and incomes more, if the interest rates charged reflect the scarcity of credit and repayment is strictly enforced. These conditions would also make it harder for China's rural credit institutions to discriminate against loans to households and in favor of loans to collective or state-sponsored activities (Annex 2, paras. 3.45–3.46). And they would discourage uneconomic mechanization.[9]

Areas for Increased State and Collective Activity

The preceding discussion has identified a number of areas—pricing, marketing, input allocation—in which less extensive or direct government involvement in managing China's household agricultural system could be advantageous. At the same time, there are a number of areas (identified in Annex 2) where increased government activity would be highly desirable. Given overall limitations on government resources for agriculture, moreover, it may in fact be essential to curtail some activities in order to expand others with larger economic benefits.

Among the areas for increased state activity identified in Annex 2 are agricultural research, education, and extension services (paras. 3.48–3.58), range management (paras. 4.48–4.51), fertilizer utilization studies (para. 3.25), and seed testing and certification (para. 3.27). Equally important, state support—both directly and by encouraging collective and individual provision—is

needed to improve rural transport, storage, and marketing facilities (Annex 2, paras. 3.61–3.70). At present, China's rural road network is less than half the size of India's; there are fewer trucks per capita in rural China than in the impoverished Sahelian countries of West Africa; and there is less cold storage capacity in the whole of rural China than in northwest India (with a population of 50 million). Improvements in these aspects of China's agricultural infrastructure would almost certainly be a better use of Government resources than, for example, direct state investment in animal husbandry, which in most countries is inefficient compared with household production (Annex 2, para. 4.70).

Expansion of collective activities in certain areas—especially marketing and input supply—could also make an important indirect contribution to the development of household agriculture. The original collective principles of China's supply and marketing cooperatives are being revived, but they could be given a much larger role in the commercial system. Both in perishable crops and in animal husbandry, including dairying, cooperative marketing facilities in other countries have very effectively stimulated and facilitated production, as well as increasing farmers' incomes.

Agricultural Incomes Policy

Increased state and collective activity in these various areas, by helping farmers to increase production, to reduce costs, and to market their output, could make a vital contribution to raising agricultural incomes over the next two decades. So could more economically rational allocation and pricing of agricultural inputs. But are there other measures that could help to close the large gap between agricultural and nonagricultural incomes? (Policies toward very low and very high incomes within agriculture are considered in Chapters 5 and 9, respectively.)

Economic forces are, by themselves, unlikely to lead to an early reduction in this gap. Indeed, experience from other countries suggests that the gap is more likely to widen—even in proportional terms—during the low- to middle-income transition. The basic problem—in China as in other countries at a similar stage of development—is that agricultural labor productivity does not increase fast enough to close the gap, even when agricultural output grows quite rapidly, unless or until agricultural employment starts to shrink absolutely. In the QUADRUPLE pro-

---

9. Especially in poorer localities, where it would aggravate the labor surplus, with (as in other countries) potentially unfortunate social and economic consequences. In richer localities, shrinking agricultural labor surpluses will make mechanization more attractive to farmers, but the alternative of permitting more movement of labor from poorer to richer areas may be beneficial to the national economy (this issue is discussed in Chapter 5).

jection, for example, although gross agricultural output increases at 4.5 percent per year, agricultural employment also rises (at 0.9 percent per year). Thus, although average gross output per worker in agriculture almost doubles over the period 1981–2000, it increases more slowly than in other sectors. Even in the BALANCE projection, where faster growth of employment in services causes slower growth of agricultural employment (0.2 percent per year), agricultural labor productivity—net of increased outlays on inputs such as fertilizer—increases slightly more slowly than in other sectors.

Agricultural employment tends to continue to expand in the early phases of development fundamentally because it constitutes such a large initial share of total employment. The absolute number of farmers can therefore be reduced only by extraordinarily rapid growth of nonagricultural output (as in South Korea in 1960–80, with industry growing at around 15 percent per year) or by unacceptably slow growth of nonagricultural labor productivity (Chapter 2). But in the twenty-first century, the situation in China will become more favorable, mainly because agriculture's share of the total labor force will have shrunk. In 2000–2020, for example, if the total labor force were to grow at 1 percent per year,[10] and nonagricultural employment were to continue to grow at the same rate as in QUADRUPLE (3.5 percent per year, from a share of 41 percent in 2000), the agricultural labor force would decline from 370 million to 255 million, or 33 percent of the total labor force. The corresponding extrapolation for BALANCE, with faster growth of nonagricultural employment, would be from 330 million to 85 million, or 11 percent of the labor force (similar to Japan in 1980).

For the remainder of this century, however, the Government may need to intervene actively to prevent the gap between agricultural and nonagricultural incomes from becoming (or remaining) unacceptably wide. Price adjustments are one obvious mechanism for transferring the benefits of nonagricultural productivity growth (in both rural and urban areas) to agricultural workers, rather than giving them mainly to nonagricultural workers in the form of higher wages. To illustrate this, the macroeconomic projections specifically assume that the relative price of agricultural output adjusts so that agricultural earnings per worker remain a constant proportion—about one-half—of nonagricultural wages. In QUADRU-PLE, for example, the relative price of crops has to increase by 17 percent over the period 1981–2000 to prevent the earnings gap from widening. In BALANCE the required relative price increase for crops is 6 percent.

Larger increases in agricultural prices could in principle reduce the gap in earnings between agriculture and nonagriculture. But they might conflict with other objectives of China's agricultural price policy, including the need to balance demand and supply for particular agricultural products, which—as emphasized earlier—will be very important in managing China's new system of household agriculture. Demand and supply forces, coupled with foreign trade policies, may require agricultural price increases—as for example in Japan, where high agricultural prices are a concomitant of the Government's policy of limiting agricultural imports. But this will not necessarily be so, or not to a sufficiently great extent. And the experience of Western Europe, where artificially high agricultural prices are maintained specifically to boost farm incomes, has not been favorable, because of the financial cost of stocking the resulting surpluses or exporting them at a loss.

In China, however, additional room for maneuver is provided by the two-tier agricultural pricing system. Even following the recent decision to unify the state procurement prices for grain, cotton, and oilseeds (based on weighted averages of the former quota and above-quota prices), procurement prices will generally differ from the market prices for above-contract sales and purchases. These market prices will strongly influence farm household decisions to increase or decrease production of particular commodities, and hence are the prices relevant to balancing demand and supply. But the state procurement prices will powerfully affect the average price that farmers receive and hence their incomes. In the past, state procurement prices have generally been below market prices—the difference being an implicit tax on agriculture. But the Government apparently envisages that the new unified procurement prices for major crops will be above their market prices (otherwise it would not be possible to replace compulsory procurement quotas with voluntary contracts).

The immediate impact of the latest price and procurement reforms on farm incomes will depend on whether the market prices for the crops concerned turn out to be above or below their unified procurement prices. But in the longer term, regardless of whether market prices are initially above or below procurement prices, the Government could in principle boost the incomes of farmers by increasing procurement prices, while allowing market-determined above-contract prices to equate supply and demand for the various agricultural commodities. To finance its increased expenditures on procurement, the government would of course have to raise additional revenues (or reduce other expenditures or subsidies), largely at the expense of the nonagricultural population. But the same would be true of any redistributive scheme to narrow the agriculture-nonagriculture income gap by a given amount. The key issues are rather (a) how much redistribution from the nonagricultural to the agricultural

---

10. This is similar to the fastest of the three labor force projections in Table 8.3.

population is desired; and (b) whether increasing procurement prices within a two-tier system is the best of the various alternative redistributive schemes available.

Although the first of these issues is fundamentally a political matter, it is complicated by the fact that the incomes of suburban farmers—who are in close proximity to the urban population—are generally substantially higher than those of the majority of farmers in more distant rural areas. Redistributive schemes that raise the incomes of all farmers across the board are thus more likely to provoke an unfavorable response from the nonagricultural population than schemes whose benefits are concentrated on farmers with average and below-average incomes. This could be a disadvantage of redistribution through two-tier pricing—although it could be minimized (as appears to be the Government's intention) by excluding the most important suburban agricultural products, such as meat and vegetables.

Redistribution through two-tier pricing would also be technically quite complicated, especially if it were to be done on a large scale and if serious inequities among farmers in different places and situations were to be avoided. This is because its impact depends crucially on the allocation of procurement contracts among individual farm households—an administratively costly process, with wide scope for abuse, especially since considerable discretion would have to be given to local officials. Direct income supplements to broad categories of farm households would be an alternative means of redistribution that might pose fewer administrative problems, because of its greater simplicity and transparency.

Another means of redistributing nonagricultural productivity gains to farmers that would probably pose even fewer administrative problems is increased government expenditure on development of agricultural infrastructure and support services. Greater budget expenditure on rural social services, particularly education and health, would constitute yet another approach, as would subsidies to a rural social insurance scheme that provided pensions and other welfare benefits (discussed in Chapters 8 and 10). All these approaches naturally have some limitations, especially as to the amount of money that could usefully be spent and the possibility of spreading it equitably within the agricultural population. But, in conjunction with two-tier pricing or otherwise, they offer substantial scope for economically efficient government action to raise agricultural incomes.

4

Energy Development

Energy, though a much smaller sector than agriculture, is just as critical to China's future growth and subject to similar uncertainties. There is uncertainty about energy supply prospects, particularly for oil and gas, but also for coal and electricity, whose successful development will require much investment and planning. Uncertainty also surrounds both the magnitude of potential economies in energy use (by reducing waste, modernizing technology, and changing industrial structure), and how much of this potential China will be able to realize without compromising standards of living. Equally important, coal is likely to remain in China—unlike almost all other countries—the overwhelmingly predominant source of energy. To harness it cleanly and efficiently in an unusually wide range of uses will be a major challenge.

This chapter, which is based largely on Annex 3, first reviews overall energy demand and supply prospects and targets to the year 2000. It then looks at issues and policies in specific energy subsectors, with special reference to the production, transport, and use of coal. Finally, it reviews possible investment requirements in the sector and the future role of planning and demand management. Two common themes—which will echo through subsequent chapters—are the importance of more general improvements in the efficiency of resource use in China and the need for economic as well as technical analysis in choosing among options. Both will require the strengthening of economic planning and intersectoral coordination as well as increased reliance on market regulation.

Demand and Supply: Trends and Balances

Coal already dominates energy consumption in China. In 1980, it accounted for about three-quarters of primary commercial energy consumption and one-half of total primary energy consumption (including biomass), the highest share for coal in any major country. Biomass fuels—used mainly in rural households—are the second most important energy source (more than 25 percent of primary consumption). Oil—all domestically produced—accounts for approximately one-fifth, and natural gas for less than 3 percent, of primary commercial energy consumption. Electricity in 1980 accounted for just 18 percent of final commercial energy consumption, a far lower share than in most countries.[1]

Industry—especially metallurgy, chemicals, and building materials—accounts for at least half of the final consumption of coal, oil, and gas, and three-quarters of electricity consumption. Households and commerce together accounted for only 20 percent of final commercial energy consumption in 1980—but, including biomass, for approximately 43 percent of final energy use (the same share as for industry). The transport sector's share of final commercial energy consumption (8 percent) is low compared with other large developing countries, because of the small role of road transport.

Energy Intensity

Cross-country comparisons suggest exceptionally high consumption of both commercial and total primary energy per unit of GDP in China. This can be explained partly by China's high share of industrial output in GDP and by space heating requirements. But energy consumption per unit of gross output value in Chinese industry is also exceptionally high compared with most other countries. Although the share of energy-intensive subsectors in industry is not significantly different from other countries, Chinese industrial output is weighted toward energy-intensive goods. High energy consumption in industrial production is also explained by relatively backward

---

1. Final energy consumption excludes transformation losses in electric power and other energy sectors (about 15 percent of primary commercial energy use in 1980); commercial energy excludes biomass fuels (about 27 percent of total primary energy use in 1980).

technology, the small scale of industrial plant, and the type of fuel used (particularly coal). Low energy prices and insufficient cost consciousness among enterprises and planners also appear to have contributed substantially to the low efficiency of energy use in China.

In recent years, steps have been taken to reduce both the growth of overall energy consumption and energy use per unit of output. These steps have so far consisted mainly of regulations concerning the amount of energy use per unit of output, reductions in energy supply quotas, and bonuses for energy use below established quotas. Conservation centers have been established to provide technical assistance. A larger share of investment funds has recently been allocated for technical transformation of existing enterprises and in particular energy conservation measures. Financial incentives are now receiving greater emphasis, and there has been some movement toward rationalizing the energy price structure.

As a result, during the past five years an impressive reduction in energy use in relation to economic activity has taken place. Energy consumption per unit of gross value of industrial and agricultural output (GVIAO) was reduced by 7 percent per year during 1979–81 and by 3 percent per year during 1982–83. Preliminary data indicate a further reduction of almost 7 percent in 1984. Technical and operational improvements are estimated to have accounted for about 40 percent of these energy savings. The other 60 percent came initially from a decline in the relative importance of heavy industry and the closure of some inefficient small-scale plants, but since 1981 mainly from structural changes within major industrial subsectors.

Demand and Supply Prospects

To investigate the future growth of demand for various types of energy in China, the projections made with the multisectoral economic model (discussed in Chapter 2) were combined with a plausible range of assumptions about changes in unit energy consumption in particular sectors. The resulting estimated annual average growth rates of primary commercial energy demand between 1980 and 2000 range from 3.4 percent to 5.5 percent. Projected elasticities of growth in energy demand relative to growth in GDP range from 0.6 to 0.85, which is far lower than the past trend in China (1.5 in 1965–78), though higher than the elasticities realized during the past few years (0.2 in 1978–81 and 0.5 in 1981–84).

In the QUADRUPLE scenario (which involves the quadrupling of GVIAO), the projections indicate that total primary commercial energy demand could be expected to grow at 4.2–5.5 percent per year, depending on the degree of success in reducing unit energy consumption. In the BALANCE scenario (which has the same rate of growth of GDP, but with slower growth in manufacturing output, faster growth of services, and greater efficiency in

resource use), energy demand grows significantly more slowly—by 3.8–5.0 percent per year from 1980 to 2000. In the MODERATE scenario (with GDP growing at 5.4 percent per year, as compared with 6.6 percent in QUADRUPLE and BALANCE, and with the same emphasis on expansion of manufacturing output as in QUADRUPLE), energy demand grows more slowly still—by 3.4–4.6 percent per year.

The Government's original tentative target was to quadruple GVIAO between 1980 and 2000 while only doubling the production and use of energy (to somewhat less than 1,300 million tons of coal equivalent of primary commercial energy). This was to involve doubling the production of coal, oil, and natural gas (output levels of 1,200 million tons for coal, 200 million tons for oil, and 25 billion cubic meters for gas by 2000). Preliminary forecasts by the Ministry of Water Resources and Electric Power (MWREP) suggested that electricity generation would increase from 301 terawatt-hours in 1980 to 1,000–1,200 terawatt-hours by 2000—with some 230–280 terawatt-hours from hydro and nuclear power.

The energy demand projections discussed above, and more recent government estimates, suggest that it will probably be necessary to increase the production of energy somewhat faster than originally envisaged (Table 4.1). For example, even under optimistic assumptions about improvements in energy efficiency, the estimated growth in energy demand resulting from quadrupling GVIAO (4.2–5.5 percent per year) would be more than could be accommodated by doubling energy production (which implies a growth rate of about 3.5 percent per year). Increasing oil and gas production substantially above the original targets is a possibility that cannot be relied on, and it would be extremely difficult to increase primary electricity production much faster than already planned. For these reasons, and because the need for more than the originally anticipated amount of energy production is concentrated on fuel, the burden of bringing energy production into line with demand is likely to fall mainly on coal (oil distillate and total electricity production plans conform reasonably well with the demand projections).

In the QUADRUPLE and BALANCE projections discussed in Chapter 2, it is assumed that coal production in 2000 will reach 1,400 million tons—a figure regarded as feasible by relevant agencies in China, even allowing for the need to develop additional transport facilities and other infrastructure. How much coal will in fact need to be produced, however, will depend heavily on the rate of economic growth, on the sectoral structure of the economy, and on the degree of success in reducing energy intensity within individual sectors.

In QUADRUPLE, production of 1,400 million tons would meet coal demand only on the most optimistic assumptions about reductions in energy consumption per

Table 4.1 Energy Supply and Demand, Alternative Projections, 1981–2000

Component	Fuel (millions of TCE)[a]	Oil distillates (millions of tons)	Electricity (terawatt-hours)	Total primary commercial energy (millions of TCE)[a]
Projections of demand				
QUADRUPLE	1,135–1,455	100–140	1,060–1,285	1,385–1,765
MODERATE	955–1,225	85–115	885–1,070	1,180–1,500
BALANCE	1,030–1,315	90–130	955–1,150	1,270–1,610
Production levels in line with original targets	1,020	112	1,000–1,200	1,275–1,295

a. Fuel includes coal, fuel oil, and natural gas for power generation, for other energy industries, and for final consumption. TCE indicates tons of coal equivalents.
Source: Annex 3, Chapter 2.

unit of output in each sector. On the least optimistic (but not implausible) assumptions about unit energy consumption, coal demand in QUADRUPLE in 2000 would exceed 1,800 million tons. Even in MODERATE, with significantly slower economic growth, coal demand in 2000 would on these less optimistic assumptions approach 1,500 million tons. In BALANCE, with slower growth of industry compensated by faster growth of services, and higher overall economic efficiency, projected coal demand is substantially lower than in QUADRUPLE—1,400 million tons on intermediate assumptions about unit energy consumption, and 1,200 million tons on the most optimistic assumptions.

Coal Production, Transport, and Utilization

In any event, the share of coal in commercial energy use by 2000 is likely to remain exceptionally large—some 70–75 percent (compared with 30–35 percent worldwide). Even if oil production reaches 200 million tons by 2000, it would still account for less than one-quarter of commercial energy production. If the target of doubling gas production by 2000 is achieved, natural gas would continue to account for only 2–3 percent of primary energy consumption. Even if the gas production target were exceeded, which is quite possible, it is extremely unlikely that its share of energy consumption in 2000 would exceed 5 percent. (By contrast, natural gas provides close to 20 percent of primary energy in most major industrial countries, and 30 percent or more in the United States and the U.S.S.R.) China thus inevitably faces some unusually substantial challenges in coal production, transport, and utilization.

Coal Mining

China has abundant reserves of good-quality coal that can be mined at relatively low cost. Economically recoverable reserves are concentrated in the North, which accounts for two-thirds (Shanxi province alone for one-third) of the total. The populous southern and eastern regions

together contain only 10 percent of the economically recoverable reserves, but by international standards are comparatively well endowed; recoverable reserves in these two regions are sufficient to sustain 1980 production levels (210 million tons) for more than 300 years.

Production costs are low by international standards. Operating costs are typically less than Y 20 per ton, while capital costs average about Y 110 per ton of capacity.[2] But geological conditions and mining costs vary widely among different coal producing areas. For example, costs[3] are as low as Y 30 per ton for extracting the few deposits amenable to open-cast mining in remote areas of Nei Monggol and Shanxi and are approximately Y 40 per ton for the huge underground reserves at moderate depth in Shanxi province. But smaller and less favorable deposits close to major consumption centers in the South and East might have production costs of up to twice those in the North.

Between 1965 and 1979, coal production grew at an average rate of almost 30 million tons per year. Coal production fell by 15 million tons in 1980, however, and remained at the same level in 1981, because of insufficient attention to mine development during the 1970s and the economic adjustment program of 1980 which sharply reduced investment allocations. Production has since picked up, increasing by about 45 million tons per year during 1982–84.

An average increase of about 40 million tons per year would be required to reach an annual production level of 1,400 million tons by the year 2000. To achieve this will require further strengthening of production incentives, a stepped up program of project preparation (including

2. Y 140–150 per ton for large-scale central mines and Y 75 per ton for small and less mechanized local mines (excluding social infrastructure).

3. Including an appropriate charge for capital recovery, for example, 15 percent of invested capital per year (based on an interest rate of 12 percent, reflecting the opportunity cost of capital and an economic life of fifteen years).

mine infrastructure), and coordination between the Ministry of Coal Industry (MOCI) and the transportation ministries to increase coal transportation capacity more quickly than originally planned. Organizational changes for central mines could also help to speed project implementation. State-imposed design norms leave little flexibility for taking account of geological conditions in the design of specific coal mining projects, which can lower the cost effectiveness of some projects. Time required for mine construction is currently longer than in other countries for similar work (construction time is more than six years for central mines) and could be shortened by better coordination among the many government entities involved in project execution.

Equally important is the balanced development of central and local mines. Central mines, primarily operated by MOCI, and local state and collective mines each accounted in 1984 for about one-half of production. Because local mines are smaller and less mechanized they require only about half as much capital spending per unit of output as large-scale central mines. And because they are more widely scattered across the country they put less pressure on transport infrastructure than the large-scale mines in the major coal basins (one-third of the coal produced by local mines comes from south of the Chang Jiang, as compared with only 3 percent of coal produced by MOCI mines). In recent years, the existence of a market for coal supplies beyond plan allocations has contributed to the development of local mines, which accounted for most of the overall increase in coal production in 1979–84. If, in addition, access to investment funds and transport facilities were improved, local mines could continue to play an important role in meeting energy demand, especially in areas with less favorable coal deposits and in supplying local needs. There is also considerable scope for improving mining techniques in local mines, with selective introduction of mechanization and greater attention to mine safety. However, large coal deposits are often more suitable to large-scale development with higher mechanization, lower costs, and better safety and resource recovery.

Coal Transport

Transport costs greatly affect the optimal spatial pattern of coal production and utilization. Just as coal mining costs vary considerably in China, depending on the type of deposit, coal transport costs also vary widely depending on factors such as the available transport mode (rail, ship, road), degree of capacity utilization, and topography. For example, long-run marginal costs (LRMC)[4] for transport over a 1,000 kilometer distance by double-track railway may be some Y 20 per ton, but about Y 30 per ton on a single-track railway line. Coastal shipping over several thousand kilometers may be Y 20–30 per ton, but road transport costs might be as high for a distance of only 200–300 kilometers. If several modal transfers (for example, rail to ship to rail to road) are required to transport coal, say, from Shanxi to an inland city in the South, total transport costs could be Y 40–60 per ton, justifying coal production in the South even under unfavorable conditions and at high costs (up to Y 80–100 per ton—or 2 to 2.5 times the production costs at the more favorable deposits in Shanxi province).

Nonetheless, the concentration of China's coal reserves in the North requires increasing large-scale, interregional coal transportation. At present, railway transport is probably more of a constraint on energy supplies than coal mine development, because of insufficient railway investments in the past and the slow replacement of inefficient steam locomotives by electric or diesel traction. It will take several years to complete the railway projects that were recently initiated to alleviate critical bottlenecks between major mining areas and the coast. If coal production were to reach 1,400 million tons in the year 2000, as much as 450 million tons might need to be transported out of Shanxi and adjacent areas in Nei Monggol and Shaanxi, even if current plans for developing mine-mouth power generation were implemented. To handle this traffic, it would probably be necessary to construct an additional new double-tracked electrified line for heavy unit trains (similar to the new Datong-Qinhuangdao line currently planned) in a southeastern direction and to increase capacity on existing lines through double tracking and electrification. Slurry pipelines might ease the pressure on the railways, but water shortages in Shanxi could constrain their widespread use.

Since a considerable part of incremental coal production (an additional 250 million to 350 million tons) will be for electric power generation, coal-fired power generation in mining areas in conjunction with long-distance transmission of electric power to load centers represents one alternative to transporting large quantities of coal. Current preliminary plans are to locate roughly half of thermal power capacity additions during 1986–2000 in coal mining areas. The relative economics of electricity transmission compared with rail transportation of coal are project-specific, as costs vary substantially. However, in most cases, rail transport of coal would be less expensive than long-distance transmission of electric power (see Annex 3, Appendix E). The optimal mix of mine-mouth power generation and load-center–based power plants will therefore be determined mainly by other factors such as the availability of low-quality coals or middlings from coal preparation plants (discussed later), the availability of water for mine-mouth power plants, and the potential for cogeneration of electric power and heat or steam for

---

4. Total costs including capital construction, operating, and maintenance costs, calculated by using an appropriate factor to reflect the opportunity cost of capital.

Table 4.2 Share of Solid Fuels in Commercial Energy Use in Selected Countries, 1960, 1980, and 2000
(percent)

Country	1960	1980	2000
United States	24	23	..
Japan	54	19	..
Germany, Fed. Rep.	78	33	..
South Korea	79	36	..
U.S.S.R.	64	33	..
China	96	77	70–75

Source: United Nations, *Energy Statistics Yearbook* (New York, 1982); Annex 3.

industrial or space heating uses in the case of power plants located near load centers. These economic choices need to be thoroughly studied before long-term plans can be finalized.

While railway transport of coal is likely to remain a constraint on energy supplies for some years to come, it nevertheless remains one of the most economical means of energy transport in China, as other technologies (water transport, slurry pipelines, power transmission) are either not as widely applicable or more costly. Lead times for railway investments need not be longer than for other alternatives. But long-term investment plans for railways and other transport facilities need to be closely integrated with coal mining development, and sufficient resources will have to be allocated, especially to ease critical bottlenecks. An optimal coal development and transportation strategy must also incorporate measures to reduce transport requirements, for example, through balanced development of large-scale coal mines in major coal basins remote from demand centers and mining under less favorable conditions and at higher costs in smaller deposits closer to consumption centers. Other means to reduce transport requirements include optimal location of raw material processing industries and more extensive use of coal preparation to reduce transport of inert material, possibly in conjunction with mine-mouth power generation. Realignment of coal and transport prices to reflect economic costs and greater enterprise autonomy in arranging supply could greatly facilitate development of least-cost solutions for coal production and transport.

Coal Utilization

Improving the efficiency of coal use could much reduce the amount of coal that will need to be mined and transported. Even so, projected increases in coal consumption will have serious implications for environmental pollution—and hence high welfare and health costs—unless improved environmental protection measures are adopted. This is particularly important in China because coal is expected to remain the dominant fuel, whereas in most industrial countries coal accounts today for only 20–40 percent of energy consumption (Table 4.2), and even less in most developing countries. Coal use in other countries is thus by and large limited to large-scale uses such as electric power generation, the steel and cement industries, and large industrial boilers, where environmental control measures can be more easily implemented and are less costly than in small-scale uses in industry or the residential and commercial sectors.

In some respects, energy utilization patterns will have to remain quite different in China from those prevailing in most other countries today. But a number of industrial countries used to have a similarly high share of coal use twenty to thirty years ago and are now again increasing the role of coal, albeit not to the high levels that are likely to prevail in China. The main issue in China will be how to use coal in environmentally acceptable *and* affordable ways, especially in urban areas where air pollution has in many cases already reached very high levels. Making coal use environmentally acceptable will require many things, but will often involve replacing decentralized and uncontrolled combustion of coal with combustion in large facilities with better environmental controls, and distribution of clean energies (for example, steam and hot water) from these facilities to final consumers. However, these distribution networks are usually very costly, and careful studies need to be carried out to minimize costs and to avoid duplication (for example, between district heating and gas distribution). Particularly uncertain is the extent to which coal conversion (coal gasification and liquefaction) technologies can be justified at present, given the cost and availability of alternative clean fuels or alternative ways to make direct coal combustion cleaner and more efficient (for example, cogeneration and district heating).

High priority will have to be given to the transfer, development, and introduction of coal utilization technologies including coal preparation and cleaning, improved boiler systems, heat recovery equipment, process controls, cogeneration systems, district heating technology, coal briquetting technology, and emission control devices such as electrostatic precipitators and bag filters. Improved coal utilization also will require greater coordination throughout the entire coal production, beneficiation, distribution, and consumption chain, calling for greater interaction between the many agents involved (for example, coal producers, transportation ministries, the power sector, commercial departments, municipal governments, and industrial enterprises). Many of the options for improving the utilization of coal (for example, cogeneration, district heating, coal gasification) cut across the responsibilities of many different institutions. Increased cogeneration could result in major energy savings (see Box 4.1), but would require institutional arrangements for power generation to be more flexible.

Coal beneficiation through washing has been slow to develop in China (about 18 percent of China's coal was

Box 4.1 Cogeneration for Industry and District Heating

Cogeneration, or combined heat and power (CHP), is the combined production of two forms of energy—electricity or mechanical power plus useful thermal energy—in one technological process. The total amount of fuel needed to produce both electricity and thermal energy in a cogeneration plant is less than would be needed to produce the same amount of electric and thermal energy separately. Cogeneration is used intensively in Western and Eastern Europe, accounting for up to 30 percent of installed electric power capacity, and is about evenly split between industrial and district heating uses, but its use for district heating has recently expanded. In West Germany, for example, cogeneration for district heating doubled over the past ten years while industrial cogeneration stagnated, as industrial restructuring and improved energy conservation reduced industrial heat requirements. In the United States, the role of cogeneration is small and limited to industry. In China, the role of cogeneration is relatively small (Box Table 4.1A), and its technology not very advanced by international standards.

Box Table 4.1A. Estimates of Installed Cogeneration Capacities in Selected Countries

Country	Total (gigawatts)	Percentage of electric power generating capacity		
		Total	Industrial	District heating
United States	14.9	2.3	2.3	(.)
West Germany	16.0	17.9	9.6	8.3
United Kingdom	2.5	3.6	3.6	(.)
Finland	3.2	29.4	16.5	12.8
U.S.S.R.	76.6	27.3	..	..
China	4.9	7.1	..	..

Source: Union Internationale des Distributeurs de Chaleur (Zurich); International District Heating Conference, Kiev, 1982; World Bank staff estimates.

Industrial Cogeneration. The pulp and paper, steel, and chemical industries typically account for a very large share (up to 80 percent) of industrial cogeneration. In the pulp and paper industry, large amounts of burnable wastes are generated and used to fuel combined heat and power plants, as are blast furnace gases in the steel industry. In other industries, a lack of waste fuels has limited cogeneration. With increased fuel prices, many industries have found it more profitable to invest in energy-saving measures, rather than in cogeneration schemes. However, if clean fuels are not available (as in China) cogeneration of electricity and steam for industrial uses might be consider-

ably more attractive, especially if environmental benefits are considered, and could justify construction of large CHP plants in industrial estates to supply steam within a radius of, say, five kilometers.

District Heating. District heating has recently received renewed interest in view of sharply increasing prices of clean fuels such as distillate oil or natural gas. District heating is also a way to increase the use of coal and other lower-grade fuels to meet residential and commercial energy requirements in an environmentally acceptable way. Although network costs for district heating are high (depending mostly on urban density), the superior efficiency of heat extraction from large CHP plants usually more than compensates. Improved materials and network construction techniques have reduced the cost of heat distribution. At the low temperatures required for district heating (70–140°C), cogeneration is particularly efficient, with incremental fuel requirements for heat extraction equivalent to only about one-fifth of conventional boiler fuel requirements. In Europe, a large share of new coal-fired electric power plants are now being built as CHP plants. New CHP plant designs have been aimed at increasing efficiency of heat extraction and maximizing flexibility between electric power and heat dispatch.

Market penetration of district heating has reached very high levels in Eastern Europe and Scandinavia (up to 50 percent of total space heating requirements). Apart from climate, market penetration of district heating is related to availability and costs of alternative clean fuels, particularly natural gas. Countries that rely mostly on market mechanisms in energy supply have found that the most important obstacles to wider use of district heating are existing natural gas distribution networks that make market penetration for a new and costly distribution system very difficult. But district heating is often the lower cost alternative if natural gas is scarce and gas distribution networks do not yet exist, and if urban densities and space heating requirements are sufficiently high. These conditions appear to be fulfilled in northern Chinese cities.

Cogeneration and district heating require close coordination between electric power generation, urban planning, and industrial location decisions. Transfer pricing mechanisms between electric power utilities, cogenerators, and district heating utilities are crucial and should reflect the costs and benefits of cogeneration as accurately as possible. Otherwise, potential industrial cogenerators will not find cogeneration a profitable investment. In market economies, large CHP plants are often owned and operated jointly by the electric power and district heating utilities to facilitate coordination and render transfer pricing arrangements more transparent.

washed in 1983) and needs to be expanded. Increased coal washing can substantially improve end-use efficiencies in combustion and reduce the amount of inert material that must be transported. The optimal role of coal washing must be carefully evaluated, however, because capital costs are high and energy losses are significant, depending on coal characteristics. In the United States, though, some electric utilities have found that the cost of coal preparation and coal cleaning is compensated by higher utilization rates and lower maintenance costs of electric power plants. Whether this would also apply to China will depend among other things on the combustion characteristics of the particular coal being used and would need to be studied further. The development of local uses for washery tailings from coal preparation plants is of particular importance, to minimize energy waste and hence reduce the cost of coal beneficiation. In countries where large proportions of coal output are washed (for example, West Germany), washery development is closely linked with thermal power development and production of coal briquettes. China's planned thermal power development in coal mining areas such as Shanxi should be well integrated with washery development—washery throughputs of 300 million to 400 million tons in 2000 would produce tailings that could fuel 20–30 gigawatts of power generating capacity.

Further development of fluidized bed combustion (FBC) is of particular importance if coal mining and coal washery wastes are to be used in mine-mouth power plants. While China has a larger number of FBC boilers operating than any other country, most are small industrial FBC boilers using low grade coals, and only a few mine-mouth power plants with somewhat larger FBC boilers (25 megawatts, electric) are in operation, using coal mining wastes. One of the reasons that larger units are not used more widely is that transfer prices for electric power are not sufficiently attractive for sales to the power grid and limit power generation by coal mines to internal use. Again, institutional changes for electric power generation, and in particular appropriate transfer pricing arrangements, would be required to improve the efficiency of coal utilization. Mine-mouth power plants using coal wastes could be operated by the the power grids, the coal mines, or jointly. Appropriate economic incentives will be required to make cogeneration attractive.

Environmental Issues

China fortunately has very substantial resources of relatively high-quality (low-sulfur) coals,[5] and total emissions of sulfur dioxide and nitrogen oxides are still low, comparable to, for example, the United States around 1920–30 (or one-half and one-quarter, respectively, of present U.S. levels). Nonetheless, air pollution from coal burning, especially particulates (dust and soot) is already a serious problem in urban China, particularly in the North. In

some cities, air pollution has already reached a multiple of internationally accepted standards. The largest and most noticeable source of street-level pollution is the direct burning of coal in household stoves and numerous industrial and commercial boilers without even simple environmental control equipment. In Beijing, for example, average dust (total suspended particulate) levels were reported at 0.5 milligrams per cubic meter, or about seven times greater than U.S. air quality standards. Despite large reserves of low-sulfur coal in North China, sulfur dioxide levels in Beijing are also very high, as coals of unusually high sulfur content are used by households for space-heating and cooking.

There are several options for making the use of coal in the residential and commercial sectors cleaner and more efficient. Over the long run, these include greater development of district heating, electric cooking, and possibly coal gasification. Over the short- and medium-term, pollution problems associated with small-scale combustion of coal in urban areas could be alleviated by greater use of higher-quality coals, in particular anthracite, and dissemination of improved coal stoves. Under the present coal allocation system, some of the least desirable coals (for example, briquettes from coal fines with high volatile matter and high sulfur content) end up in urban areas. This could be remedied by allocating high-quality coals (anthracite) to urban areas and restricting the use of less desirable grades of coal.

Urban air pollution could also be alleviated by locating energy-intensive heavy industries outside densely populated areas. The construction of large cogeneration plants can be justified in urban areas, however, provided adequate environmental protection measures (dust and noise control) are adopted. As low-sulfur coal is available in substantial quantities, expensive flue-gas desulfurization equipment may continue to be unnecessary, but much more attention will need to be given to installing improved particulate removal systems. Installation of such equipment in new coal-fired plants is now standard practice in most countries. Fly ash collected from power plants and industrial enterprises can be used profitably as an input in cement manufacturing (up to 40 percent of the raw material required) or as a substitute binder for building materials, as is already done to some extent in China.

In a number of industrial countries that have experienced environmental damage from acid depositions ("acid rain") it is now believed that these effects are probably due to a complex interaction of different pollutants, involving not only sulfur and nitrogen oxides but,

---

5. Most Chinese coals have a sulfur content of 0.4–2 percent, probably averaging less than 1 percent, but a few deposits have high sulfur content (3–5 percent).

in a key role, ozone and other photochemical oxidants formed by reactive hydrocarbon compounds, emitted primarily by petroleum refineries and other chemical plants. Although there are still large scientific uncertainties about the mechanisms and effects of acid depositions, these deserve attention in the choice of energy utilization technologies. Large-scale coal gasification is of particular concern because pollutant emissions from coal gasification plants are similar to those from refineries. Some of the most serious environmental effects of air pollution in Eastern Europe are believed to be related to large-scale coal gasification.

The experience of other countries indicates that enterprises are often unwilling to make substantial investments in pollution control equipment without direct government intervention in the form of financial incentives or administrative measures, such as a system of enforced penalties for exceeding specific industry-by-industry standards. In China, the development of adequate pollution regulations and enforcement provisions is necessary and will become even more important as state enterprises gain more autonomy and independence. Lack of attention to pollution control at the time of installing new plants may ultimately result in higher costs. Investments required to rectify the situation could be higher than if adequate measures had been taken at the time of plant construction. In view of rapidly increasing energy use and remaining uncertainties about causes and effects of environmental damage, it would also be highly desirable to sharply increase the extent and quality of environmental monitoring. This could be instrumental in determining cost-effective environmental pollution control measures in the future.

Oil and Gas

Oil Production

China's largest oil fields have already passed their peak productivity. The extent of their natural rate of decline is being reduced somewhat by a program of infill drilling, well stimulation, and secondary recovery. China's success in meeting its goals for petroleum production in 2000, however, will be largely determined by the extent of new discoveries and the speed with which they can be developed. By 2000, most of the fields producing today will be twenty-five to forty-five years old, and it is unlikely that they will provide more than a small share of the production target of 200 million tons. A large share of total production by the year 2000 will have to come from new reserve additions during the next eight to ten years.

China's prospective oil areas onshore and offshore are extensive, geologically complex, and largely unexplored. To achieve the 200 million tons per year production target by the year 2000, China will have to develop a long-term strategy for exploration, which could determine the most promising areas for immediate exploration, establish priorities for future exploration, and formulate policies on the use of foreign technology and capital. Moreover, although exploration, development, and production practices have been improved considerably in recent years, China's techniques and practices will need to be brought closer to international standards. In the recent past, petroleum exploration and development have been characterized by too much attention to short-term production targets. Reservoir management has sometimes also been less than optimal, with many fields producing at rates that reduce ultimate total recovery of oil from the reservoirs.

To meet its petroleum production targets, China must upgrade equipment, technology, and management at all stages of exploration and development. Current operation and maintenance practices, particularly for field equipment, need to be improved substantially. Future discoveries of the magnitude envisaged probably can only be located by drilling in the deeper parts of sedimentary basins, in more complex geological structures, and in more remote locations where access is difficult. All this will require, in addition to imports or joint venture manufacturing of equipment, more intensive personnel training, both on the job through service contracts and abroad in accredited institutions and with operating companies. International oil companies (IOCs) are already involved in China's offshore oil activities and recently the Government decided to expand IOC activities to limited onshore areas through joint venture contracts. Appropriate legislation needs to be prepared before contracts can be finalized. Such involvement would allow the Government to share the risks of development and exploration with foreign investors and might facilitate technology transfer.

The transportation of crude oil, petroleum products, and natural gas does not appear to face major bottlenecks at present, but the options and costs of future transport systems should be analyzed. Increased use of pipelines could help to reduce the burden on the railways and improve refinery utilization. Transport will be an important factor in developing the hydrocarbon reserves that may be discovered in the western basins, as transportation costs will be critical in determining the economic viability of such efforts.

Natural Gas

Natural gas production is targeted to increase to 25 billion cubic meters by the year 2000—roughly double the current level. A significant part of this increase is expected to be achieved by doubling production from the Sichuan Basin to 10 billion cubic meters and through development of new onshore and offshore finds such as the recent Zhongyuan and Hainan Island discoveries. Nonassociated gas production by 2000 could be as much as four times greater than the current level of 5 billion cubic meters. If, in addition, the oil production target is reached, total gas production could reach 35 billion to 40 billion cubic meters, or three times current levels. If exploration efforts for nonassociated natural gas are stepped up, production could be even higher, and some estimates indicate that it could reach as much as 5 percent of total commercial energy requirements. There is also an urgent need to increase gas exploration in older producing areas where production declines are leading to shortages of gas for existing plants.

In many feedstock and fuel applications, natural gas has a relatively high value per unit of energy compared with other energy sources. Evaluating its optimal use, however, is highly complex and needs to be pursued on a site-by-site basis, taking into account regional variations in demand, in the opportunity cost of alternative fuels or feedstocks, and in the costs of gas transmission and distribution. Given the characteristics of natural gas, it is necessary to make a comprehensive plan that includes requirements for exploration and development as well as transport and use. To accommodate uncertainties about gas reserves, production rates, and the size of the market, this plan should be flexible, with staged construction to permit continuous revisions as new information becomes available. The value and use of natural gas is likely to be very location specific. Given the projected small share of natural gas in commercial energy production and use, natural gas is likely to be used primarily for high-value industrial uses such as feedstocks. Nonetheless, some uses of natural gas which may be regarded as "low value"— electric power generation, for example—should not be excluded as they could be instrumental as initial uses to develop gas production and pipeline networks. Household use for cooking and heating could be rational in some areas.

Petroleum Refining

The demand for oil distillates[6] is projected to grow from 34 million tons in 1980 to between 90 million and 140 million tons in 2000. The attainment of both oil production and economic growth targets might result in a balance between oil distillate supply and demand around the midpoint of the projected demand range with approximately the same refinery complexity as today (Table 4.1). If crude oil production levels were to reach only 150 million tons in 2000, either major imports would be required to satisfy domestic demand for distillates or refinery distillate yields would have to be increased to their technical maximum by installing more sophisticated (and expensive) secondary conversion facilities.

If road freight and passenger transportation both grow at close to 10 percent per year during 1980–2000 (implying significant increases in the share of road transportation in total transport), the demand for transport fuels would grow from about 10 million tons in 1980 to be-

tween 30 million and 50 million tons in 2000, even with major improvements in energy efficiency. Transport fuel requirements thus would account for one-fourth of targeted oil production, or more if oil production falls short of the target. Policies to restrain the growth of road transport could of course reduce growth in distillate demand, but at high costs in terms of the efficiency and dynamism of economic development, especially outside large cities (see Chapter 5).

While the projected high share of transport fuels in total petroleum product demand is not unusual by international standards, the bulk of Chinese crude oil is relatively heavy with, on average, more than 70 percent residuals in primary distillation. Chinese crude oils are particularly deficient in very light fractions (naphtha and gasoline). Consequently, about 35 million tons per year of secondary conversion capacity has been installed, primarily catalytic cracking (24 million tons per year) and thermal cracking. Refinery complexity in China (secondary conversion equivalent to 35 percent of primary distillation capacity) is thus already high in comparison to most other countries, except the United States (48 percent). Refinery throughput is about 80 million tons per year (80 percent capacity utilization), and refinery losses have been reduced from 8 percent in 1980 to about 6 percent in 1984. Exports of crude oil have increased to over 20 million tons in 1984, and product exports have averaged some 5 million tons in recent years.

The major issue for China's refinery industry in the future is how to match domestic demand, geared toward transport fuels and other distillate products, with China's domestic resources of heavy, high-wax (but low-sulfur) crude oils. While some degree of flexibility regarding domestic burning of residual fuel oil appears justified, given the high costs of converting plants originally designed to burn oil to use coal or the high costs of coal handling equipment for small boilers, there is little doubt that it will be more economical in most cases to increase coal supplies to meet boiler fuel demand and to either export or further refine much of China's residual fuel oil.

While it is technically feasible to convert Chinese crude oils to transport fuels and other distillate products by secondary conversion, yielding virtually no residual fuel oil, these processes are inherently very capital intensive and expensive. Considerable savings from the present strategy of self-sufficiency in petroleum products for domestic consumption could be achieved by greater integration into the international oil market. Other countries in the region and elsewhere have a different demand structure, and other crude oils are available with very different

---

6. Defined to include gasoline, diesel, kerosene, lubricants, light petrochemical feedstocks, and liquefied petroleum gas (LPG). See Annex 3.

characteristics. Refineries elsewhere are meeting product demand not only by installing conversion facilities, but also by optimizing the mix of crude oil feedstock and by trading some refined products in international markets. Some of the options that should be considered before investments in further secondary conversion facilities are finalized include: (a) importing foreign crude oils in exchange for increased exports of Chinese crude oils to increase the yield and quality of products (for example, transport fuels or asphalt) in which Chinese crude oils are deficient; (b) importing (or exporting) deficient (or surplus) products to meet domestic demand; and (c) contracting for the processing of a marginal share of China's crude oil in international refining centers with excess capacity.

Institutional changes would be necessary for more rational investment and production decisionmaking in the refining industry. While distillate prices are more or less in line with international prices, crude oil prices are low, making oil refining a very profitable industry. This has led to duplication of investments in the past, as different localities and organizations tried to maximize their revenue from oil refining. The consolidation of virtually all refining and basic petrochemical production in one state corporation (SINOPEC) in 1983 has helped to rationalize the refining and petrochemical sector and has made transfer pricing of petroleum products and petrochemical feedstocks less cumbersome and controversial. However, some problems remain. For example, the present preference for product rather than crude oil exports is apparently mainly related to the allocation mechanism for foreign exchange. Less than optimal export patterns (and resulting revenue losses) could be avoided if domestic prices for crude oil and products were set at international prices and if foreign exchange allocation mechanisms were improved. Decentralization of the petroleum industry would become possible only after price reform.

Electric Power

Electric power development in China has proceeded rapidly during the past three decades. By the end of 1983, total installed capacity reached 76,000 megawatts, compared with less than 2000 megawatts in 1949. Approximately one-third of generating capacity in 1983 was hydro, while the remaining two-thirds was thermal. No nuclear power plants have been commissioned. There were thirteen power grids with capacities of more than 1,000 megawatts each; four of these had capacities exceeding 10,000 megawatts. The combined installed capacity of the thirteen largest grids accounted for more than 80 percent of the national total. Between 1965 and 1979, total generation increased at an average rate of 10.7 percent per year, but has slowed down in recent years, increasing by 5.8 percent per year during 1979–

84, and the power sector has been unable to meet demand fully.

Demand Projections

Electricity demand growth could average 6.0–7.5 percent per year during 1980–2000, with the projected range depending to a large extent on the rate of growth of manufacturing industry (Table 4.1). Generation requirements in 2000 would be 960–1,290 terawatt-hours, which is quite consistent with MWREP's preliminary estimates of 1,000–1,200 terawatt-hours. The share of electricity in final commercial energy consumption is projected to continue to rise from 18 percent in 1980 to 26–27 percent in 2000 (excluding cogeneration in industry), but the elasticity of growth in electricity demand relative to growth in GDP is expected to decline to 0.9–1.15. Electricity use in transportation and households is expected to grow particularly fast (14–15 percent per year and 11–13 percent per year, respectively, from 1980 to 2000); though this is from a low base in both sectors, it may result in increased peak load generating requirements. The manufacturing sector is projected to continue to account for at least three-quarters of final power consumption, although electricity use per unit of gross manufacturing output value is likely to fall slightly, because of changes in the structure of manufacturing output.

Investment Planning

No official long-term development program for electricity development for the remainder of the century has yet been prepared. The present mix of generating capacity, however, is not expected to change much over the next two decades. By the end of the century, nuclear power would supply less than 4 percent of total generation, while hydropower would stabilize its share of supply at 18–19 percent (or 22–23 percent if small plants are included). Thermal power will account for the balance, and under current plans all new capacity will be based on coal. The bulk of additional hydropower is expected to come from four large-scale river basin development schemes, which have already been the subject of substantial study.

China's exploitable hydropower resources are among the largest in the world, but the bulk of undeveloped potential is in the Southwest and Northwest, where large-scale development would require transmission of electricity over distances of 1,200–1,500 kilometers to major industrial load centers. Gestation periods for the large-scale projects are relatively long (eight to ten years from project approval even under ideal conditions) and have been further extended in some recent projects because of unexpected geotechnical problems, shortages of funds, and other unanticipated problems. Higher infrastructure costs and rising costs due to inundation are also increasing the costs of large-scale hydro projects, and careful economic analyses will need to be carried out in selecting sites and timing of large-scale hydro projects, taking into account economic effects on agricultural production, inland water transport, and other users of water resources.

MWREP's preliminary power production profiles for 1985–2000 suggest a commissioning of 5,000–8,000 megawatts of nuclear capacity by the end of the century. Because of relatively low-cost coal and competing demands for financial resources, it is unlikely that a nuclear power program beyond MWREP's targets could be justified, at least in the medium term. The high capital costs, long lead times, and uneven performance of nuclear plants in some countries underscore the importance of evaluating the parameters that determine the economics of nuclear generation in relation to the costs of other alternatives (particularly coal, but possibly also natural gas). Commissioning of a few nuclear units in China could be justified in certain circumstances, for example, in locations far from low-cost coal mines and on the basis of the continuing need to develop technical expertise and operating skills. The competitiveness of large-scale nuclear power development could probably be enhanced by the experience gained from a modest-size program and by careful planning—foreign experience shows that a well-designed and well-paced program could reduce capital costs.

Nuclear power requires a major long-term commitment to developing manpower and infrastructure. It involves technically complex plants, severe economic consequences in case of operational failures, and strict safety requirements, all of which are unique to this type of power. Major investments of effort, time, and resources are needed to develop the technology and standards for equipment manufacturing in the early stages of the program, as well as autonomous safety and regulatory institutions to provide essential oversight functions. Particularly important over the long term is that plants be based on a standard design that has been carefully selected and developed.

Under current plans, conventional thermal power generation based on coal will continue to provide at least three-quarters of total generation at the end of the century. Probably the most important issues are those of plant location and transmission network planning. For example, the location of many plants will have to be determined by the relative advantage of development at coal mine sites—requiring high-voltage transmission to major load centers—versus development near load centers and port areas where large quantities of coal would be transported by rail or water. Decisionmaking should include consideration of factors such as the regional distribution of coal resources, availability of low-grade fuels from coal preparation plants, regional differences in coal development costs, relative costs of coal transportation and power transmission, environmental implications, and other external factors such as increased use of cogeneration.

The demand for power currently exceeds supply in all of China's major grids, and the cost of interconnecting most regional grids, which requires transmission lines of 1,000 kilometers or longer, may not be justified by reductions in reserve requirements and load diversification alone. However, with large-scale hydropower development and construction of some mine-mouth power plants, greater interconnection will become more compelling and eventually imperative, because large amounts of power will have to be transmitted from West to East. In addition, integration will allow wider use of modern, large-scale generating equipment with improved technical and economic results. Currently, China has adopted a step-by-step approach to grid expansion and integration, with plans to establish a national integrated power grid by the end of the century.

Increased efforts to optimize investment planning by focusing on long-term, least-cost development programs will be essential. Of particular importance is the need to consider the full economic costs of large-scale projects with long lead times (for example, nuclear or large hydro projects). Such projects clearly can provide major benefits, but the opportunity costs of money invested and the costs of sacrificing flexibility need to be more carefully evaluated. The adoption of up-to-date system planning techniques also will help in the evaluation of broad strategic decisions about the generating plant mix, power plant location, and grid architecture. Modern computer models allow planners to look beyond the unit cost of energy in determining least-cost sequences; they take into account such factors as demand patterns, variation in hydrology, and random outages of generation and transmission facilities. These models are not without their limitations, however, and much training is required to use them appropriately.

Rural Energy and Biomass

According to Chinese estimates, the consumption of biomass fuels (that is, fuelwood, crop byproducts, and dung) by rural households was about 220 million tons of coal equivalent in 1980, thus accounting for more than 25 percent of total primary energy use. Crop byproducts and fuelwood each account for roughly one-half of consumption, while dung contributes an almost negligible share. Biomass fuels provide some 85 percent of the total energy consumed by rural households. In many areas, biomass fuel supplies fall short of demand, but supply even at current levels no longer can be sustained by the agricultural system and local environment through traditional means without serious adverse consequences. While the production of crop byproducts has probably doubled since the first half of this century, the proportion used as fuel has increased from about 50 percent during the early 1930s to 60–80 percent today, inhibiting their use as animal fodder, organic input for soil improvement, and construction material. Increased demand on local nonagricultural land to produce other types of biomass fuel has exacerbated long-standing water and soil conservation problems, as traditional fuel collection methods have often gone unchecked and immediate fuel needs have impeded efforts to reforest local areas. Hence, China faces major challenges in developing alternatives to traditional supply and use practices. Continued reliance on traditional patterns of biomass supply and use to meet rural household fuel needs will result not only in greater disparity between supply and demand, but also in greater disruption of local agricultural and ecological systems.

Current rural energy policies emphasize the development of local energy resources for local needs and improvements in the efficiency of energy use. In 1980, an initiative was launched to promote the production of fuelwood in private woodlots in areas that have suitable uncultivated land. By 1984, small plots had been allocated to almost one-half of China's rural households for this purpose. The development of local coal resources continues, for use by local households and industries and for sale to consumers in other areas. Solar cookers have been popularized in a few areas and, where conditions for small-scale hydropower development are particularly favorable, the use of electricity for cooking is beginning to be promoted. Despite past setbacks in the biogas program,[7] the promotion of family-size digestors continues, with greater emphasis on quality construction. In some areas, larger, community-size digestors are now being promoted to supply gas for household use. A major program to develop and disseminate more efficient rural cooking stoves was started recently, and by early 1984 had put into use more than 40 million improved stoves.

The potential and the economic viability of the different options vary dramatically from area to area, depending on local conditions. Moreover, even the implementation of seemingly simple solutions can be quite complex. In the case of biogas generation, for example, the economic viability of the higher-quality but more expensive digestors currently being promoted hinges on a wide range of local direct and indirect factors (for example, local slaughtering rates, winter temperatures, sanitation problems). Experience in other developing countries suggests that, while the benefit of energy conservation derived from improved stoves appears attractive relative to the costs involved, dissemination can be difficult. For example, acceptance can be hindered because the new stoves may compromise convenience in cooking or may prove inappropriate for preparing certain traditional foods. In China, household heating needs, which are often met by traditional stoves, must also be considered.

Given the importance of local conditions, central policies should be highly flexible and should emphasize continued strengthening of local capabilities for both technical development and economic evaluation of alternatives. All options should be considered, including increased reliance on supplying energy to households from outside a given locality.

Investment, Planning, and Prices

Investment Requirements

The energy sector is one of the most capital-intensive sectors in any country, and efficient use of existing and new plants is of utmost importance for the efficiency of the sector and the economy at large. The average annual investment requirements for developing the coal, petroleum, and electric power industries are estimated on the basis of current government goals to increase from about Y 11 billion in the Sixth Five-Year Plan (1981–85) to Y 30 billion to 40 billion during 1986–2000. If petroleum production targets are to be achieved, a significant increase in investment for exploration and production development will be required. Investments in the power sector will need to be sharply increased if electric generating capacity is to be installed to meet forecast demand. While the power sector accounted for less than 40 percent of original energy sector investment allocations for the Sixth Five-Year Plan, power will need to account for two-thirds of energy investments according to Western definitions, or 60 percent according to Chinese definitions of capital construction (Table 4.3). Actual spending for electric power during the Sixth Plan has been considerably higher than originally planned.

PETROLEUM. On the basis of knowledge of some Chinese fields and using some international yardsticks, the minimum investment required to discover and develop the additional reserves required to meet China's production targets can be estimated at Y 30 billion and Y 70 billion for exploration and development, respectively, over the next twelve to fifteen years. Considering the risks and uncertainties associated with petroleum investments, this estimate simply provides a benchmark. Major adjustments in investments targeted for the sector may be required as risk assessments and estimates of development needs change. Petroleum sector investment targeted under the Sixth Five-Year Plan amounted to Y 15.5 billion (an annual average of Y 3.1 billion), 70 percent of which was for petroleum development and 30 percent for exploration. Thus a future average investment figure of Y 6

---

7. Of the 5 million family-size biogas digestors constructed in Sichuan during the 1970s, only about one-third are reported to be in operation.

Table 4.3 Estimated Investment Requirements in the Energy Sector, 1986–2000

Component	Amount (billions of yuan)	Percentage of energy sector investment
Coal mining[a]	50–70	12–13
Petroleum	80–120	20–21
Exploration	20–40	5–7
Development	60–80	14–15
Electric power	280–370	66–68
Generation	200–270	48–49
Other	80–100	18–20
Total	410–560	100
Energy-related investments in industry and transport		
Coal transport	40–50	—
Refineries	20–40	—

a. Assuming coal production of 1.2 billion to 1.4 billion tons by 2000. Includes only direct production-related investment. Associated social infrastructure (housing, schools, etc.), which is included in Chinese estimates, would add at least Y 20 billion to 30 billion.
Source: Data provided to the economic mission.

billion to 8 billion a year represents about two or three times the recent level of expenditure. The foreign exchange requirements for substantial imports of sophisticated tools, material, and equipment, along with the proposed involvement of foreign contractors, would likely amount to US$15 billion to 20 billion over the next twelve to fifteen years.

ELECTRIC POWER. Preliminary estimates of the investment required for capacity and grid expansion to generate 1,000–1,200 terawatt-hours in the year 2000 have been made by MWREP. Given the increasing unit costs expected in the sector, a dramatic increase in average annual investments will be required if capacity is to be expanded not only to relieve current supply constraints, but also to provide the additional power required to meet the needs for rapid economic growth. Under the Sixth Five-Year Plan, the average annual investment for the power sector has so far been about Y 4.2 billion. Average annual investment requirements are estimated to grow to some Y 13 billion to 15 billion during 1986–90 and Y 22 billion to 29 billion during 1991–2000. This implies a major increase in the share of the power sector in total domestic investment compared with recent years.

The share of power sector investment has been lower in China than in many other developing countries. The increased share estimated for the future (about 2 percent of GDP) is not unusual by international standards. The World Bank estimates that power sector investment requirements in all developing countries together will represent about 2 percent of GDP from 1982 to 1992. (Electric power investments of industrial countries have generally been about 1 percent of GDP or less, mainly because of lower growth rates of electric power demand.)

COAL. The average yearly financial requirements for capital expenditures to produce 1,400 million tons by 2000 (also in 1983 prices) are expected to rise to about Y 4 billion to 5 billion for mine development plus Y 2 billion to 3 billion for social infrastructure. This may be compared with, for example, the 1983 state budget for capital expenditures in coal for MOCI mines (Y 3.6 billion including social infrastructure, or about Y 2.2 billion excluding social infrastructure). The Government's program for coal price increases should provide more incentives and financial resources to increase coal production, particularly in mines operated by local governments and collectives. Resources made available to MOCI are being increased under the Seventh Five-Year Plan (1986–90) to more than Y 6 billion a year (including social infrastructure). To supplement domestic funds, efforts are also being made to mobilize foreign investment resources in the form of foreign loans as well as direct foreign investment.

Planning and Coordination

To achieve optimal energy production and efficient use of energy, decentralization of decisionmaking and greater use of prices and other economic levers will be essential. At the same time, however, long-term planning and intersectoral coordination will need to be improved. In particular, economic evaluation of specific development alternatives to reflect all relevant costs and benefits could help to avoid serious economic distortions. For example, economic evaluation of a coal gasification scheme for urban cooking should take into consideration all economic costs, including gasification, gas distribution and consumer hook-ups, and the relative costs and benefits of other alternatives, for which different institutions may be responsible.

Beyond specific project analysis, long-term energy planning should consider explicitly the impact of broad aspects of economic development strategy on energy demand, as well as long-term programs for energy production and distribution and improvement in energy efficiency. Potential tradeoffs between the achievement of short-term gains and attainment of long-term goals may exist, for example, in cases where emphasis on increasing short-term energy production compromises ultimate reserve recovery or overlooks preparation for long-term needs. Tradeoffs may also arise where the deployment of outdated technology in new industrial capacity provides an easier and faster way to meet pressing current demands, but ultimately may compromise goals to improve energy efficiency.

Because effective long-term planning for energy production, distribution, and utilization involves so many interrelated and intersectoral issues, an integrated approach to energy planning is essential. The development of markets in various sectors and regions must be considered along with the development of energy production, transportation, and distribution. Major imbalances may be avoided through review and coordination of long-term plans for specific projects in the various economic sectors. Better energy planning also requires an improvement in the quality and quantity of statistics relating to energy production and consumption.

Intersectoral coordination has been difficult in the past, for example, in relation to the location of large coal mines and power plants and to the distribution of natural gas and the development of its market. To meet even greater needs for such coordination in the future, institutional mechanisms at both central and regional levels must be strengthened. Prices that fully reflect production costs and scarcity are the most important tool for ensuring intersectoral coordination, but market research by producers and interagency coordination at all levels are also important.

Technology Transfer and Development

The rapid transfer and development of energy-efficient technologies will also be crucial because the power plants and energy-using industrial equipment that are now being built will last for several decades and will determine the efficiency and environmental effects of energy use into the next century. With rapid economic growth, the degree of energy efficiency of new plants will be more important for energy conservation over the long term than energy savings in existing plants. Moreover, the most energy-efficient technologies available abroad are not necessarily more costly, particularly if attributes such as better reliability, product quality, and environmental controls are considered.

Technology transfer is critical for thermal power plants, combined heat and power plants and district heating, small- and medium-scale industrial boilers, heat recovery equipment, industrial process controls, transport equipment, and a long list of other industrial equipment. At least as important is the transfer of disembodied technology, for example, modern management and organizational techniques (see also Chapter 7). Importation of disembodied technology through manufacturing licensing agreements, service contracts, joint ventures, and other procedures is one of the most economical means of transferring technology, as is job training in conjunction with technology service imports. An important example of the need to import disembodied technology through service contracts in the energy sector is the transfer of petroleum exploration, development, and reservoir management techniques that could considerably enhance the efficiency of China's petroleum sector (Annex 3, Chapter 5)—a critical element if petroleum production targets are to be reached.

Demand Management and Pricing

Energy in China has been—and still is, despite recent reforms—largely allocated administratively, with market forces playing only a minor role. Financial constraints have not been a critical consideration for most enterprises, whose overriding objective has been to meet physical output quotas. Energy prices in China likewise have been primarily determined by administrative decisions, some made decades ago. As a result, most energy prices today reflect neither scarcity nor production costs—petroleum refining is very profitable, for example, while official prices for coal barely cover operating costs. Some improvements have recently been made by permitting market-related prices for above-quota supplies. This two-tier pricing system has spurred production (for example, from small coal mines under local control) and may also have helped to reduce energy consumption.

Overall, administered energy prices are low in relation to economic costs, with the exception of some petroleum products and electricity for residential consumers. Compared with the structure of international prices, the prices of coal, crude oil, and fuel oil are particularly low. Average electricity tariffs are much lower for nonresidential than for residential consumers. Centrally allocated coal is priced at about 60 percent of long-run marginal costs, and heavy fuel oil at only one-third of international prices. There is little information on the level and structure of natural gas prices, although they appear to be low in relation to the economic costs of competitive fuels.

Although recent measures (mentioned earlier) have been effective in promoting energy savings, a quota-based energy allocation system is fundamentally unsuited to achieving large and economically rational reductions in energy intensity over the longer term. Enterprises are discouraged from reducing energy consumption because quotas are related to past consumption levels, and unnecessarily large quotas are sought for security or stockpiling, or for sale or exchange for other commodities. The inflexibility of the administrative allocation system also makes enterprises reluctant to introduce new products and processes, including energy-saving measures, where these would involve changes in the required level or pattern of energy supply. Enforced reductions in energy quotas, for lack of information, have to be imposed too uniformly on all enterprises, with insufficient regard to the widely varying economic costs of reducing energy consumption.

The two-tier pricing system now in operation for some forms of energy, and under consideration for others, is a considerable improvement on the pure quota system, since the market-determined prices of above-quota supplies give more appropriate signals to producers and users of energy. But for the two-tier system to operate effectively, quotas need to be set and regularly revised so that all producers and users are obliged to make significant use of the above-quota market. This is difficult, especially because production potential and energy consumption requirements change constantly and often cannot be directly and reliably ascertained. Indeed, the two-tier pricing system itself increases the incentives for energy producers and users to supply misleading information to the authorities responsible for setting quotas.

There would thus be clear advantages to phasing out the whole quota system gradually, with more autonomy for individual enterprises, and the establishment of a unified energy price structure that reflects the relative scarcity of competing fuels (see Chapter 10). Two key advantages of higher energy prices as compared with administrative regulation are: (a) that they are passed on in higher product prices and hence reduce consumption of energy-intensive products; and (b) that reductions in energy use occur automatically where the economic cost of reductions is least, provided that other prices are rational and enterprises are profit sensitive. For internation-

ally tradable fuels, such as petroleum, prices should be set at world prices plus or minus transport margins, unless there are limits to imports or exports (as, possibly, in the case of coal), in which case domestic prices should float to clear the market, especially if there are many producers and markets that could be competitive. For electric power, tariffs should on average at least cover long-run marginal costs that fully reflect investment costs and the opportunity cost of capital. Lower tariffs may be set at off-peak periods, and higher tariffs are needed to bring demand efficiently into line with supply in periods when generating capacity is insufficient. An appropriate electric power tariff would make physical rationing of electric power unnecessary, as users would restrict their demand if the costs of electricity consumption exceeded the benefits, particularly in peak-load periods. An appropriate electric power tariff would also promote development of efficient cogeneration schemes and mine-mouth power generation.

Spatial Issues

5

Spatial aspects of development will play a critical role in how efficiently and equitably China makes the transition from a low- to a middle-income country. First, China's sheer size and past emphasis on local self-sufficiency offer opportunities for large gains in national economic efficiency through increased specialization and trade among regions and between urban and rural areas. Second, remaining poverty and inequities have a major spatial dimension—personal incomes are much higher in urban than in rural areas, and poverty is concentrated in specific rural localities.

To increase internal specialization and trade and to further reduce rural poverty will require a lot of investment—and some basic changes of orientation—in transport and commerce. It will also require changes in the system of economic management and in the roles of different levels of government. For example, to ensure that the spatial decisions of households, farmers, and (increasingly) autonomous enterprises are efficient, special attention will need to be given to economic levers such as transport tariffs and land use charges, as well as to removing barriers to competition and trade among localities. Direct government intervention in some spatial decisions—and of course in infrastructural development—will continue to be necessary. But the appropriate degree and form of direct intervention, and the level (or levels) of government that should intervene, will need to be reassessed.

This chapter—which unavoidably deals more with general principles than with geographical specifics—looks first at policies and instruments to guide specialization and trade in agriculture and industry. It then considers associated changes in the volume, pattern, and efficiency of transport, and in commerce and related services. Next, it discusses some implications of structural change and specialization for the pace and pattern of urban and rural development. It concludes with a review of measures to reduce rural poverty and regional inequality.[1]

Table 5.1 Dispersion of Production Activities among and within Provinces, 1982

Production activity	Number of provinces involved in activity (out of 29)	Number of prefectures or municipalities involved in activity		
		Jiangsu (out of 14)	Hubei (out of 14)	Gansu (out of 13)
Foodgrains	29	14	14	13
Cotton	21	11	12	3
Coal	27	9	7	. .
Cement	29	14	14	13
Pig iron	27	9	3	2
Steel	28	13	8	4
Steel products	28	14	7	. .
Fertilizers	28	14	12	6
Machine tools	28	13	9	2
Cloth	28	14	14	4
Bicycles	26	12	6	1
Sewing machines	24	. .	8	0
Watches	24	11	. .	0

Source: State Statistical Bureau, Statistical Yearbook of China, 1983 (Hong Kong: Economic Information and Agency, 1983); data provided to the economic mission.

Specialization and Trade

China's past emphasis on local self-sufficiency rather than specialization has resulted in all twenty-nine provinces, and hundreds of prefectures, being involved in a wide range of production activities (see Table 5.1). In fact, almost all provinces and many areas within provinces produce not just basic foodstuffs and materials such as cement—whose production is dispersed in most countries—but also iron and steel products and consumer du-

---

1. This chapter draws on the fuller discussion of transport in Annex 6 and on Background Papers 1–3, which cover rural nonagricultural development, urbanization, and international economic strategy.

rables, whose production in other countries tends to be much more concentrated because of large economies of scale. In many areas of China, production is small scale, high cost, and frequently of such low quality that commercial bureaus can sell the output only by restricting imports from other localities. Partly as a result, there is wide variation among provinces in the profitability of enterprises in particular industrial subsectors (Table 5.2).

The diversity of production in most localities in China does not imply an even distribution of output. In fact, industrial output is quite concentrated, especially in Shanghai (Table 5.3). And there are large differences in per capita output between, and also within, regions and provinces (see Map 5.1 and Figure 5.1). Both per capita agricultural and industrial output tend to be much higher on the coast than in the interior.[2] The difference, for instance, between Jiangsu, a prosperous coastal province, and Gansu, a poor province in the interior, is substantial: per capita gross agricultural output is Y 390 in Jiangsu and Y 160 in Gansu; per capita gross industrial output is Y 820 in Jiangsu and Y 410 in Gansu; and per capita net

2. The interior is defined to include the provinces of Shaanxi, Gansu, Qinghai, Ningxia, Xinjiang, Sichuan, Guizhou, Yunnan, and Xizang.

Table 5.2 Gross Output and Profits of State-Owned Industry, by Province and Subsector, 1982
(percent)

Subsector	Gross output				Profit rate[a]			
	Jiangsu	Hubei	Gansu	National average	Jiangsu	Hubei	Gansu	National average
Metallurgy	3	17	16	11	22	17	10	23
Power	6	5	9	5	38	19	24	23
Coal	2	..	3	4	−4	−10	1	3
Petroleum	4	6	17	7	137	36	51	74
Chemicals	15	10	13	12	37	20	18	38
Machine building	18	22	20	19	34	14	14	21
Building materials	3	3	3	3	33	20	17	21
Forest industry	..	1	1	2	48	36	15	22
Foodstuffs	15	11	..	13	88	101	..	93
Textiles	28	19	5	16	100	58	54	81
Paper making	1	1	..	1	50	17	7	33
Other	5	5	13	7	49	29	25	37
Total	100	100	100	100	45	23	19	32

a. Defined as profits plus taxes divided by net value of fixed assets.
Source: Data provided to the economic mission.

Table 5.3 Industrial Concentration, by Region and Key City, 1982
(percent)

Region and city	Gross industrial output shares			Population shares		Ratio of output to population	
	Total (1)	Heavy (2)	Light (3)	Total (4)	Urban (5)	Total (1):(4)	Urban (1):(5)
Three municipalities[a]	19.3	17.8	20.8	2.8	8.8	6.9[b]	2.2[c]
Beijing[d]	3.9	4.3	3.4	0.5	2.7	7.8	1.4
Tianjin[d]	3.7	3.2	4.2	0.5	2.5	7.4	1.5
Shanghai[d]	9.0	8.0	10.0	0.6	3.0	15.0	3.0
Other provinces	80.7	82.2	79.2	97.2	91.2	0.8	0.9
Other key cities[e]	15.9	17.0	14.7	3.1	15.1	5.1	1.1
Total, all provinces	100.0	100.0	100.0	100.0	100.0	1.0	1.0
Total, all key cities	32.5	32.5	32.3	4.7	23.3	6.9	1.4

a. Includes some rural counties surrounding the cities of Beijing, Tianjin, and Shanghai.
b. The equivalent ratios for some major cities in other countries are: Chicago 2.6 in 1914 and 1.4 in 1977; Bangkok 3.7 in 1978.
c. The equivalent ratios for some major cities in other countries are: Chicago 1.2 in 1914 and 1.1 in 1977; Bangkok 0.6 in 1978.
d. Excluding the rural counties.
e. Includes Shenyang, Dalian, Changchun, and Harbin in the Northeast; Taiyuan in the North; Jinan, Qingdao, and Nanjing in the East; Wuhan and Guangzhou in the Central South; Xian and Lanzhou in the Northwest; and Chengdu and Chongqing in the Southwest.
Source: State Statistical Bureau, *Statistical Yearbook of China, 1983.*

Map 5.1 Per Capita Net Material Product, by Province, 1982

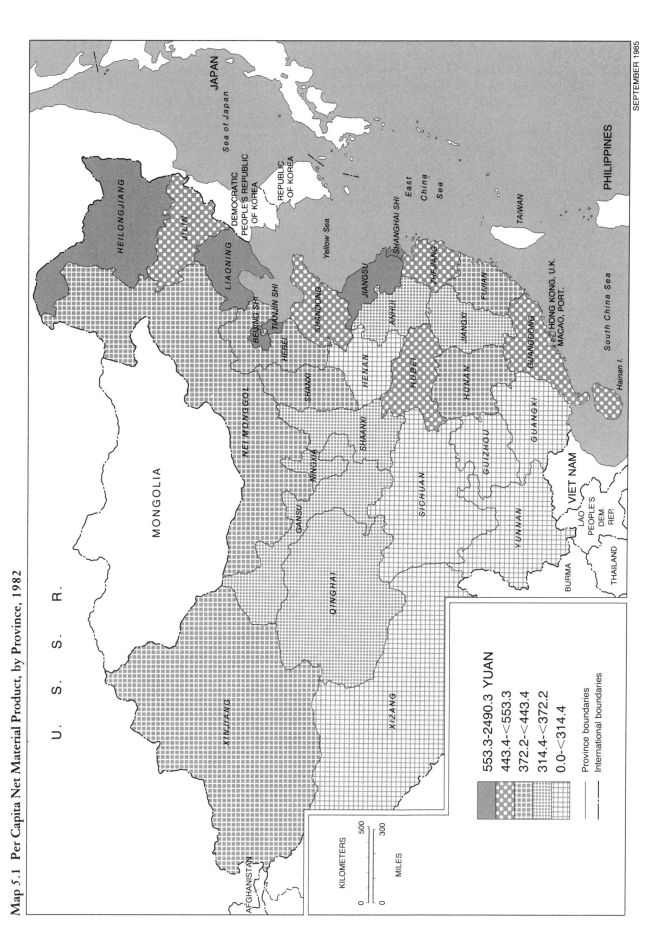

SEPTEMBER 1985

553.3–2490.3 YUAN

443.4–<553.3

372.2–<443.4

314.4–<372.2

0.0–<314.4

Province boundaries

International boundaries

KILOMETERS

500

0

MILES

300

0

75

Figure 5.1 Variations in Per Capita Gross Agricultural and Industrial Output, 1982

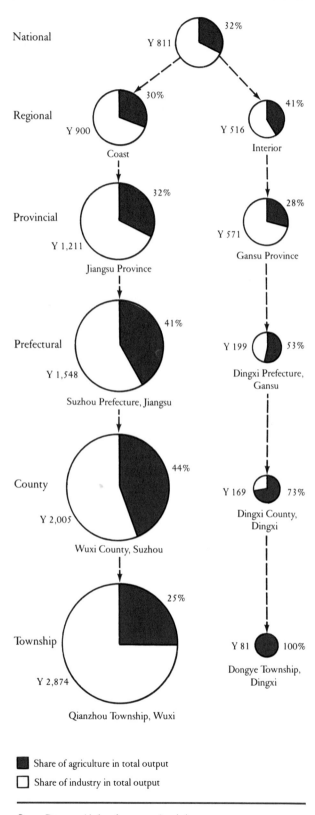

Source: Data provided to the economic mission.

■ Share of agriculture in total output
□ Share of industry in total output

material product is Y 550 in Jiangsu and Y 320 in Gansu.[3] Differences in per capita output within individual provinces (which themselves are as large as most middle-size countries) are even more substantial. In Gansu, for example, per capita gross output ranges from Y 94 in the county of Qinan to Y 2,685 in the city of Lanzhou, while in Jiangsu even some rural areas have per capita gross output levels of nearly Y 3,000.

Despite fiscal and other redistributive measures, these inequalities in per capita output result in substantial, though smaller, interregional variations in personal incomes. The gap in personal incomes between Jiangsu and Gansu, for example, is 1.4 to 1; between Wuxi County, Jiangsu, and Dingxi County, Gansu, it is 2.8 to 1; and between Qianzhou Township, Wuxi, and Dongye Township, Dingxi, it is over 10 to 1.[4] The challenge will thus be to increase efficiency through greater internal specialization and trade, while simultaneously reducing the poverty associated with these substantial income inequalities.

Agricultural Specialization

In recent years, rapidly increasing agricultural specialization in China has contributed to both growth and poverty reduction. The specialization has mainly involved changes in the location of nongrain agriculture (with continuing, though diminishing, emphasis on local self-sufficiency in foodgrains). In the case of industrial crops, provincial specialization according to comparative advantage may now be more characteristic of China than of India.[5] Further specialization both within and between provinces will, however, be critical for future agricultural growth.

An efficient spatial pattern of agricultural development will require increasing concentration of production in areas where agroclimatic conditions are most conducive to high yields. But land and transport costs will also play an important role. For example, areas close to cities and towns will usually have higher economic land values than areas farther away, because there are much greater possi-

3. The gap in per capita NMP between the richest province (Shanghai) and the poorest province (Guizhou) is 11.1 to 1; if the three municipalities are excluded the gap falls to 3.2 to 1 between Liaoning and Guizhou. These gaps compare with a 3.3 to 1 gap in U.S. state per capita domestic product in 1950 (between Delaware and Mississippi); a 1.8 to 1 gap in U.S.S.R. national per capita income in 1970 (between Lithuania and Turkmenia); and a 2.5 to 1 gap in Indian state per capita domestic product in 1975-76 (between the Punjab and Bihar).

4. The gap in personal per capita income between Shanghai and Gansu (the richest and poorest provinces by this measure) is 2.4 to 1. This compares with 3.1 to 1 in the United States in 1950 between Delaware and Mississippi; 1.9 to 1 in the U.S.S.R. in 1965 between Estonia and Azerbaidjan; and 1.7 to 1 in India in 1967-71 between the Punjab and Orissa.

5. See Annex 2, Appendix B, for an interprovincial comparison of cropping patterns in China and India.

Although dairy production in China is still quite limited, the sector is characterized by a wide range of systems, from individual farmers grazing one or two dairy cows on low-quality natural pastures to large suburban dairies that rely on feed concentrates and are often closely integrated with other agricultural activities. During the next two decades, demand for dairy products in China is expected to increase rapidly. Some of this demand can and undoubtedly should be met through increased imports (in view of the very low prices of powdered milk products on the international market), but the Government also wants to develop a more efficient domestic dairy industry.

International experience suggests that there are three basic systems for dairy production: (a) the system common in most developing countries, where dairy cattle obtain most of their feed nutrients from low-quality roughages, such as crop residues or natural pastures; (b) the system used in Australia and New Zealand, based mainly on improved high-quality pastures; and (c) the system used in the United States, Western Europe, and Japan, which is based on relatively high levels of concentrate feeding. The much higher unit production costs for system (c) over system (b) have resulted in farmgate prices for milk ranging from US$0.12 per liter in Australia and New Zealand to US$0.23 per liter in the United States and Western Europe, and to as much as US$0.35 per liter in Japan.

In China, efficient expansion of dairy production is likely to involve increasing the quantity and quality of roughages, with roughage feed supplemented by concentrates. The location of dairies based on such a feeding system needs to be considered in relation to the sources of feed supplies and the locations of markets for milk and other dairy products. Major markets are likely to be in urban areas. Nevertheless, roughage, which has a very low return per hectare, is likely to be most efficiently grown in remote and hilly areas with few alternative land uses. The

optimal location for a dairy will thus depend crucially on whether it is more efficient to transport feed a long distance and dairy products a short distance, or vice versa. International experience suggests that it may be more economical to locate the dairy where the roughage is produced, because the quantity of feed is much greater than the quantity of dairy products. In fact, three or four tons of feed (roughage and concentrate) are generally required for every ton of milk (or about 100 kilograms of cheese, 131 kilograms of whole milk powder, and 435 kilograms of condensed milk). Unit transport and handling costs may, of course, be higher for milk and dairy products than for feed, but the difference is unlikely to affect the choice of location.

A more major issue may be the transport and marketing of dairy by-products, including manure, which has sometimes been used as a justification for locating dairies in suburban areas and integrating them with fish farming or fruit growing. However, there are other sources of manure, and the costs and benefits of such integrated operations need to be closely compared with alternatives such as integrated pig or poultry raising and fish farming.

Clearly there is no simple answer to the issue of the optimal spatial pattern of dairy production, and careful sector and project analysis, to determine where alternative systems can be most efficiently developed, should precede any major investment decisions. In addition, potential constraints to the efficient spatial distribution of dairy production include the transport, storage, and marketing systems, which may make it feasible to develop only a suburban-based dairy industry dependent on feed concentrates, and planning and management systems, which need to ensure that municipalities do not develop integrated dairy operations when production in outlying areas for sale in the municipality would be more economical.

bilities for nonagricultural development. However, the economic cost of transport in areas close to cities and towns will usually be lower than in areas farther away because chemical fertilizers and other agricultural inputs are frequently transported through cities, and the main markets for agricultural products are usually in urban areas. Accordingly, areas close to cities and towns will need to specialize in activities (such as cultivation of vegetables and some perishable fruits) that have relatively high returns per hectare and high transport costs. Foodgrain production, which is characterized by relatively low unit transport costs and returns per hectare compared with activities such as vegetable growing, should probably be moved increasingly away from areas close to cities and

towns, and toward more outlying plain areas. Finally, in hilly or mountainous areas, pasture and livestock development, coupled with tree crops on gentler slopes and forestry on steeper lands, will frequently be the most economical pattern of agricultural development.

It is not easy, however, to predict the precise directions of efficient agricultural specialization, as Box 5.1 (on the location of dairy production) indicates. The development of a flexible and economically rational system of agricultural management is therefore very important (see Chapter 3). The 1979–80 rural reforms, which gave farm households more autonomy in deciding what crops to grow, have already done much to facilitate agricultural specialization and should continue to do so. To ensure that the resulting specialization is economically efficient, however, the incentive system must provide appropriate signals to farmers on what crops to grow and what other agricultural activities to develop.

The most important incentives are output and input prices. On average across all regions, these should be such as to balance the demand and supply of particular commodities and to encourage optimal input use (see Chapter 3). In addition, variations in agricultural prices from one region to another should reflect variations in the economic costs of transport. The prices of products marketed through the collective and individual sectors already reflect prevailing differences in the actual costs of transport, but there are differences between actual costs and economic costs that need to be reduced by adjusting the prices of items such as fuel and trucks. In the state sector, in contrast, input and output prices may not even reflect the actual costs of transport, because, for example, procurement prices for agricultural products may be set at higher levels in more remote or mountainous areas than in high-productivity crop production bases. Such practices help to raise incomes in poor areas, but can also hamper agricultural specialization. It may be more efficient to replace these practices with other policies and measures that benefit poor areas, including improved transport.

Recently announced agricultural price reforms should make it possible to do without (from 1985 onward) most mandatory production planning—including quotas for sown area and procurement of grain, which have been major obstacles to agricultural specialization. In Jiangsu, for example, farmers living close to urban areas want to specialize in activities that have a high value per unit of land, and township authorities have had to pay them fifty fen per jin of grain (three times the state price) to ensure that they grew enough grain to meet the state procurement target. But, while many such forms of directive planning can and should be abolished, economic levers will need to be supplemented by administrative measures in some situations. In hilly areas, for example, some types of annual cropping may produce large short-term benefits but have major long-term costs for the natural environment. The development and enforcement of regulations on land use should therefore remain an important responsibility of both national and local authorities. The Government will also need to continue providing special assistance, including relief grain, to poor areas and to develop special programs to stimulate their development (discussed later).

Agricultural specialization in China will also be greatly affected by the adequacy of transport and trade facilities (also discussed later). The development of individual and collective enterprises, as well as of state enterprises, in transport and commerce is already assisting specialization. But transport infrastructure remains a bottleneck. Gansu, for example, has a sunny climate and fertile soil, which could provide the basis for high-value horticultural crop production: indeed, melons and deciduous fruit from Gansu sell at high prices in Hong Kong, while Chinese cabbage procured in Gansu for Y 0.02–0.04 per kilogram sells in northeastern cities for more than Y 0.20 per kilogram. These price differentials suggest that better transport might well enable some farmers in Gansu to specialize in horticulture rather than grain production, purchasing their foodgrain from elsewhere. More generally, improved transportation would permit more rational use of suburban land, reduce input supply problems, distribute perishable products more widely, and allow a broader spectrum of China's farmers to reap the income gains of high-value agricultural production.

Industrial Specialization and Location

In contrast to agriculture, and despite recent policy changes and reforms, China's rather low degree of local industrial specialization does not seem to be increasing. Specifically, although some localities already specialize to some extent in particular industrial products (Wuxi in textiles and clothing, for example), transport problems, shortcomings in commerce and material supply, price distortions, barriers to competition, and the fiscal system combine to provide strong incentives for local self-sufficiency in a variety of other industrial products. Each provincial and municipal planning bureau accordingly continues to emphasize the development of a wide range of industrial activities on a scale tailored to local needs, rather than concentrating its resources on large-scale low-cost production of a narrow range of commodities for export to other localities. Because this could have a serious adverse impact on China's overall investment efficiency, there is an urgent need for measures to reduce the present conflict between what seems rational for a particular locality and what is rational for the whole economy.

Specialization of medium-size and smaller cities in particular industries is usual in other countries (large cities tend to be more diversified).[6] But because in other countries much of a city's labor force is engaged in commerce and other services, the proportion of employment in the industry of specialization rarely exceeds 40 percent and is typically only 10–20 percent, though sometimes with a significant percentage of other workers engaged in support activities for this industry. Even so, difficulties in the industry concerned could depress the whole local economy, which means that specialization has risks as well as benefits. In China, moreover, the past pattern of industrial investment will limit the speed of movement toward greater specialization of localities, since it will often be

---

6. The experience of other countries is discussed in greater detail in Background Paper 2.

economically rational to keep a diverse range of existing enterprises in operation for some time, rather than to close them all down straightaway (see Chapter 7). What is crucial, though, and what does not yet appear to be happening, is that new industrial investment should become much more specialized.

Location decisions for heavy industry have in many countries been based as much on historical and political considerations as on current economic conditions. But China's spatial pattern of heavy industrial development seems to have unusually little economic rationale. In recent years, many of the small and inefficient heavy industrial plants have been closed. Yet industries such as iron and steel—where economies of scale are critical—still have many small, locally operated plants producing at high cost (see Box 5.2). Moreover, medium-size and large heavy industry plants are still concentrated in very large cities (see Table 5.3), despite the fact that these industries have very large spatial needs, create substantial environmental problems, and do not always require the many services and other benefits that come with a large-city location. Specific decisions on relocation of heavy industries can be made only after a detailed industry-by-industry assessment. But measures to concentrate production in fewer enterprises—located away from the largest cities and often closer to resource deposits—could not only improve national efficiency, but also benefit poorer interior provinces, which currently produce raw materials for processing elsewhere (see Chapter 5).

Concentrating some types of heavy-industry production in fewer enterprises, as a means of realizing economies of scale, implies that many small rural enterprises might eventually need to be closed—and some already have been. However, only some 6 percent of China's rural labor force is now employed in manufacturing, compared with 3 to 15 percent in other Asian countries (see Table 5.4). And only 24 percent of rural manufacturing workers in China are employed in the food processing, textile, and clothing industries, compared with 40 to 60 percent in other Asian countries.[7] Accordingly, while there may be a decline in output from some types of rural industry, both national efficiency and equity could be enhanced by measures to promote rapid growth in other types of rural industry, including coal mining (Chapter 4), and cement and bricks (which enjoy a high degree of natural protection), as well as agroprocessing and some other light industries.

The efficient location of many light industries depends less on location of raw materials than on the cost of other inputs and the location of markets. Those industries serving a broad market and not subject to scale economies may be widely dispersed, with rural as well as urban plants, while those that can benefit from scale economies will probably be most efficiently located in urban areas. A critical issue, however, is the size of city or town most

Table 5.4 Extent and Composition of Rural Nonagricultural Activities in Selected Countries
(percent)

Component	China, 1982	Thailand, 1975–76	Indonesia, 1980	Other Asian developing countries
Share of rural labor force involved in nonagricultural activities	13.8	16.6	34.7	15–35
Composition of rural nonagricultural labor force				
Manufacturing	45.2	. .	23.1	15–39
Construction	8.9	. .	7.5	4–14
Commerce	12.2	. .	29.7	12–29
Transport	4.6	. .	5.5	5–10
Other services	29.1	. .	34.2	25–45

Note: Data for China have been adjusted to conform with the adjustments to total employment made in other sections of this report.
Source: Background Paper 1 and World Bank Reports 3906-TH on Thailand and 3586-IND on Indonesia.

appropriate for different types of light industry, because size affects economic costs and benefits. The economic costs of land, for example, are much higher in larger cities (and in the center of the city than in the suburbs) because the land has a greater number of alternative, high-value, uses. The economic costs of materials and of housing, commuting, and food for workers also tend to be higher in larger cities because of higher transport and land costs. For some activities, however, there may be additional benefits as well as costs to locating in larger rather than smaller cities. These benefits (often referred to as urbanization economies) arise from having immediate access to other industries, diverse labor markets, large local consumer markets for product testing, and the diverse environment that accompanies increasing urban size.

Light industrial enterprises producing standardized products such as bicycles (see Box 5.3) tend to benefit much more from economies of scale arising from the size of their own industry than from urbanization economies; it is therefore likely to be more efficient to locate them in smaller cities. But high-technology industries and advanced service industries benefit much more from urbanization economies, which are frequently sufficient to offset the additional economic and social costs of location in a large city. Some of the activities now located in large cities like Shanghai and Tianjin should thus be progressively transferred to smaller cities and towns. But these activities should be replaced by new activities such as electronics (and services), which are only now assuming importance in the national economy. As a result there

7. See Background Paper 1 for further discussion of these issues.

Box 5.2 Locational Issues in the Iron and Steel Industry

China's iron and steel industry consists of approximately 2,000 state and collective enterprises, varying from small enterprises that produce less than 5,000 tons of steel per year to the large integrated Anshan Steel Company in Liaoning, which in 1982 produced 6.1 million tons of pig iron, 6.8 million tons of steel, and 4.4 million tons of steel products. The industry varies widely by technology used (31 percent of steel production still comes from open hearth furnaces) and costs of production (pig iron production costs, for example, vary from Y 138 per ton for large enterprises to Y 192 per ton for medium-size enterprises and Y 304 per ton for small enterprises). The industry is also very dispersed, with all provinces except Xizang and Qinghai producing pig iron and all except Xizang producing crude steel and steel products.

Efficiency improvements in the iron and steel industry depend in part on changes in the structure and location of enterprises, including increased concentration of production in a few large integrated enterprises. China already has ten integrated enterprises with a crude steel-making capacity of 1.0 million tons per year or more, but these account for only 60 percent of total steel production. Moreover, the minimum efficient scale for an integrated enterprise producing steel by the basic oxygen system and rolling a fairly comprehensive range of products is likely to be nearer to 8 million tons per year. International experience suggests that there will also be economic justification for some small nonintegrated steel mills producing light, non-flat steel products, and relying either on iron and steel scrap or on directly reduced iron if cheap sources of energy are available locally.

Efficient location of iron and steel plants depends critically on transportation costs for a few inputs (iron ore, scrap, coal, and electricity) and for finished products. Integrated steel enterprises are involved in a weight-reducing activity, and transport cost considerations are likely to justify locating such enterprises close to sources of raw materials, even though the economic costs of transport are generally higher for a ton of finished products than for a ton of material inputs. China's largest iron and steel enterprises tend to be located in the North, Northeast, and Central South regions, close to abundant supplies of iron ore, coal, and limestone, and future development of the industry should probably involve expansion of existing enterprises and construction of new ones in these locations. The only major exceptions are the Baoshan iron and steel plant, which will depend on imported ore once port facilities have been developed, and another large enterprise

in Shanghai, which currently uses pig iron transported from other parts of the country and which in the future should probably switch to imported materials. There are, however, many plants in other parts of the country which should ultimately be closed down unless they are producing light, nonflat products and using iron and steel scrap.

Decisions on the structure and location of iron and steel plants ought to be based on sound sector planning, which takes account of the interdependence of decisions on the mix of final products, the size of productive units, and the choice of technology, as well as the location of productive units. Efforts to strengthen planning in the industry are therefore critical. Several other constraints to efficient spatial development need to be addressed. One major issue concerns the relationship between different administrative levels of government in planning and managing the industry. Gansu, for example, has one national iron and steel enterprise located close to major iron ore and coal deposits, and one provincial enterprise in the provincial capital, which depends on supplies of pig iron transported from the national enterprise over 1,000 kilometers away. From a national economic point of view, it would almost certainly be more efficient to close the provincial enterprise, but because of uncertainties concerning expansion plans for the national enterprise and the disposal of its output, the provincial government decided to continue operating and even to expand the provincial enterprise. In Hubei, because of problems of coordination between administrative levels, four iron and steel enterprises were built in one town, each with similar output but reporting to different administrative levels (national, provincial, municipal, and county). All but the national enterprise were small scale, experienced problems in obtaining raw materials, and showed poor economic results.

The material supply system also appears to be a constraint to optimal spatial development in the iron and steel industry. This is particularly apparent in Jiangsu, which has a diversified and rapidly expanding industrial sector that includes a significant iron and steel industry, even though the province has only minimal iron ore and energy resources. Local authorities view the iron and steel industry as critical to overall industrial development in the province and are even willing to subsidize the industry because it ensures regular supplies of steel products to the many commune, brigade, and other enterprises that are outside the plan and have no guarantee of receiving steel products through the normal materials allocation process.

may be no overall decline in the relative importance of larger cities.

To increase industrial specialization, and more generally to improve the economic rationality of industrial loca-

tion, will require action on several fronts. Of fundamental importance will be systemic reforms (see Chapter 10) that increase the cost-consciousness of enterprises, especially state enterprises, and expose them to stiff competition, especially from enterprises in other localities. Also important will be improvements in transport and commerce (discussed further below), without which competition would be limited and localities unable to rely on external sources of supply for essential goods. General price reforms and changes in the system of public finance are also needed, to reduce the incentive for local authorities to set up (and preserve) their own small enterprises in profitable or highly taxed industries.

Since the changes now under way in the system of nonagricultural economic management will increasingly delegate decisions to relatively autonomous enterprises, price reform will also be essential to give enterprises appropriate guidance on what industries to develop and where to develop them. This is true both of prices in general and of some specific prices that crucially influence location decisions—transport tariffs, land use charges, and wages.

As in agriculture, industrial enterprises must be sensitized to variations in the economic cost of transport, for both inputs and outputs. Although most enterprises already pay for transport, there are apparently large differences between actual and economic tariffs. Recent increases in rail tariffs (including the latest decision to charge more for short hauls) are a step in the right direction, as is the pricing flexibility allowed to individual and collective transport undertakings. But studies are needed to establish economic user charges for state-operated rail, road, and other transport services, based on long-run marginal costs.

Perhaps even more vital will be a system for charging enterprises for the use of land that takes account of varying land values among regions and localities. Experience from other countries suggests, for example, that the economic cost of land can rise by as much as 25 percent per kilometer as one moves from agricultural land on the edge of an urban area to core land in the inner city. If the economic cost of agricultural land on the edge of a Chinese city is assumed to be Y 0.8 per square meter, the economic cost of land in the city center would be about

Y 10 per square meter for Wuxi, for example, which has a radius of about ten kilometers, but would be as much as Y 120 for Shanghai, which has a radius of twenty kilometers.

Enterprises must be made to feel these wide variations in the opportunity cost of land when making spatial decisions. This could be done through a system of land taxes, under which the assessed tax varies according to the features of each locality (rural versus urban, small versus large urban area, suburbs versus center, and so on). Other methods consistent with public ownership of land, such as a system of rents determined by competition among those who need the land,[8] could also be considered. In introducing either a land tax or a rental market, however, the whole system of local public finance would need to be reconsidered, to ensure that both enterprises and local governments were subject to consistent and appropriate fiscal incentives. For example, given their present direct dependence on enterprise profits, local urban governments might have mixed feelings about levying a land tax that would drive some enterprises away.

The cost of labor can also powerfully influence enterprise location decisions. Even if there were no restrictions on labor mobility,[9] interlocality differences in the economic cost of labor would remain, corresponding to differences in the economic cost of living. Experience from other countries shows that these differences can be quite substantial: in the United States, for example, wages must rise by 0.33 percent for each 1 percent increase in the population of an urban area to maintain the same consumer standard of living. In southern Brazil, the corresponding ratio has been estimated at 0.66 percent, implying that wages must be at least twice as high in cities of more than 200,000 as in cities of under 50,000 to ensure similar living standards. In China, however, enterprises are not yet affected by such issues because rent and food prices and wages are all fixed at fairly uniform levels. To the extent that price reform involves more local variation in consumer prices, enterprises will be obliged to reflect at least some of this variation in wages. But if price reform does not involve such changes, then other measures (including local variations in tax rates) could be used to influence enterprise decisionmaking.

Even with prices, taxes, and wages such as to provide appropriate signals to autonomous, cost-conscious enterprises, some decisions on spatial development would still have to be made by industrial bureaus or ministries. For example, in subsectors such as cement and fertilizers, it may be economically most efficient to determine the location and scale of several plants simultaneously, to minimize transport plus production costs. In other subsectors, such as automobiles and electronic chips, one very large plant might be able to satisfy much of the national market, but with no obvious choice as to its location. In cases where administrative interventions are desirable, however, it is important to base them on careful investment planning including, where necessary, use of planning models that take account of the interdependent nature of decisions on location of productive units, size of productive units, choice of technology, time phasing of the stages of the project, and mix of final products. (Planners also need to bear in mind that profitability calculations based on current wage, capital, and zero land costs can be very misleading as indicators of the relative economic efficiency of alternative locations.)

Transport, Commerce, and Other Services

During the past three decades, China has made major investments in transport, especially railways, and has developed a substantial system of commerce and material supply based on administrative allocation of key commodities. In the decades ahead, rapid economic growth will undoubtedly require further expansion of these basic supporting sectors. But rationalization of the spatial pattern of economic activity, together with other structural changes and systemic reforms, could significantly alter the pace and pattern of development in both transport and commerce.

Transport Needs

Difficulties and delays in transportation are already an important concern in China, as is the longer-term possibility that transport shortages may hold down the overall speed of economic growth, especially given the length of time needed to construct new railways, roads and other infrastructure.[10] It is extremely difficult, however, to predict how rapidly the total volume of freight transport will in fact need to grow, given any particular assumption about the future trend growth rate of national income. This is largely because by international standards China currently uses an exceptionally large amount of freight transport—more than three ton-kilometers per dollar of GNP, as compared with well under two ton-kilometers in India, Brazil, and the United States. The Soviet Union, though, is even more freight-intensive (over four ton-kilometers per dollar of GNP) than China.

Though the freight-intensity of particular countries is affected also by their specific geography, these comparisons suggest that future growth of transport demand in China could vary widely, depending on the pattern of economic growth, both in terms of sectoral structure (for

8. A system of rents determined by competitive bidding among enterprises would, in principle, be more efficient than a land tax system and would avoid the administrative problem of deciding on appropriate tax levels.

9. These restrictions are discussed in detail later in this chapter.

10. Annex 6 contains a fuller discussion of transport issues.

example, industry is more transport-intensive than services) and in terms of spatial location (which influences average transport distance). It will also be affected by system reform, which will, on the one hand, tend to increase transport requirements because of increased specialization and exchange, but, on the other hand, could greatly reduce wasteful use of transport facilities, for example through less cross-hauling, more preliminary processing of materials, and more rational location decisions. The possible magnitude of the combined impact of changes in the growth pattern and system reform is illustrated not only by international comparisons but also by China's own experience: in 1952–77, freight transport volume increased 55 percent faster than national income, but in 1979–84 about 26 percent slower than national income.

Within the framework of the macroeconomic projections introduced in Chapter 2, alternative projections of freight transport volume are presented in Annex 6. In QUADRUPLE, with continuing strong emphasis on material production, and with industry and agriculture using transport only moderately more efficiently than in the past, freight volume could reach 3,200 billion ton-kilometers by the year 2000. In BALANCE, by contrast, with the same growth of national income achieved through faster expansion of services and slower expansion of industry, and with somewhat greater efficiency in transport use, freight volume in 2000 would be 2,400 billion ton-kilometers. Even in the latter case, China's projected freight-intensity (2.4 ton-kilometers per dollar of GNP in 2000) remains high by comparison with other countries, which suggests that the possibility of an even slower growth of freight volume cannot be ruled out.

But although the overall volume of transport requirements in the longer term is highly uncertain, changes in the industrial and spatial pattern of development will certainly require a new and different mixture of transport investments, as well as changes in organization and management. Intraprovincial specialization in agriculture and industry, for example, will involve the movement in fairly small lots of a great variety of goods, many of which are perishable, over short to medium distances (5 to 100 kilometers), to and from dispersed origins and destinations. To help meet these diverse and growing demands as efficiently as possible, a major expansion of the transport network linking rural and urban areas will be essential. In parts of southern China, richly endowed with dense networks of rivers and canals, water transport can continue to play an important role. But in most parts of the country, roads will be the critical constraint. One major task will be to expand the rural road network, which currently totals 300,000 to 500,000 kilometers, compared with 900,000 kilometers in India, 1.2 million kilometers in Brazil, and more than 100,000 kilometers in Thailand (which is smaller in area than Sichuan). In addition, a

major program for paving and upgrading intraprovincial highways will be necessary.

Greater industrial specialization will also involve a very large increase in interprovincial and interregional transport of light industrial goods. Currently, most roads in China radiate from provincial capitals, forming separate networks with few interconnections; rail is therefore the only effective link between provinces and regions. As a result, light industrial goods are usually transported short distances by road to the rail network and then by rail across provincial and regional boundaries. However, light industrial products, which often have high value-weight ratios or are quite fragile (and liable to be damaged by transshipment), are more efficiently transported by road than by rail, even over long distances. Developing the intercity and interprovincial road network for the transport of light industrial goods should therefore be a high priority in transport investment. (Improvements in the volume and quality of air freight services could also make a significant, though much smaller, economic contribution.)

It is widely recognized in China that road transport should and will play a larger role in the future. Yet there seems to be no strategic plan to bring this about. Indeed, during the past few years, there has been little road construction, and the situation is unlikely to improve substantially so long as roads remain almost entirely a local government responsibility. This is partly because the present price and fiscal systems make directly productive investment (especially in industry) generally more attractive to local governments than investment in roads and other infrastructure. But it is also because the interest of each locality in contributing to improvement of the road network linking it with other localities is reduced in the absence of higher-level coordination and cost-sharing among localities. For this reason, in many countries, the finance, planning, and coordination of road development has been made a responsibility of higher (national and provincial) levels of government, with delegation of responsibility only for actual construction and maintenance to local governments.

As regards sources of finance for road development in China, the issuance of bonds (as in some other countries) has recently been encouraged, and rural labor contributions are increasingly being commuted into cash payments. But much more use could be made of road-related taxation. Since direct road user charges (tolls) often have undesirable effects on traffic patterns, most countries have adopted a system of road user charges based on vehicle and fuel taxation. The tax component of gasoline and diesel motor fuels is often very substantial (up to 50 percent, and in some countries even more), and vehicle taxes based on axle loads recoup the high share of road maintenance costs caused by heavy trucks. Such a system of road user charges in China could generate sufficient

Box 5.4   Trade, Pricing, and Transport of Cement

In most countries, the raw materials for cement production are widely available, and the industry consists of
many plants located close to major markets in order to
minimize delivery costs, which are very high in relation to
the value of the commodity. In the United States, for
example, the ratio of freight cost to production cost is
about 0.5 for cement, compared with 0.04 for steel. China's cement industry is also characterized by many plants
and dispersed locations, but average transport distances are
significantly higher than in the United States primarily
because the North and Northwest have little local cement
production and must trade with provinces that have surpluses, especially Liaoning in the Northeast, which accounts for 9 percent of national output. More important,
however, cement production in China is divided between
centrally and locally controlled plants, with output from
centrally controlled plants priced much lower than local
output and frequently of higher quality. As a result, and
even without accounting for quality differentials, centrally
controlled cement delivered by rail can compete with local
cement delivered by road well beyond the distances found
economical in other countries (see Box Table 5.4A).

Box Table 5.4A   Local and Centrally Controlled Cement Prices
(yuan per ton)

Component	Local cement delivered by road, 50 km	Centrally controlled cement delivered by rail	
		2,500 km	3,000 km
Cement price	80.0	50.0	50.0
Transport tariff	10.0	35.2	42.3
Delivered price	90.0	85.2	92.3

Source: Data provided to World Bank staff.

Improving the efficiency of cement distribution will depend in part on further dispersing production from its
original concentration in the Northeast, and efforts to
achieve this are already under way. But dispersed production is efficient only if local demands are actually met by
local production. Some provinces with centrally controlled
plants are now obliged to send most of their cement output to other provinces, but then have to buy cement from
locally controlled enterprises in other provinces. This
wastes a lot of transport. Reforms in the trade and pricing
system for cement are therefore critical.

funds for an accelerated road construction program, as
well as contributing to an economically appropriate division of traffic between road transport and other modes of
transport.

To develop China's road transport system to a sufficient extent, various other steps would also have to be
taken, some of which would require greatly increased
horizontal coordination among different government
ministries and agencies, and possibly the establishment of
a superior agency specifically charged with road transport
development. These steps include production of different
(smaller as well as larger) and more fuel-efficient trucks,
better management and utilization of truck fleets, upgrading of fuel quality, improvement of fuel distribution systems, and rationalization of the motor fuel price structure. For example, eliminating the large subsidy on diesel
fuel for agricultural use would help to clear rural roads of
walking tractors, which slow down all traffic as well as
being highly energy-inefficient by comparison with small
pickup trucks. But this would be difficult because plans to
develop the production of small trucks (and fuel for
them) have lagged far behind growth of demand.

Railways will remain the most efficient mode for transporting raw materials and most heavy-industry products
over long distances. But the extent of these movements,
and hence the railway expansion program, will depend
not only on the overall growth and pattern of industrial

output and on the extent of industrial specialization but
also on how quickly the materials supply system can be
improved. Currently, for example, centrally allocated materials at state prices are more competitive than local
materials available at market prices, even when delivered
over long distances. The result is excessive interprovincial
movement of materials, because some provinces are
obliged to send out materials under centrally administered allocation and then purchase similar materials from
other provinces at higher prices (see Box 5.4). In these
circumstances, a change from administered to market distribution of key materials could significantly affect interprovincial movement of raw materials and hence the required railway investment program.

Since increased energy requirements in China will have
to be met largely by coal (see Chapter 4), and since water
and road transport of coal can increase only to a certain
extent, the amount of coal transported by rail will continue to grow. Rail transport distances for coal are also
likely to continue to increase, as coal mining will be
increasingly concentrated in the North, and in particular
in Shanxi province. With coal production increasing to
1,400 million tons by the year 2000, the share of coal
would be likely to increase to about 40–50 percent of
total rail ton-kilometers (up from 32 percent in 1980),
depending on the extent of transport rationalization for
other commodities—for example, processing of wood

and ores before shipment and greater use of coastal and inland water transport because of more appropriate location of new heavy industry plants.

Total rail freight transport in the year 2000 might grow to about 1,300 billion ton-kilometers under the BALANCE scenario, and 1,700 billion ton-kilometers under the QUADRUPLE scenario (see Annex 6), increases 2.3 and 3.0 times 1980 levels, respectively. These increases in rail transport capacity seem quite feasible, especially given the demonstrated capacity of the Ministry of Railways to secure finance and implement investment projects. For example, with a modest increase (15 percent) in the total railway network, to 60,000 route kilometers by 2000, the required increase under the BALANCE scenario could be achieved if average freight density were to double, from 12 million ton-kilometers per kilometer of rail route in 1980 to 24 million ton-kilometers per kilometer of rail route by the year 2000. In the U.S.S.R., a comparable increase in traffic density was achieved between 1960 and 1975 by switching from steam to electric and diesel traction, combined with double-tracking of about one-third of the railway network. Steam traction declined from 85 percent in 1955 to 15 percent in 1975 and has since vanished completely. By contrast, 70–75 percent of total traction in China is still provided by inefficient steam locomotives, and only 18 percent of the rail routes are double tracked. The investment cost of network expansion, double-tracking, and electrification to meet projected traffic demand to the year 2000 would be large, but not prohibitive—perhaps Y 5 billion to 7 billion per year in the BALANCE scenario, and Y 7 billion to 9 billion in the QUADRUPLE scenario.

Despite expansion in recent years, domestic water transport is still not used to its best economic advantage. The network of navigable inland waterways has decreased by over one-third since 1960, partly because of dams built to generate electricity and provide irrigation under the responsibility of a different ministry than that controlling water transport. With a great increase planned in hydropower development to the end of the century, the use of waterways for transport must be recognized and included at an early stage in the planning and evaluation of hydropower sites. Coastal shipping—which offers an economic alternative to north-south railways—has likewise grown more rapidly in recent years, but is still underdeveloped, most notably by comparison with Japan. Much greater use of coastal and inland water shipping could be made if more heavy industries were in future located so as to avoid the need for inland transport to and from ports.

Considerable efficiency gains could be made in the entire transport system through better intermodal coordination, which has thus far been impeded by the vertical and largely self-contained organization of China's transport and other sectoral agencies. Better choices need to be made regarding interfacing of different modes, including technical solutions and standards to facilitate intermodal transfer or avoid unnecessary transshipment. Examples include increased containerization for high-value products, self-unloading ships to reduce the need for port facilities, and ocean-going barges to avoid transshipment between coastal shipping and inland water transport. To realize the potential efficiency gains from intermodal coordination requires prices and tariffs that reflect the full cost of each transport mode, but also more competition and specialization of transport modes. In market economies, where intermodal coordination is achieved mainly through pricing and competition, many specialized entities provide transport, storage, and transfer services. There are also many joint ventures among enterprises operating in different transport modes to facilitate intermodal transfers (for example, jobbers, storage companies, and companies leasing containers, railcars, trailers, and other equipment).

Despite a rapid rise in recent years, personal mobility in China is still low by international standards, and passenger transport can be expected to grow fast. Rural economic development has lately generated a lot of demand for short-distance travel. Increased internal economic specialization and trade will also require far more personal contacts and business trips, and experience in other countries shows that people like to spend a considerable fraction of income increases on travel to visit relatives or for recreation. This demand for greater mobility has invariably been accompanied elsewhere by demand for private vehicles (motorcycles as well as cars). Public passenger transport will shift toward (lower-cost and more flexible) buses, as well as aircraft, with a decline in the share of the railways. This strengthens the case for improvement of China's road network, as well as of rural and intercity bus (and air) services, although rail passenger transport capacity will also have to expand quite fast. Within towns and cities, too, public transport will need to be strengthened.

Developing Commerce

Like transport, commerce has an essential role in facilitating specialization, both of localities and of enterprises, as well as providing the infrastructure of market regulation (Chapter 1). To accomplish this, however, China's commercial system would need to become much more flexible, responsive, and diversified, which would entail basic changes in organization and management. It would also need to become much larger, especially in terms of employment, but also in terms of fixed assets (although it might need less circulating capital than at present—see Chapter 2). For example, in the QUADRUPLE projection, where the pattern of development resembles that of the Soviet Union and of China in 1950–80, employment in commerce remains exceptionally small by comparison with other countries—under 5 percent of total employment in 2000. In the BALANCE projection, reflecting more fundamental changes in the system of economic management, it increases to 10 percent of total employment.

Development of collective and individual commerce in recent years has already contributed to expanding and improving retail trade, as has greater freedom of choice of suppliers in the (still overwhelmingly dominant) state-operated retailing system. The efficiency of wholesale trade—especially in key materials—has also been improved by reductions in the scope of centrally administered allocation. Many enterprises are now allowed to sell some of their output themselves, and unregulated wholesale markets for producer goods and industrial consumer goods have been established in many cities. But the proportion of goods involved is still small. Centralized allocation has frequently been replaced by provincial- or county-level allocation, and shortages and bottlenecks remain, especially in the availability of materials for small collective and commune and brigade enterprises. As a result, many localities still feel obliged to develop local materials production capacity. There are also undesirable pressures to enlarge the scope of administrative planning to incorporate small urban and rural collectives.

In accordance with the Government's intentions, there should continue to be a steady shift from administrative to market allocation of both essential and other commodities, in parallel with a decline in the proportion of industrial production subject to obligatory quotas. There should also continue to be a steady increase in the relative importance of individual and collective commerce, whose motivation, initiative, flexibility, and responsiveness to customer needs is generally superior to that of state-run commerce (which could, however, improve significantly if stimulated by competition). Individual and collective enterprises, moreover, should not remain confined to retail trade in consumer goods, but should probably also eventually play a major role in wholesaling and material supply. To do this, they would need to be given much better access than at present to premises, credit, skilled labor, and transport facilities.

Even with a more market-regulated system of commerce, the powers of different levels of government to control interlocality trade would remain a major issue. Despite the growth of collective and individual commerce and instructions from the central government, local governments continue to protect local industries by restricting purchases of certain types of goods from outside the locality. This sort of problem is by no means special to China: local governments in most countries and historical periods (for example, the city guilds of medieval Europe) have also sought to protect local producers from external competition. But to overcome it requires strong action by the central government. In addition to general prohibitions on administrative barriers to interlocality trade,

there is also need for some legal process or institution with the power to impose large fines and compel compensation, to which any enterprise or individual subjected to local government interference could appeal directly.[11]

However, removing commerce from the control of localities may not be sufficient so long as localities in China own many of the enterprises and can influence the buying and selling decisions of enterprises in such a way as to protect other local enterprises. Of course, in some circumstances, there may be good reasons from a national viewpoint for providing special assistance to local industries (Chapter 5). But the power to grant such assistance, and the conditions under which it is granted, must be very clearly specified by the central government—otherwise interlocality specialization may be seriously harmed.

Development of services other than commerce (discussed in Chapter 1 and 2) will also shape, and be shaped by, changes in China's spatial pattern of economic activity. This is so for social services and public administration, for personal services such as restaurants and hairdressers, and for financial and other enterprise support services, including law, telecommunications, and technical consultancy. Some of these service activities contribute to specialization and exchange in material production, especially by increasing the flow of technical, and commercial information. Some—colleges and centers of local government, for example—in other countries constitute the main specialized activities of particular small cities. And some sophisticated financial, technical, and commercial services benefit from clustering together in large cities. But most services need to be spatially dispersed, close to their customers. As a result, most localities in other countries do not specialize in particular services, as they do in particular industries, but provide a wide range of services to meet local needs.

Urban and Rural Development

Despite controls on rural-urban migration, the distribution of China's population between urban and rural areas appears to be quite similar to other low-income countries (see Table 5.5). The urbanization rate may even be above the low-income country average if account is taken of

---

11. The importance of reducing obstacles to interlocality trade in China is well demonstrated by the recent national report of a member of a self-employed household in Sichuan who was asked to buy lumber for his township's mechanized brickyard. It took him fifty-four days and Y 1,453 for seven permits to transport thirteen cubic meters of used building materials, which he bought for Y 3,300, a mere sixty kilometers. The unreasonable expenditure raised the cost of the lumber, which was consequently rejected by the brickyard.

Table 5.5   Urbanization and Economic Development in Selected Countries

Country	Per capita GNP, 1982 (dollars)	Percentage of the population living in urban areas		Percentage of the urban population living in cities of 500,000 or more	
		1960	1982	1960	1980
China	310	18	21	42	45
India	260	18	24	26	39
Other low-income countries	250	12	20	19	40
Average for lower-middle-income countries	840	24	34	28	47
Average for upper-middle-income countries	2,490	45	63	38	51

Source: World Bank, *World Development Report 1984* (New York: Oxford University Press, 1984).

Table 5.6   Per Capita Income in Urban and Rural Areas, 1982

Area	Urban		Rural		Total	
	Per capita income (yuan)	Percentage of population	Per capita income (yuan)	Percentage of population	Per capita income (yuan)	Percentage of population
National average	574	21	269	79	333	100
Shanghai municipal average	668	63	437	37	582	100
Jiangsu provincial average	593	16	309	84	354	100
Wuxi County[a]	572	7	412	93	423	100
Qianzhou Township[a]	. .	. .	560	100	560	100
Hubei provincial average	550	18	286	82	334	100
Gansu provincial average	648	15	174	85	245	100
Dingxi County[a]	562	9	108	91	149	100
Dongye Township[a]	. .	. .	55	100	55	100

a. Data are for 1983.
Source: Annex 5, Appendix I; data provided to the economic mission.

differences in definitions.[12] However, the differentials in output and investment per capita between urban and rural areas appear to be larger than in most other low-income countries and as a result urban areas account for an unusually large share of output and investment.

The distribution of personal incomes between urban and rural areas of China is also somewhat different from that in other developing countries. The policy of national uniform wages has resulted in extremely small income differences among (as well as within) urban areas. But large differences in average incomes remain between urban and rural areas, especially in poorer regions (see Table 5.6). In Jiangsu, for example, the ratio of urban to rural per capita income is 1.9; in Gansu it is 3.7; and in Dingxi county, over 5. Moreover, these urban-rural income gaps reflect differences in real living standards and not just differences in costs of living. The average urban household for example owns 1.3 bicycles, 2.1 watches, 1.2 radios, and 0.4 televisions, whereas the average rural household owns 0.5 bicycles, 0.6 watches, 0.8 radios, and 0.06 televisions.

In most countries, the low- to middle-income transition has involved a significant increase in urbanization. In China, though, the Government for many years sought to limit urbanization, emphasizing rural industrialization instead. The current policy is much less restrictive, since it is now generally accepted that increased urbanization will be an essential element of structural change and specialization. But some elements of the former policy persist, especially regarding the growth of large cities and movement of population into formally designated urban areas. The rationale for these continuing restrictions, which could have significant economic and social costs, merits careful consideration. So does the question of whether the restrictions should apply to people, or to directly productive investment, or to investment in infrastructure. More generally, it will be important to devise a

12. China now classifies as urban both the agricultural and the nonagricultural population of all towns with 3,000 or more permanent residents, at least 70 percent of whom are engaged in nonagricultural activities. Previously, the agricultural population was excluded—hence the lower urbanization rate quoted in the World Bank's first economic report on China. However, the Chinese definition of "urban" may still be more restrictive than the definitions used in many other countries. For a detailed discussion of China's urban definitions and how they compare with definitions used in other countries, see Background Paper 2.

Figure 5.2 Distribution of Employment, Capital, and Gross Output, Alternative Projections, 1981–2000

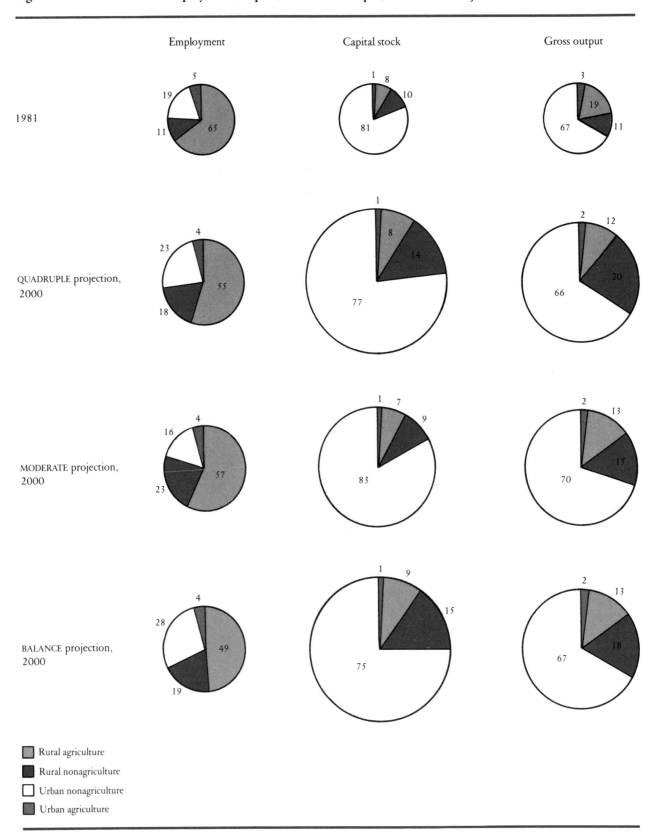

Rural agriculture

Rural nonagriculture

Urban nonagriculture

Urban agriculture

Note: For more detail, see Annex 4, Chapter 6.
Source: World Bank projections.

Table 5.7   Distribution of Employment and Population, Alternative Projections, 1981–2000
(percent)

Measure and projection	Employment			Population		
	Rural	*Urban*	*Total*	*Rural*	*Urban*	*Total*
Shares of total						
1981	75.8	24.2	100.0	79.8	20.2	100.0
2000						
QUADRUPLE	73.2	26.8	100.0	75.0	25.0	100.0
MODERATE	79.7	20.3	100.0	81.1	18.9	100.0
BALANCE	67.8	32.2	100.0	70.0	30.0	100.0
Average annual growth						
QUADRUPLE	1.6	2.3	1.8	0.7	2.2	1.0
MODERATE	2.0	0.8	1.8	1.1[a]	0.7[a]	1.0
BALANCE	1.2	3.3	1.8	0.3	3.1	1.0

a. These growth rates are the same as the projected natural growth rates of the rural and urban population and therefore imply no rural-urban migration.
Source: World Bank projections.

management system and set of policies that generate an economically and socially efficient pace and pattern of urbanization.

Urban-Rural Balance

Although the macroeconomic projections discussed in Chapter 2 are not uniquely associated with particular patterns of urban and rural development, Figure 5.2 illustratively connects each of these projections with a specific urban-rural distribution of employment, capital, and output.[13] In QUADRUPLE it is assumed that the overall target of quadrupling the gross value of industrial and agricultural output is accompanied by a strong emphasis on the development of nonagricultural activities in rural areas. This emphasis is reflected both in an increased rural share of the nonagricultural capital stock and in an increase in the share of nonagricultural employment in total rural employment from 14 percent in 1981 to 25 percent in 2000, which is in the high range for lower-middle-income countries. However, urban employment is still assumed to grow more rapidly than rural employment. In MODERATE it is assumed that lower macroeconomic efficiency relative to QUADRUPLE is accompanied by greater restrictions on urban employment growth than in QUADRUPLE and no shift of capital away from urban areas. As a result rural nonagricultural output growth is seriously constrained, while urban areas respond to labor shortages by adopting more capital-intensive techniques. In BALANCE, in contrast, it is assumed that the rapid growth in services and greater economic efficiency relative to QUADRUPLE are accompanied by faster growth of urban employment, which further reduces the need for accelerated (and from a national economic viewpoint inefficient) automation of urban production.

Growth of urban employment at the rate assumed in BALANCE, though more conducive to raising national economic efficiency than the lower rates assumed in QUAD-

RUPLE and MODERATE, would involve substantial rural-urban migration. This is because large fertility differentials between urban and rural areas have developed in recent years, which will result in a natural growth rate of both the total and the working-age populations that is much higher in rural than in urban areas over the next two decades. Indeed, while the natural growth rate of the working-age population in rural areas will decline from about 3.3 percent at present to 1.1 percent per year by the late 1990s, the corresponding decline in urban areas will be from 2.1 percent to virtually zero. Accordingly, only under the MODERATE scenario, with the urban share of total employment falling, would no migration be required (see Table 5.7, which assumes a rate of migration just sufficient to meet employment requirements). Even the modest growth in urban employment assumed in QUADRUPLE would require substantial rural-urban migration—and the pace of migration would have to be even greater if China were to achieve the urban employment growth rate assumed in BALANCE. Even then, urbanization in China in the year 2000 would still be well below the 34 percent average for lower-middle-income countries.

In order to efficiently manage the overall process of rural-urban migration, the Government will almost certainly have to rely much more on pricing and other economic measures, and much less on administrative measures than in the past. At present the Government provides only a relatively small number of people with official permission to move to cities of more than 200,000 inhabitants. It is also trying to limit the number of people moving to small or medium-size urban areas by stipulating that workers who move usually may not bring

---

13. The assumptions behind each of the urban-rural balance scenarios are discussed in more detail in Annex 4 (Chapter 6).

Table 5.8 Average Annual Growth of Urban and Rural Income, Alternative Projections, 1981–2000
(percent)

Measure and projection	Urban	Rural	Total
Earnings per worker			
QUADRUPLE	4.5	4.5	4.6[a]
MODERATE	3.7	3.7	3.5[b]
BALANCE	4.5	4.6	5.0[a]
Per capita income			
QUADRUPLE	4.6	5.4	5.4
MODERATE	3.8	4.6	4.3
BALANCE	4.6	5.5	5.8
Ratio of labor force to population	0.1	0.9	0.8

a. The average earnings growth rate is above the urban and rural rate because the share of urban employment (which is higher paid) increases overall.
b. The average earnings growth rate is below the urban and rural rate because the share of rural employment (which is lower paid) increases overall.
Source: World Bank projections.

their families with them or be granted urban registration (which deprives them of the subsidies normally available to urban residents). However, growth in employment opportunities in collective and individual activities and other changes (such as the availability of foodgrains in urban free markets) have made it much easier for people to ignore such administrative regulations; already an estimated 5 to 10 percent of the labor force in some large cities are there unofficially. In these circumstances, economic efficiency as well as intraurban equity could probably be enhanced by replacing such administrative regulations with measures to reduce the existing huge incentives for rural-urban migration to more economically rational proportions. One way of doing this would be to increase the costs of locating activities and employing workers in urban areas (especially large cities) through the land use charges and other pricing measures discussed earlier.

The alternative urban-rural balance scenarios also have major implications for investment flows and how these flows should be managed (see Chapters 9 and 10). Both QUADRUPLE and BALANCE, for example, assume that there would be an increase in the share of rural areas in the nonagricultural capital stock. This would probably require changes in the composition of accumulation, especially as between government, enterprises (retained profits, including those of collective and individual enterprises), and households and in the institutions and policies that channel the savings of particular sectors into investment in other sectors.

The alternative urban-rural balance scenarios result in quite large variations in the growth of output per worker between urban and rural areas. But, in order to assess the implications of such variations for urban-rural income disparities, it is necessary to take account both of the relationship between growth in output per worker and growth in earnings per worker and of the relationship between labor force and population growth. For example if, as is assumed in the macroeconomic projections, intersectoral variations in the growth of gross output per worker are offset by relative price and tax changes, and earnings per worker increase at the same rate in all sectors (see Chapters 2 and 3), urban-rural differentials in earnings per worker would probably change very little (Table 5.8).

However, the labor force in relation to population will be increasing much more rapidly in rural than in urban areas over the next two decades, primarily because the effects of family planning policies and slower population growth will be felt much later in rural than in urban areas (see Table 5.8). As a result, significant reductions in urban-rural income disparities could occur even if urban and rural earnings per worker increased at the same rate (see Table 5.9). Nonetheless, the projected income disparities in 2000 are still large; additional measures to reduce them should be considered (see Chapters 3, 8, 9, and 10).

Development of Towns and Cities

Over the next two decades major changes will take place not only in urban-rural balance but also in the number, size, and structure of rural towns and of small, medium, and large urban areas. The precise changes will depend in part on the type of urban-rural balance strategy China follows, but some major features are already apparent. Within rural areas, small towns were neglected for many years and need to develop rapidly. In some cases this is already happening. In Jiangsu, for example, many small towns actually experienced a fall in population during the 1950s and 1960s, as service and other activities were increasingly taken over by the state. In recent years, however, movement of people into these towns has been actively encouraged, and many of the towns now qualify as urban areas.

Table 5.9 Urban-Rural Income Disparities, Alternative Projections, 1981–2000

Year and projection	Average per capita personal income (yuan)	Urban per capita personal income (yuan)	Rural per capita personal income (yuan)	Ratio of urban to rural per capita income
1981	290	554	223	2.5
2000				
QUADRUPLE	788	1,302	606	2.1
MODERATE	645	1,125	524	2.1
BALANCE	846	1,326	617	2.1

Source: World Bank projections.

Compared with other large countries, China also appears to have a lower proportion of its urban population in cities with fewer than 100,000 inhabitants (32 percent, compared with 47 percent in India, 42 percent in Brazil, and 41 percent in the Soviet Union), and the Government's emphasis on the rapid development of small and medium-size urban areas seems appropriate. In addition, though, an increase in the number (and major changes in the structure) of large cities will be required as part of the overall process of structural change and development of high technology and service activities.

The expansion and efficient development of towns and cities will depend, among other things, on the quality and quantity of public infrastructure and support services. For example, if small towns are to become effective commercial centers for surrounding rural areas, transport links must be greatly improved, more marketing facilities established, and public utilities (including water supplies, electricity, and telephones) greatly expanded. There will also be a need to improve rapidly the quality of education, health, and other social services and to provide more housing in these small towns if they are to constitute a socially viable alternative to larger towns and cities. In urban areas in general, the quality of education and health services tends to be much better than in surrounding rural areas, but the stock of housing is small[14] and poorly maintained (in part because of low rents), the transportation system is very congested, and there are serious environmental problems.

Developing appropriate financing mechanisms (including user fees) for public infrastructure and support services will be a major issue, particularly in rural towns. Social labor—which rural households are still obliged to contribute—and the retained profits of local enterprises are at present the main resources available. With the development of the rural production responsibility system, the obligation to supply social labor is becoming increasingly inconvenient, and in some of the richer and more rapidly growing rural areas can be avoided by paying the village or town the daily wage equivalent. Improved systems of local taxation and pricing of services are needed, however, to strengthen the financial base of rural towns.

In county towns and larger urban areas, more formal systems of resource mobilization already exist, including grants from higher administrative levels, surcharges on industrial and commercial taxes, shares of industrial and commercial enterprise profits, as well as utility fees. But the adequacy and appropriateness of these resources must be viewed in relation to likely future expenditure responsibilities. In many countries, efficient and equitable development of urban services has been seriously constrained either by fragmented and unclear allocation of responsibility among different administrative levels or by failure to ensure that revenue sources available to towns and cities have the potential to grow in line with population and incomes, as well as with service demand.

In China, special attention needs to be given to the ways in which broader reforms (see Chapter 10) may require or facilitate changes in the system of local public finance. At present, directly productive investment—especially in industry—absorbs an unusually large proportion of local expenditure, while economic and social infrastructure and related services are comparatively neglected. In the future, however, responsibility for financing directly productive investment may shift increasingly to enterprises and to banks. At the same time, the present social responsibilities of enterprises (for housing, education and health) may be shifted increasingly to government at various levels; increases in the complexity and specialization of the economy may require more sophisticated and expensive urban infrastructure and services. In these circumstances, to minimize duplication and gaps, it will be important to assign particular expenditure responsibilities to particular levels of government.

On the revenue side, greater independence of enterprises from administrative control may reduce the share of receipts from direct enterprise ownership in local government budgets. To offset this, there could be greater reliance on land taxes (or rents, as mentioned in Chapter 5), which are the main source of revenue for local governments in other countries. Local income taxes, which are used extensively in the United States, might also be considered. In addition, with the important exception of basic social services such as education and health (Chapter 10), the cost of providing urban services should as far as possible be recovered by charging fees to users and beneficiaries. And to the extent that revenues from these various sources do not match assigned local expenditure responsibilities, arrangements for revenue sharing with higher levels of government will need to be reconsidered, as will the possible powers of local governments to borrow for capital expenditure.

Rural Poverty and Regional Inequality

The rural reforms and policy changes introduced in recent years have already reduced rural poverty. Many of the poorest rural areas were among the first to introduce the production responsibility system and have benefited from rapid growth in crop production. Poor areas of eastern and southern China that were previously obliged to grow foodgrains under unsuitable agroclimatic conditions have been able, in recent years, to switch to other crops (such as cotton), which produce much better re-

---

14. The average amount of urban housing per person is less than five square meters compared with twelve square meters in rural areas.

Table 5.10 Rural and Provincial Poverty, 1982

(percent)

Type of area	Jiangsu	Hubei	Gansu	National average
Urban	0	..	2	1
Rural	3	3	41	13
Total	3	..	35	11

Note: Data are percentages of the population with per capita incomes below Y 167 in urban areas and Y 140 in rural areas.
Source: Annex 5, Appendix I.

turns. Some poor rural areas, however, appear to have benefited much less, if at all; interprovincial variations in the incidence of poverty remain very large (see Table 5.10); and there is increasing concern that the per capita output and income gap between the coast and the interior could widen significantly. The Government would like to ensure that increased specialization and trade, and changes in urban-rural balance, help to further reduce the incidence of poverty and stimulate development in the interior. But this will require both a detailed assessment of prevailing conditions in poor areas and the development of an overall strategy of systemic changes, investments, and other interventions.

There are, of course, many circumstances under which reforms and investments that facilitate specialization and trade will also contribute to poverty reduction. For example, in some poor rural areas, investments in supporting infrastructure for agriculture (such as irrigation and transport) may show better returns than additional investments in richer areas that already have relatively high yields. In many poor areas and regions, industrial development could be stimulated by the pricing and commercial reforms needed to enhance specialization and trade. Changing the current practice whereby the state procures most agricultural products for processing in large state enterprises would enable many poor areas to establish local agroprocessing industries. Further expansion and diversification of commerce, together with improvements in transport, would help some poor rural areas to compete better with state and collective enterprises in other parts of the country. Reform of the material allocation system should also help to ensure that mineral resources are no longer mined in the interior and allocated to coastal provinces for processing when it would be more efficient to process them locally. Finally, a system of economic charges for land should help stimulate development in poor rural areas and in the interior, where land values will generally be much below national averages.

Other aspects of system reform and specialization, however, may have a negative effect on poor areas and provinces, particularly those where the physical resource base is poor and the level of human resource development low. Dingxi County in Gansu, for example, is on

the Loess Plateau, where basic agricultural conditions are extremely difficult, and much further research and extension work may be necessary before suitable technical packages can be developed and agricultural development stimulated (see Box 5.5 and Table 5.11). In the meantime, cash incomes from agriculture could even fall, if there were decreases in output prices and increases in input prices to better reflect the economic costs of transport. The limited prospects for agricultural development will also constrain nonagricultural development, and improvements in trade and transport will bring competition from outside that will threaten existing industrial activities. There is also a danger that levels of human resource development in poor areas could fall: the adoption of fee-for-service medicine (following the introduction of the production responsibility system) may lead to the relative neglect of preventive measures; and school enrollment ratios and attendance may fall if parents have to pay more for, or see little advantage to, their children's education. Finally, a less direct role for the government in rural commerce may make it more difficult to provide relief grain to poor and disaster stricken areas.

To ensure that poverty is reduced while national efficiency is increased, all levels of government will need to review very carefully both the prospects for poor localities and the measures that would most efficiently increase the incomes of their populations. Of fundamental importance will be measures to improve the human resource base, including both health and education levels. China now needs to extend to poor areas and regions the improvements in health that have occurred in most parts of

Table 5.11 Rural Development in Dingxi County (Gansu) and Wuxi County (Jiangsu), 1983

Measure	Dingxi	Wuxi
Rural per capita income (yuan)	108	412
Rural population (percentage of total)	91	93
Rural labor force		
Percentage in farming, forestry, or livestock	91	51
Percentage in other activities	9	49
Arable land per agricultural worker (mu)	14	3
Percentage irrigated	6	96
Percentage grain crops	79	87
Grain yield (kilograms per mu)	85	400
Per capita GVIAO (yuan)	169	2,005
Farming, forestry, or livestock	118	357
Brigade and team industry	5	535
County and commune industry	46	1,113
Primary school enrollment ratio (percent)	80	..
Hospital beds per thousand people	0.6	2.3

Source: Data provided to the economic mission.

Chinese agriculture and civilization first developed on the Loess Plateau,[1] but continuous farming over many millennia has totally changed the landscape and caused major environmental problems. The original vegetation has been completely removed, and the loess (a dust of minute yellowish-grey grains that covers the entire plateau from depths of a few meters to more than a hundred meters) breaks down with alarming ease. As a result, hillsides, though extensively terraced, are affected by serious gully and sheet erosion problems. The region is subject to bitterly cold winters, hot summers, and low rainfall (generally below 400 millimeters per year). Cotton, wheat, and (more recently) corn are grown in irrigated areas, but these account for only a small proportion of the total cultivated area. In nonirrigated areas, millet and *gaoliang* are the major crops, but yields even in a good year are very low. The incidence of rural poverty in these areas is as high as anywhere in China, and most households survive only by having access to relief grain from the state.

Efficient development of the plateau is likely to require some investments in irrigation, if these can be shown to be economical, and, more important, reforestation and development of improved pastures in rainfed areas. But there are many constraints to such developments. For example, irrigation projects in the Loess Plateau require especially careful design and appraisal because of the extremely difficult topographical and agroclimatic conditions, but comprehensive and reliable data necessary for such work are often unavailable. More woody and forage species that are suited to the varying conditions of rainfed areas need to be found and developed, but worldwide searches for suitable materials and local programs of genetic selection and plant breeding appear to have been very limited. Yields in both irrigated and dry land areas of the Loess Plateau could probably be increased by more appropriate fertilizer use, but programs of field experimentation, soil testing, and extension are still very weak. Perhaps the major constraint, however, is a very serious shortage of the qualified technical and professional personnel needed to develop research, and extension programs that can form the basis of future agricultural development on the plateau.

Programs of agricultural education, research, and extension will take time to develop, so that improvements in agricultural and environmental conditions on the Loess Plateau may only be realized in twenty years or more. An overall strategy for raising incomes on the plateau should take this into account. To achieve significant income increases in the meantime might require programs for outmigration.

1. The plateau covers Shaanxi, parts of Gansu and Ningxia, western Shanxi, and western Henan.

the country. Mortality and morbidity due to infectious diseases are frequently high in poor areas, substantial undernutrition remains, and the level of health services is much below the national average. Overcoming these problems will require careful analysis of prevailing health problems in poor areas, development of plans to address those problems, and provision of the necessary manpower and financial resources to carry out such plans. Financing issues will be of particular importance, because of the collapse of the rural cooperative health insurance systems in many poor areas and the need to ensure that everyone can receive a minimum basic level of health care and that preventive activities (including health campaigns) are not neglected.

Primary and secondary school enrollment ratios are unsatisfactorily low in many poor areas. This problem is of long standing, but has apparently been aggravated by the production responsibility system (Chapter 1): in a village an hour's drive from the provincial capital of Gansu, for example, the primary school enrollment ratio in early 1985 was only 50 percent. There is thus an urgent need to improve both the quality of education and access to schools in poor areas (Chapter 8). In addition, parents must be convinced by specific results that education will lead to a socially and economically better life for their children. In this regard, the contrast between Wuxi (Jiangsu) and Dingxi (Gansu) is striking. In Wuxi, parents are determined to keep their children in school because the children need a basic education to get jobs in the rapidly growing rural industrial sector. In Dingxi, by contrast, the rural industrial sector is not expanding, and parents see much less value in their children's education.

In many of the poorest rural areas, population levels are already high in relation to the quality, as well as the quantity, of natural resources and are increasing quite rapidly (high birth rates more than offset relatively high death rates). For these areas, the Government needs to consider the potential role of outmigration in increasing income levels, both for those who move and for those who remain. International experience suggests that migration to urban areas and to other rural areas can play an extremely important role in reducing poverty, providing it is appropriately managed and does not involve movement of too many of those with the best education and entrepreneurial talent (see Box 5.6). Although migration has been more limited in China than in other countries,

The effects of migration on communities of origin appear to have varied greatly not only among countries but also within one country at different periods, and even within one country at the same time. Much depends on the characteristics of the community and the migrants, as well as on the scope, costs, and limits of migration. While it is very difficult to generalize, some important issues emerge from a comparison of experience in different countries.

From 1950 to 1970, the state of West Virginia in the United States experienced both a population decline of 13 percent (as outmigrants more than cancelled out the excess of births over deaths) and a rate of economic and social development much in excess of the national average. Per capita income went up 14 percent faster than in the United States as a whole, school enrollments for youths age sixteen to seventeen rose 53 percent faster, and the percentage of people employed in agriculture dropped by 79 percent—9 percent faster than the national average. It seems most unlikely that the pace of development would have been as great if the migrants had not left.

Experience from some developing countries, however, is not as encouraging about the potential benefits of outmigration for communities of origin. In particular, experience from northeast Brazil and certain regions of Mexico suggests that the younger, more skilled, and better educated population groups tend to migrate, leaving behind an older and less well-trained group. As a result, some communities of origin have lost the very resources that could stimulate their vitality and development, and total (and even per capita) output has declined.

Clearly, the potentially positive effects of outmigration on communities of origin are not realized automatically—and indeed the ultimate impact of outmigration is likely to depend very much on overall development policy. If outmigration is one element in an overall strategy to raise the level of human capital and labor productivity in poor areas, supplying regions may gain greatly. But if appropriate investments are not made in human and other capital in poor areas, they may even suffer through outmigration.

---

people were moved in the 1950s from densely populated rural areas, such as Shandong, to the much less densely populated Northeast. Within Gansu, the possibility of moving people from Dingxi to Hexi, which has better agricultural prospects, is being considered. Poor rural areas are also being encouraged to form construction teams that can work on a temporary basis in other parts of the country, and the recent lifting of restrictions on the use of hired labor may provide further opportunities for temporary migration from poorer to richer agricultural areas.

The Government also needs to assess the costs and benefits of larger programs of permanent migration from poor rural areas to urban areas or to richer rural areas, and to study how such programs might be implemented. For example, as labor market conditions tighten in more rapidly growing rural areas, and more and more people move out of agriculture and into nonagricultural activities, national efficiency and equity could both be enhanced by some permanent rural-rural migration, from slowly growing to more rapidly growing areas.

Even with some temporary or permanent migration of unskilled labor out of poor rural areas and perhaps out of the interior, surplus labor is still likely to be greater, and the economic cost of labor lower, in these areas for many years ahead. Currently, however, large interregional differences in the economic cost of labor are not reflected in state and large collective enterprise wage levels, nor even in commune and brigade enterprise wage levels (see Table 5.12). Indeed, in many cases wage levels may even be

higher in the interior than in coastal provinces as a result of efforts to establish uniform nationwide real wages in the face of regional cost of living differences. Consequently, enterprises in the interior have little incentive to employ more labor and face more difficulties in competing with enterprises on the coast. In the past year there have been indications that wage levels at the commune and brigade enterprise level are increasing more rapidly in richer than in poorer areas (bonuses are much higher in Jiangsu than in Gansu, for instance). But the competitiveness of urban state and large collective enterprises in poor areas also needs to be improved. One possibility would be to make changes in the current policy of national

Table 5.12   Wage Levels, by Province and Type
of Unit, 1982
(yuan per worker per year)

Type of unit	Jiangsu	Hubei	Gansu	National average
State-owned units[a]	748	760	936	836
Collectively owned units in cities and towns[a]	626	657	649	671
Commune and brigade enterprises	488	443	604	493

a. These variations result both from interprovincial differences in the composition of the labor force and from interprovincial differences in the cost of living.
Sources: State Statistical Bureau, Statistical Yearbook of China, 1983; Ministry of Agriculture, Animal Husbandry, and Fisheries, Agricultural Yearbook of China, 1983 (Beijing, 1983).

Map 5.2 Provincial Budget Expenditures and Revenues, 1982

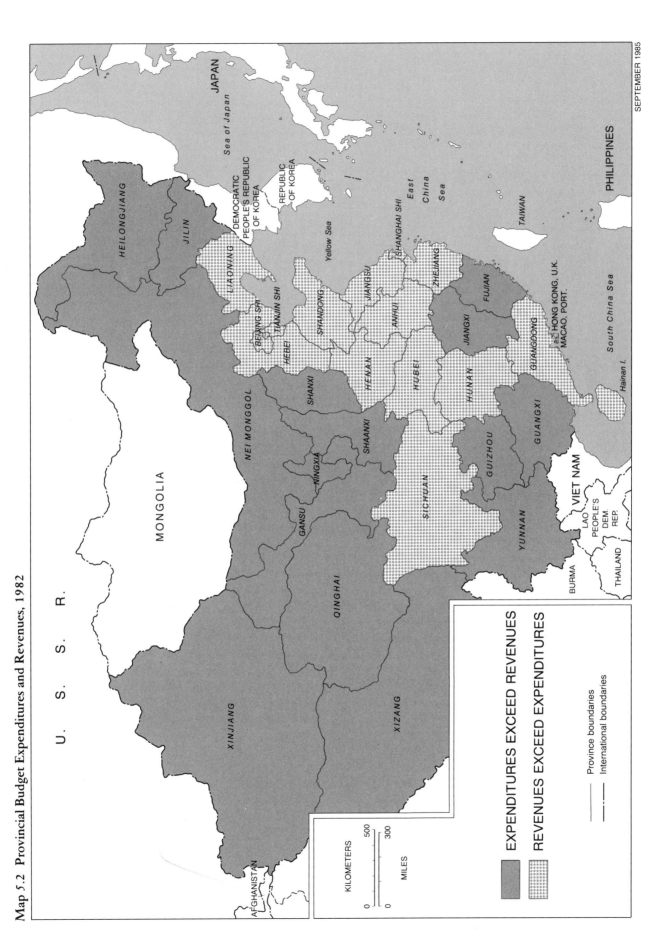

SEPTEMBER 1985

95

uniform real wages for employees of these enterprises. Alternatively, the policy could be maintained, but enterprises in poorer areas could be provided with wage subsidies.

Efficient development of poorer areas and provinces over the long term will also require some major improvements in the skilled manpower and technical resource base of such areas. Currently, for example, enterprises on the coast appear to be better managed and better able to take advantage of new technologies than enterprises in the interior. But this is more a consequence of manpower and technology policies than of location. There is a clear need to increase the availability of skilled labor in the interior—through increases in the number of higher education institutions located there and through increased incentives for skilled labor to work there. It may thus be necessary to modify the wage system so that scarce skilled labor is paid more and surplus unskilled labor is paid less in the interior than on the coast. In addition, poorer areas need to be given better access to technical developments, both domestic and international. This could be accomplished by providing more incentives for enterprises to cooperate with and diffuse technology to enterprises in other provinces and by developing consulting and other agencies that specialize in diffusion of technology (see Chapter 7). More mobility of skilled labor across provincial boundaries would also help spread new ideas and technology.

The development of agriculture and industry and the improvements in transport, education, and other services that are essential to overall economic development and income growth in poor areas and provinces will all require substantial financial resources. Although some resources can and should be raised locally, large contributions from higher levels of government will also be essential. In recent years the revenue-sharing system appears to have been quite effective in transferring fiscal resources to poorer areas and evening out state budget expenditures (see Map 5.2 and Table 5.13). But the pricing system probably continues to transfer resources away from poor areas (for example, because interior provinces such as Gansu get a low price for their minerals). Moreover, fiscal resources are only part of total financial resources: special funds outside the budget and funds channeled through banks and other financial intermediaries are increasing in importance; the Government will need to take steps to ensure an adequate net flow of nonbudgetary finance to poorer localities.

There are thus many measures that the Government could and should introduce that would help poorer localities while at the same time facilitating specialization and national efficiency improvements. But some of them— such as improvements in education, expansion of the transport system, and development of agricultural research and extension—will take many years to implement

Table 5.13 State Budget Revenues and Expenditures in Wuxi and Dingxi Counties, 1983

Measure	Wuxi	Dingxi
Rural per capita income (yuan)	412	108
Revenues per capita (yuan)	157.7	13.9
Expenditures per capita (yuan)	39.4	28.8
Ratio of expenditures to revenues	0.25	2.07

Source: Data provided to the economic mission.

and even longer to have an effect. The effects of increased internal trade and competition, however, are likely to be felt much more quickly, with some activities being stimulated while others are destroyed. Many of the existing activities in poorer areas could never be made economically efficient and ought to be phased out, but others could in the long run be competitive, though requiring some protection in the short and medium term.

To protect local economic activities, as mentioned earlier, poorer (as well as richer) provinces frequently prohibit commercial organizations from purchasing goods produced elsewhere or force them to buy local products that are inferior in quality and price. However, there may be other ways of providing some temporary protection for local activities at less cost in terms of national economic efficiency. Probably the most efficient measure would be a straight subsidy for specific activities that could be phased out according to a prearranged schedule. Another possibility would be to impose taxes on goods brought into a locality and to provide subsidies for goods leaving the locality, both on a temporary basis. If the tax and subsidy rate were set at 10 percent of final product value, for example, all industrial activities in the interior with costs no more than 10 percent higher than elsewhere would still find it financially profitable to expand and even to export to other regions. Implementation of such a system would, however, be administratively quite difficult, requiring all goods moving into and out of a locality to be checked and then taxed or subsidized.

The issue of the appropriate level or levels of government to be responsible for approving and implementing such measures of local protection is also important. If specialization and national efficiency are not to be seriously compromised, only the central government should be vested with the power to approve subsidy or other protectionist measures, because only that level of government can adequately assess potential tradeoffs between national efficiency and local development. Moreover, central government approval should be required for measures to protect industries in specific counties as well as in specific provinces, since both affect national efficiency. Appropriate lower levels of government could still, however, be responsible for implementing protectionist measures.

International Economic Strategy

6

In choosing among alternative international economic strategies, China cannot avoid tension between the wish to guide and protect the character of internal development and the wish to take advantage of the gains possible through contact with the external world. Greater involvement in the international economy could undoubtedly raise efficiency and income in China. But it could also increase economic instability and regional disparities. A central theme of this chapter is that an economic system that responds quickly and flexibly to changes in both domestic and international conditions will be critical in realizing the benefits, as well as in minimizing the costs, of more trade and contacts with the outside world.

The chapter begins by discussing the general issue of external economic contacts and management, in light of expected international and domestic economic trends. It then looks more specifically at China's foreign trade prospects and policies, and at options for use of foreign capital. It concludes with a discussion of the possible regional implications of a more open external orientation.[1]

China in the World Economy

After a long period of inward-directed development that accentuated the normal tendency of all very large countries to export only a small fraction of national product and import a correspondingly small fraction of national supplies, China has begun in recent years to adopt a much more open orientation toward the world economy. This more open orientation is reflected in part in the rapid growth in foreign trade. Exports of goods and nonfactor services now account for 9–10 percent of GDP, a ratio above that of India and similar to large middle- and upper-income countries such as Brazil and the United States (see Figure 6.1). Inflows of direct foreign investment and foreign borrowing are also being actively encouraged, and tourism, purchases of technology, overseas training of Chinese nationals, and other sorts of external contacts are increasing rapidly.

For the future, there are two large and related issues. The first is how much, and in what directions, to further increase these contacts. The second is how best to manage such contacts, and in particular whether to establish a truly "open door" between China's economy and the rest of the world, or whether to maintain the present "airlock" of administrative intermediation and separate price systems, which insulates the domestic economy from the world outside. In both respects, the choice will depend partly on expected developments in the structure and management of the world economy, and partly on internal economic objectives and reforms.

External Environment

The general consensus at present is that over the next two decades the industrial market economies, which still account for about 60 percent of total world income and trade, will grow (in terms of real GDP) at a trend rate around 3.5 percent per year—slower than in the 1950s and 1960s, but somewhat faster than in the 1970s and early 1980s. Inflation in these countries is also expected to persist, but at lower rates (perhaps 5–6 percent per year) than in the 1970s. Difficulties in adjusting the economic structure of those countries in the face of changing economic and technological circumstances—particularly the need to shift many industries to developing countries and to replace them with newer industries and services—will also persist, and hence so will the tendencies toward protectionism in these countries.

Nonetheless, world trade is expected to grow faster than production, implying further increases in economic interdependence. Trade among industrial market countries will still account for a large share (currently over 40 percent) of total world trade, but developing countries will continue to increase their share, with particularly rapid growth of manufactured exports (8–10 percent per

---

1. This chapter draws on Annex 4 and Background Paper 3.

Figure 6.1 Exports of Goods and Nonfactor Services in Selected Countries, 1978–82

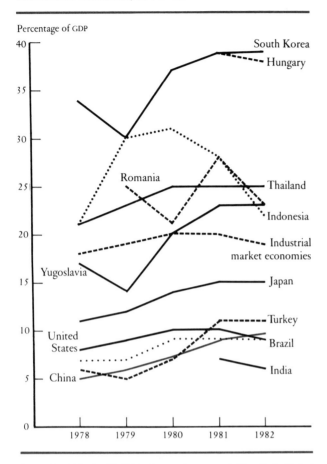

Source: World Bank, *World Development Report 1984* (New York: Oxford University Press, 1984).

year). Partly as a result, production (real GDP) in developing countries is expected to grow at an average trend rate around 5 percent per year—faster than in the industrial market economies, although this will be canceled out by faster population growth, with little narrowing of the large gap in per capita income. Some developing countries, moreover, will grow much more slowly, because of persisting external debt difficulties or fundamental internal problems, while developing countries in East Asia are expected to continue growing more rapidly than the average.

These global projections should be treated with caution. Previous long-term projections have often been wrong: in 1950, most economists envisaged recession in the following two decades, and there was a boom; in 1970, most economists projected the boom to continue, and it did not. Much will depend on reform and improvement of the systems for managing the world economy, but the extent to which countries will be guided by multilateral or regional rules and procedures remains very

uncertain.[2] Moreover, around the projected trends there will undoubtedly continue to be cyclical fluctuations whose timing and amplitude are unpredictable.

Such uncertainties and instabilities in the world economy should not discourage China from expanding its external economic contacts. China will always be a large and diverse economy, with a relatively small foreign trade sector, which greatly reduces the possible damage that unexpectedly unfavorable external developments could inflict, relative to the more predictable costs of isolation. However, international uncertainties should cause China to favor a flexible and responsive system for managing its external economic contacts.

Benefits and Costs of External Economic Contacts

To achieve rapid, sustained growth, China needs to introduce more modern technology (Chapter 7), but also—more importantly—to increase the efficiency with which all resources are used. External economic contacts are desired in China primarily as a source of new technology. But they can also contribute to greater efficiency. Indeed, if they do not, the transfer of technology in the broadest sense will itself be impaired.

Foreign trade can increase efficiency through specialization and realization of economies of scale—concentrating resources in low-cost production for export, and importing goods that can be purchased internationally more cheaply than they could be produced domestically. This source of efficiency gains is less important for China than for smaller countries, because the domestic market is in many sectors large enough for several competing plants of optimal scale (although, as discussed in Chapter 5, small, high-cost, low-quality, protected local enterprises continue to proliferate). China's potential gains from international specialization should not be underestimated, however. Within agriculture, other countries with limited cultivable land (the Netherlands being a prominent, if small, example) have made themselves much better off by exporting high-value, land-intensive products and importing in exchange lower-value products such as grain. Within industry, countries much larger than China (in economic terms) find it advantageous to engage in specialization and exchange on a huge scale.

There are many other ways in which increased external economic contacts could be of benefit to China. Of particular importance are the new products, new technology, new standards and ideas, as well as assistance in mastering them, that can come with a more open exter-

_____

2. At present a multilateral system provides the institutional framework (rules and regulations) for most transactions of industrial market economies and some transactions of developing countries. A separate system (the Council for Mutual Economic Assistance) governs economic relations among East European nonmarket economies.

nal orientation. External trade can also provide some much needed competition for domestic producers and thereby further stimulate improvements in domestic economic efficiency.

Increased external economic contacts could, however, have some serious disadvantages in terms of China's internal economic objectives. One potential disadvantage is that immediate foreign competition could stifle infant industries—activities in which China could produce economically, but only after a period of learning—or industries of strategic importance. Others include the possible transmission into the domestic economy of primary product price volatility, general inflation, and fluctuations in world demand for industrial products; increased regional inequalities; and the possible emergence of undesirably large trade deficits or surpluses and unwanted inflows and outflows of capital.

Managing an Open Economy

To achieve the benefits of increased external economic contacts it may be necessary to endure some of the costs. But the establishment of a sound management system and skillful use of appropriate policy instruments can soften this tradeoff—minimizing the costs while securing many of the benefits. Different countries (Box 6.1) have opted for different management systems and for different sets of instruments, however, and China has to make its own choice. The following paragraphs will focus on ways of indirectly regulating a decentralized external trade and finance system as a possible alternative to the present administratively managed and relatively centralized system. This is not of course China's only option, but it is the option that (in various forms) most other countries have eventually chosen, and the one that seems most consistent with the direction of reform of the system of economic management within China.

International experience strongly suggests that decentralization to the enterprise level can be very important in helping realize the potential benefits of increased external economic contacts. Direct exposure of exporting firms to foreign buyers and competitors has proved elsewhere to be an extremely effective way not just of learning in the abstract about new and better products and processes, but also of learning how (and being put under pressure) to introduce them in practice (see Chapter 7). Similarly, greater freedom for enterprises—including commercial

---

Box 6.1   Contrasting Types of International Economic Strategy

The table below (drawn from Background Paper 3) summarizes five orientations with country examples. The categories are not narrowly defined; each spans a multitude of detailed differences yielding widely varying results for countries with the same general orientation.

Box Table 6.1A   International Economic Strategies

Strategy	Examples
1. Highly open economies with little protection against imports and few restraints on foreign investment.	
a. with little government intervention to limit poverty or guide investment	Chile, 1973–82
b. with considerable domestic intervention for social objectives	Singapore from 1967
2. Relatively open economies, emphasizing export promotion, particularly for industrial products, but with considerable use of protection and government control of the economy	Japan Republic of Korea from 1962 Brazil from 1964 Yugoslavia from 1964 Hungary from 1968
3. Regional groupings with relatively free trade for industrial products inside the region, but with protection of agriculture in each country and moderate protection from outside manufactures	European Economic Communities
4. Highly protected economies without strong orientation toward exports, but with attempts to promote industrialization and some foreign investment	Brazil to 1964 Columbia to 1967 India
5. Relatively closed economies with tight restrictions on trade and investment	Burma from 1962 Sri Lanka to 1976 China to 1977 U.S.S.R.

Source: Background Paper 3.

enterprises—and consumers to choose directly between imported and domestically produced goods could greatly increase competitive pressure on Chinese producers to introduce new, better, and cheaper products. Direct contacts between domestic and foreign enterprises would also facilitate the process of specialization, much of which takes place within finely classified product categories.

Decentralization of decisionmaking would make it impossible for the government to predict or control the actions of individual enterprises or the details of external transactions. To ensure that these actions were in accordance with China's overall economic interests, and broadly consonant with government strategy, internal reforms to make enterprises more sensitive to costs, to customer requirements, and to profits and losses would therefore be essential, as would an appropriate system of prices and other indirect levers. Of particular importance is the relationship between domestic and world prices, which greatly affects the economic rationality of decentralized export and import decisions. In many respects, the more direct the linkage the better, since external prices, mediated through an appropriate exchange rate (discussed later), can provide appropriate signals to Chinese producers and consumers about the value (for exports) or cost (for imports) of particular goods to China in world markets. They provide incentives to produce more (and use less) of items that can be exported at a profit to the economy or that it would be unnecessarily costly to import; and to produce less (and use more) of items that could be exported only at a loss or could be more cheaply imported. Such direct linkages could also contribute in China to a much-needed widening of price differentials between low- and high-quality products, without which enterprise incentives to innovate and improve quality will remain small.

Certain modifications to direct price linkages may also be valuable, however (even when domestic prices and costs are economically rational, as is not at present the case in China—see below). Import tariffs are a widely used and quite efficient means of providing infant or strategic industries with a certain degree of protection from foreign competition—though it is easy to miscalculate the amount of protection provided.[3] Their main disadvantage is that they discourage infant industries from exporting, thus slowing their technological advance, unless complemented with export subsidies or replaced with production subsidies (both of which, however, are liable to provoke retaliation by foreign countries, unless consistent with international rules—which permit indirect tax rebates). This bias against exports has in many countries been compounded, and other serious economic distortions introduced, by indiscriminate use of high tariffs as a substitute for exchange rate adjustments. Taxes on some exports could also be used to discourage Chinese exporters from driving down prices to an unprofitable ex-

tent where the world market for a product is limited—rice and many of China's other traditional agricultural exports being examples (see Chapter 3). It may also be appropriate to prevent short-term fluctuations in the world prices of primary commodities from influencing the domestic economy, by interposing a system of stabilizing taxes (when prices are low) and subsidies (when they are high) on exports and imports—although it is often difficult to distinguish fluctuations from trends.

Many countries, including such economic successes as Japan and South Korea, as well as some conspicuously unsuccessful ones, have supplemented indirect regulation through taxes and subsidies with direct quantitative controls on imports and exports. Explicit upper limits (including outright prohibitions) have frequently been imposed on imports of particular products, while the import of others has been deliberately obstructed by government and state industry procurement practices, product safety laws, complex administrative procedures, and so on. Upper limits have sometimes also been imposed on exports, and in some cases enterprises have been given formal or informal export quotas (a crude but effective method of offsetting the bias noted above).

China should thus not necessarily eschew direct quantitative controls on foreign trade, but should use them sparingly. They are almost always a less economically desirable means of achieving a given result than equivalent taxes and subsidies (for example, because some exports under quotas are needlessly costly—either to produce or to withdraw from domestic consumption—and because some imports under quotas are either inefficiently allocated or resold at a high profit). Yet because they can be more directly and precisely applied, they can sometimes be a useful means of implementing a strategy—such as building up a particular industry or obtaining a foothold in a particular external market—that is itself economically sound, in the sense that it would ultimately be viable without these controls. In most cases elsewhere, however, quantitative controls on trade (as well as taxes and subsidies) have been applied without any such strategy.

A common reason for indiscriminate use of quantitative controls, as of tariffs, has been inappropriate exchange rate policy, and in particular maintaining too high an exchange rate (in terms of dollars per unit of domestic

---

3. Even an apparently small nominal tariff can often provide a high degree of effective protection to domestic producers, mainly because value added and profits are only a fraction of gross output. For example, if the ratio of material inputs to output (at world prices) were 70 percent, a 10 percent tariff on output, with no tariffs on inputs, would provide an effective rate of protection of 33 percent (by increasing value added per unit of output at domestic prices by this proportion).

currency), which encourages excessive imports, by making them cheap, and discourages exports, by making them unprofitable. By contrast, countries that have maintained a competitive or even undervalued exchange rate have been able to intervene much more selectively and purposively and have not suffered from the chronic shortages of foreign exchange that have plagued most developing countries. However, too low an exchange rate can create its own problems, including unwanted trade surpluses, inflationary pressures, and discouraging the production of useful nontraded goods and services.

Especially following the recent unification of foreign exchange arrangements (the internal settlement rate was abolished at the beginning of 1985), and given the current account surpluses of recent years, large reserves, and the ready availability of external capital, China appears extraordinarily well placed to move toward a selectively and mainly indirectly regulated open door system, without the problems (of external insolvency or internal inflation or deflation) that many other countries attempting a similar move have simultaneously had to contend with. To do this immediately, at one stroke, would probably be unwise: most Chinese enterprises are not yet appropriately motivated and price sensitive; even if they were, there are still distortions in domestic prices, taxes, wages, and interest rates that could lead them in economically undesirable directions. But devolution of export and import decisions to enterprises could proceed in parallel with internal economic reforms.

During this transitional period, and subsequently, the suitability of the exchange rate should be carefully monitored and necessary adjustments made. This is partly because there is no way of telling in advance whether the present exchange rate would, following internal reforms and dismantling of the external airlock, generate approximate balance between imports, on the one hand, and exports plus desired capital inflow, on the other. It might turn out to be too high—with an excessive trade deficit—or too low—with too little net capital inflow or a trade surplus. It is also because China's optimal exchange rate would not usually remain constant over time, for two reasons. One is differences between internal and external inflation rates: to the extent that there are differences in these inflation rates, the (nominal) exchange rate would need—other things being equal—to be changed regularly by the difference between the average world inflation rate and the internal inflation rate.

The other reason is fundamental changes in economic circumstances, which may gradually or occasionally alter the real exchange rate needed to attain any desired long-run level of capital inflow (with reasonably full utilization of domestic productive capacity). Possible examples of such changes would be a steady improvement in China's technological level relative to other countries, including developing country competitors in export markets; or a

sudden but enduring change in the price of a major commodity (such as oil) or in the openness of a major market (such as might be caused by war or political realignment). Changes in the desired long-run level of net capital inflow could also require alteration of the exchange rate.

Temporary fluctuations in global economic activity are an additional source of problems, though one that is almost as serious with an administrative airlock as with an open door. They cause export revenues to fluctuate (often requiring offsetting oscillations in reserves or external borrowing), which in turn can cause internal fluctuations in economic activity, especially by affecting production in export-oriented manufacturing. In principle, these fluctuations can be damped by countercyclical changes in domestic fiscal and credit policies (which, however, may aggravate the fluctuations in the foreign trade balance) or in the exchange rate and trade incentive system. In practice in other countries, this has proved hard to do on more than a limited scale, at any rate without sacrificing longer-term objectives. Less stability in the domestic economy may therefore be a concomitant of greater contact through trade with the world economy. This is a much less significant problem for China than for smaller countries, but particular industries and localities could experience quite sharp swings in prosperity.

Foreign Trade Prospects and Policies

Although the size of the foreign sector in relation to national income has increased considerably in most countries over the past two or three decades, it tends to be no greater in large high-income countries than in large low-income countries (in small countries, it is significantly greater at higher income levels). China's trade ratios have recently risen to levels well within the 6–15 percent range of other very large countries. In the macroeconomic projections introduced in Chapter 2, these ratios increase only modestly in the next two decades (see Table 6.1), but the model used to make the projections is not well suited to addressing foreign trade issues,[4] and larger—or smaller—increases might turn out to be possible or desirable.

China's present composition of foreign trade (see Figure 6.2) is in many respects quite similar to those of other low-income economies, specializing in primary product and textile exports to industrial countries and in such

---

4. In primary sectors, as explained in Chapter 3 (agriculture) and Annex 3 (energy), as well as in Annex 4, the trade balance is just a residual—indicative of tendencies and problems to be solved, rather than of likely actual outcomes. In other sectors, there are no explicit efficiency-seeking or learning mechanisms, and the results are governed largely by assumptions about sectoral self-sufficiency, openness and export composition.

Table 6.1 Total Foreign Trade Ratios, Alternative Projections, 1981–2000
(percentage of GDP)

Measure of trade	1981	2000 Quadruple	2000 Moderate	2000 Balance
Exports	8.4	11.0	10.6	10.3
Imports	8.1	11.4	10.9	10.7
Foreign trade deficit	−0.3	0.4	0.3	0.4

Source: World Bank projections; Annex 4.

services as tourism, which are exchanged for machinery and transport equipment and other manufactured goods and services. However, China, like India, has a high percentage of exports of manufactured goods compared with other low-income economies and is highly self-sufficient in machinery. China is also not an oil-importing country.

In the following paragraphs, some future possibilities and options for the growth and composition of China's foreign trade are reviewed, together with related policy measures and reforms. The quantitative projections for specific products and groups of products that are mentioned should be regarded as subject to a wide margin of error. Of much greater importance will be the capacity of China's system of economic management to generate an efficient overall level and pattern of trade in the face of changing internal and external circumstances.

Primary Products

China is currently a net exporter of primary products (a trade surplus on energy more than offsets a trade deficit on other primary products). Whether China should remain a net primary products exporter will depend to a large extent on domestic cost and international price developments. Primary product prices on average, and in real terms, have been falling for at least the past fifty years, since developments in production technology have more than kept pace with the growth in demand; most recent studies of the world economy expect this trend to continue. The markets for primary products will, however, continue to be characterized by great price variability, instability, and uncertainty.

In the case of energy, for example, most studies of the world economy now predict that the resource and technological capacity either exists, or is likely to be developed, to meet expected growth in world demand. Incremental advances in technology could soon make exploitation of nontraditional oil and gas resources (such as tar sands, bituminous shales, and frozen natural gas) economical, thereby extending use of oil and gas as major energy resources well into the next century. World coal reserves are much greater than oil and gas reserves, and coal usage is likely to increase as oil and gas usage declines. Use of nuclear energy will also increase, and re-

search on new forms of energy has been initiated. (This does not mean, however, that energy prices will necessarily remain stable or fall over the next two decades). In view of the relatively low cost of exploiting its huge coal reserves, China is likely to find it economically advantageous to remain basically self-sufficient in coal and petroleum, though some two-way trade in crude oil and petroleum products may be attractive (see Chapter 4).

In the case of agricultural raw materials, better and wider application of existing technology and scientific discoveries in the area of biotechnology are expected to result both in greatly increased world production capacity and in continued falls in the real prices of most agricultural products. In the medium term, China's comparative

Figure 6.2 Trade in Goods and Nonfactor Services, 1978–83

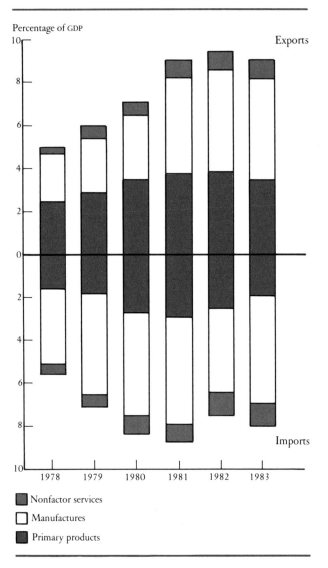

Source: Bank of China, International Monetary Fund, and World Bank estimates.

advantage may still lie in expanding exports of some agricultural products such as rice (even if this contributes to a fall in world prices), in importing other agricultural products including coarse grains, and in achieving an overall surplus on agricultural trade (see Chapter 3). But China is not well endowed with agricultural resources. Thus in the longer term, as domestic costs increase and the real prices of agricultural products on world markets continue to fall, China's comparative advantage may lie in becoming a net importer of agricultural products.

In an effort to make primary products trade more efficient and responsive to international as well as domestic economic developments, the Government has recently initiated a further stage of management decentralization. Initially, management of primary products trade was decentralized from the Ministry of Foreign Economic Relations and Trade (MOFERT) to national foreign trade corporations. Some of these corporations have proved to be very efficient. The Chinese national food trading agency, CEROIL, for example, is among the most astute grain buying and selling operators in the world and has saved China substantial amounts of foreign exchange. However, other national trading corporations in China are much less efficient. The Government has therefore decided to decentralize trade in many primary products to local and often more specialized corporations.

This will make it all the more necessary to develop an incentives system that provides appropriate signals to producers and consumers, as well as importers and exporters, as to the level and pattern of production and consumption and hence the level and pattern of primary products trade. Internal pricing policies (see the discussion of agriculture and energy in Chapters 3 and 4) will be especially important. The Government will also need to closely monitor current and prospective world prices for key primary products and provide market information to prospective buyers and sellers. In addition, it will need to consider carefully the implications of alternative levels and patterns of primary products trade for investments in infrastructure and other support services, many of which may be both large and product-specific.

Manufactures

In both large and small countries, rising per capita incomes are usually associated with a rising share of manufactures in total exports (see Table 6.2). Moreover, trade in manufactures has usually been more effective than primary products trade in fostering diversification of production, in promoting new technology and ideas, and in stimulating improved efficiency in the domestic economy. In recent years, China has been able to rapidly expand exports of textiles and other manufactures despite the slow growth of the world economy, and trade surpluses on these types of manufactures have partially offset trade deficits on machinery and equipment. But China is

Table 6.2 Share of Manufactures in Total Merchandise Exports, 1960 and 1981
(percent)

Country of origin	All manufactures		Machinery and transport equipment	
	1960	1981	1960	1981
United States	63	70	35	44
Germany, Fed. Rep.	87	86	44	45
France	73	73	25	34
Japan	79	97	23	57
Yugoslavia	37	79	15	29
Uruguay	29	30	(.)	2
Hungary	66	65	38	31
Brazil	3	41	(.)	18
Chile	4	10	0	2
South Korea	14	90	(:)	22
Thailand	2	27	0	5
Sri Lanka	(.)	21	0	(.)
China	. .	53	. .	5
India	45	59	1	8
Burma	1	. .	0	. .

Source: World Bank, *World Development Report 1984* (New York: Oxford University Press, 1984), pp. 236–37.

already beginning to be affected by market constraints for certain types of manufactured exports, and the rapid pace of change in both domestic and international industry makes it difficult to forecast future trading patterns.

One major issue for China is how open the manufacturing sector should become in terms of the ratios of exports and imports to output and demand. The higher these ratios, the more opportunities there will be for domestic enterprises to participate in and benefit from involvement in foreign trade. But higher ratios may also increase the potential for world market uncertainties to affect the domestic economy. In the macroeconomic projections—whose limitations in respect of foreign trade were noted earlier —it is assumed that the Government aims for higher sectoral export and import shares in BALANCE than in QUADRUPLE and MODERATE (see Table 6.3).[5] In QUADRUPLE, however, even maintaining a ratio of manufactured imports to domestic manufacturing demand of 6 percent requires a significant increase in the ratio of manufactured exports to domestic production in order to offset the projected net deficit on primary products trade (see Tables 6.4 and 6.5). In MODERATE, in contrast, continued surpluses on primary products trade would reduce the required increase in the ratio of manufactured exports to output. And in BALANCE, also with a

5. The higher target shares are in metallurgy, chemicals, machinery, and other manufacturing; target export and import shares in other sectors remain unchanged.

103

continuing primary products surplus, the objective of a higher ratio of manufactured imports to domestic demand could be satisfied with the same ratio of manufactured exports to output as in QUADRUPLE. The growth rates of manufactured exports in all three projections are quite substantial, ranging from 7.3 percent per year in MODERATE to 10.1 percent in QUADRUPLE, but comparable with the World Bank's projections of worldwide developing country growth in manufactured exports of 7.5–9.7 percent per year for 1985–95.[6]

Whatever the overall growth rate of manufactured exports, it seems that China will have to change the compo-sition of its manufactured exports very significantly over the next two decades. The textiles and clothing sector, for example, has provided many countries with the first step on the ladder to export-oriented industrialization and has been a key element in China's recent rapid growth of manufactured exports.[7] As a result, China now accounts for 5 percent of world trade in textiles and clothing and for a much larger share of world trade in certain (generally lower-quality) textile products. Although it is difficult to predict future technological developments, China's cotton production potential (see Annex 2) and its relatively low economic cost of labor are likely to give it a clear comparative advantage in textile and clothing exports for many years to come. China could therefore take over a much larger share of the world market, if allowed to do so. However, expansion of Chinese textile exports is already being curtailed by voluntary export restraint agreements with the United States and member countries of the European Economic Community and by the provisions of the Multifibre Arrangement. There is still considerable scope for boosting textile and clothing export earnings by upgrading product quality, and China should also continue to press in international forums for relaxation of the restraints on trade. But China's textile and clothing exports will probably grow by no more than 6 percent per year (in real terms), and their share in total manufactured exports will decline.

To offset the likely slow growth in textile exports, China should more rapidly expand exports of other manufactures, including machinery and metal products,

Table 6.3 Sectoral Foreign Trade Ratios, Alternative Projections, 1981–2000

Measure		2000		
of trade	1981	Quadruple	Moderate	Balance
Exports (percentage of gross output)				
Primary products	2.6	2.3	3.4	3.3
Manufactures	6.0	8.3	6.5	8.3
Machinery	3.8	10.7	8.2	8.9
Textiles[a]	10.1	8.3	6.5	8.2
Other	4.7	6.4	5.2	7.8
Imports (percentage of domestic demand)				
Primary products	2.2	3.9	3.5	3.0
Manufactures	6.7	6.0	6.1	8.0
Machinery	8.3	8.0	8.0	12.0
Textiles[a]	6.2	2.0	2.0	2.0
Other	5.9	6.4	6.8	7.9

Note: Data are calculated at constant (1981) domestic prices.
a. In this and subsequent tables, textiles includes clothing.
Source: World Bank projections; Annex 4.

6. See World Bank, *World Development Report 1984* (New York: Oxford University Press, 1984), p 35.

7. Includes Standard International Trade Classification categories 65 and 84.

Table 6.4 Average Annual Growth of Foreign Trade, Alternative Projections, 1981–2000
(percent)

	Quadruple		Moderate		Balance	
Measure of trade	Constant yuan	Current dollars	Constant yuan	Current dollars	Constant yuan	Current dollars
Exports						
Primary products	5.3	9.1	6.4	11.3	7.1	11.4
Manufactures	10.1	16.4	7.3	13.6	8.8	15.2
Machinery	15.2	21.6	12.1	18.4	12.8	19.1
Textiles	6.1	12.0	3.4	9.1	4.9	10.8
Other	9.8	16.3	7.4	13.8	9.6	16.3
Imports						
Primary products	9.3	15.2	7.4	14.4	7.4	14.2
Manufactures	7.3	14.4	6.2	12.6	7.9	14.2
Machinery	8.4	14.5	7.1	13.1	9.9	16.0
Textiles	0.8	6.5	−0.3	5.2	−0.2	5.4
Other	8.5	16.9	7.6	14.6	8.3	15.2

Source: World Bank projections; Annex 4.

Table 6.5 Structure of Foreign Trade, Alternative Projections, 1981–2000

Measure of trade	1981	2000 Quadruple	2000 Moderate	2000 Balance
Exports				
Primary products	44.6	19.1	35.4	29.8
Manufactures	55.4	80.9	64.6	70.2
Machinery	10.5	35.0	26.9	25.0
Textiles	25.0	17.5	13.7	15.1
Other	19.9	28.4	24.0	30.1
Imports				
Primary products	24.4	38.3	32.6	26.3
Manufactures	75.6	70.3	74.6	81.7
Machinery	29.4	31.4	32.0	42.7
Textiles	19.2	5.2	5.3	4.5
Other	27.0	33.7	37.3	34.5

Note: Data are percentages of total merchandise exports in current dollars.
Source: World Bank projections; Annex 4.

which currently account for less than 20 percent of manufactured exports and which in many countries have played a key role in overall export growth. Developing countries currently absorb 85 percent of China's machinery exports (see Figure 6.3) and will probably remain an important market. Substantial increases in machinery exports to industrial countries should also be possible. This, however, would involve manufacture of parts and components, and in some cases assembly of imported components, as much as sales of complete equipment wholly manufactured in China. An extensive and flexible network of subcontracting and other cooperative agreements between Chinese and foreign enterprises would therefore be vital, but would be hard to establish through China's present airlock of administrative intermediation. (East European exporters of machinery and equipment, subject to a similar airlock, have done much less well than the newly industrializing countries of Asia and Latin America—Background Paper 7.)

Both within the machinery category, and in the wide and promising range of other nontextile manufactured exports, sales of high-value consumer goods to industrial and upper-middle-income countries constitute an especially attractive market. But competition from other developing countries will be intense, and improvements in the quality of Chinese products essential. Experience elsewhere suggests that quality improvements could be assisted by allowing Chinese exporters to import freely if materials, components, and equipment available from domestic suppliers are not up to international standards. Chinese enterprises will also need to develop the capacity to meet individual buyers' requirements and to ship products that are packaged and labeled, ready for sale.

Rapid growth in manufactured exports will make possible rapid growth of manufactured imports, whose de-

Figure 6.3 Direction of External Trade, 1983

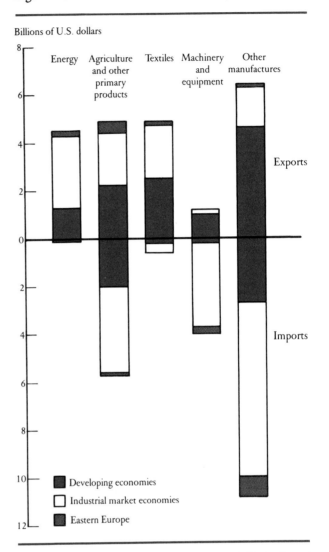

Source: Ministry of Foreign Economic Relations and Trade; General Administration of Customs.

tailed composition should change continuously as China learns to produce particular goods domestically, while constantly adding new imports to provide the basis for future learning. In recent years, China has placed most emphasis on intermediate and capital goods imports to ease energy and other domestic supply constraints, to stimulate technological development and improve efficiency in domestic industries. In metallurgy, for example, domestic steel supplies have been increasingly supplemented by imports, which in 1983 accounted for 24 percent of steel product demand. Much the same has happened in chemicals, and machinery imports have resumed their upward trend. Rapid expansion of such intermediate and capital goods imports is likely to continue, and quite large deficits in energy-intensive metallurgy and chemicals subsectors may persist.

China's strategy with regard to consumer goods imports still appears to be influenced more by considerations of self-sufficiency than of economic efficiency and technological progress. Despite recent relaxation in some sectors where demand has far outstripped production capacity, imports of most consumer goods remain strictly controlled. This helps protect domestic consumer goods industries. It also has the possible social objective of limiting the availability of expensive goods that only a few consumers can afford. However, international experience strongly suggests that a relatively closed orientation toward consumer goods imports is likely to result in the development of a highly inefficient domestic consumer goods industry, and that the competition and new technology that come with a more open import orientation may be just as important in consumer goods as in other industrial sectors.

If China is to expand its trade in manufactures rapidly and efficiently and reap the full benefits from such trade, domestic firms will need to be allowed more freedom to choose between domestic and foreign suppliers and more direct contacts with foreign markets and firms. A much wider and more competitive range of foreign trade enterprises—probably including collective and individual enterprises—will also be needed to provide specialized commercial and other services. These changes will be important not only in enabling Chinese enterprises to compete effectively in external markets but also in ensuring that there is a real transfer of technology and other benefits to China. In recent years the Government has tried to grant enterprises greater autonomy and has encouraged foreign trade corporations to act more as agents than as principals in external transactions. But the pattern of exports and imports still appears to be determined more by administrative decisions at the industrial bureau or foreign trade corporation level than by incentives at the level of the individual enterprise, and direct contacts between Chinese and foreign enterprises remain quite limited.

It is important to reiterate that effective decentralization of manufactured goods trade to the enterprise level must be accompanied by and not precede the overall process of enterprise reform. At present many enterprises in China still appear to care relatively little about the quality and cost of inputs and about whether or not they are able to sell their output. In such circumstances the development of direct contacts between local and foreign firms could easily result in inappropriate trade patterns and even in serious trade and balance of payments difficulties for China.

As the management of manufactured goods trade begins to be decentralized to autonomous and price sensitive enterprises, the Government will need to consider further the use of price, tax, exchange rate, and other regulatory levers. One major issue concerns China's present practice of setting prices for manufactured goods relatively high, as a means of generating large enterprise profits and hence large profit tax and remittance revenues for the budget. These high domestic prices reduce the incentive for Chinese enterprises to export. They could be offset by subsidies for manufactured exports, but such subsidies may result in charges of "dumping" by other countries and may make it more difficult for China to participate fully in such multilateral trading arrangements as the General Agreement on Tariffs and Trade. This provides an additional reason for changes in China's price and fiscal systems. Among other things, movement away from profit taxes and remittances and toward indirect taxes (including a value added tax—see Chapter 9) would make it easier to address dumping charges, because rebates of indirect taxes are generally more acceptable under international rules than export subsidies.

Services

In recent years, world trade in services has been increasing rapidly and in some—mostly industrial—countries, service exports are now substantial relative to merchandise exports and GDP. They include activities ranging from transport and insurance services, which are often closely related to merchandise trade, to banking and financial services, which are closely related to investment and borrowing policies.[8] But changes in the structure of the world economy (including the increased importance of the information and service sectors) are expected to result in continued rapid growth of trade in services.

At present China's main service receipts are transport and tourism. Chinese enterprises also have overseas construction contracts, especially for projects in the Middle East, and payments for labor services have increased sharply. In South Korea this type of service export has been very important for the overall growth of exports, leading to other types of service export, such as licensing and technical agreements and consulting services, and also helping stimulate exports of machinery and equipment, many of which are directly related to construction and other contracts.

China could benefit from substantial further increases in imports of technical information and other services from industrial countries. In industries in which China already has substantial technological capability, licensing or purchase of technological assistance could help fill the gaps in local knowledge and capabilities and could up-

8. The principal services involved in international trade are: banking and financing services; insurance; freight transport and port handling; passenger transportation and tourism; architecture, construction and engineering, repairs and maintenance; films, communications, data processing, printing, professional services (technical, health, education, legal, accounting); and other services (franchising, leasing).

grade technology quickly. China has increased its use of licenses and other disembodied technology sharply in the last few years, but still spends relatively little on these items. Licensing often covers only older technology and may carry restrictions on use, but it could help overcome critical shortcomings in domestic capability (for example, components for machine tools). Advanced countries also find licensing an effective means of upgrading technology: the United States and Japan, for example, conduct a large mutual trade in licenses.

External Balance and Finance

Many developing countries, as well as many industrial countries at earlier stages of development, have used foreign trade deficits and net capital inflows as a means of maintaining a higher long-run rate of investment than could be sustained using domestic savings alone.[9] But such a strategy is economically beneficial only if the productivity of the additional investment, at the macroeconomic as well as the project level, exceeds the cost of foreign capital. China's current account surpluses of the early 1980s (see Figure 6.4) may therefore have been an appropriate economic response to a situation in which international interest rates were very high in real terms and the capacity of the domestic economy to absorb imports efficiently was limited by the lack of sound feasibility studies for major investment projects.

The Government's longer-term policy, however, is to incur moderate foreign trade deficits, with increased but cautious reliance on external finance. Accordingly, in the macroeconomic projections it has been assumed that foreign borrowing adjusts gradually upward toward a ceiling imposed by a 75 percent ratio of debt to exports.[10] However, the ceiling is not reached within the projected period (see Table 6.6). In all three projections, trade and current account surpluses change to trade and current account deficits, but the deficits in relation to GDP remain at or below 1 percent and fall to 0.7–0.8 percent by 2000. The projected levels of debt in 2000 appear large at current prices, but at 1981 prices they would be only one-third as large (that is, $56 billion in QUADRUPLE, $46 billion in MODERATE, and $54 billion in BALANCE).

---

9. In the nineteenth century net capital inflows to the United States hovered around 1 percent of GNP and reached 7–8 percent of GNP in Canada, Australia, and some other now developed countries. *World Development Report 1985* surveys the recent as well as historical experience of many countries in using external finance. It also analyzes current problems and future prospects and options in this area.

10. If an average interest rate of 10 percent per year and an average repayment period of ten years is assumed, this corresponds approximately to a 15 percent debt service ratio.

Figure 6.4 External Balance, 1978–84

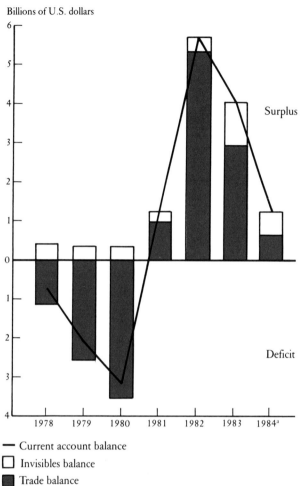

a. Preliminary estimate.
Source: Bank of China, International Monetary Fund, and World Bank estimates.

Table 6.6 Foreign Trade Balance and Debt, Alternative Projections, 1981–2000
(billions of dollars)

Measure	1981	2000 Quadruple	Moderate	Balance
Exports f.o.b.	22.5	279.0	216.6	261.8
Imports c.i.f.	21.7	289.6	223.0	271.5
Trade balance	+0.8	−10.6	−6.4	−9.7
Net interest	−0.1	−11.1	−9.2	−10.7
Net transfers and other services	0.6	1.6	1.6	1.6
Current account balance	+1.2	−20.1	−14.0	−18.9
Net debt [a]	0.9	158.3	128.4	151.9

Note: Data are at current prices, assuming international inflation at an average of 5.6 percent per year.
a. Debt outstanding and disbursed, less foreign exchange reserves.
Source: World Bank projections; Annex 4.

The appropriate future level of China's foreign trade deficit and net capital inflow will depend in part on the availability and cost of foreign capital. In the 1960s and 1970s, capital flows to developing countries at moderate real interest rates increased significantly and in many countries played an important role in facilitating structural adjustment and in accelerating economic growth. Since 1981, however, the supply of foreign finance has declined, real interest rates have increased greatly,[11] and the dollar (in which most developing country debt is denominated) has appreciated significantly against other currencies, causing serious debt servicing problems for many countries. These circumstances make it difficult to predict the future supply and cost of foreign capital. But a significant reduction in current high real interest rates is likely only if industrial countries can reduce their presently large budget deficits.

The appropriate size of China's foreign trade deficit and net capital inflows will also be affected by the ongoing process of economic reform aimed at improving the efficiency of investment. It would not be in China's economic interests to borrow at real interest rates of 5 percent to undertake a project whose economic rate of return was only 2 percent—indeed this would actually make China worse off. And there are many examples of countries (in Eastern Europe, for example) that were once, like China today, very cautious in their foreign borrowing programs, but then moved too quickly to more active use of foreign capital and now face balance of payments and debt service problems. Careful control and monitoring of China's increased use of external finance will thus be necessary. Of particular importance are the regulations governing which entities may engage in foreign borrowing. In the long run, increasing the access of enterprises to foreign capital will probably be in China's national economic interests, but it is essential that such decentralization of foreign borrowing not precede effective reform of enterprise management. Whatever the rules of access, it is also essential that the central government develop a debt information and monitoring system for provinces and enterprises.

There are, of course, many different types of capital flow—including direct foreign investment, official lending, and commercial bank lending—each with particular advantages and disadvantages. As a result, some situations may justify net inflows of certain types of capital and net outflows of others. Indeed, China has been in just such a situation in recent years, when current account surpluses allowed early repayment of commercial bank debt but the Government still encouraged net inflows of foreign investment and official loans.

Among the potential benefits of direct foreign investment to China are increased access to export markets and to the very latest technology in some fields. However, the latest product or process design may not be the most

appropriate for China, and foreign investors may operate as an enclave within the domestic economy rather than as an integral part of it. Judicious policy intervention is thus needed to induce foreign investors to link their activities to those of local enterprises. For example, many countries have used domestic content legislation to force automobile companies to make greater use of domestic suppliers, and component manufacturers have thereby been assisted in upgrading product quality and increasing efficiency. Direct foreign investment can also aggravate some of the problems caused by domestic price distortions, including those associated with inappropriately high protective tariffs or quotas: these can allow foreign as well as domestic enterprises to earn high profits from activities that are economically inefficient (sometimes even with negative value added at world prices, or a net loss of foreign exchange).

Although the appropriate solution clearly lies in internal price reform rather than restriction of foreign investment, official fear of problems of this kind seems to have impeded direct foreign investment in China. In addition, and despite recent improvements, the number of administrative hurdles that prospective foreign investors must surmount is unnecessarily large. In this context, the recent widening of the officially permitted scope for foreign investment—now covering far more geographical areas, as well as a broader range of consumer goods and services—seems wise. This is because, in China's circumstances, foreign investment is desirable not only for the foreign exchange and advanced technology that it may bring, but also for the demonstration effect of modern management techniques. The example of, and competition from, well-run foreign companies can help domestic firms to identify weak links in management, product design, material supply, and quality of service and can spur them to make changes they might otherwise never consider. The greater the dispersion of foreign firms among sectors and localities, and the more they are integrated into the domestic economy, the larger these demonstration effects are likely to be.

In recent years, China has increased its use of concessional and nonconcessional lending from official sources (mainly Japan and the World Bank Group), but the costs and benefits of such lending also need careful evaluation. On the positive side, official flows are usually accompanied by technical and institutional assistance and sometimes by policy assistance. In addition, official flows are usually of longer maturity than commercial borrowing and are often at lower interest rates. However, official lending can also have both direct and indirect costs; in-

---

11. The average real London interbank offered rate, or LIBOR (deflated by the U.S. GNP deflator) was 5.6 percent during 1979–83, compared with 0.34 percent during 1974–78.

deed, even concessionary aid could prove costly to China if tied to a particular technology or project that was not economically efficient.

In addition to direct foreign investment and official lending, China would probably have to use commercial bank lending and other types of capital inflow to finance part of the current account deficits projected in Table 6.6. During the 1970s, commercial banks played a critical role in linking developing countries (particularly middle-income developing countries) with international capital markets, by providing syndicated loans and short-term trade finance, as well as medium-term export credits guaranteed by governments. They also assisted many developing countries to manage reserves and other commercial activities. But since 1981, voluntary lending by commercial banks has declined sharply, and the future availability of commercial bank finance to developing countries remains very uncertain. Other sources of external finance could be considered, including the international bond markets, which traditionally offer long-term money at fixed rates of interest, but which are very averse to risk and require a consistently high level of creditworthiness.

Regional Issues

China's more open orientation of recent years has benefited coastal areas more than the interior. Procurement of goods for export has been increasing much more rapidly in coastal provinces like Jiangsu than in interior provinces like Gansu, and in 1982 the level of export procurement in relation to net material product reached 12 percent on the coast (and as much as 31 percent in Shanghai) compared with only 4 percent in the interior. Provincial differences in the degree of openness are partly a result of the transport advantages enjoyed by the coast, and so long as most external trade continues to be waterborne the coast will retain these advantages. Nonetheless, various domestic and external policy measures could help spread the potential benefits of an open external orientation to more regions and provinces.

Many of the measures needed to stimulate development in poorer regions (Chapter 5) would also enable those regions to gain more from international trade. For example, the introduction of a system of economic charges for land use could affect the choice between locating a land-intensive export activity (or foreign investment) in a large coastal city and locating it in a less densely populated or interior region. Increases in unskilled wage differentials to better reflect interregional variations in the economic cost of labor could also facilitate the development of labor-intensive export activities

in poorer provinces and regions. In addition, improvements in the transport system, particularly roads, will allow interior provinces to participate more in external trade.

Changes in external sector management, and particularly in the extent of regional autonomy, could also facilitate greater involvement by interior provinces in external economic activities. At present the extent to which external sector management has been decentralized varies widely among regions. It is greatest in the four special economic zones established in 1980 (Shenzen, Shantou, Zhuhai, and Xiamen) and in the fourteen coastal cities and surrounding regions (including the four provinces adjacent to Shanghai) that were recently given many of the same privileges. But some coastal provinces, such as Guangdong and Fujian, have more autonomy than others, and the more remote interior provinces, such as Gansu, have the least autonomy. The degree of autonomy varies not only in regard to trade in particular product lines, but also to acceptance of foreign investment and signing of cooperative arrangements and to control of foreign exchange.

International (as well as recent Chinese) experience confirms that the establishment of special zones that are less subject to tariffs and other import restrictions, that have good infrastructure and service facilities, and that specialize in production for export can be a useful initial step in developing a more open external orientation for the whole economy. However, because these zones are enclaves within the domestic economy, the spread of new technology and ideas tends to be limited. Policies and practices initially applicable only to special zones and to export activities, where these prove to be beneficial to national interests, need subsequently to spread to other parts of the country and to other sorts of economic activities, with a decline in the significance of special zones.

Long isolation and distorted domestic prices have probably increased the potential costs (as well as benefits) to China of a more open orientation. Initiating a more open orientation on an experimental basis and in limited areas has therefore been appropriate. Equally, however, the recent major expansion of the geographical scope of these open areas seems an appropriate response to their initial success (despite some unresolved problems), and further expansion to include the interior provinces should be considered. But to make this decentralization of external economic management a success, in coastal and interior provinces alike, it must be closely matched by internal reforms to motivate and guide enterprises to respond rationally to the challenges of a more open economy.

7 *Managing Industrial Technology*

China's long-term economic objectives can be attained only by combining extensive growth, which means following the past pattern of expansion through duplication of existing production, with intensive growth, which involves reducing costs, increasing productivity, and introducing new and better products. The need to use inputs more efficiently is obvious. Improved products are equally important. Obsolete or low-quality producer goods raise costs and reduce quality in the industries that use them. Inferior products also limit expansion of exports and lower living standards.

This chapter, which focuses on industry (though much of it applies equally to other nonagricultural sectors), first discusses the role of technology in intensive growth. It then deals with strategic planning for technological advance, means of acquiring technology from abroad, and domestic research and development (R&D). The discussion turns next to ways of stimulating the application and diffusion of innovations, and finally to policy on obsolete products and processes. A recurring theme is that the key to intensive growth in China lies not only in better access to modern technology, but also in systemic reforms that would generate constant and spontaneous pressure on enterprises to make sound investment decisions, to cut costs, and to introduce new and improved products.[1]

Technology in Perspective

China has made tremendous strides in industry since 1949. With one of the highest sustained industrial growth rates in the world (8.5 percent per year in 1957–82), a full range of production has been built up in nearly every industrial sector. This has been accomplished despite prolonged international isolation, by mastering available technology, improving it, and modifying it to suit local conditions. As a result, however, and despite some notable technological successes, industrial technology in China has generally lagged behind that of industrialized and newly industrializing countries. One Chinese study estimates that only 20 percent of China's present industrial technology is of 1960s and 1970s vintage, another 20–25 percent is backward but can still serve present needs, and the remaining 55–60 percent should be replaced.

Technological self-reliance has been sought not just at the national level, but also by individual ministries, provinces, localities, and even enterprises (many of which, for example, manufacture their own machinery and design their own products). This has been extremely wasteful of both physical capital and human resources. Enterprise machine shops are usually equipped with inefficient general-purpose machine tools and are chronically underutilized. Equally serious, the talent of China's scarce technical personnel is wasted through duplication of effort.

Productivity performance has been disappointing. In most rapidly developing countries, a considerable proportion of output growth is due to growth of total factor productivity (TFP), that is, to output growing faster than the total of all inputs.[2] But in China's state-owned industry, TFP apparently increased in 1952–57, then stagnated or declined in 1957–82 (see Table 7.1). Increases in capital per worker raised labor productivity (output per worker), but this was more than offset by a decline in capital productivity.

Product innovation and quality improvement have also been slow in China. Many product designs have remained unchanged since their introduction decades ago. For example, the ubiquitous Liberation truck is based on a Soviet model, which in turn was based on a U.S. model from the 1930s; Chinese ball bearings last only one-fifth to one-half as long as the best of foreign ones; and 40

---

1. Background Papers 5–8 contain a fuller treatment, with more references to other work, of the issues discussed in this chapter, including the experiences of other developing countries, the Soviet Union, and Eastern Europe, and technological development in electronics.

2. See Chapter 1 and Annex 5.

Table 7.1 Index of Total Factor Productivity in State-Owned Industry, 1952–82

Measure	1952	1957	1978	1982
1. Net output	37.6	100	673.3	798.4
2. Labor input	68.2	100	406.6	468.3
3. Capital input	44.3	100	948.7	1,299.8
4. Total factor inputs (40% labor, 60% capital)	53.9	100	751.8	967.2
5. Total factor inputs (60% labor, 40% capital)	58.6	100	623.5	800.9
6. Labor productivity (1 ÷ 2)	55.1	100	165.6	170.5
7. Capital productivity (1 ÷ 3)	84.9	100	71.0	61.4
8. Total factor productivity (1 ÷ 4)	69.8	100	89.6	82.5
9. Total factor productivity (1 ÷ 5)	64.2	100	108.0	99.7

Note: Net output in constant prices was estimated by multiplying the ratio of net to gross output in current prices of all industry by the index of gross output at comparable prices of state-owned industry. Capital is the original value of fixed assets. Lines 4 and 5 present alternative estimates of total inputs, assuming different weights, and lines 8 and 9 present correspondingly different estimates of total factor productivity.

Source: State Statistical Bureau, *Statistical Yearbook of China, 1983* (Hong Kong: Economic Information and Agency), pp. 7, 13, 22, 126, 216.

Figure 7.1 Output and Cost of Production of the JA 1-1 Sewing Machine, by Enterprise, 1980

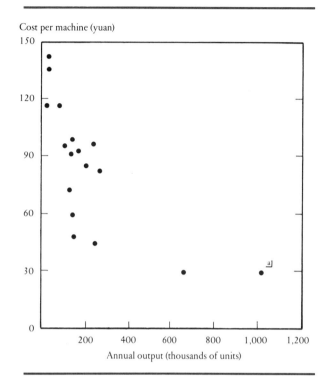

a. Includes production of both JA-1 and JA 2-1 models.
Source: State Economic Commission, Investigation and Research Office, "An Analysis of the Economic Efficiency of the Sewing Machine Industry in China," *Jingji Diaocha* (Economic investigations), no. 1 (October 1983), p. 25.

percent of Chinese nitrogen fertilizer is still low-quality and unstable ammonium bicarbonate.

It is widely believed in China that the way to solve these problems of stagnant productivity, high costs, and low product quality is to introduce modern technology. But in formulating policy, it is essential (a) to recognize that in many cases new technology is neither necessary nor sufficient to improve productivity and product quality, and (b) to have a clear understanding of how technological improvement takes place and how it contributes to economic progress.

Other Determinants of Efficiency and Quality

Productivity and product quality in Chinese industry could often be dramatically improved without new technology, whose introduction may indeed divert attention from more elementary problems. A case in point is the Tianjin Elevator Company's joint venture with the Otis Elevator Company of the United States,[3] where quality problems have prevented elevators from being exported. Some officials of the Tianjin company believe that these problems would be solved by replacing electromechanical controls with sophisticated microprocessors. The immediate problem, however, lies more in work practices and the quality of material supplies. Workers now hold metal pieces for drilling rather than using clamps, measure pieces manually rather than mechanically, and move partially assembled pieces by dragging them rather than using a conveyor. The result is that holes do not line up and parts are damaged or do not fit together. Moreover, castings supplied by other factories are of low quality, thus

causing waste and excessive wear on tools. Solving these basic problems would probably contribute more than the proposed introduction of sophisticated controls to achieving the joint venture's export targets.

Similarly, the large differences in performance among firms in a given industry often depend more on management and organization than superior equipment. Two of the largest, oldest, and best-managed watch factories in China may be used as an example: the Tianjin Watch Factory has more and better equipment and nearly as many workers as the Shanghai Watch Factory, yet it produces only 35 percent as many watches at a cost 27 percent higher. And the gap between the Shanghai factory and many new factories is much greater. In the sewing machinery industry, costs of production for one model are nearly five times as great in the highest cost enterprise as in the lowest (Figure 7.1). Even among the five enterprises producing 124,000–135,000 units,

3. See *Asian Wall Street Journal*, August 10–11, 1984.

which probably have similar techniques of production, the cost differential is more than two to one.

Failure to exploit economies of scale (see Figure 7.1) has also denied—and continues to deny (Chapter 5)—China an important source of productivity growth and product improvement. For example, in 1978, 130 enterprises, in twenty-six provinces and under the jurisdiction of several ministries, produced 150,000 motor vehicles. Consolidation of production could have a major impact on product cost and quality even without sophisticated machinery and automated production, by standardizing parts, allowing longer production runs for individual parts, and introducing more specialized machine tools. Production costs of bicycles, refrigerators, and watches are also unnecessarily high because of "small and comprehensive" production units in these industries. The solution is not necessarily large and comprehensive units. In some industries, economies of scale in production may be limited (for example, in the clothing industry) or may be offset by high transport costs (for example, in the cement industry). Moreover, small specialized firms can be an important source of growth (as will be discussed later). In the auto industry of industrial countries, a few very large-scale units produce key parts and undertake assembly, while numerous (often small-scale) units produce components and provide specialized services.

Economically Efficient Technology

Experience in China and other countries alike confirms that there can be no quick technological fix to problems of high cost and low product quality. New technology improves economic results only when carefully selected and appropriately applied over a long period.

Some innovations may actually increase China's production costs, especially if they substitute expensive and electricity-intensive imported machinery, such as fully automatic looms, for inexpensive and abundant labor power. Associated improvements in product quality may sometimes justify the additional cost, but because of distorted prices (including the cost of capital and product quality differentials), enterprises now often make choices that are wrong for the whole economy. Such investment in automation could also be economically rational in the longer term if the machinery could be satisfactorily—and more cheaply—manufactured in China, and if the initial imports provided models for domestic manufacturers. But this should not be assumed to be so without careful investigation.

Deficiencies in China's existing technological capability may also prevent some new technology from being efficiently absorbed. One Chinese study of large and medium-size projects completed during 1980–82 concluded that "among the nine projects imported from foreign countries, six have poor economic results."[4] Another study of more than thirty major turnkey projects undertaken in the 1970s concluded that only one-third met the three criteria of short construction periods, high utilization rates after the start of operations, and good operational results.[5] (For some of the problems encountered in steel, see Box 7.1.)

Similar problems in absorbing foreign technology have been encountered and studied in other countries. Technology, it appears, cannot simply be transferred, since it cannot be thoroughly codified in blueprints or embodied in capital equipment. Considerable effort and investment are needed to master any technology and to make adaptations in complementary production, in management, and in the technique itself. Studies of "learning by doing" have shown that improvements in productivity often come through experience in production. There is a learning curve following the introduction of a new product or process, in which unit costs first fall steeply as total cumulative production increases and then level off. Moving down the learning curve does not happen automatically, however, but requires a conscious effort and investment. Production experience needs to be complemented by systematic improvements in the basic technological knowledge and skills of individual enterprises and specialized agencies.

Two other, related, lessons of technological advance in other countries also seem of great relevance to China. First, the cumulative effect of successive small innovations (including modifications, adaptations, and changes of materials and work practices) on both production cost and product quality is larger than that of completely new products or processes. It is therefore more important that enterprises should hunt every single day for small ways of improving performance than that they should make occasional radical innovations. Second, a large gap exists in every industry and country between the newest (or "best-practice") technique and the average technique in use. Since it is the average that determines the economy's overall performance, narrowing the technology gap between the leaders and the laggards in an industry is as vital to cost reduction and product improvement as the pace at which the leaders acquire new technology.

Planning for Technological Development

Good investment decisions—for both radical and small innovations—are crucial for upgrading technology. An important element is sound investment project analysis,

4. Ma Hong, "Do a Good Job in the National Economic Appraisal of Construction and Renovation Projects," *China Report: Economic Affairs*, no. 366 (July 20, 1983), pp. 1–7, translated from *Jishu Jingji yu Guanli Yanjiu*, no. 1 (March 1983), pp. 9–12.

5. Chen Huiqin, "The Orientation of Technology Import Must Be Changed," *Economic Management* (April 1981), pp. 22–25.

Box 7.1 Continuous Casting of Steel

Development of continuous casting in steel production offers an instructive example of how to open up a new technological path through selection of domestic and foreign technological elements. The Wuhan Iron and Steel Company (WISC) prepared design criteria and requirements for a continuous casting plant in 1970. The Government approached a West German firm to help build the plant, and an agreement was signed in 1974. The agreement called for the German firm to provide all of the equipment and for the Chinese to construct the building, with collaboration in designing the building and erecting the plant. More than 200 people were sent to Germany for training. Construction began in August 1975, the plant was completed in October 1978, and trial operations were conducted for four months, followed by full load acceptance tests. The plant was approved for operation by the state in 1980. Initial problems with the control system were solved by German technicians still in China.

The continuous casting unit was thus operating smoothly from early 1980. However, the plant reached only 50 percent of capacity in 1980, 60 percent in 1981, 66 percent in 1982, and 79 percent in 1983. The bottleneck was in production of liquid steel because of a shortage of oxygen supply for the converters and poor-quality refractory material, which resulted in excessive down time of the converters. These problems finally appear to have been solved by bringing in a manager from the Capital Iron and Steel Company in mid-1983. This illustrates the limitations of using radical new technology to solve production problems. Upgrading production capability in the better-known technology of steelmaking proved to be as important for raising productivity as attaining production capability in the more radical innovation of continuous casting. Through an intelligent blending of foreign and domestic technological elements, WISC was able to master the continuous casting process, but its success was marred by slow mobilization of domestic expertise to solve production problems in the supposedly well-known steelmaking process.

The introduction of continuous casting was also successful in another way. China has used the experience of WISC to develop investment as well as production capability in continuous casting. The Echeng Steel Mill, a provincially run enterprise near Wuhan, is planning an investment in continuous casting, for which the design work is being done by the Ministry of Metallurgy and the Wuhan Iron and Steel Design Institute on the basis of what has been learned in WISC. The equipment will be jointly manufactured by German and Chinese companies in China and will be entirely installed by a Chinese construction company that participated in the installation of two other billet-casting units elsewhere in China. Training for the Echeng plant will be done in Chinese factories. Thus, through forward planning, China has been able to substitute increasingly more domestic for foreign technological elements in continuous casting. There may have been some tradeoff between the development of investment capability and diffusion of continuous casting production, however.

---

undertaken by efficiency-conscious enterprises and planners, using methods that are well established in other countries.[6] But major investment decisions should also be taken within a sectorwide strategic framework. And conventional cost-benefit analysis should be supplemented by evaluation of alternative technological paths. This can be illustrated by an example from the watch industry. China mostly produces mechanical watches, and its best factories produce these efficiently by world standards. A large domestic market and a modest export market for mechanical watches will probably continue to exist for many years. However, other countries have largely shifted to production of electronic watches and production costs are falling. At present, China could only produce electronic watches cheaply by using imported electronic components, because of the high price and low quality of domestic components. Should China plan to expand mechanical watch production or shift to production of electronic watches? If the latter, should China replace existing mechanical watch production or only produce electronic watches for incremental demand? Should electronic watches use domestic or imported components? These questions require careful analysis of existing cost differences and judgments about the future direction of technological change. Because electronic watch production might open up new technological paths for the economy, dual technological development (continued production of mechanical watches and experimental production of electronic watches) undoubtedly makes sense for a time.

China faces some unusual strategic choices. The normal sequence of developing technological capability is first to develop production capability, then investment

---

6. The China Investment Bank has produced an "Appraisal Manual for Industrial Credit Projects," which adapts these methods to Chinese conditions. A similar manual has also been prepared by the Agricultural Bank of China.

capability, and finally innovation capability.[7] But China already has a full range of industries, from machinery to final products, and needs to upgrade technology in nearly every one. Where to break out of this circle of low productivity? Should China import foreign technology to upgrade production capability for final consumer products, or give attention first to upgrading technology in producer goods industries? For which industries should technology be imported and for which could existing technology be upgraded through domestic R&D? And in which product lines should China, for the time being, rely entirely on imports?

Issues of strategic choice are best approached industry by industry, looking at all the stages of production from producer goods to intermediate components to final goods. An objective comparison should then be made of the effects on production costs and product quality of using existing domestic equipment, importing equipment embodying a newer technology, and attempting to manufacture more up-to-date equipment in China. For example, it makes sense in a relatively mature industry such as textiles to concentrate first on upgrading production capability in textile machinery. Improved domestically produced textile machinery could then be used to upgrade textile production capability. More generally, since China

is a large-scale machinery producer, upgrading the production of general-use machinery (such as machine tools and boilers, see Box 7.2) should have high priority.

In high-technology industries such as electronics, different strategic considerations apply, distinguishing between the advantages of *use* and of *production* of electronics products. It is the use of electronics products in many industrial processes that offers the greatest potential for productivity gains. The advantages of electronics production are secondary. Even in the United States, high-technology industries have accounted for only 3 percent of

---

7. Capabilities needed to acquire, assimilate, use, adapt, change, or create technology can be placed in three categories: production, investment, and innovation. Production capability is needed to operate productive facilities. It is reflected in technical efficiency and in the ability to adapt operations to changing market circumstances. Investment capability is needed to establish new productive facilities and expand existing facilities. It is reflected in project costs and in the ability to tailor project designs to suit the circumstances of the investment. Innovation capability is needed to create new technology or introduce existing technologies in a new environment. It is reflected in the ability to introduce processes or services that are less costly or to develop new products or services that better meet specific needs.

the new jobs created during the past fifteen years. Many smaller advanced countries have almost no electronics production, but use imported components to reduce costs and improve products in other industries.

China may eventually be able to produce electronics products competitively because of its large internal market and low labor costs, and the low material intensity of production. Moreover, starting production now may speed the process of learning and make it easier to catch up later on.[8] But China's technological capability is far below that of world leaders, who in turn are still moving down their learning curve, and Chinese electronics products are now extremely high in price and often of poor quality.[9] Obliging Chinese industry to use domestically manufactured electronics products would thus limit their use and sacrifice many potential cost reductions and quality improvements.

One way to help resolve the conflict between fostering the use and fostering the production of electronics products is to concentrate on mastering production of selected products and solving key production problems before the production base is broadened (see Box 7.3). For example, use of computers in the Chinese economy could be increased most quickly and effectively by importing finished systems. Domestic manufacture of a complete computer system is unattractive, especially since it would not function well unless all parts of the equipment development program were successful. Moreover, a domestically produced system would be greatly out of date by the time it had been developed. But for various reasons, including actual or potential restrictions on the supply of foreign-made computers, China may feel obliged to move

---

8. However, it may also be possible—and cheaper—to wait until the world industry learning curve has begun to level off and then try to catch up, skipping some of the stages gone through in other countries. This would have to be evaluated industry by industry.

9. For example, the price of an advanced integrated circuit in China is eighty times greater than the world price for the same circuit. Other Chinese electronics products are typically five to ten times the world price and of lower quality.

Box 7.3   A Successful Strategy in Electronics

Many developing countries have promoted their electronics sectors over the past two decades; South Korea has been one of the most successful. By 1981, South Korea's production was, for instance, estimated at around four times that of India, a country with comparable levels of production and technology in the early 1960s, and South Korea's technological expertise has moved decisively ahead.

In South Korea, the thrust was on rapidly acquiring production know-how, initially for assembly of final products and later for the production of parts and subassemblies. The South Korean electronics industry has been free to make product and technology choices and to respond to market and technological trends. It concentrated initially on consumer items and components, but has recently moved into industrial electronics, as well as some high-technology semiconductor processing. In some other developing countries, such as India, the government restricted the growth of consumer electronics and promoted the development of producer electronics.

The South Korean electronics industry has been heavily export oriented. Import protection was provided for several consumer electronic products, but competition in world markets gave enterprises a great incentive to reduce costs and improve efficiency and an opportunity to learn from demanding users. In contrast, the Indian electronics industry, for example, has essentially been oriented toward the domestic market, and the heavy protection from imports is often held responsible for inadequate effort by the industry to grow out of its "infant" status.

The electronics sector in South Korea has been able to reap economies of scale and break out of the constraints imposed by a small domestic market. The production of consumer electronics in some other developing countries, such as India, has been concentrated in small-scale enterprises; limiting the scale of operation has been uneconomic for some activities and for many dynamic firms. Moreover, small-scale enterprises are often ill equipped to undertake significant technological development.

Choices about modes of technology acquisition and the nature of capabilities acquired by the South Korean electronics sector have apparently been economically appropriate, given the needs of the sector as it evolved and the availability of know-how within South Korea and abroad. It has imported both "disembodied know-how" (for example, product designs and licenses) and technology embodied in capital equipment, as well as parts and components that could not be manufactured domestically to international standards. The government has encouraged diffusion, especially through the development of local suppliers. Attention was also paid to the development of applied engineering capabilities, which is essential for the assimilation of more advanced foreign technologies as well as the rapid translation of know-how into better products and processes. In this regard, the South Korean Institute of Electronics Technology played an important role.

toward domestic manufacture. In these circumstances, it might be best to concentrate initially on developing production of certain key components (such as the central processing unit and monitor) and import those components (such as the disk drive and printer) for which good-quality domestic production would be difficult. Domestic production could later gradually diversify to replace imported components. The objective, as in other areas of electronics production, should be to match international price and quality standards in whatever is produced and to avoid producing items in which China cannot become competitive.

Sectoral investment strategies have figured prominently in the development process in Japan, the only backward country to catch up with (and in some cases overtake) the technological leaders. What lessons are there for China?

One lesson—abundantly confirmed by experience elsewhere—is that neither planners nor enterprises can pick technological winners consistently. Japan's Ministry of International Trade and Industry (MITI) is sometimes credited with extraordinary foresight and power; in fact MITI has just helped create a favorable environment for technological advance, by facilitating information flows among producers and reducing the risk of investments that followed its consensual "vision" of future development. But it has not forced producers to conform to its plans. Some large enterprises (such as Sony and Honda) often pursued strategies at odds with official objectives: private automobile producers, for example, made automobiles one of Japan's leading exports despite MITI's initial decision not to support development of autos as an export industry. There have also been failures, as when both MITI and private producers wrongly expected petrochemicals to become a competitive industry; and sometimes private producers alone tried but failed to develop industries that MITI did not want to back (for example, commercial aircraft). A second lesson of Japanese experience is thus that planning for long-term technological transformation need not, and indeed generally should not, be mandatory.

Two other features of Japanese industrial strategy have been critical. First, the criterion of success has been ability to compete in the international market after a period of infant industry protection, and second, enterprises themselves have borne the risks of failure and reaped the rewards of success. The careful attention MITI has given to developing internationally competitive industries is often compared with the attention a mother gives a student preparing for an entrance examination. Japan has thus had a flexible system of strategic planning that allows for mistakes and for experiments with alternative technological paths, and a system in which competition—domestic as well as international—provides a strong incentive to seek out promising technological paths and retreat quickly from paths that lead nowhere.

The Make or Buy Decision

China has a wide network of research institutes with proven ability to develop new technology. These have often matched or improved upon advances in other countries, and they have also shown considerable skill in adapting techniques to China's special conditions. But excessive self-reliance has undoubtedly impeded China's technological progress in the past. China has preferred to develop known technologies by copying imported equipment or through completely independent research and development, rather than by importing technological know-how. The strategy of creating, and often recreating, technology contrasts sharply with the absorptive strategy of Japan, which aimed to assimilate and adapt foreign technology as fast as possible. The absorptive strategy has many advantages for a technological latecomer, because selectively importing or borrowing technology generally involves lower risks, a shorter time lag, and a lower cost of acquisition.

The issue is not whether China should upgrade technology through its own research or through imports. Studies in other countries have shown that these two routes are complementary. Countries (and enterprises) with a strong R&D capability can make more productive use of imported technology because they can unpackage the technology and be selective in importing. They can use the information developed from their own research to strengthen their bargaining position, use imports to strengthen their own research, and through their own R&D adapt foreign technology to local conditions. The issue, then, is the right balance between domestic R&D effort and importing technology.

Importing Technology

Selectivity is the key to using imports in upgrading technology. In the past, China has tended to alternate between the extremes of importing turnkey plants or relying wholly on domestic R&D. But there are many intermediate options. Elements of unpackaged technology that can be imported include licenses, designs, key equipment, and consultants to help solve management, marketing, or engineering problems. Recent Chinese policy has stressed the need to import "software" (know-how) in addition to, or instead of, "hardware" (equipment). This is an important advance in technology policy, because it recognizes that individual elements of technology can be traded and that equipment is not necessarily the most important element.

Import policy should remain flexible, however. It is less important *how* foreign technology is obtained than *what* is being obtained and *why*. The appropriate mode of acquisition will depend on the objectives being pursued: to gain production capability in a radically new technology, import of a turnkey plant may still be the cheapest and most effective option; to develop investment capability in producing better chemical equipment, it may be enough to purchase an overall design and certain specialized parts. The objectives will determine the specific elements to be acquired and the mode of acquisition; within each mode of transfer, considerable scope exists for negotiating conditions tailored to promote the objective.

Two important modes of acquiring technology, direct foreign investment and licensing or purchase of technical assistance, were discussed earlier (Chapter 6). Other modes can also be effective. One is the "apprentice" pattern of development, in which the the first plant in an industry is built on a turnkey basis with substantial training of, and observation by, local staff. In subsequent projects, domestic technological elements can be substituted for foreign elements and assimilation of investment capability becomes more important than mastery of production capability. Many developing countries have effectively used this approach to upgrade local technological capability in several industries, as has China in large-scale nitrogen fertilizer production and in continuous casting of steel (see Box 7.1).

"Informal" means of acquiring foreign technology can also be important. A survey of 112 South Korean exporting firms in 1976 showed that the most important sources of process technology, both domestic and foreign, were overwhelmingly informal. Formal means (licensing, technical assistance, and government-supported institutes) were important only 28 percent of the time. Informal means, particularly assistance from suppliers or buyers, and hiring personnel with experience abroad (including foreign managers—for example, in shipbuilding) or in domestic firms, were much more important. The role of overseas buyers in providing information on innovations is an important extra benefit of exporting and partly explains why the fastest-growing economies in East Asia, with their strong export orientation, have been able to upgrade technology quickly.

Copying imported equipment is another informal means of acquiring technology, but one that must be used carefully. Even when it is technically possible to copy foreign machinery, it may be uneconomic to do so. For example, the Shanghai Boiler Factory and Shanghai Number 3 Machine Tool Plant jointly designed a special deep-bore drill. The drill matches the technical quality of an imported product and may even have cost somewhat less, but it took several years to produce and will not be produced again. This illustrates the tendency to concentrate only on the technical rather than the economic aspects of innovation. But while copying is sometimes uneconomic and can never be the only means of acquiring technology, it can be effective in some industries (particularly simple mechanical industries). The Shanghai Bicycle Company has matched and even surpassed advanced European standards for some bicycle manufac-

turing equipment, by copying foreign equipment or using its own designs. The company imported a West German electric resistance welding machine in 1962 and through its own R&D efforts has since tripled the machine's speed, essentially matching improvements made in Europe. The company also developed a rim-making machine based on a study of the technical literature starting in 1976. According to company sources, this machine is superior in most respects to comparable equipment produced by a leading French bicycle machinery manufacturer. China has also begun to participate in international subcontracting and is sending study tours and students abroad, as well as attracting back overseas Chinese with technical or business experience. All of these international contacts should increase the flow of information into China.

Research and Development

In China, central government agencies and ministries, with their research institutes and superior resources, have traditionally been considered the best agents for determining what innovations are needed (though R&D proposals from below are in practice usually approved). For example, the State Science and Technology Commission selected thirty-eight key research projects and identified several innovations to popularize during the Sixth Five-Year Plan. Central agencies can certainly play an important role in informing bureaus, corporations, and enterprises about technological developments abroad and in progressive Chinese enterprises. They could also usefully monitor costs and the physical productivity of key processes and provide enterprises with feedback on their individual performance in comparison to best (domestic and international) practice.

There are severe limitations, however, to the top-down, "technology-push" approach to innovation. International experience indicates that bottom-up, "need-pull" innovation is generally much more successful. A study of major U.S. innovations by source during 1953–73 showed that 80 percent of new ideas came from within the enterprises that produced the innovation, three-quarters of them from the producing division or department itself. Less than 5 percent came from universities and government laboratories. A European study also showed that over 70 percent of the main ideas for innovation came from within the innovating company and that by far the highest proportion of successful ideas came from commercial rather than technical staff (Table 7.2). Market feedback is thus the most important source of ideas for innovation.

The traditional organization of R&D in China puts too much emphasis on technology-push rather than responding to the demands of users for innovation. Only 10–30 percent of research results are utilized in production. Moreover, research results passed to production units are often incomplete and prototypes require additional devel-

Table 7.2 Sources of Successful Innovations in European Firms

Source	Number of cases	Commercial success	Commercial failure	Technical failure	Failure rate (%)
Technical staff	31	8	19	4	74
Commercial staff	60	33	21	6	45
Top management	6	1	4	1	83

Source: *The Economist* (June 26, 1982), p. 96, based on data from the European Industrial Management Association.

opment work that the production unit cannot handle. In addition, because of administrative compartmentalization in China, potentially beneficial innovations are often not easily integrated into production if they require the cooperation of other ministries to develop new materials, components, or ancillary machinery.

User feedback is very important in the machinery sector, but China's system does not usually allow sufficient interaction between machinery users and producers. If an enterprise's request for equipment is approved, a machinery manufacturer is assigned to produce the equipment from a design of its own or of a design institute. Users often cannot convey their special requirements to machinery producers, and many resort to designing or manufacturing their own machinery, which is a far from satisfactory solution. Innovations by machinery manufacturers would be much more frequent if users had not only direct contact with suppliers, but also, and more importantly, the freedom to choose their suppliers—including foreign suppliers if they can show that this would be economically rational. This freedom should include the right to manufacture their own equipment, though this option would undoubtedly be chosen less often than at present. In fact, during the readjustment period in 1981, equipment users did have much more freedom of choice in suppliers, with clear beneficial effects (discussed later); subsequently, as markets have become tighter, restrictions on choice have been reimposed.

Several changes have recently been made in R&D policy and organization. Most are potentially beneficial, but their impact will depend largely on how they are implemented. Research institutes are now being encouraged to form closer links with production, through contract research, technical assistance on a fee-paying basis, and joint research-production teams. Research-production associations in the Soviet Union, however, have had a minimal impact on innovation; integration has been nominal only, and the activities of research institutes and production units have continued to be separate. Contract research and technical assistance offer considerable potential for making research more responsive to the needs of

users. A danger, however, is that linkages between enterprises and research institutes will be emphasized at the expense of linkages among enterprises. Moreover, research institutes often do not have sufficient production experience to make an effective contribution.

Pilot plants are being established in some industries to link research and production. A prominent feature of Japan's early industrialization strategy was government-sponsored pilot plants, although these were turned over to private industry once they reached a certain level of efficiency. China, too, has in the past established small-scale pilot plants for many products, some of which have been successfully scaled up for commercial production (for example, the production of benzine for use in polyester fiber). More recently, research institutes have embarked on full-scale production of some products; for example, the Beijing Machine Tool Research Institute now assembles Japanese numerical control devices for sale to machine tool enterprises.

The move toward commercially applicable R&D is commendable, but should not be applied to basic research, or even to all applied research. Most basic and some applied research produces results, which—because they are either universally or only indirectly applicable to production—would not be ordered or purchased by fee-paying users, even if they would benefit the whole economy. Stressing financial self-sufficiency might result in too few resources being devoted to research, or in research institutes becoming mere production units, to the neglect of research that has no immediate commercial payoff.

Nonetheless, consideration should be given to transferring some applied R&D from research institutes to enterprises. Most R&D in industrial capitalist countries takes place within productive enterprises. Governments fund a large proportion of this research, partly to further defense objectives, but mainly because the risks involved, and the difficulty of patenting or commercially exploiting certain research results, would otherwise lead to inadequate R&D effort. But even publicly funded research is usually located in enterprises in order to respond to user needs and take advantage of the enterprises' production experience. Locating applied research in enterprises is also consistent with the greater importance, mentioned earlier, of technological advance through cumulative small changes than through radical innovations. To do this successfully in China, however, would require greater applied engineering capability within enterprises, so that they could adapt and apply innovations introduced from research institutes, foreign sources, or other enterprises. Enterprises would also have to be given appropriate incentives.

Incentives for Innovation and Diffusion

Despite the extensive talent and tremendous drive to innovate of its technical personnel, China's planning and incentive system has traditionally been strongly biased against innovation. An enterprise's most important production targets have been for physical output or gross value of production. Few enterprises therefore have been willing or permitted to interrupt (or risk interrupting) current production by introducing new products or processes, even when the longer-term benefits would be large. Secondary plan targets for cost reduction, material use, and product quality have done little to offset the bias against innovation. Market pressures have been equally ineffectual. Price differentials between high- and low-quality products have been small or nonexistent. Enterprises have usually had no responsibility for sales. And with goods generally in short supply—a seller's market—almost any product has found a buyer.

The experimental reforms of industrial enterprise management in the past few years have not basically changed the situation. Experience in the Soviet Union and Eastern Europe confirms that minor modifications to the planning and incentives system have little impact on innovation and productivity. Special targets or bonuses for cost reduction or new products do little to offset the overwhelming importance attached to quantitative production targets. Profit targets and profit retention schemes offer only a weak incentive to innovate when enterprises can sell everything they produce without innovating. Moreover, distorted prices encourage enterprises to produce the wrong products or to use scarce inputs wastefully. Increased price flexibility for new products tends to stimulate cosmetic product changes to justify price increases, generating inflation with little meaningful innovation. The most significant change that has occurred in China has been in marketing. Since 1980, not all output has been guaranteed an outlet through planned purchases by commercial departments or the material supply network; part has had to be sold directly to users. This change, at least for a time and in some industries such as machinery, has created a buyer's rather than a seller's market. Enterprises therefore have had to pay attention to product quality and customer preferences to maintain sales and profits, which has led to some changes in product mix and an increase in product innovation in several industries.

For China to catch up with the world's technological leaders, far more radical changes in the system of incentives for innovation would be required—with far-reaching economic and social implications. The changes required include: (a) greater enterprise and managerial accountability for financial performance, with heavy and unrelenting penalties for poor performance as well as large rewards for success; (b) rationalization of prices, to ensure that profit and loss reflect cost efficiency and the economic benefits of what is produced, and (c) greatly increased competition among enterprises. These essential and basic reforms of the system of economic manage-

ment, and how they might be implemented, are discussed at length in Chapter 10. The same chapter discusses ways of dealing with some of the social problems that might arise with stronger positive and negative incentives for innovation—including closure of enterprises and high managerial and entrepreneurial earnings.

Diffusion of Technology

Diffusion is one of the weakest aspects of China's technology system. Although China is justifiably admired for making economic use of older technologies, especially in rural enterprises, it also seems that innovations introduced in particular enterprises usually spread uneconomically slowly to the rest of industry. Even in the steel industry, one of the best organized for spread of information, China has been rather slow to adopt energy-saving innovations such as continuous casting and conversion from open-hearth to oxygen steel production. China has also lagged in converting cement production to the dry process (60 percent is still wet production), introducing high-efficiency boilers, and upgrading quality or reducing costs in backward enterprises in consumer durable industries, such as watches, bicycles, and sewing machines. Diffusing best-practice techniques, including management techniques, already in use in China may, as discussed earlier, be more critical to productivity growth than introducing more advanced technology into a few leading enterprises.

China's institutions and policies for diffusion of technology have followed the Soviet model, which stresses the benefits of a free flow of knowledge. Specialized research institutes have usually developed innovations, which can then be passed to production units free of charge. Similarly, approved new products and techniques developed by enterprises can be diffused to other producers at no charge. The Soviet Union and China have both recorded impressive technological achievements in areas in which they have concentrated the considerable resources of their R&D systems, but they have been much less successful in diffusing a wide variety of improvements throughout industry.

One important reason for failure to diffuse technology is the general lack of incentives for innovation discussed earlier. Other reasons are also systemic, but relate to the nature of technology. Technology is not machinery or blueprints that can be simply passed from one user to another, but is rather a whole method for doing something, which requires understanding of associated work procedures and organization and which can be assimilated only with considerable effort, cost, and sometimes substantial adaptation. Three examples of failure to diffuse innovations in China illustrate shortcomings of the present system.

EXAMPLE I. A Shanghai foundry producing small castings for machine tools successfully copied (achieved two-thirds of the speed of) a Danish automatic molding process. This innovation was not diffused. Some years later, a research institute developed a similar machine, which was then made available to other foundries. In this case, diffusion occurred from the research institute, but not from the enterprise. In general, innovations have sometimes been successfully diffused to subordinate units, but they are rarely diffused horizontally (there is little communication with other ministries or regions producing similar products).

EXAMPLE II. The Shanghai Bicycle Company (SBC) is not only one of the leading bicycle producers in China,[10] but also a producer of bicycle machinery that is advanced by world standards. However, SBC is not interested in producing bicycle machinery either for other plants in China or for export. The Shanghai Light Industry Bureau has set up a specialized factory to produce bicycle machinery, which may use SBC designs but will have only minimal access to SBC specialists. Since much technological knowledge cannot be explained in manuals, but rather is embodied in people, the bureau's factory is unlikely to be as proficient as SBC and is certainly less likely to have the export potential of SBC. In other countries, SBC would spin off a specialized company to produce machinery, or its engineers would set up their own company or be hired by the new producer, thus diffusing the technology of machinery production.

EXAMPLE III. The Shanghai Number 6 Textile Mill achieved national recognition for its success in developing computer monitoring of looms. About fifty other textile producers in China have built or will build a similar system, many with the assistance of the Number 6 mill. Thus diffusion is occurring because of the organization and communications within the Ministry of Textiles. The Number 6 mill now proposes to develop, in cooperation with a research institute, an online microprocessor control system, but neither unit has any staff specially trained in microprocessors. Since it is difficult for the textile industry to hire an electronics engineer or to get support from the Ministry of Electronics, the two units will mostly rely on training their own staff through seminars given by the city.

CONCLUSIONS. Several improvements could be made to remove the barriers to technology diffusion in these examples. Examples I and III illustrate the problem of poor communications between ministries, regions, and enterprises. Though this problem can never be wholly overcome in an administratively regulated economy, joint ventures across administrative boundaries could diminish it. For example, as part of the plans for cooperation within the Yangtze Delta zone (established to break down provincial barriers to development), SBC has formed a joint venture with the Suzhou Bicycle Factory for associate production of the Forever brand bicycle. SBC will provide technical assistance to improve the quality of the main parts produced by the Suzhou plant, as well as of several small components made by other manufacturers. This should expand the market share of the superior Forever brand at the expense of the lower-quality Suzhou bicycle, but without loss to the workers in the Suzhou factory.

Examples I and II show that enterprises that innovate successfully need incentives to diffuse new technology to other producers. A change in the right direction now being made is the introduction of patents, internal licensing of technology, and fees for technical assistance.

Examples II and III suggest that greater labor mobility would enhance diffusion. Hiring of experienced technicians and managers is perhaps the most important source of new knowledge for enterprises in most countries. (Excessive labor mobility, however, can create a disincentive for enterprises to invest in training.) Japan is a notable exception to this general rule, at least in the large-scale manufacturing sector. Japan apparently substitutes for this means of diffusion partly through MITI's efforts to bring industry experts together to share experience and to develop a consensus on future development and partly through informal contacts among people who went to the same school or university but now work in different companies. Even so, Japanese enterprises have far more flexibility in hiring than Chinese enterprises, so that a textile enterprise, for example, can hire electronics engineering graduates. China is now introducing some flexibility in its hiring procedures, though far more is needed (Chapter 8). Professional associations based on individual membership have also been revived, thus encouraging engineers and scientists in different industries and fields to make contact.

These examples also show that China needs to encourage specialization. Special agents can mediate between producers and users of technology or provide missing technological elements. In Example III above, consultants with expertise in electronics and some familiarity with textiles could probably have provided a fast and cost-effective alternative to staff training or interministerial coordination. Consultants and other specialized agents, moreover, have an incentive to speed diffusion whereas competing enterprises may wish to limit it (for instance, in Example II, SBC might not wish to assist other bicycle manufacturers by selling them improved machinery, but a specialized enterprise spun off from SBC would have a strong interest in selling better equipment).

---

10. Its Forever brand bicycles are in very high demand and must be rationed in the domestic market. SBC also exports bicycles to Sears, Roebuck & Co. in the United States.

China has recently begun to encourage the formation of consulting companies, using experts from research and design institutes, universities, and ministries. But much more needs to be done to facilitate the creation of new enterprises and organizations that specialize in production of technology-related goods and services, and indeed also of other things. In other countries, units providing services such as repair and maintenance often spin off from their parent firm to provide services on a contract basis to both the parent and other firms, which helps make firms in most industrial capitalist countries less comprehensive than Chinese firms.[11] Large Japanese firms likewise often help set up trusted employees in business as subcontractors. The specialization that results from spinoffs is one of the main vehicles of productivity growth.

The Role of Small Enterprises

Greater reliance on small enterprises for innovation could also contribute more generally to China's technical progress. Studies in other countries have shown that small industrial enterprises are just as innovative as large ones, especially in sectors such as specialized machinery, electrical and other consumer goods, and in small computers and related software. Even in sectors where large-scale production is optimal, such as basic chemicals and metallurgy (and, in electronics, semiconductors), small specialized firms have contributed many useful innovations, sometimes in the role of subcontractors to the larger firms. (Chinese visitors to foreign countries are often given a misleading impression in this regard, because they are usually taken only to well-known, large enterprises.)

In China, by contrast, it is generally assumed that small firms are necessarily technologically backward, while large firms must be the technological leaders. As a result, collective and individual enterprises, which already have strong incentives to innovate, are denied access to the skilled manpower, modern equipment, and foreign exchange they need to innovate. State enterprises, which have far less incentive to innovate, have exclusive access to the necessary resources.

Diverting a substantial fraction of China's skilled manpower, technology imports, and research support to small enterprises on a competitive basis would unquestionably speed China's technical advance. Moreover, the social problems posed by strong incentives for innovation could be less serious in the context of small than of large enterprises. High individual or collective earnings from successful innovation may sometimes be more acceptable than large payments to managers and researchers insulated from risk in big organizations. Similarly, the failure of a small enterprise (in other countries, most small enterprises fail within a year or so of starting up, although those involved often try again) affects only a few workers and a small amount of capital and has little effect on the prosperity of its locality.

Obsolescence and Scrapping

Old and new processes and products coexist in all countries, since it is rarely economic to scrap and replace recently acquired equipment or recently introduced products the moment new processes and products become available. Thus, although China has deliberately chosen to use old and new technology simultaneously as one aspect of the strategy of "walking on two legs," it could also be said that the typical economy walks on far more than two legs: it is like a centipede, with the newest products and techniques at the front, the oldest at the back. The creature moves forward steadily, innovating at the head, abandoning old products and processes at the tail. But it always remains quite long: the vintages of equipment in use may span two decades or so, with corresponding variations in enterprise profitability, while outputs of widely varying quality are sold at different prices to different segments of the market.

What is unusual about China is the length of the technological centipede, and indeed its tendency to get longer and longer. As new processes and products are introduced, the head moves forward, but the tail does not move. There is very little scrapping of equipment and abandoning of old products, even when it makes good economic sense to do so. Antique vintages of equipment are not merely used, but continue to be reproduced and embodied in new investment on an enormous scale by China's machine-making industry.[12] Equally remarkable is the coexistence of high- and low-quality products selling at the same price, with the result that, for example, inferior bicycles accumulate in inventory while "famous name" brands continue to be rationed.

There are various reasons for this unusual pattern. Some of them are connected with aspects of China's system of economic management mentioned in earlier sections of this chapter—few incentives for innovation, little competition, chronic shortages, irrational prices. There is also a widespread, deep-rooted aversion to the "waste" involved in scrapping equipment that still functions, or any product that might still serve some purpose. This is coupled with intense reluctance to displace workers, largely because of fear that they would become unemployed. These apprehensions have some foundation, but are in important respects misconceived and exagger-

---

11. In Switzerland, watch companies do not have their own machine shops or provide all of their components as in China. In Japan, steel companies contract out many services, such as changing refractory linings in furnaces, that are provided within Chinese enterprises. Some steel companies in less developed countries even contract for this difficult operation internationally.

12. An eminent Chinese economist, Sun Yefang, was the first to describe China's machinery industries as reproducers of antiques.

ated; they will need to be dispelled if China is to make rapid technological progress.

The Government, recognizing the outmoded state of much of China's industry, is at present stressing technical transformation of existing enterprises rather than wholly new construction. In line with this approach, it needs to be more widely understood in China that the economic life of equipment is usually shorter than its physical life.[13] It would also seem worth disseminating certain well-established rules for deciding whether an old process is still economically viable, or whether it should be upgraded or scrapped, with or without replacement. Specifically, an old process should in principle be scrapped and replaced if the total cost of production using new equipment (including interest and depreciation on the new capital employed) would be less than present operating costs (materials, energy, and wages). It should be upgraded if the saving in operating costs would be greater than the capital cost of the upgrading investment. And it should be scrapped without replacement if both the operating cost with existing equipment and the prospective total cost with new or upgraded equipment exceed the product price.

These principles are logically powerful and could assist in choosing technical transformation projects, many of which are now selected more on the basis of engineering enthusiasm than economic calculation. But they are not easy to apply in present Chinese circumstances, mainly because prices, wages, and charges for the use of capital do not reflect the true value to the economy of the items concerned. Cheap fuel, for example, would on the principles outlined above encourage uneconomically slow replacement of energy-intensive equipment, while capital grants, cheap loans, and unduly high wages for unskilled labor would all lead enterprises to scrap and replace equipment sooner than economically desirable. Nor is there an adequate market in used equipment, which could allocate items abandoned by one enterprise either to other enterprises that could use them economically or to the scrapheap. In this situation, in the near term, enterprises and their supervisory bureaus might be obliged to use shadow prices set by some central agency to make economic audits of their equipment and decisions about replacement and other technical transformation. In the longer term, price reform and related measures would help enterprises spontaneously to make appropriate decisions on old equipment.

Similar principles exist for scrapping and replacement of products, but are also not easy to apply in present Chinese circumstances. In the case of producer goods, the test is whether the higher cost (because of the additional investment required) of supplying a new and better item would be more than offset by the cost reductions it would permit users to realize. Again, though, the test is valid only if prices are rational. And there are additional problems with consumer goods, where the higher cost of the new item has to be weighed against its benefit to consumers. Willingness to pay, reflected in the price differential between new and old products, is the measure of consumer benefit in a market economy. But at present in China, consumer prices are not allowed to move freely enough to serve this purpose. Even if they were, the Government, like others in developing countries worried about the spread of costly Western consumerism, might not see them as an appropriate guide to the allocation of technological resources.

The possible adverse effects of scrapping on employment should also be put in perspective. Much of the replacement process can occur within existing enterprises: in Japan, for example, lifetime employment in large firms has proved compatible with high rates of product and process innovation, and much the same has been true in other countries. At the same time, the experience of smaller firms in Japan and elsewhere makes clear that evolutionary competition between old and new products and processes would inevitably lead to the closure of enterprises, with consequent loss of jobs. In general, however, the closure of old enterprises actively stimulates the expansion of technologically more advanced enterprises, creating new jobs to absorb the displaced workers. This is because the continued existence of backward enterprises—as in China—acts as a drag on progressive enterprises, by depriving them of materials, skilled labor, capital, and markets that they could put to more productive use.

Over time, and looking at the economy in aggregate, both economic logic and the experience of other countries suggest that high rates of scrapping and replacement cause faster, rather than slower, growth of modern industrial employment. This may require many workers to change jobs more frequently, sometimes with transitory periods of unemployment; it may also, more seriously, cause certain workers and localities to experience protracted unemployment. There are policies and institutions that could alleviate the economic hardship of displaced workers and assist in their retraining and reemployment. But, as in any society undergoing rapid change, the losses of particular individuals and groups from technical advance would still have to be weighed against the gains of the majority.

---

13. It is sometimes argued in China that raising the depreciation rate, which is at present only 3–4 percent per year, would bring about a more appropriate pace of scrapping. Such a step might indeed help to overcome some irrational resistance to abandoning things before the end of their physical life. But, as explained in the text, the magnitude of accumulated accounting depreciation does not enter into an economically sound calculation of whether or not a particular item should be scrapped at a particular time. Only the operating costs of installed equipment are relevant to decisions regarding its future use.

Human Development

8

People are both the means and the ends of economic development. Their numbers, health and nutrition, education and training, allocation among economic activities, effort, and initiative will largely determine the pace and pattern of China's development. People's well-being, however, is the whole object of development—to enable them to enjoy greater consumption of material goods and services, improved health, increased opportunities to shape their own lives, and a greater sense of security and social worth.

China's future human development policies—especially in education, employment, and wages—must take account of the need for structural change. At the macroeconomic level, rapid growth will require and bring about substantial changes in the sectoral pattern of employment. At the microeconomic level, as discussed in Chapters 1 and 7, structural change should be even more rapid, as newer and better processes and products displace older ones, causing constant shifts in the relative efficiency of different enterprises and in the pattern of demand for labor. A central theme of this chapter is that China's presently rigid, compartmentalized approach to the development and use of human skills could prove a major obstacle to rapid and equitable growth.

The first part of the chapter addresses some key issues in education and training, including the role of manpower planning.[1] The discussion then turns to employment, productivity, and wages, with special reference to labor surpluses and shortages, allocation of workers, and payment systems. The final section deals with some potential problems of the twenty-first century arising from changes in the size and composition of China's population, whose solution would require action within the next decade or so.

Education and Training Issues

By comparison with other low-income countries, China's present stock of educated manpower has an unusual com-

position (Table 8.1). The proportion of the population with primary education is exceptionally high. But, largely because of the Cultural Revolution, which stopped or hampered higher, upper secondary, vocational, and technical education for ten years, the number of people with advanced educational qualifications is small—smaller, indeed, in the twenty-five to thirty-four age group than among those over thirty-five. China's many years of isolation have also contributed to the smallness of the stock of people equipped to apply or teach the up-to-date skills essential for modernization.

Basic Educational Priorities

These deficiencies in advanced, high-quality education have—rightly—been the focus of China's educational strategy in the past few years, when great efforts have been made to restore academic standards, to expand both formal and informal higher education, and to plan for its further substantial enlargement over the next two decades. These efforts should not, however, divert attention from basic education, where problems have emerged in recent years.

INTERNATIONAL EXPERIENCE. China's long-standing commitment to widespread basic education has a sound economic, as well as social, foundation. Some other countries, such as Mexico or Brazil, have industrialized quite rapidly with relatively low levels of basic education. But their development has been characterized by much inequality of incomes, partly due to the high earnings of the educated minority, and has been unduly oriented toward capital-intensive, not very efficient, industry. By contrast, widespread basic education in some East Asian

---

1. Annex 1 contains a fuller discussion of recent educational developments and of issues in primary and secondary education, technical and vocational education, teacher training, and education costs and financing.

Table 8.1 Educational Attainment of the Population, by Age and Sex, in Selected Countries

| Country | Percentage of persons who have completed at least: | | | | | | | |
| | Primary school | | Lower secondary school | | Upper secondary school | | Postsecondary school | |
and age group	Male	Female	Male	Female	Male	Female	Male	Female
China, 1982								
Total,15 years or more	79.1	51.1	42.9	26.0	13.3	8.3	1.0	0.3
15–24 years	95.1	82.2	71.0	53.6	23.5	17.8	0.1	0.1
25–34 years	88.8	61.9	48.0	26.4	13.4	7.6	0.8	0.4
35 years or more	63.2	24.6	21.5	7.5	6.4	2.4	1.6	0.5
Other low-income countries								
India, 1971								
Total,15 years or more	37.2	14.7	21.3	7.1	10.3	3.0	1.6	0.4
15–24 years	53.6	27.4	35.5	15.1	15.6	6.4	1.2	0.7
25–34 years	39.4	14.4	23.4	6.5	13.1	3.1	2.7	0.7
35 years or more	26.4	7.1	12.0	2.4	5.9	0.9	1.3	0.2
Pakistan, 1973								
Total,15 years or more	30.8	9.5	..	..	12.5[a]	3.9[b]	1.9	0.5
15–24 years	44.8	18.0	..	..	17.0[a]	7.3[b]	1.5	0.9
25–34 years	34.8	8.8	..	..	15.2[a]	3.7[b]	3.4	0.8
35 years or more	20.8	4.8	..	..	8.7[a]	2.1[b]	1.5	0.2
Sri Lanka, 1971								
Total, 15 years or more	59.6	44.8	..	..	7.7[a]	6.6[b]	0.7	0.3
15–24 years	69.8	65.0	..	..	7.5[a]	7.7[b]	0.1	0.1
25–34 years	66.5	53.6	..	..	12.2[a]	10.8[b]	1.6	0.9
35 years or more	49.1	30.8	..	..	5.7[a]	3.6[b]	0.8	0.2
Middle-income countries								
Brazil, 1970								
Total, 15 years or more	33.6	31.7	..	..	9.9[a]	9.1[b]	1.5	0.5
15–24 years	41.5	41.6	..	..	10.8[a]	11.6[b]	0.1	0.1
25–34 years	35.0	31.8	..	..	11.8[a]	10.6[b]	2.1	1.0
35 years or more	26.7	23.5	..	..	8.2[a]	6.3[b]	2.3	0.6
Colombia, 1973								
Total, 15 years or more	80.7	79.0	..	..	26.0[a]	23.7[b]	4.1	1.6
15–19 years	87.5	89.8	..	..	36.0[a]	36.2[b]	0.7	0.7
20–29 years	86.4	86.5	..	..	34.4[a]	30.7[b]	7.4	3.6
30–39 years	81.4	78.2	..	..	22.4[a]	18.2[b]	5.2	1.5
40 years or more	71.1	65.6	..	..	14.6[a]	12.3[b]	2.8	0.4
Mexico, 1970								
Total, 15 years or more	31.3	27.7	10.8	7.0	6.4	4.1	3.8	1.5
15–24 years	44.4	39.7	15.1	10.4	6.8	5.1	3.2	1.7
25–34 years	31.5	27.5	11.6	7.1	8.5	5.0	5.6	2.0
35 years or more	20.5	17.8	6.9	4.2	5.0	2.8	3.3	1.2
South Korea								
Total, 15 years or more	82.3	66.3	44.5	22.4	23.7	8.9	6.2	1.6
15–24 years	97.5	95.9	55.9	39.3	23.2	13.1	1.6	1.5
25–34 years	94.9	85.7	57.9	29.6	37.2	14.2	11.7	3.4
35 years or more	63.7	37.7	28.2	8.2	16.3	3.6	6.6	0.7

a. All secondary school, male.
b. All secondary school, female.

Source: Ten Percent Sample of China Population Census (Beijing: State Statistical Bureau, 1983); *Country Demographic Profiles* (Washington, D.C.: U.S. Bureau of the Census, Center for International Research Division), selected issues.

economies has helped achieve both unusually high output per unit of physical capital and an unusually equal sharing of the benefits of rapid development.

Western specialists now believe that developing countries may have overemphasized higher education at the expense of primary education and in some cases also secondary education, from the viewpoint of both equity and efficiency.[2] Failure to achieve basic literacy is a condemnation to utter poverty: strong evidence links pri-

2. See World Bank, *World Development Report 1980* (Washington, D.C., 1980; reprinted by the World Bank in 1982 as *Poverty and Human Development*) for references to detailed studies.

mary education and the ability to earn an income, in both rural and urban settings. Economic rates of return on educational expenditure, viewed as an investment, appear to compare favorably with rates of return on physical capital; they are generally higher for primary than for secondary education, and for secondary than for tertiary education. Furthermore, educating women encourages and assists them to have fewer children and contributes to their children's health and educational attainments.

PROBLEMS IN CHINA. International experience should thus reinforce concern about the drop (discussed in Chapter 1) in primary and secondary school enrollment rates in China's rural areas in the early 1980s, mainly as a consequence of the production responsibility system (PRS). The declines have been most marked in secondary education and for girls in poor areas; this is apparently related to employment opportunities. Thus school attendance in the richer parts of Jiangsu has not been much affected, although the productivity of additional child labor on a family holding might be quite high, because a junior secondary education is necessary for a job in a local commune or brigade enterprise. Furthermore, education can contribute more to raising agricultural output in areas such as Jiangsu where technological advance is rapid.

In the poorer parts of China, however, where there is little technological advance in agriculture or opportunity for nonagricultural employment, the economic return to education must seem very low. Peasant households in these areas tend to have large families, so a twelve-year-old daughter can help around the house or look after younger siblings without seeming to jeopardize her prospects. But taking a longer-term view, the same daughter may be in the labor force forty years from now, when economic opportunities will be very different. Moreover, if there is to be significant migration out of the poorest parts of China (Chapter 5), a good basic education will be essential to enable migrants to adapt to a new economic and social environment.

The Government has taken steps to reverse the enrollment decline, apparently with more success in primary than in secondary education. But increased local financial self-reliance in basic education seems to have aggravated the already substantial problems of poorer areas (see Chapters 5 and 10). Moreover, the factors that caused the enrollment decline could be a serious obstacle to attaining the Government's target of making nine years of basic education universal by the end of the century. This is an important target—essential if China's full potential for growth is to be realized, and its benefits equitably distributed between town and country and between backward and more advanced localities. It is also an affordable target, because of the prospective decline in the primary school age group. But it will not be achieved

unless parents actually enroll their children in school and encourage their continued attendance.

The campaign to publicize the benefits of basic education should clearly be continued. But the Government should also direct more financial support to schools in poorer areas. This money could be used to reduce some of the obstacles to school attendance, including fees, distance (by building more schools or providing free transportation), and the quality of staff and buildings. Finally, and especially insofar as there is a conflict between the interests of parents and children, serious consideration should be given to making attendance compulsory, as is normal in industrial countries and already practiced in a few places in China. This is not a simple solution, since it creates administratively (and often morally) difficult, and costly, enforcement problems. But China's relatively high degree of social organization would make it less difficult than for most other developing countries.

KEY SCHOOLS. Education defines subsequent opportunities to an unusual degree in China. Examinations determine whether a child will attend senior high school, and thus whether he may take the unified national university examination. This examination determines the institution to be attended, if any, and the course of study to be followed, which in turn has normally determined the graduate's life-long job assignment. Examination results are thus of momentous individual significance; and they may be greatly affected by the quality of the school a child attends. It may therefore be questioned whether China's key-school policy, which deliberately increases quality differences among schools by concentrating resources in the better schools, is desirable, or whether it unnecessarily increases inequity and widens the gap in educational access between rural and urban areas.

Research has shown that the educational system has an inherent tendency to perpetuate the economic advantages and disadvantages of particular families from generation to generation, which is unlikely to be absent in China, even though differences in family background may be smaller. This tendency is aggravated by the uneven quality of secondary, as well as higher, education even in the richest countries. Schools with the highest achievement rates are located in cities and hence are more accessible to children from urban families. All countries also eventually abandon the principle of equality in higher education in order to concentrate students, staff, and facilities in centers of excellence, because of the costs involved in scattering them among all institutions of higher learning.

Given the low enrollment ratios, poorly qualified or over-age staff, shortage of library facilities, and obsolete equipment in China's higher education, some scarce resources should probably be concentrated in a few "key" universities. But the gains in educational quality or cost-effectiveness from such a policy at the secondary and especially at the primary level are questionable. Concentration of resources in certain privileged schools encourages the educational system to classify children too hastily as high or low achievers, which leaves much potential ability untapped. Many countries, capitalist as well as socialist, have rejected such policies in basic education as contrary to both equity and economic efficiency.

Specialized versus General Education

The Government's present policy is to reduce opportunities to go to general senior secondary schools and to promote vocational education, by adding vocational courses at some general secondary schools and wholly converting others into vocational secondary schools. This policy is a reaction to the heavy pressures on university entrance and the general difficulties of absorbing new labor force entrants into productive jobs. However, enrollment in general upper secondary education is not high in China compared with other rapidly growing developing countries, and its contribution to raising the productivity even of pupils who do not go on to university should not be underestimated.

Vocational secondary education, moreover, has been controversial in many countries since the beginning of this century. In the 1920s, for instance, Strumilin argued that sound general education supplemented by brief vocational training was the most efficient form of training for skilled workers.[3] For China, this argument is reinforced by the need for rapid structural change over the next few decades, which will require constant alterations in the skill composition of the labor force, and by the slow prospective growth of the labor force in the twenty-first century (discussed later), which will reduce the scope for changing skill composition simply by changing the pattern of training of new labor force entrants. Providing workers with good general education, which is the best foundation for retraining as circumstances change, is thus likely to yield large economic benefits.

Any vocational training should be in skills adaptable to a wide range of occupations, but vocational training in China suffers from one of the acknowledged weaknesses of the Soviet system on which it is modeled: overspecialization. China now offers 700–800 training programs (the Soviet Union in the early 1970s offered about 1,100). Most vocational training, and even higher education, is carried out by enterprises or under the auspices of sectoral ministries and tends to be excessively narrow and job specific.

The administrative compartmentalization of training also reduces quality and raises costs. Enterprises or sectoral agencies now seek self-sufficiency in key skills because trained manpower has been scarce, the assignment process does not meet their needs, and they cannot hire employees away from other enterprises. They may even attempt to provide all their own manpower; for example, the Ministry of Railways has a medical school to train physicians for employment in its hospitals and clinics. This "small but comprehensive" approach, even where it does not result in overspecialized courses, is wasteful because it passes up potential economies of scale.

Given the apparent shortage of skills, the recent fall in enrollments at—the mainly enterprise-run—schools training skilled workers is surprising, especially because the disincentive to enterprise training that worker mobility creates in other countries is much less in China (an enterprise can select the best trainees from its own schools). The causes of this decline, which could be related to the new emphasis on profitability (although some enterprises are using part of their retained profits to supplement the 1.5 percent of the wage bill they may use for training), should be investigated, as should its consequences. This is partly because upgrading and relearning of skills will continue to be badly needed (the state of China's impressively large and capable, but outmoded, stock of human resources strongly resembles that of its physical capital stock and requires just as much "technical transformation"). It is also because enterprise-sponsored vocational training, despite the danger of excessive narrowness, can ensure close contact between the trainers and users of trained manpower and provide opportunities for training on the latest equipment, thus overcoming problems of irrelevance and obsolescence that have plagued vocational training elsewhere.

This advantage of enterprise-sponsored training can also be captured by schools in close touch with enterprises, but funded by local governments, several of which already exist in China. Representatives of local enterprises can be on the boards of directors for the schools and can arrange for on-the-job training using relevant equipment.[4] These schools can provide broader training

---

3. S. G. Strumilin, "The Economic Significance of National Education," in *Readings in the Economics of Education*, edited by Mary Jean Bowman and others (Paris: Unesco-IIEP, 1968), pp. 413–50. Despite Strumilin's opposition, the Soviet Union did eventually develop formal vocational education. Various attempts were also made to integrate vocational and general education, but none was successful. See Irene Blumenthal and Charles Benson, *Educational Reform in the Soviet Union: Implications for Developing Countries*, Staff Working Paper 288, (Washington, D.C.: World Bank, 1978), pp. 32–50.

4. In Romania, after several reforms of education and training, a reportedly cost-effective, successful system has been developed. All vocational schools are jointly administered and operated by a nearby enterprise and a government institution. The enterprise subcontracts the manufacture of product components to school workshops. However, these must fit into the training programs and modules prepared by the Ministry of Education, which ensures that training is not narrowly specialized. See Andreas C. Tsantis and Roy Pepper, *Romania: The Industrialization of an Agrarian Economy under Socialist Planning* (Washington, D.C.: World Bank, 1979), pp. 151–64.

than enterprises normally do and are less likely to lose economies of scale. They could also fill the void created by the proposed phasing out of apprenticeship programs (now involving more than 2 million young workers). Other countries, however, in particular both East and West Germany, have found apprenticeship schemes, with a minority of time spent in the classroom, to be an effective way of training skilled workers.

The Role of Manpower Planning

Planning of both the level and the composition of expenditures on (especially advanced) education and training in China is linked to manpower forecasting. However, manpower forecasting elsewhere has proved very unreliable (though less so in projecting needs for teachers and doctors than in other areas). Manpower forecasts in countries particularly active in the field some time ago— Canada, France, India, Italy, Nigeria, Sweden, the United Kingdom, the United States, and Zambia—were especially inaccurate more than two or three years ahead. Forecasts were usually based on estimates provided by enterprises of the numbers of workers with particular skills (especially in scientific and technical areas) they would require. But only very large firms regularly forecast personnel requirements; moreover, they can only guess at their individual relative shares of the total market, so that the forecasts of individual firms may be quite inconsistent and cannot be aggregated into a forecast for the whole economy.

More complex manpower planning methods—which attempt to calculate labor requirements (by occupation, sector, and industry) based on output and productivity forecasts and to convert them into an educational structure through estimates of the level of formal education required for each occupation—have been no more successful. Converting information about occupations into educational needs is difficult partly because it involves aggregating varying amounts and kinds of formal and nonformal education. But the main problem of this approach is its neglect of the possibilities for substitution: depending on prices, wages, and availability, enterprises produce given amounts of output with widely varying mixes of labor and machinery, of different occupational skills, and (within occupations) of different educational qualifications. As a consequence, extensive research has been unable to relate output forecasts (which are themselves problematical) to educational needs.

Manpower planning in China is likely to suffer from all these problems, but the consequences of error could be much more serious, at least if skilled labor continues to be administratively allocated (discussed later). In other countries, inaccurate manpower forecasts are less worrisome, because both individuals and enterprises can respond more flexibly to errors: for example, if 1,000 doctors had been trained while only 500 were needed, the 500 best

doctors would find medical employment, while the others sought retraining or jobs requiring more general skills. By contrast, with administrative allocation, the forecasting error would be less conspicuous, but enterprises that really needed a doctor and an engineer would find themselves with two doctors and no engineer.

Recognizing the difficulties of manpower forecasting, it would be desirable for postsecondary schooling to offer several routes to any given educational qualification. For example, rather than having an indivisible four-year university course for engineers, an individual might become a "technician" in, say, two years and an engineer in another two. Under this system, the requirements for both technicians and engineers need be forecast only two years ahead. Revising forecasts annually or biannually could steer the educational system in line with labor requirements.

The considerable flexibility of higher education in China, achieved for example through correspondence colleges and television universities, is offset to some extent by excessively specialized fields of study. It is less difficult, for example, to forecast the demand for chemists than for organic chemists, inorganic chemists, and industrial chemists. The difficulties of manpower forecasting thus strengthen the case for broad curricula, with highly specialized skills acquired after, not during, formal study.

Employment and Productivity

The preceding discussion revolved mainly around shortages. Just as much thinking in China, however, has revolved around surpluses, especially of less-skilled labor. China's labor force will continue to grow, though less rapidly in the 1990s than in the 1980s. In absolute terms, the numbers are staggering: an increase between 1981 and 2000 of about 250 million in the population of working age, and perhaps 180 million in the labor force, requiring on average nearly 10 million additional jobs each year.

Faced with these statistics, and with evidence of existing labor surpluses, many people in China are worried that there could be—also partly because of the PRS— widespread open unemployment in the countryside, with serious social and political consequences. There is likewise fear of urban unemployment, which, for example, has led the Government in the past five years to cram many young people (especially those who returned from the countryside) into enterprises that were already grossly overmanned—and whose labor productivity has deteriorated as a result. More generally, a strong desire to preserve and multiply jobs is reflected in reluctance to take steps that would raise productivity. These legitimate and important concerns raise many policy issues requiring careful analysis of both the facts and the principles involved.

Productivity and Growth

Economic growth is, overwhelmingly, productivity growth. Since the ratio of the labor force to the total population will change little, growth of average per capita income will be almost entirely determined by growth of average output per worker. And, as in other countries (chapter 1), although part of the increase in average labor productivity will come from movement of labor out of agriculture into other sectors, most of it must come from higher productivity within each sector. For these basic reasons, measures that restrict labor productivity growth will slow China's overall economic growth. Slower growth, moreover, means slower accumulation of capital and expansion of demand in the modern sectors, and hence over the longer term less of precisely the sorts of employment that the Government is seeking to provide by holding down labor productivity.

This is not to deny that increases in productivity may lead to the loss of particular jobs. Indeed, as discussed in Chapter 7, rapid and intensive growth depends on this happening on a large scale, with obsolete or uneconomic activities and products being replaced by new and better ones. Displacement of old jobs by new jobs can take place largely within existing enterprises—in other countries, employment tends to grow faster rather than slower in enterprises with above-average rates of innovation and productivity growth. But part of it must involve movement of workers from one enterprise to another (raising possible issues of unemployment, discussed below).

Nor is productivity growth incompatible with the "labor-intensive" development path that some successful developing countries have followed. High labor intensity in the relevant sense is not low output per worker. It is making the best use of scarce capital, land, materials, and skills by using them in conjunction with large amounts of unskilled labor, thereby achieving the highest level of output (and hence average labor productivity) that available resources permit. In countries that have, like China, concentrated scarce resources in capital-intensive enterprises, labor productivity in those enterprises has sometimes been high, but average labor productivity in the economy has been reduced.

Urban Employment

The situation regarding current and prospective urban labor surpluses and shortages in China seems to be remarkably varied. Despite general concern about surpluses there is rapid absorption of labor into small rural towns. Some larger towns and cities—for example, Changzhou in Jiangsu and Shashi in Hubei—are also experiencing general labor shortages. And the projections discussed in Chapter 5 imply that this will happen more frequently unless greater migration is permitted.

Within enterprises, in localities of general surplus and general shortage alike, the picture is even more mixed. A manager may complain that he is obliged to employ far too many veterans, females (especially in heavy industry), and children of current or former employees, but also that he is short of competent, well-trained, able-bodied workers even at relatively low skill levels. Shortages and surpluses of specific types of labor coexist in other countries, too, but, as with goods, the degree to which this is so in China is unusual.

The acuteness of the mismatch between labor demand and supply in China is partly due to rigid labor allocation and wage policies (possible implications for these policies are discussed later in this chapter). But it, and the general predominance of labor surpluses in urban areas, also owes much to the unbalanced sectoral and institutional structure of production.

The smallness of employment in the service sectors in China, especially commerce and miscellaneous business and personal services, and the possible economic advantages of its much faster expansion in the future, have been discussed in earlier chapters. The range of future possibilities may be illustrated by comparing Chapter 2's QUADRUPLE projection, in which service sector employment increases by the year 2000 to 14 percent of the labor force (90 million workers), with the BALANCE projection, in which—with the same growth rate of GDP—it increases to 25 percent of the labor force (155 million workers), most of the increment being in commerce and miscellaneous services. Service sector employment in QUADRUPLE in 2000 is only 70 percent of industrial (manufacturing and mining) employment, which is similar to the Soviet Union in 1959 (80 percent). In BALANCE, service sector employment is 150 percent of industrial employment, which is the same as Japan in the early 1950s, though less than in the average lower-middle-income country today (200 percent, which is the product of a similar-size service sector but less industrial employment).

Service sector activities, being more labor intensive (combining more workers with a given amount of capital and materials), could create more jobs and hence reduce the overall urban labor surplus. These jobs would, moreover, disproportionately employ the categories of labor that are now in surplus in urban China. In the United Kingdom in 1970, for example, women made up 52 percent of the labor force in commerce, finance, business, and miscellaneous services (as compared with 30 percent in manufacturing), partly because of the greater scope for part-time employment.[5] The service sectors in other countries also absorb many males who lack the skills, physical strength, or tolerance of monotony needed for manual work in modern industry. Expansion of the ser-

---

5. In the U.K. data, 36 percent of the women in the service sectors worked part time, as compared with 22 percent in manufacturing.

vice sectors could thus permit many people who now contribute little or nothing to output in China's factories to move to more productive work. So could expansion of transport (see Chapter 5), especially road transport, which is much more labor intensive than rail transport.

Closely associated with China's presently unbalanced production structure is the smallness of the individual sector—including self-employment, partnerships, and sole proprietorships with a few workers—which in other countries plays a dominant role in commerce and miscellaneous services, although it is important also in industry, construction, and transport. In China in 1984, this sector employed about 2.5 percent of the urban labor force. By comparison, to take some representative examples of cities in other developing countries, the equivalent "informal sector" is estimated in the early 1970s to have employed 31 percent of the urban labor force in Abidjan, 40 percent in Jakarta, and 30–40 percent in Lima.[6] Even in other socialist countries, the proportion is much higher than in China: for example, the proportion of the industrial and industrial-handicraft labor force employed in private, semiprivate, and cooperative enterprises in the early 1970s was 8 percent in Romania, 11 percent in East Germany, 17 percent in Hungary, and (in 1980, with services included) 29 percent in Yugoslavia.[7]

It is increasingly recognized in China that many services and specialized products are more efficiently provided by small, flexible enterprises and that such economic activity complements, rather than threatens, the state sector. Since 1980, young job-seekers have been officially encouraged to organize small collective enterprises. Self-employment and the development of family enterprises have been promoted, and the taking of apprentices and hiring of labor (up to eight employees) have been permitted. Although still very small, the individual sector has grown rapidly. In 1984, privately owned industrial and commercial undertakings employed more than 13 million people, of whom about 3 million were in urban areas, a twentyfold increase over 1978. The majority are in commerce, where the Y 28.8 billion turnover was 8.6 percent of total retail sales.[8]

Further expansion seems desirable. Indeed, to take fuller advantage of the employment-creating and productive potential of individual and small collective activity in China would require few positive actions, since the sector tends to grow spontaneously to meet demand once restrictions are removed. It would be necessary, however, to further improve its access to premises, materials, skilled labor, and credit and to make sure that the workers involved have access to public services such as housing, health care, and pensions. (Policy toward the individual sector is discussed further in Chapter 10.)

Underutilized Rural Labor

The scope for expansion of service sector and individual nonagricultural enterprise activities is of course not confined to urban areas. The degree to which such activities expand will also have a powerful effect—probably as great an effect as the overall pace of growth—on the number of workers in agriculture, which is likely to remain the residual employer of labor over the next few decades.

In the QUADRUPLE projection, with continuing rather slow growth of the service sectors, the proportion of the labor force in agriculture declines from 70 percent in 1981 to 59 percent in 2000; the number of agricultural workers increases by 56 million. In the BALANCE projection, with faster growth of the service sectors, employment in agriculture drops to 52 percent of the total, but the number of agricultural workers still rises by 13 million. This is a normal pattern by international standards. A marked decline in China's agricultural labor force over the next two decades could be achieved only if nonagricultural labor productivity grew unsatisfactorily slowly (Chapter 2).

Thus although the agricultural labor force could shrink rapidly in the twenty-first century (Chapter 3), surplus rural labor in the next twenty years is probably unavoidable. The ratio of farmworkers to cropland in China is very high indeed by international standards, with Chinese sources generally estimating that about one-third of the agricultural labor force is superfluous.[9] In considering

---

6. Heather Joshi, Harold Lubell, and Jean Mouly, *Abidjan: Urban Development and Employment in the Ivory Coast* (Geneva: International Labour Office, 1976); S. V. Sethuraman, "The Urban Informal Sector: Concept, Measurement and Policy," *International Labour Review*, vol. 114, no. 1 (July–August 1976), pp. 69–81; C. Wendorff, "El Sector Informal Urbano en el Peru: Interpretacion y Perspectivas" (paper presented at a seminar on employment problems in Peru, Catholic University, Lima, Peru).

7. The figure for Romania excludes small-scale private firms and is therefore an understatement. The figure for Yugoslavia includes transport, communications, catering, tourism, construction, and artisan work. David Granick, *Enterprise Guidance in Eastern Europe* (Princeton, N.J.: Princeton University Press, 1975), p. 486; Harold Lydall, *Yugoslav Socialism* (Oxford: Clarendon Press, 1984), p. 268.

8. *China Daily*, March 16, 1985.

9. Labor use in China is very high, even compared with other parts of East Asia, which in turn is usually greater than elsewhere in the world. For example, Japanese agriculture used nearly 525 man-days per hectare in 1956, and well over 600 man-days in some areas. See K. N. Raj, "Preface," in *Labor Absorption in Asian Agriculture*, by Shigeru Ishikawa (Bangkok: International Labour Office–Asian Regional Team for Employment Promotion, Asian Employment Programme, 1978), p.v. A recent study of thirty production teams in Nantong County, Jiangsu, suggested that a wheat-cotton rotation required 92.3 labor-days per mu (1,384 per hectare) and that a wheat-rice rotation needed 77 labor-days per mu (1,155 per hectare). See Song Linfei, "Village Labor Surplus *(continued)*

what to do about this, it may be unhelpful to think of some specified proportion of agricultural workers as surplus, the rest as necessary. Instead, the problem could be viewed as most agricultural workers making a small incremental contribution to production—or, as Western economists would say, generally low marginal productivity. Because farmers are poor and ingenious, this contribution is rarely zero—if it were, parents would not (as they are now doing in China, and have always done in other developing countries) keep their children out of school to work on the land. Marginal productivity may even have been increased in recent years by the PRS—for example, cotton used to be picked only once, but is now picked repeatedly. And the continuing reorientation of the sector away from grain toward other crops and animal husbandry may raise the marginal productivity of agricultural labor over the decades ahead. But it will in most places and activities remain exceedingly small.

This does not necessarily mean low or stagnant agricultural incomes. For although in other countries low marginal productivity would mean low wages for landless laborers, peasant incomes in China depend instead mainly on average productivity—the amount produced on the household plot divided by the number of household members. In some localities, and for some households, average productivity also will be very low. But for the agricultural sector as a whole, average productivity is likely to increase quite substantially over the next two decades (Chapter 3).

From the viewpoint of efficiency, though, agricultural labor with very low marginal productivity is an underutilized resource. It has often been argued in other developing countries that utilizing such labor for rural public works could increase output and investment, as well as raising the incomes of some of the poorest members of society.

There has also been much skepticism about this possibility. Although a few rural construction projects could use unskilled labor and need very simple tools, most rural investment needs other equipment. Using labor-intensive methods can also be very slow, especially if the work is only done in the off season. Partly finished projects are like unutilized capital assets—it may be worth using higher-cost methods to complete them quickly. Some projects might be completed by using very large amounts of labor at once, but this requires considerable organizational skills, which are not costless. Furthermore, labor participation in public works projects requires the payment of reasonable wages, at least to justify the travel and work effort involved. If this is not to be inflationary, additional taxes need to be collected. In short, these proposals for using surplus labor require investment decisions based on careful evaluation of the benefits and costs involved.[10]

China has made considerable progress in solving the

organizational problems of public works. The difficulties encountered with extensive rural mobilization during the Great Leap Forward demonstrated the limits to this approach, mainly because workers were diverted from agricultural production. During the Cultural Revolution, excessive emphasis on large projects that did not justify the effort involved also led to a reaction against labor-intensive construction methods. But aside from these two periods, China has effectively used rural labor in the slack season for such things as the maintenance and upgrading of irrigation facilities and terracing. The obligation to perform "social labor" is a tradition that preceded the People's Republic and has not been ended by the PRS, although it can now often be commuted into a tax payment.

Neither seasonal public works nor the general utilization of very labor-intensive methods in rural construction is likely to be a panacea for underutilized rural labor. But China could, over the next two decades, use labor-intensive public works to improve rural infrastructure, especially roads. Even the roads linking substantial towns and cities are often poor, and the even lower quality of the rural road network poses a serious obstacle to economic development (Chapter 5). The abundance of underutilized agricultural labor could, with proper management and planning, provide an opportunity to tackle this problem, while contributing directly and indirectly to increasing rural incomes.

Allocating and Motivating Workers

To realize the full potential of China's human resources, it will be essential not only to provide appropriate education and training and to create the right jobs, but also to

and Its Outlet," *Chinese Social Science*, no. 5 (1982), pp. 121–33. Even with this intensity, however, and with a significant amount of sideline and collective enterprise activity, this particular county had a great deal of surplus labor. There were only 1.6 mu per head of the agricultural labor force; the study argued that about 4 mu per worker would be needed to avoid surplus labor. This is actually a substantially higher estimate of labor requirements than many others used in China. For example, forecasts of national agricultural manpower requirements by the Ministry of Agriculture, Animal Husbandry and Fisheries use an average cropping intensity of 9 mu (0.6 hectare) per worker in crop production as an estimate of full employment. On official estimates of the cultivable area, this would suggest that crop production itself could fully employ only about 160 million workers.

10. See Shahid J. Burki and others, *Public Works Programs in Developing Countries: A Comparative Analysis*, Staff Working Paper 224 (Washington, D.C.: World Bank, 1976); and Basil Coukis and others, *Labor-based Construction Programs: A Practical Guide for Planning and Management* (New York: Oxford University Press, 1982).

be successful in matching workers to jobs and getting them to perform well in those jobs. China's traditional system of allocating and motivating workers has serious shortcomings, but changes to achieve greater economic efficiency will raise difficult issues, especially of equity. In agriculture, fundamental and highly beneficial changes in the system of motivation have already tied household earnings to household effort and initiative. This section will thus focus on labor allocation and motivation in nonagricultural and urban activities, which will predominate over the longer term.

Employment Choices of Enterprises and Workers

China's system of labor allocation allows individual employers and employees uniquely little freedom of choice—far less even than in the Soviet Union and Eastern Europe. Until recently, all young people were administratively assigned to particular jobs—college graduates by the central government, secondary school graduates by local labor bureaus—with little attention to their preferences or the preferences of employers. The assignment was typically for life: with few exceptions (generally dictated from above rather than a result of individual or employer preferences), workers could not move from one enterprise to another. Enterprises, moreover, were not permitted to discharge workers, even if they had more employees than they needed, and even if particular employees were habitually absent, lazy, or negligent.

In the last few years, there have been some changes. The system of unified assignment has been dropped for youths with limited training, and enterprises may now examine prospective employees assigned to them by labor bureaus. Some jobs are now advertised. It was recently announced that the best graduates of two universities (Qinghua and Jiaotong) may choose their own employers. From mid-1984, an experimental "job invitation" scheme has allowed a few organizations to offer jobs which they may later terminate to particular individuals, the individual also having the right to refuse the offer or subsequently to withdraw. Another experiment, covering 300,000 workers in early 1984, involves "job contracts" between enterprises and new employees, often for three to five years, specifying mutual obligations in regard to wages, performance standards, contract renewal, and severance. Enterprises are now in principle allowed to dismiss unsatisfactory employees. Finally, there has been rapid growth of the commune and brigade and individual enterprise sectors, where employment decisions are subject to little administrative regulation.

These and other reforms, though beneficial, have not basically changed the system. The unified assignment scheme is still used for virtually all those with any postsecondary training and for some skilled manual workers. Enterprises can seldom hire badly needed skilled workers from other enterprises where their skills may be less valu-

able; they are still obliged by the labor bureaus to accept "packages" containing both wanted and unwanted recruits; they cannot discharge redundant workers; and they have been allowed to dismiss unsatisfactory workers only in a few instances, involving extreme absenteeism or malfeasance. It appears imperative to consider further, more radical, changes.

INDIVIDUAL CHOICE OF JOBS. A fundamental weakness of the present assignment system is its failure to take account of the the fact that individual job performance is as much a matter of individual interest and motivation as of qualifications. Nor is monetary reward the only motivator of effort and initiative. Freedom of choice about where to work not only increases individual satisfaction, but also productivity, since people are likely to be more enthusiastic in a job they have chosen to do. There are therefore many advantages to allowing all workers, skilled and unskilled, new graduates and experienced people, to choose and change jobs freely.

Most governments assign graduates only for compelling reasons. For example, a few with training in much-needed skills might be asked to work in remote areas for a fixed period. Centrally planned countries assign some graduates to their first job: for example, Hungary assigns doctors and teachers; its chief manpower planner found the idea of extending this procedure to all graduates "inconceivable."[11] Hungary, Romania, and the Soviet Union all allow some choice of assignment, at least to the best students, which provides an incentive for good performance at school. Furthermore, these assignments usually last only three years. Many workers then choose another job (perhaps because they were poorly assigned, or perhaps because the assignment process is used to fill inherently unattractive positions). In the Soviet Union, the first year of assignment became a probationary period. The enforcement of assignments, which was once very strict, is now rather lax.

Allowing experienced workers to change employers also has advantages. It diffuses technological knowledge (Chapter 7) and reduces overspecialization. Workers can move to jobs where their particular skills will contribute more to production than in their present jobs. Furthermore, people like variety and are often challenged and stimulated by new situations. (At present in China, the employing unit has to give permission for an employee to move: it will obviously consider its own needs more than those of other enterprises or the whole economy and is likely to deny permission to those with the greatest energy and aptitude for tackling a new job.) Besides, workers forced to remain in jobs where they are bored or

11. János Timar, *Planning the Labor Force in Hungary* (White Plains, N.Y.: International Arts and Sciences Press, 1966), p. 137.

unhappy are generally unproductive. Even large Japanese enterprises, which typically provide lifetime employment, though only to about a quarter of Japan's labor force, encourage periodic reassignments among different departments. They also oblige their workers to "retire"—usually to other jobs—at about age fifty-five.

A possible disadvantage of individual freedom in job choice could be that the resulting pattern of employment was not in accordance with national economic priorities, particularly because many skills are now extremely scarce. This is indeed a real danger in China's present circumstances, but mainly because enterprises are not yet subject to appropriate motivation and economic signals. Without enterprise responsibility for profit and loss, product market competition, or rational prices, employer willingness to pay to secure or retain particular employees would be a poor guide to their potential economic contribution (the changes in the wage system that might be required are discussed below). But these problems should be corrected through wider system reform, which, except for a few projects of great scientific or strategic significance, could make it unnecessary and inefficient for the Government to intervene directly in the allocation of labor.

The other possible disadvantage of giving individuals more freedom to choose and change jobs is excessive labor turnover, which could disrupt production and prevent employees from acquiring enough experience in particular jobs, as well as deterring employers from offering training (unless subsidized or obliged to do so). Though there is controversy about its extent and causes, labor turnover in the Soviet Union is generally believed to be high by international standards and to impose substantial economic costs. By contrast, the Japanese model of mutual lifetime commitment between worker and employer in large enterprises is widely believed to have contributed to the country's economic success. Nevertheless, substantial labor turnover in most countries does not seem to have been particularly disruptive. Even in Japan, 13 percent of all workers leave their enterprises each year, and South Korea has been economically successful despite very high rates of turnover, especially in the labor-intensive export sectors.

ENTERPRISE CHOICE OF WORKERS. The possible advantages of allowing enterprises to compete for workers (new graduates or workers in other enterprises) have already been mentioned. There would also seem to be advantages in allowing enterprises freely to reject potential recruits they do not want, to release redundant workers, and to dismiss unsatisfactory workers.

Dismissal of unsatisfactory workers is already an accepted principle in China. The issue is, rather, what constitutes unsatisfactory performance. This varies from country to country, as do the legal and procedural rights

of workers threatened with dismissal. But the virtual immunity of employees from dismissal in China is unique, and the comparative experience of Hong Kong and foreign businessmen who have established enterprises in China abundantly confirms that it substantially reduces worker effort and initiative. Positive incentives that kindle enthusiasm for work and reward diligence are essential. But it is vital to complement them with the threat of dismissal for poor (and not merely atrocious) performance.

Inevitably, some dismissals will be unfair. Because of mistaken perceptions or personal dislike, employers sometimes dismiss satisfactory workers unless they have to go through a prohibitively elaborate administrative or judicial review process. Moderate safeguards, such as the right to appeal to a tribunal containing some worker representatives, would be essential, but could not avoid all injustice.

Dismissal will also often cause economic hardship—unemployment and loss of income—which, though fair for the idle or negligent worker, is not so for his children. For if dismissal involves no hardship, it loses most of its force, as, for example, in the Soviet Union, where chronic labor shortages mean that dismissed workers have little difficulty in getting other jobs. Even in industrial capitalist countries, where a dismissed worker risks protracted unemployment and may be ineligible for unemployment insurance benefits (which are commonly confined to those who lose their jobs through no fault of their own), he would usually be eligible for some form of public assistance, especially if he had dependent children. Some such compromise between making dismissal a toothless sanction, and making it distressingly onerous, would have to be struck also in China.

Policy toward workers an enterprise would like to discharge (or reject), not because they are idle or negligent, but because they are simply not needed for production, involves yet harder choices. Indeed, even the principle that enterprises should be allowed to do this (or, more drastically, to close down altogether) is not generally accepted in China, mainly because it would inevitably lead to open unemployment. This is seen as wasteful of human resources, and also inequitable because those who lose their jobs may have been conscientious workers (though clearly employers will let the least diligent go first). It would also inflict unusual hardship in China, where there is at present not only no unemployment insurance, but also workers depend on their enterprises for housing, pensions, much education and medical care, and so on. These objections deserve careful consideration.

Long-term, large-scale unemployment is unquestionably wasteful, especially where, as at present in the industrial capitalist countries, large numbers of young people are affected. In China, moreover, where the actual wages of many urban workers may be above their potential contribution to production in alternative employment, employers might on the basis of profitability calculations want to release more workers than would be rational from the viewpoint of economic efficiency. For example, if the wage were Y 100 per month, profit-oriented enterprises would release all workers contributing less than Y 100 to monthly production, even though the alternative jobs for these workers might raise production by only Y 50—thus clearly lowering total national production. (The implications of this for China's wage policy are discussed below.)

Nonetheless, the waste associated with unemployment has to be weighed against the waste associated with the present employment system. To some extent, this system simply transfers unemployment from the streets into the factories, which is no less wasteful. The resulting sense of labor surplus in many enterprises, moreover, discourages managers from improving work habits and increasing the pace of work. The rigidity of the system is also an obstacle to long-term technological advance and productivity growth, both by impeding the replacement of old products and processes with new ones (Chapter 7) and by obstructing the movement of particular workers to jobs in which they could be more productive. For these reasons, allowing enterprises to release or reject redundant workers could on balance lead to fuller use of China's human potential, despite transitory unemployment. This would be particularly likely if the state provided displaced workers with retraining and assistance in finding suitable new jobs.

There are also ways of reducing the hardship that unemployment would otherwise impose on workers released or rejected by Chinese enterprises. These, which are discussed in Chapter 10, include establishing a system of unemployment insurance and transferring much responsibility for housing, pensions, and social services from enterprises to the Government. However, setting the level of unemployment benefits (including housing and social services for unemployed workers) involves an insoluble dilemma. If these benefits are set low, relative to wages, then people who become unemployed through no fault of their own, and their families, suffer unacceptable hardship. But if they are set high, people have little incentive to work and may even prefer to be unemployed rather than take, to gain a little extra money, a monotonous or arduous job. The strength of this disincentive to work remains controversial. But most economists agree that generous unemployment benefits, both by providing a disincentive to work and by raising wages in low-skill jobs, have contributed significantly to the high levels of long-term unemployment that now afflict, in particular, some West European countries. These benefits have thus also changed unemployment from a problem of poverty into one mainly of wasted human resources.

The arguments for and against allowing enterprises to release or reject redundant labor hinge ultimately on the probability of released workers finding new jobs, paying acceptable wages, within a short time. This probability—which, if high, would make unemployment much more acceptable—should not be underestimated in China. Many workers released by one enterprise would be able to find work in other enterprises simply because employer needs for particular types of labor are now poorly matched with labor allocations. Other released workers would find work after retraining in accordance with the revealed pattern of shortages and surpluses of particular skills (which is at present hard to ascertain). The elimination of old jobs and inefficient enterprises actively contributes to the creation of new jobs and the expansion of employment in efficient enterprises (Chapter 7). There is great potential for creating productive jobs in the service sectors and the individual economy.

But even under the most optimistic assumptions, free release of labor would cause an appreciable number of unlucky individuals—and localities—to suffer long-term unemployment, or (as is more usual in developing countries without unemployment insurance schemes, and consequently with little open unemployment) to experience sharp wage reductions. The increases in unemployment in industrial countries since about 1970 are not encouraging: although unemployment rates are still only 2–4 percent in Austria, Japan, Norway, and Sweden, they are over 13 percent in Belgium, the Netherlands, Spain, and the United Kingdom (where 5 percent of the labor force has now been without jobs for more than one year). There is also appalling urban poverty in some developing countries. Thus, even though most unemployment in other countries is in fact temporary, freedom for Chinese enterprises to release or reject redundant—as distinct from idle or negligent—labor would have both advantages and risks and should probably be approached cautiously and gradually.

Efficiency, Fairness, and Stability in Wage Determination

For most of the past three decades, China's wage system has been just as rigid as its labor allocation system— though more similar to the Soviet and East European systems. There are centrally determined basic wage scales, varying among occupations, industries, and localities. Enterprise managers have had virtually no discretion over where to place individual workers on, or how fast to move them up, these scales—indeed, individual wages might be frozen for a decade or so, causing, for instance, a rapidly promoted minister to be paid less than a longer-serving junior official. Bonuses, piecework, and other forms of payment by results were for many years prohibited. Moreover, a large fraction of worker remuneration has been provided in kind (housing, social services, subsidies), more or less equally to all employees.

In recent years, there have been some changes, most notably the reintroduction of piecework and bonuses, which now have no upper limit for individual workers, though enterprises making payments above specified levels are in principle subject to stiff taxes. Under various "floating wage" schemes, most or all of the basic wage follows the standard eight-grade scale, but bonuses and a part (usually 20–30 percent) of the basic wage are linked to the profit or output of the firm or to performance targets for the individual job.[12] A related scheme is the "floating wages and grade system," under which a worker is promoted for good performance but can only retain the higher grade after three years of sustained good performance. Some state enterprises set aside up to 1.5 percent of the wage bill for "labor emulation" or "labor competition" awards, and honorific titles and privileges are offered for good work performance or innovation. In addition, there has been rapid expansion of commune and brigade and individual enterprises, which have considerable freedom to set their own wages.

As with labor allocation, however, these reforms have not basically changed the system. Bonuses have become general wage supplements, distributed to workers and staff in almost all organizations, often with little regard to the performance of either the organization or the individual. Managers still have little discretion regarding promotion (or demotion). Floating wages apply to a tiny minority—in Jiangsu in early 1984, only 1.4 percent of workers were covered by such schemes. Moreover, even with floating wages, the main determinant of earnings remains the centrally prescribed wage scales, which have changed very little and are most egalitarian by the standards of other countries, especially as regards the smallness of the differentials between manual workers and technical, managerial, and professional staff.

These continuing characteristics of China's wage system cause serious economic problems. It is hard for enterprises to reward good work—including, very importantly, that of their managers—with higher pay or promotion, or to penalize poor work with lower pay. The low, fixed pay of skilled or other scarce labor contributes to misallocation and waste, because employers who need such labor cannot attract it, and because wages that do not reflect its economic value offer no disincentive against employing such labor unnecessarily. Conversely, the relatively high wages that must be paid to unskilled workers are a deterrent to their employment and would become even more so if employers were given more freedom of choice in hiring and firing. More generally, the rigidity of the wage structure is an important cause of the striking coexistence, mentioned earlier, of labor shortages and surpluses in urban China. (The problems caused by limited interregional differences in wage levels and structure were discussed in Chapter 5.)

The Government is therefore actively considering fur-

ther steps toward a more flexible, less egalitarian wage system, in which demand and supply, as well as individual contributions to production, would play a greater role in determining the earnings of particular employees and occupations. It must be stressed that in few other countries are wages freely determined by market forces: even in capitalist nations, there is usually some mixture of market forces, collective bargaining by trade unions, minimum wage legislation, and—within large organizations—administered wage scales influenced by considerations of hierarchy and fairness. (The rigidity that these nonmarket elements introduce into the wage structure is widely thought to have contributed to both unemployment and inflation in the industrial countries.) Moreover, for China, the economic benefits of a more flexible wage system would be relatively limited without more general reforms of enterprise motivation and prices, which would align the financial interests of enterprises more closely with the economic interests of the nation.

Objections to more wage flexibility—which could be accomplished partly by reform of the state enterprise wage system, partly by relative expansion of the less regulated nonstate enterprise sector—are mainly connected with equity. Although the Communist Party's Central Committee has recently stressed that China needs more than the present degree of wage inequality,[13] both very high and very low earnings may be considered contrary to socialist principles. Another concern is that more flexibility might lead to wage inflation, with adverse consequences for the budget or the overall price level. These possible disadvantages of further substantial reform of China's wage system merit careful consideration.

HIGH WAGES. It is essential to distinguish between two quite different forces that would tend, with a greater role for market regulation, to increase the relative pay of certain individuals and occupations. The first is the nature and magnitude of their work: jobs that are particularly arduous or unpleasant, or involve disagreeable risks or responsibilities or long training, must be better paid than other jobs requiring comparable skills to persuade enough people to work in them (this is true even now in China, where mining and remote or hazardous jobs command a wage premium); and people who work longer hours, or faster, or more conscientiously will tend to be paid more. These causes of high earnings seem fully com-

12. See, for example, Qiu Yang, "On the Basic Direction for the Reform of the Wage System of Enterprises," *Jingji Guanli*, no. 9 (September 5, 1983), pp. 20–23 (Joint Publications Research Service 84603, October 24, 1983). Also Zhuang Qidong, "Comments on Floating Wages Being Tried Out in China," *Renmin Ribao*, December 9, 1983.

13. Communique of the Third Plenary Session of the Twelfth Central Committee of the Chinese Communist Party, October 20, 1984, Decision on Reform of the Economic Structure, Article VII.

patible with the socialist principle of payment according to work.

The second source of high wages in a market setting is scarcity. This may arise from a limited supply of innate talent—outstanding artists, sportsmen, and businessmen being examples. Or it may arise from bottlenecks in the education and training system, which cause shortages of certain sorts of labor—at least for a while—even though more than enough people would be willing to undergo the necessary training. Unexpected changes in demand and supply—including those associated with other aspects of system reform—can also cause temporary shortages of particular types of labor in particular places. These sorts of scarcity tend to generate high earnings, which, while they may be economically efficient, are much harder to defend as fair. However, progressive personal income taxation can help to reconcile efficiency with equity by driving an increasingly large wedge between the wage paid by the employer (whose high level encourages efficient use of scarce skills) and the wage received by the employee.

China already has a progressive personal income tax, aimed primarily at resident foreigners; this could be more widely applied as greater wage flexibility is introduced. (A progressive payroll tax paid by the employer on wages above a certain level could achieve similar results.) But the progressive tax would have to be levied on high earnings due to effort as well as on those due to scarcity, since there is no administratively feasible way of discriminating between them, and could thus deter hard work and initiative. For this and other reasons (discussed in Chapter 9), the personal income tax rate structure in China, as in all countries, would have to be a compromise between conflicting objectives.

LOW WAGES. The conflict between principles of efficiency and of equity is generally sharper, and harder to resolve, for low relative wages than for high relative wages. In China, as in other developing countries, unskilled labor is in such abundant supply that profit-oriented employers may only be willing to pay a wage below the minimum necessary for a decent existence.

China's approach to this problem thus far has consisted mainly of keeping unskilled wages above their economic level while obliging employers to take on more unskilled (and other categories of surplus) labor than they want. This approach is not altogether inefficient, since many of the "unwanted" workers in state enterprises are engaged in low productivity activities, much as if they had been voluntarily hired at a lower wage. But it has some serious disadvantages in the context of wider economic reform: it runs counter to the spirit of making enterprises manage their own affairs and cut costs; and it makes it hard for state enterprises to compete effectively in product markets with nonstate enterprises, which in turn encourages administrative restrictions on competition. The budget-

ary burden of subsidies to overmanned loss-making enterprises is also a disadvantage.

If unskilled wages were allowed to float downward, the problems of employment associated with a more flexible system of allocating labor, discussed earlier, would be reduced: profit-oriented employers would want to release fewer unskilled workers than at the present, higher, wages; and it would be easier for those released to find employment elsewhere. But this gain, and other associated increases in economic efficiency, could involve a socially and politically unacceptable drop in unskilled wage levels. There are various ways of easing this problem; none offers a perfect solution.

One is to move gradually, so that there is little or no absolute reduction of unskilled wages even though they decline in relative terms. This could be done on an individual basis, with the guarantee that workers' wages will not be reduced, even though new recruits will be paid less. This would, however, create tension between "old" and "new" workers. Another approach would be to establish a legal minimum wage at the present unskilled level, and then (this would be the vital but difficult part) not to raise it in real terms for perhaps twenty years, even though average earnings—especially those of skilled workers—were increasing. For example, if the unskilled wage were initially three-quarters of the average wage, and the average wage increased at 4 percent per year (as in the QUADRUPLE projection in Chapter 2), a constant absolute unskilled wage would, after twenty years, have declined to one-third of the average wage.

A related strategy would be to increase the cost to employers of other inputs to production, thus making use of unskilled labor relatively more attractive. Obvious examples are increases in the cost of capital (higher profits or taxes on machinery, higher interest rates, fewer grants), energy, raw materials, and of course skilled labor. But beyond a certain point, such increases might be economically irrational, although they could perhaps be complemented with targeted payroll subsidies to employers of low-wage labor. (Payroll taxes or employer social insurance contributions on unskilled wages would of course have the opposite effect.)

The association between low-wages and household poverty is weakened by varying labor force participation. Some low-wage earners are members of households with reasonable average incomes, either because there are few dependents or because other family members earn higher wages. Conversely, some households are poor even though their working members earn reasonable wages, because they have many dependents. Rather than attempting to boost or supplement low wages as such, it may thus be more equitable—and more efficient—to provide direct state income supplements to poor households. This possibility—and some of its other advantages and disadvantages—are discussed in subsequent chapters.

WAGE STABILITY. Recent experience in China, as well as in other socialist and capitalist countries, substantiates the concern that a more flexible wage system might cause excessive increases in average and total wages—and hence budgetary or macroeconomic management problems. In capitalist countries, the main sources of wage-push inflation have apparently not been market pressures, but institutions such as collective wage bargaining and legal minimum wages. These can not only push up wage rates despite balance or surplus in labor markets, they also make it difficult for any wage rate to fall in money terms, so that relative wage adjustments can be achieved only through wage increases. In socialist countries, workers also exert pressure on managers to raise wages, and managers are often disinclined to resist, partly for ideological reasons, partly because they are not concerned to hold costs down. As a result, there has always been some form of wage control from above in the Soviet Union and Eastern Europe, although its form has varied.

If China were to move toward a more flexible, market-regulated, wage system, control of wages in the individual and collective sectors would probably not be needed for overall wage stability (although wage bargaining by trade unions is a potential problem). But in the state sector, unless or until managers are made highly profit-conscious (see Chapter 10), wage control from above will still be necessary. This is partly because workers in large organizations can exert collective pressure for wage increases, partly because, as the Hungarians have discovered, it may be politically inexpedient to encourage conflict over wages between the managers and workers of state enterprises. In China, the case for continuing state sector wage control is further strengthened by the large size of the present gaps between wages (and benefits) in state and nonstate enterprises and between urban and rural incomes, which should probably be gradually narrowed.

The precise form of wage control is itself a difficult issue. The Soviet Union and Eastern Europe have moved increasingly toward limits on the enterprise's total wage bill, leaving managers considerable discretion over how many workers of particular types to employ and how much to pay them, and toward linking the overall wage bill to measures of the enterprise's economic performance, such as growth of net output. Such an approach could have advantages for China, too. But it would be desirable to retain limits on growth of average (per worker) earnings in each enterprise, as well as on the total wage bill. Workers and managers may, otherwise, find it in their interests to restrict or reduce employment to an economically undesirable level, which would have more serious consequences in China than in the labor-short Soviet Union. These limits on earnings increases should, moreover, be enforced administratively, and not merely through tax penalties, whose efficacy in China is much

reduced by poor accounting and managerial indifference to financial results.

In addition, formal linkages between worker remuneration and enterprise (as distinct from individual or group) performance should be approached with caution. This is partly because irrational prices and limited competition make profitability a poor measure of economic performance at present in China, partly because alternatives measures such as labor productivity are fraught with ambiguities of definition and calculation. But it is mainly because there is no way to determine how much of the variation among enterprises in the level or growth of profits or productivity is due to variation in worker effort and initiative, as opposed to variation in technology or managerial skill, which are generally more important. Some improvements in enterprise performance, moreover, are simply a reflection of unacceptably poor prior performance. Larger wage increases for workers in enterprises whose profits or productivity increase more rapidly are thus often (and justifiably) perceived as unfair by workers in other enterprises, who then exert pressure on their employers to secure similar increases by manipulating the statistics and bending the rules. (For example, rules relating wage increases to enterprise productivity increases seriously undermined an overall policy of income restraint in the United Kingdom in the late 1960s.)

Current government proposals to establish formal linkages between average remuneration and financial performance (tax or profit remittances) in individual state enterprises could therefore cause problems. An alternative approach might be to have rather uniform guidelines for average wage increases in state enterprises, related to an overall strategy regarding wage differentials between the state sector and other sectors (including agriculture—see Chapter 3), as well as to economywide labor productivity increases. These overall limits should as far as possible be combined with stronger linkages within enterprises between the remuneration and performance of particular individuals and groups, and with greater flexibility in setting the pay of scarce, skilled categories of staff and workers. But there will inevitably have to be compromises between the need for continuing administrative restraint of total wage bills and the need for more microeconomic flexibility and incentives. Moreover, the managerial indifference to profitability that makes administrative restraint of total wages necessary is obviously also an impediment to establishing an economically efficient and nonegalitarian distribution of the wage bill within particular enterprises.

Population Issues beyond the Year 2000

China's low rate of population growth, by comparison with most other developing countries, is one important reason for China's unusually favorable per capita income growth prospects (Chapter 2). It has been achieved through widespread female literacy and primary health care (see footnote 2 in this chapter), as well as strong birth planning policies. The Government's target for the year 2000 is a population of 1,200 million. This will require a substantial drop in rural fertility from its present level, which will not be easy to achieve. But the target seems broadly feasible, as well as desirable, and its attainment has been assumed in the various economic projections presented in earlier chapters.

The focus of the present section, however, is on demographic and related issues in the twenty-first century. Its objective is not to offer predictions or prescriptions, nor even a comprehensive account of possible outcomes and their determinants and implications, but rather to draw attention to certain issues that may need to be considered and acted on within the next few years.

Figure 8.1 and Table 8.2 present and extend to the year 2100 a demographic projection (B) which almost exactly attains the Government's population target for the year 2000, as well as two alternative projections (A and C).[14] In Projection B, fertility falls below the replacement level during 1985–90, reaches a low point in the first half of the 1990s, and rising again, remains at replacement after the year 2000. Its population of 1,196 million in the year 2000 stabilizes by the year 2100 at an unchanging level of about 1,500 million. Projection A assumes a rather slower decline of fertility, never falling below replacement level; but it, too, assumes that replacement fertility will be achieved in the year 2000 and then maintained indefinitely. Its population of 1,273 million in the year 2000 eventually stabilizes at about 1,700 million. In contrast,

Figure 8.1 Population, Alternative Projections, 1980–2100

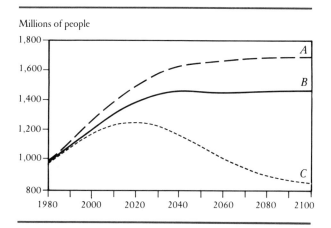

Source: World Bank projections.

Projection C reaches the same low fertility rate as Projection B in the early 1990s and maintains it until the year 2040, when it returns to replacement level. Its population is 1,180 million in the year 2000, falling to about 800 million by the time it stabilizes. (There are no good historical precedents for such a decline, except in conditions of acute economic distress, as in nineteenth century

14. These projections follow the World Bank's standard methodology. See My T. Vu, *World Population Projections 1984* (Washington, D.C.: World Bank, 1984).

Table 8.2 Population Growth, Alternative Projections, 1980–2100

	Projection A			Projection B			Projection C		
Year	Population (millions)	TFR[a]	Average annual growth (percent)[b]	Population (millions)	TFR[a]	Average annual growth (percent)[b]	Population (millions)	TFR[a]	Average annual growth (percent)[b]
1980	980.3	—	—	980.3	—	—	980.3	—	—
1990	1,112.4	2.3	1.3	1,093.8	2.1	1.1	1,093.8	2.0	1.1
2000	1,273.0	2.2	1.4	1,196.3	1.7	0.9	1,179.7	1.5	0.8
2010	1,392.1	2.2	0.9	1,312.3	2.2	0.9	1,232.7	1.5	0.4
2020	1,495.0	2.2	0.7	1,379.4	2.2	0.5	1,245.9	1.5	0.1
2030	1,583.4	2.1	0.6	1,436.8	2.1	0.4	1,224.8	1.5	−0.2
2040	1,626.3	2.1	0.3	1,461.1	2.1	0.2	1,158.1	1.5	−0.6
2050	1,646.8	2.1	0.1	1,449.7	2.1	−0.1	1,085.6	2.1	−0.6
2060	1,663.8	2.1	0.1	1,446.7	2.1	−0.0	1,002.6	2.1	−0.8
2070	1,679.3	2.1	0.1	1,454.8	2.1	0.1	938.4	2.1	−0.7
2080	1,682.6	2.1	0.0	1,461.0	2.1	0.0	893.9	2.1	−0.5
2090	1,685.7	2.1	0.0	1,459.9	2.1	−0.0	859.3	2.1	−0.4
2100	1,687.8	2.1	0.0	1,462.1	2.1	0.0	843.0	2.1	−0.2

a. Total fertility rate; i.e., the average number of children born to women who experience the prevailing pattern of fertility during their child-bearing years.
b. Growth rates are averages over the preceding ten years.
Source: World Bank projections.

Ireland, but some Chinese demographers have suggested an ultimate population target as low as 700 million, to be reached as rapidly as possible).[15]

In the next two decades, the economic implications of these alternative projections are quite limited. The difference in population of about 93 million between Projections A and C in the year 2000 is of course striking, especially since neither projection is based on extreme assumptions. But, though very large in absolute terms and by the standards of other countries, it is a difference of less than 10 percent, and the difference in the average annual growth rate of the population during 1985–2000 is only 0.5 percent. The higher figure would cause per capita income in the year 2000 to be somewhat lower, and probably also the pattern of food consumption and agricultural trade to differ (Chapter 3), but not to a large extent.

In contrasting Projections A and C over the longer term, however, the differences in population size are astounding. A nation of 1.7 billion people would differ in very many ways—physical and social, as well as economic—from one less than half that size. To assess the long-run optimal size of China's population would be difficult and perhaps impossible, since there is no basis for predicting the state of technology more than a century ahead. But it is possible to examine the more predictable consequences of alternative population growth paths for the age structure of the population and some of their economic and social implications. These will probably be quite small in the next fifteen years, but could be very large in the twenty-first century.

Changes in the Age Structure

POPULATION OF SCHOOL AGE. The difference between Projections A and C in the number of children age five to fourteen is 29 million at the end of this century; thereafter, the gap widens until by the year 2040 there are 106 million five- to fourteen-year-olds in Projection A and only 50 million in Projection C.

A smaller number of children would offer the potential for significant savings or quality improvements in education. But the cost reductions would not be proportionate to the difference in population size, since there could not be a proportionate elimination of classrooms and schools or dismissal of teachers. Even in industrial countries, with much more urbanization, better public transport, and a stronger tradition of dismissing redundant employees, it has proved difficult to consolidate educational facilities in the face of declining educational needs. China already has fairly modest primary student-teacher ratios (averaging 25:1 in 1983) and average class sizes (thirty-four pupils per class in 1983), with an average of about five classes per school, which, with a five-year curriculum, gives little opportunity for consolidation. At the secondary level, a smaller age cohort would offer an opportunity for improving enrollment ratios, but recent falls in enrollment suggest that capacity is not currently the main constraint on enrollment.

POPULATION OF WORKING AGE. All three projections show growth in the population of working age (here taken as age fifteen to sixty-four) until after the year 2010 (Table 8.3). The anticipated growth of the labor force is slower under Projections B and C, but even under Projection A, the rate is not high by past Chinese or developing country standards.

Eventually fewer people enter the labor force than retire from it. In Projection C, the population of working age (and hence presumably the labor force) begins to shrink after the year 2010. Under the other projections, this drop comes somewhat later and is less marked. The problem is especially acute in 2030–40 when the large cohorts of the mid to late 1960s and early 1970s retire, and all three projections show declines in the working age population. Negative labor force growth might have some economic advantages. It could cause rapid increases in productivity through faster abandoning of old plants, and stronger incentives for employers to economize on the use of labor. In agriculture, the opportunities for consolidating landholdings and mechanization, and more generally the elimination of the rural labor surplus, would be welcome.

However, a shrinking labor force also inevitably causes problems of adjustment. To introduce new products and processes would require more than equal reductions of employment in older activities, which would not be economically or socially costless: the closure of some plants to preserve economies of scale in other plants might, for example, require substantial geographical movement of labor. There would be a rise in the average age of the labor force, with shortages especially of younger, more recently trained, more adaptable workers, and possibly surpluses of older workers, who find it harder to adjust to new production possibilities requiring substantially different skills. These problems—whose solution would be impossible without a flexible and responsive system of labor training and allocation, far removed from China's present system—would occur under all three projections, but would be most serious and prolonged under Projection C.

THE ELDERLY. Because all three population projections assume the same ultimate fertility and mortality rates,

---

15. Song Jian, "Population Development—Goals and Plans," in *China's Population: Problems and Prospects*, by Liu Zheng and others (Beijing: New World Press, 1981), pp. 25–31; Hu Baosheng and others, "Setting a Target for Our Country's Total Population," *Renkou Yu Jingji* (Population and economics), no. 5 (1981), pp. 15–18, 64.

Table 8.3 Population of Working Age, Alternative Projections, 1980–2100

Year	Projection A			Projection B			Projection C		
	Population (millions)	Percentage of total population	Average annual growth (percent)[a]	Population (millions)	Percentage of total population	Average annual growth (percent)[a]	Population (millions)	Percentage of total population	Average annual growth (percent)[a]
1980	584.8	59.7	—	584.8	59.7	—	584.8	59.7	—
1990	761.4	68.4	2.7	761.4	69.6	2.7	761.4	69.6	2.7
2000	850.3	66.8	1.1	850.3	71.1	1.1	850.3	72.1	1.1
2010	956.8	68.7	1.2	901.0	68.7	0.6	901.0	73.1	0.6
2020	1,020.1	68.2	0.6	944.0	68.4	0.5	894.2	71.8	−0.1
2030	1,027.6	64.9	0.1	935.2	65.1	−0.1	829.7	67.7	−0.7
2040	1,000.6	61.5	−0.3	866.2	59.3	−0.8	698.7	60.3	−1.7
2050	1,029.0	62.5	0.3	877.6	60.5	0.1	620.8	57.2	−1.2
2060	1,025.4	61.6	−0.0	899.6	62.2	0.2	570.7	56.9	−0.8
2070	1,021.4	60.8	−0.0	883.8	60.8	−0.2	532.3	56.7	−0.7
2080	1,030.0	61.4	0.1	888.8	60.8	0.1	508.6	56.9	−0.5
2090	1,024.8	60.9	0.0	894.6	61.3	0.1	505.7	58.8	−0.1
2100	1,029.4	60.9	0.0	887.2	61.7	−0.1	510.5	60.6	0.1

Note: Data are for the population fifteen to sixty-four years old.
a. Growth rates are averages over the preceding ten years.
Source: World Bank projections.

Table 8.4 Population Sixty-Five Years Old or More, Alternative Projections, 1980–2100

Year	Projection A			Projection B			Projection C		
	Population (millions)	Percentage of total population	Working-age pop. ÷ 65 + pop.	Population (millions)	Percentage of total population	Working-age pop. ÷ 65 + pop.	Population (millions)	Percentage of total population	Working-age pop. ÷ 65 + pop.
1980	45.1	4.6	13.0	45.1	4.6	13.0	45.1	4.6	13.0
1990	67.2	6.0	11.3	67.2	6.1	11.3	67.2	6.1	11.3
2000	94.5	7.4	9.0	94.5	7.9	9.0	94.6	8.0	9.0
2010	118.5	8.5	8.1	118.5	9.0	7.6	118.5	9.6	7.6
2020	172.9	11.6	5.9	172.9	12.5	5.5	172.9	13.9	5.2
2030	234.8	14.8	4.4	234.8	16.3	4.0	234.8	19.2	3.5
2040	316.7	19.5	3.2	316.7	21.7	2.7	316.7	27.4	2.2
2050	307.7	18.7	3.3	307.7	21.2	2.9	307.7	28.3	2.0
2060	323.6	19.4	3.2	275.8	19.1	3.3	275.8	27.5	2.1
2070	348.8	20.8	2.9	299.7	20.6	2.9	256.4	27.3	2.1
2080	338.3	20.1	3.0	304.6	20.8	2.9	227.4	25.4	2.2
2090	347.7	20.6	3.0	294.0	20.1	3.0	200.1	23.3	2.5
2100	350.2	20.8	2.9	305.3	20.9	2.9	179.1	21.2	2.9

Source: World Bank projections.

they all eventually converge—in the twenty-second century—to the same, unchanging age structure (Table 8.4). People age sixty-five and over constitute about 21 percent of the "stationary" population in each case. The population of working age is about 61 percent of the total, only slightly greater than the 60 percent of 1980. The ultimate ratio of dependents to the labor force is thus not very different from today. But the demographic structure of dependency is very different: in 1980 only about one out of ten dependents (excluding those age fifteen to sixty-four) was sixty-five or more; ultimately, it will be about one out of two.

Though all countries will probably eventually have a similarly substantial proportion of elderly people, China

is likely to find aging issues more serious, because the rise in the proportion of elderly people will begin at a comparatively low income level. In addition, with an irregular decline in fertility, the proportion of the elderly may even temporarily rise above its long-term stationary level. In Projections A and B, the proportion of the elderly increases slowly to its ultimate size with little fluctuation. By contrast, in Projection C, the elderly become an extremely large proportion (27–28 percent) of the population for several decades after the year 2040.

How financial support of China's prospectively large elderly population might be organized—an issue that may require important steps to be taken soon—is considered below. The other major problem posed by the aging of

The pattern of Chinese health problems has already changed from that of a low-income developing country, where typically over 40 percent of deaths result from infectious, parasitic, and respiratory causes and mortality is particularly high among infants and young children, to one where the leading causes of death are heart disease, strokes, and cancer, as they are in high-income countries. China now faces the difficult challenge of preventing and treating these chronic diseases. The conclusions of a recent World Bank study of China's health sector are summarized in the following paragraphs:

"While there are important steps [to prevention of chronic diseases] that can be taken with little further analysis—particularly control of salt intake and tobacco consumption— . . . much work needs to be done to identify and field test appropriate preventive strategies. The task is inherently far more difficult than is that of prevention of communicable disease. An essential ingredient of a second health care revolution [to tackle emerging problems of chronic disease] in China will be to recognize the difficulty and importance of that task and to commit substantial resources in a sustained way to its solution.

"Another important ingredient of the second health care revolution will be development and widespread implementation of strategies for dealing with the large number of cases of chronic disease that will, inevitably, occur. These strategies must include capacity for treatment where treat-

ment holds promise of results and can be afforded; they must pay careful attention to affordable plans for rehabilitation of individuals partially or wholly incapacitated by noncommunicable disease; and they must be concerned with humane care for the terminally ill (an area in which there have been major and quite affordable advances in Western medical practice).

"A third ingredient of the second health care revolution will be that of designing an insurance and financing structure that encourages prevention and discourages current tendencies toward overuse of facilities. Such an insurance structure should both provide strong disincentives for introduction of the high-cost procedures that would necessarily be available to only a fraction of the population; and it should (through inclusion of substantial deductibles and co-insurance rates) create incentives for both patient and doctor to utilize health resources prudently.

"Assembling the above three ingredients will, inevitably, prove to be a major challenge; but, to the extent that success is achieved, China will have become a world leader in the effective and humane handling of the burden of chronic disease without succumbing, as other countries have, to endlessly costly investments in medical technologies of limited efficacy."[1]

1. Dean T. Jamison and others, *China: The Health Sector* (Washington, D.C.: World Bank, 1984), paras. 5.13–5.16.

China's population will be health care: in the United States, medical expenditure per elderly person is roughly three times that of working-age people. Changing age structure is in fact only one of the components of China's impending second health care revolution (see Box 8.1), but it provides the clearest illustrations of the terrible choices that will have to be made about the—usually extremely expensive—treatment of chronic and terminal diseases. Britain, for example, has held down costs by denying those above a certain age access to treatments such as renal dialysis. Other countries, such as the United States, have not done this, with the result that their health care costs have risen dramatically as a share of GNP—and the proportion of the elderly in China in the next century will be far higher than the present proportion in the United States.

Birth-Planning Policy

In the past decade, the Government has shown a remarkable ability to control individual fertility decisions. China is in a good position to determine its demographic destiny. Nevertheless, even the Chinese system cannot con-

trol the level of fertility precisely. Though couples are urged to have one child, some will have more. Despite substantial economic incentives, the one-child policy is not popular in a family-oriented culture, which has greatly prized sons rather than daughters.

There are no official population targets beyond the year 2000. But the preceding analysis suggests that while the achievement of replacement level fertility (2.1 children per women) is clearly desirable, there could be disadvantages in trying to hold fertility well below this level, especially after the year 2000. Beyond a certain point, as illustrated by Projection C, the gains from achieving a smaller population in the twenty-first century could be more than cancelled out by the adjustment and transfer problems posed by the population's changing age structure.

In any event, an important issue is how eventually to achieve an orderly transition out of the one-child policy. Abandoning the policy suddenly would probably lead to an undesirable new baby boom. One measure already adopted, which is designed to emphasize that the one-child policy is only a temporary measure, is to allow children from one-child families who marry each other to have two children. Another policy modification now applied in rural areas is to permit parents whose first child is a girl to have a second child. A possible extension of this would be to permit every family to have one son, but no further children: average family size would then be about two children. Whatever route the transition takes, the present generous level of economic incentives to parents who have only one child should be maintained, at least until their removal would not excessively stimulate fertility. Indeed, the core positive incentive—a monthly payment to one-child families—might well remain, even if some of the negative incentives, which discriminate against children from families with more than one child, were removed.

Supporting the Elderly

Providing financial support to a large elderly population poses two sorts of problems. One is its economic cost. While the ultimate overall dependency ratio may be much the same as at present, elderly people have higher material consumption needs than children, especially for food and housing space. The economic cost of supporting the elderly could in principle be reduced by cutting their living standards, but China, like other societies, will want its older people to share in the increasing prosperity that they have helped to bring about. The costs involved are already causing difficulties in rich countries, even though they have a smaller proportion of elderly people than China will have in a few decades.

The other problem is how to organize and provide this support. Traditionally, in China as in other developing countries, elderly parents have lived with, and been supported by, their children; China's 1980 marriage law reiterates this filial duty. But in all countries, economic modernization—with more urbanization and mobility, rising incomes, and changing social attitudes—has reduced the number of multigeneration households. In China, the difficulty children have in supporting parents will be further increased by the one-child family policy.

China already provides some support for the elderly, but existing institutions will not be able to cope with the problems of the twenty-first century. In the countryside, the Five Guarantees provide food and clothing, shelter, medical care, and burial expenses. But the level is minimal, and people are sometimes reluctant to accept these benefits, because of the shame of indigency or because they want to retain the right to bequeath family property. In the cities, and in a few rural areas, enterprises and other employers now provide pensions for retired workers; the coverage of such schemes will increase as industrialization and urbanization proceed. However, continued heavy reliance on pensions paid directly by employers would be an obstacle to intensive growth, partly because—as experience in other countries has shown—this

reduces mobility of workers among enterprises, partly because it increases the difficulty and social cost of closing down or drastically reorganizing inefficient enterprises.

Other approaches to supporting the elderly include having the elderly support themselves, through work and through personal saving; the establishment by the state or employers of funded pension schemes; and state noncontributory (or nonfunded) pension schemes. Other countries have adopted varying mixtures of these approaches, each of which has some advantages and disadvantages.

Except for household agriculture, the degree to which the elderly support themselves through work depends on the age of retirement. In China, this is now normally sixty for men, fifty-five for women cadres, and fifty for women workers—a pattern that is not unusual by international standards, and indeed has been shaped by similar pressures, including a desire to move workers (especially women, who actually tend to live longer than men) out of the labor market at times of general unemployment. Official retirement ages are not closely related to ability to work; despite increasing longevity and improving health, the retirement age was raised in only two out of fourteen industrial countries between 1949 and 1977 (nine countries lowered it). Moreover, forcing people with the capacity and desire to make a contribution to stop work at a certain age can be bad for their health and self-respect. In the longer term, and especially when China's labor force is stagnating or shrinking in the twenty-first century, providing more—especially part-time—employment for people above the retirement age, or raising the retirement age, would be an option worth considering.

Greater personal saving for retirement also has certain advantages (governments elsewhere sometimes provide tax concessions to long-term saving schemes), including smaller administrative costs and a greater sense of independence and responsibility for the beneficiary. But because many people are either too poor, or insufficiently farsighted, or without access to appropriate financial investments, to save enough to support themselves decently in old age, personal saving will probably in China (as in most other countries) be confined to a supplementary role.

Fully funded (FF) pension schemes, sponsored by the Government or by employers, are similar to personal savings in that they receive and invest contributions during the employee's working life, with the resulting pension strictly dependent on the amount contributed and the returns earned from its investment. They may differ from personal savings, however, in receiving contributions from employers as well as from employees, or in making employee contributions obligatory.

Employer-sponsored FF pension schemes would be superior to the present Chinese system of pensions paid directly by the employer (sometimes called pay-as-you-

141

go), because the fund could and should be legally separated from the enterprise's general finances and could thus survive and meet its pension responsibilities even if the enterprise closed down. Similarly, if employees were allowed to retain or transfer their share of the pension fund to a new employer (which employers elsewhere have been reluctant to permit, partly to encourage long service, partly because of the administrative costs involved), the employees could move more easily among enterprises. But, clearly, government-sponsored pension schemes (whether funded or not) would also offer independence from enterprise finances and greater worker mobility.

FF pension schemes have the additional advantage of providing pensions as a right, with less sense of burden for both the recipient and the working-age generation. In other countries, moreover, pension funds play an important role in financial markets and could perhaps also do so in China, as well as providing a means for indirect worker ownership of enterprises (these possibilities are discussed further in Chapter 10).

However, FF pension schemes also have certain shortcomings. They provide little or nothing for those who retire within a decade or two after their introduction and indeed become fully operational only after forty years or so. Moreover, the pensions they provide are uncertain and variable in relation to the wages of current workers. This is partly because wages go on rising, while the pension depends largely on contributions from earlier—and much lower—wages, partly because the return on financial and other investments is somewhat unpredictable, especially when corrected for price inflation (which sometimes makes real returns negative).

For these reasons, which would be relevant also in China, governments and employers have often supplemented or modified FF pension schemes. To meet the needs of those retiring before the schemes are fully operational, some governments have—as in Japan—established parallel noncontributory pension schemes, while others—as in the United States shortly after the introduction of the social security system—have waived or reduced contribution requirements for these age groups. To ensure that pensions maintain a stable and equitable relationship with current wages, many government and enterprise pension schemes have made pensions dependent on the number of years during which contributions were made, the individual's terminal salary, subsequent price inflation, current wage levels, and so on—rather than on the individual's accumulated contributions.

Although benefits have increasingly been divorced from individual contributions, the principle of an independent, financially viable fund has generally been preserved, either through supplementary contributions from employers (under enterprise schemes) or the budget (un-

der government schemes), or by raising the contributions of current employees or their employers. The principle that beneficiaries should have earned their pensions through contributions remains important, if only because the elderly thus seem (and feel) less of a burden on current workers.

There is increasing concern, however, that collecting these contributions through—in effect—a substantial tax levied on wages may have an adverse effect on employment. (This could also be a problem in China, especially as regards unskilled workers.) For this reason, but also because the contributory principle is now often a matter of appearance more than substance, state pension schemes financed straightforwardly through general taxation are sometimes advocated, and have been implemented in the Soviet Union and, on a supplementary basis, in Japan and the United Kingdom. China's Five Guarantees system is similar in principle to these pension schemes.

Noncontributory pension schemes are sometimes criticized as being excessively costly and as imposing an unjust burden on current workers. This is fundamentally incorrect, since, whatever the specific institutional arrangements, the elderly are ultimately always supported by the productive activities of current workers—the real issue being at what relative level. Raising the substantial revenues required through general taxation may, however, as with payroll taxation, have adverse economic effects or be politically difficult.

For China, a central issue would be whether, when, and how to include peasant households in any pension scheme. Reform of the urban pension system would be comparatively straightforward. In rural areas, however, there would be not only more administrative difficulties, but also, and more fundamentally, the problems of an initially large gap between average urban and average rural incomes and of widely varying rural incomes. In these circumstances, should the contributory principle be applied, should contributions be compulsory and related to income, and should pensions be related to contributions—all of which would make pensions as unequally distributed as incomes and, in some cases, very low? Or should a large and fiscally expensive noncontributory element, or cross subsidies, be used to make pensions less unequally distributed than—or even unrelated to—contributions?

In planning for the support of the elderly in the twenty-first century, China has a wide range of options. The choice among them is not simple, and none (and no mixture of them) is ideal. But it will be important to consider them, to choose a system, and to put it into operation, within the next few years. Other countries have found that the problems of an aging population can be compounded by failure to look sufficiently far ahead.

Mobilizing Financial Resources

In China, as in other countries, rapid economic and social development will require (though not automatically follow from) high rates of both saving and government revenue raising. To mobilize the huge amounts of money involved, and to do so in ways that promote efficiency, improve the distribution of income, and maintain macroeconomic stability, will require much political will and administrative skill. The economic and institutional changes associated with system reform, moreover, will require constant adaptation of old financial instruments and policies, as well as experimentation with new ones.

This chapter discusses some interrelated long-term issues and options in government finance and national saving—financial intermediation and investment decision-making are discussed in Chapter 10. After reviewing alternative sources of saving, it looks at subsidies and transfer payments, then at overall government revenue needs and sources, and finally at tax reform.[1] (Though local public finance was addressed in Chapter 5, this report does not deal fully with the complex and difficult financial relationships among different levels of government in China. And it touches only very briefly—in Chapter 10—on short-term fiscal stabilization policies.)

The various topics and projections discussed in this chapter share a common macroeconomic accounting framework, summarized in Figure 9.1 (which includes estimates of the relevant magnitudes for China in 1981). The economy is divided into three institutional sectors (the government, enterprises, and households), each of which has a distinct source of income (taxes and remitted profits, retained profits, and wages and other earnings, respectively). The diagram divides the uses of national income into three main categories: household consumption, public consumption, and saving. It then shows how each of the three institutional sectors contributes to each of the three uses of national income. Government revenues, for example, finance some household consumption (through transfers and subsidies[2]), as well as public consumption (to which enterprises also contribute), and sav-

ing. Conversely, total domestic saving comes partly from the government, partly from enterprises (state, collective, and individual), and partly from households. Of this saving, part is used for self-financed investment—enterprises ploughing back retained profits into expansion and people building houses. The rest is channeled into investment indirectly, through government grants or loans to enterprises, through bank deposits being relent to enterprises, through bond sales, and so on.

Alternative Sources of Saving

The macroeconomic projections discussed in Chapter 2 suggest that to attain its long-run growth targets China will need to save something like 30 percent of national income (the numbers mentioned in that chapter range from 26 percent to 36 percent, depending on the assumptions made about investment efficiency, foreign borrowing, and the growth rate). This is a high saving rate by most international standards, though similar to those of Japan and the East European socialist countries (Annex 5, Table 3.2), and comparable to the rates achieved by China over the past three decades (Chapter 2). It is thus important to consider, especially in relation to proposals for further fundamental reform of China's system of economic management, how this high saving rate might be achieved, and in particular what might be the contributions of different institutions and sectors.

Up to now in China, the Government has been the main saver, which has meant a large overlap between saving and public finance. This pattern of saving is proba-

---

1. International experience in public finance and its implications for China are discussed in Background Paper 4.

2. Government finance of household consumption through subsidies is not explicitly shown in the figure, since uses of national income are measured at purchaser prices (which already include the price-reducing effect of subsidies).

Figure 9.1 Sources and Uses of Funds, 1981
(billions of yuan)

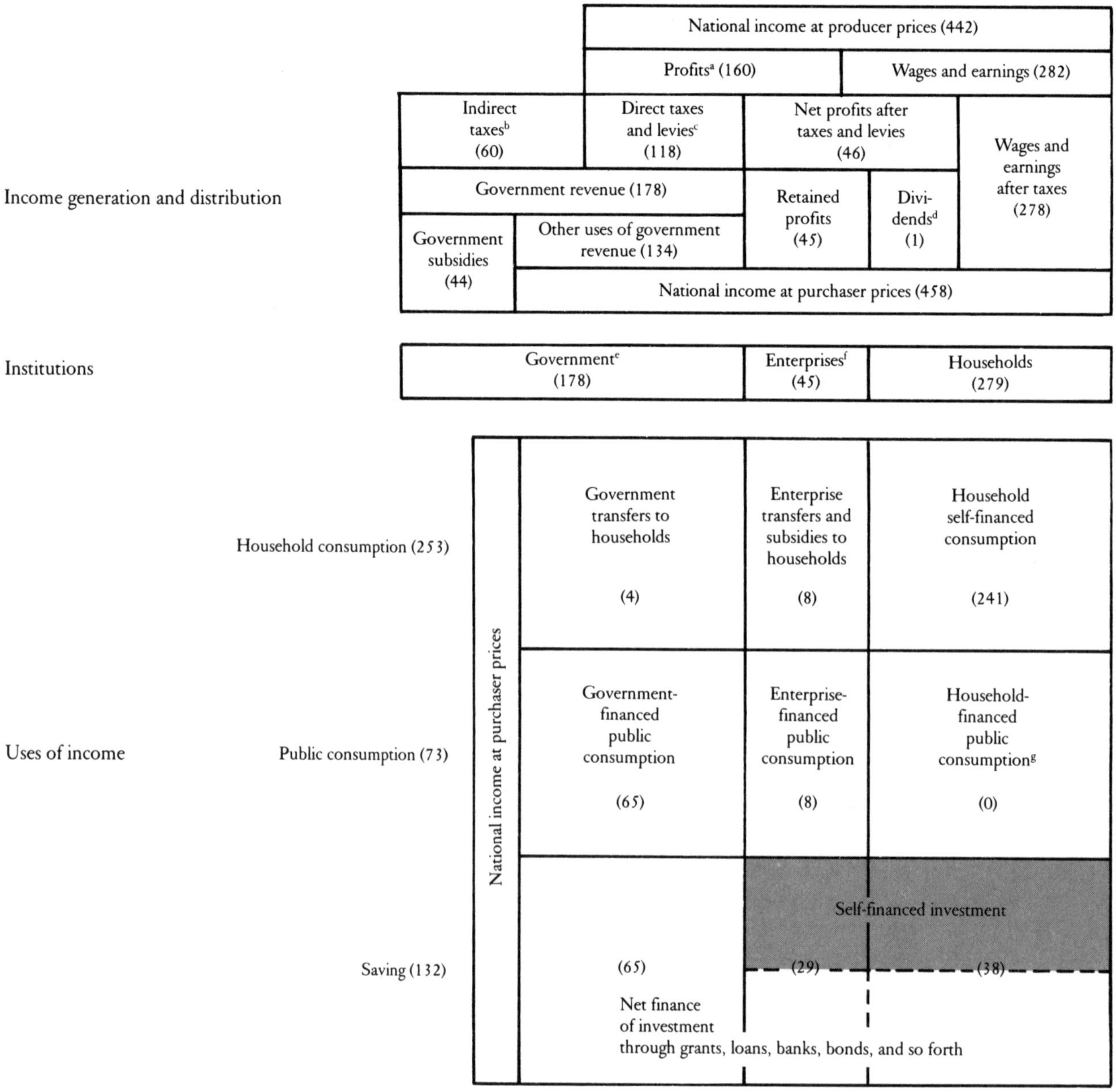

	National income at producer prices (442)			
	Profits[a] (160)		Wages and earnings (282)	
Indirect taxes[b] (60)	Direct taxes and levies[c] (118)	Net profits after taxes and levies (46)	Wages and earnings after taxes (278)	
Government revenue (178)		Retained profits (45)	Divi-dends[d] (1)	
Government subsidies (44)	Other uses of government revenue (134)			
	National income at purchaser prices (458)			

Income generation and distribution (row label, left margin)

Institutions

Government[e] (178)	Enterprises[f] (45)	Households (279)

Uses of income (left margin)

National income at purchaser prices (vertical axis label)

	Government	Enterprise	Household
Household consumption (253)	Government transfers to households (4)	Enterprise transfers and subsidies to households (8)	Household self-financed consumption (241)
Public consumption (73)	Government-financed public consumption (65)	Enterprise-financed public consumption (8)	Household-financed public consumption[g] (0)
Saving (132)	(65)	(29)	(38)

Self-financed investment

Net finance of investment through grants, loans, banks, bonds, and so forth

Note: This accounting framework can be applied to any country, but the numbers in each box are tentative estimates for China, 1981. The diagrammatic integration of the national accounts with government, enterprise, and household accounts is based on the United Nations System of National Accounts. Thus, "national income" includes not only net material product, but also nonmaterial services (which compose a large fraction of "public consumption") and depreciation (which composes a large fraction of "saving"). National income (or gross domestic product, GDP) can be measured at producer prices, reflecting the incomes actually received by the producers in the economy, or at purchaser prices, reflecting the amounts paid by households, enterprises, and the Government for the goods and services they buy. The difference between the two is indirect taxes, net of government subsidies. The sum of incomes received by the Government, enterprises, and households is equal to GDP at producer prices plus total indirect taxes (which form part of government revenue).

a. Gross of depreciation and government subsidies, but net of indirect taxes.

b. All taxes and levies on goods and services.

c. Includes income and profit taxes, asset taxes, agricultural tax, profit remittances to the budget and to government organizations, remittances of depreciation funds, and social insurance contributions.

d. Workers' bonuses paid out of enterprise profits are considered part of wages and earnings.

e. Includes extrabudgetary income and expenditures of government organizations, as well as the government budget.

f. State, collective, and individual enterprises are treated as a single sector.

g. In the conventional national accounting framework, household expenditures on education, health, and other forms of public consumption are defined as private consumption and therefore are included in the box above.

Source: Annex 5, Appendix J.

144

Table 9.1 Gross Domestic Savings in Selected Countries, 1976–80
(percent)

Measure	China, 1978[a]	China, 1981[a]	United States	United Kingdom	Japan	South Korea	India
Share of total saving							
Government	73	49	7	0	9	26	13
Enterprises[b]	12	22	58	56	37	35	22
Households[b]	15	29[c]	35	43	54	38	65
Total	100	100	100	100	100	100	100
Aggregate saving rate[d]	37	29	19	19	32	25	23

Note: Data include depreciation funds.

a. For China, government saving includes both the consolidated budget surplus of revenues over current expenditures and the nonbudgetary saving of government organizations. Enterprise saving includes state and urban and rural collective enterprises.

b. Rough adjustments have been made to the national accounts statistics in order to include the saving of unincorporated enterprises with that of other enterprises (rather than with that of households).

c. In 1981 personal saving appears to have been unusually high in China, because of large stock increases in rural areas.

d. Total saving as share of GDP at purchaser prices.

Source: Estimates based on State Statistical Bureau, *Statistical Yearbook of China, 1981* (Hong Kong: Economic Information and Agency, 1981), see Annex 5, Appendix J; United Nations, *Yearbook of National Accounts* (New York, 1981).

bly similar to that of the Soviet Union and Eastern Europe (though detailed data are not available), but is quite different from those of most other countries. In Table 9.1 for example, despite a significant change between 1978 and 1981, government saving in China is far more important than in any of the other countries. Correspondingly, the shares of both enterprise and household saving in China are the lowest in the table—although the division of saving between enterprises and households varies widely among the other countries (enterprise saving being substantially larger than household saving in the United States, for example, but substantially smaller in Japan).

For the future, one possibility for China would be continuance of the past (or East European) pattern, with government revenues as the predominant source of savings. It is also possible, however, that increased reliance on market regulation and other systemic reforms might make it preferable to further increase the shares of enterprises and households in total saving. How much to reduce the share of government saving, though, and how to divide the remainder between enterprises and households, depends on the advantages and disadvantages of each of these sources of saving.

Government Saving

Two clear advantages of government saving in the Chinese context are that it is a proven and reliable means of achieving a high and reasonably steady aggregate saving rate and that it is unquestionably consistent with social ownership of the means of production created through saving. It could also be argued that government saving is essential for financing infrastructural investment and that it permits close control of other investment. These latter arguments are not quite so compelling. China's past

heavy reliance on government saving has actually been associated with underinvestment in economic and social infrastructure; in other countries a significant fraction of such investment is financed by the savings of enterprises and households through the issuance of government bonds. Moreover, government finance of other investment does not always imply close control: recent experience in China suggests that it may in fact be difficult for the central authorities to regulate the level and composition of local government investment, especially when it is financed from extrabudgetary funds.

One clear disadvantage of heavy reliance on government saving is the strain it imposes on the public finances. Tax rates must be higher than they would otherwise have to be, other government expenditures (on public consumption or support of household consumption) lower, or some combination of the two. High tax rates in turn are disadvantageous because they weaken incentives to cut costs, innovate, and work harder and because they increase tax evasion and the administrative costs of tax collection. Reductions in other public expenditure are disadvantageous because—despite some potential for eliminating waste—there are pressing needs (mentioned frequently in this report) for greater government expenditure in many areas of social and economic importance, for which greater enterprise and household expenditure cannot or should not substitute. Another possible disadvantage of keeping government saving as the main source of finance for investment is that this might conflict with expansion of enterprise autonomy in decisionmaking. But it might be possible to channel government saving to enterprises through an efficient network of financial intermediaries (discussed in Chapter 10).

Perhaps the best approach to determining the appropriate level of government saving in China might be to think of it as the sum of two components—first, as the main source of finance for vital basic investments, and second, as bridging the gap between the total amount of saving required for rapid growth and the actual saving of enterprises and households. But even this admits a wide range of possibilities. As regards the first component, for example, if government saving were to finance only 60 percent of investment in energy and transport, 75 percent in education and health, and 90 percent in public administration and defense, its share in total saving in the year 2000 would be 20 percent (on the basis of the QUADRUPLE investment projections), but if vital basic investment were construed to mean 100 percent in these three categories plus 75 percent in industry and 50 percent in commerce and housing, the government would account for 70 percent of total saving. Similarly, the amount of gap-bridging government saving that might be needed could—on the basis of experience in other countries—vary widely, depending on the amounts that enterprises and households were able (or permitted) to save.

Enterprise Saving

In the four more developed countries in Table 9.1 enterprise saving accounts quite consistently for 10–12 percent of national income (roughly double the percentage in China). It is important, however, to distinguish among enterprises according to their ownership—and especially whether they ultimately belong to the Government or to (individual or groups of) households.

STATE ENTERPRISES. Government saving and state enterprise saving are obviously closely related: both result in state ownership of the means of production created through saving, and one can be substituted for the other—within limits—by varying the profit tax rate and the rules governing remittance of after-tax profits (and depreciation funds) to the budget. But state enterprise saving has certain advantages over government saving, especially in the context of a reformed economic system: it gives enterprise managers a stronger incentive to cut costs and increase profits, and it enables enterprises to function as autonomous economic units—since such units must control at least some investment, and at least some of their investment must be financed internally, rather than by borrowing. State enterprise saving may also have disadvantages, especially if other aspects of system reform lag behind: inappropriate motivation and distorted prices may lead enterprise managers to make bad investment decisions, and profits intended for enterprise saving may be diverted into bonuses and benefits for workers. (The advantages and disadvantages of giving more control of investment to state enterprises are amplified in Chapter 10; control of worker remuneration in state enterprises is discussed in Chapter 8.)

The potential future contribution of state enterprise saving in China naturally depends heavily on the likely future level of state enterprise profits—which will also affect the level and pattern of taxation needed to achieve government revenue targets (discussed later). In China, unlike some other countries (where poorly run state enterprises are a financial burden on the rest of the economy),[3] and despite the losses of many specific enterprises, the state enterprise sector has always generated substantial profits. A crucial question, however, is whether pricing and other reforms will reduce the average profitability of China's state enterprises. This is hard to predict: it will be the net result of several conflicting influences.

Price reform (discussed in Chapter 10) is likely to entail redistribution of profits among sectors—for example, from manufacturing to mining and commerce (there has already been substantial redistribution toward agriculture). This would reduce overall state enterprise profits if—as seems possible, given the recent expansion of collective coal mining and commerce—nonstate enterprises were more common in the sectors whose profitability was increased than in the sectors whose profitability was diminished. Equally crucial, in all sectors, will be the relative efficiency of state enterprise management and the relative wage level in state enterprises. If state enterprises were less cost- or quality-conscious than nonstate enterprises, or obliged to pay higher wages or employ surplus labor, increased competition among enterprises—something which would otherwise be highly desirable—could reduce the profits of state enterprises, and hence their capacity to generate savings.

NONSTATE ENTERPRISES. Experience in other countries suggests that collective and individual, as well as private and mixed-ownership enterprises could potentially contribute a large fraction of the savings required for rapid growth in China, and at the same time could contribute to increasing efficiency through competition and microeconomic structural change (see Chapter 1). To do so—as China's experience especially with commune and brigade enterprises confirms—nonstate enterprises must be allowed to make substantial profits (in aggregate, though some will lose money) and to invest and expand freely. They will then have a strong incentive to increase their profits through cost reduction and greater attention to customer needs and, just as important, to save and reinvest a high proportion of their profits. It is essential, however, that the owners of these enterprises should be confident that the Government will allow them to go on operating indefinitely, without expropriation or punitive taxation. In Hungary, for example, uncertainty about the future course of government policy, which now encour-

---

3. World Bank, *World Development Report 1983* (New York: Oxford University Press, 1983), Chapter 8.

ages individual and small collective enterprises, has caused these enterprises to reinvest only a small (by international standards) proportion of their profits in expansion and market development.

The main disadvantage of relying heavily on nonstate enterprises as a source of saving in China would be its potential consequences for income distribution. A considerable fraction of their after-tax profits (perhaps 50 percent, with the other 50 percent saved) must be distributed for consumption, or else the incentives for establishing and expanding these enterprises would be reduced or even eliminated. Such distribution may be acceptable for collective enterprises, where consumption out of profits is used to benefit the local community, or given to workers as bonuses, or as higher wages than they could earn elsewhere. It poses greater problems in the case of individual enterprises, where much of the profit accrues to one person or family. Other countries have used taxation to influence the division of private enterprise profits between consumption and saving (by higher rates of tax on profits distributed to owners than on reinvested profits). However, any resulting short-term reduction in consumption out of profits eventually tends to be offset by the higher rate of enterprise growth caused by more reinvestment of profits. A better approach to minimizing adverse distributional effects is thus probably progressive taxation of personal incomes and wealth (discussed later and in Chapter 10).

Household Saving

In low-income countries a large part of household saving is for reinvestment in peasant agriculture and thus shares most of the potential advantages and disadvantages of nonstate enterprise saving discussed above. (It is normally treated as household saving simply because of the practical difficulty of disentangling the various sources and uses of income within farm households.) In China, too, the introduction of the rural production responsibility system, and repeated official confirmation of its indefinite continuation, have given farm households strong incentives to make their incomes grow faster through greater saving and reinvestment. But the statistics currently available, though suggesting a high rate of rural saving (probably increased somewhat by shortages of consumer goods), do not permit an accurate assessment of the rate of reinvestment in agriculture, as opposed to nonagricultural activities and housing (Annex 2, paras. 1.13–1.18). In particular, it is unclear whether increased household investment has been sufficient to offset reduced state and collective investment in agriculture.

Apart from agriculture, household saving in other countries is partly for purchase of consumer durables and other occasional and unanticipated expenditures (and is largely cancelled out by dissaving or borrowing for such expenditures). Most, however, is connected with housing

or with provision for retirement. Saving for housing is already important in China. Peasants have apparently used a considerable part of their increased saving in the past few years to build new houses and improve existing houses. In urban areas, there is also a substantial private housing stock (mainly rather old), and some state-built apartments have recently been sold to individual families.

In the future, the greater part of China's investment in urban housing could be financed by personal saving (partly through housing cooperatives), with far less provision of workers' housing by enterprises. The Government might provide housing directly only to the minority of people unable to pay, but could assist others by selling off more existing urban housing, as well as by "sites and services" projects—planning and providing basic utilities for new individually constructed housing—coupled with technical assistance and limited subsidies or tax concessions to housing cooperatives. (These could partially replace the large existing housing subsidies, which would need to be reduced or eliminated to provide an incentive for tenants to become owners.) Experience elsewhere suggests that such a system would be a powerful stimulus to household saving, as well as to better construction standards and maintenance.

Saving for retirement (including contributions to funded pension schemes) was discussed at the end of Chapter 8. Household saving for this purpose could probably be substantially increased, though not as the sole or necessarily even the primary means of supporting the elderly. It could be encouraged by organizing funded pension schemes and other long-term saving instruments (commonly provided in other countries by life insurance companies), and possibly also by payment of bonuses to workers once or twice a year—as in Japan—rather than monthly (this might also facilitate a closer linkage between bonuses and profits).

Saving for retirement by today's workers will of course always be to some extent offset by the dissaving of retired people, although many bequeath something (often a house) to their children. The household sector's net contribution to national saving is thus influenced by the growth rate and age structure of the population, with a slower-growing, aging population (as China will have for the forseeable future) tending on balance to save less. Fast growth of per capita income, by contrast, tends to raise the household saving rate, by making the incomes of today's savers higher than those from which today's dissavers built up their savings. In this regard there is good potential for household saving in China—as in Japan, where the effect of rapid income growth appears to have more than outweighed that of an aging population.

The data in Table 9.1 suggest that household saving may be an especially important potential substitute for government saving. In particular, Japan, the only large nonsocialist country to have persistently saved about 30

Table 9.2 Subsidies, 1981

Type of subsidy	Billions of yuan
Price subsidies	37.8
Industrial inputs to agriculture	2.2
Imported agricultural products	8.8
Grain	5.9
Other	2.9
Domestically produced staple food	15.0
Grain	12.2
Edible oil	2.8
Other commodities	6.8
Nonstaple foodstuffs	2.8
Cotton	1.3
Coal	1.0
Other	1.7
Housing[a]	5.0
Subsidies to money-losing enterprises	10.2
Industrial enterprises	4.2
Commercial enterprises	6.0
Total	48.0

a. Estimated depreciation, maintenance, repairs, management, and interest (based on the cost of construction), less rent paid. About Y 1.3 billion is direct government expenditure; the rest is paid for by state enterprises.
Source: Annex 5, Appendix J, Worksheet D.

percent of national income, has done so not mainly through high enterprise saving, but through an extraordinarily high personal saving ratio (about 20 percent of personal disposable income). In most other nonsocialist countries, where personal saving ratios are around 10 percent, aggregate saving is usually only 20–25 percent of national income. In South Korea, for example, the aggregate saving rate is as high as 25 percent only because the government contributes a quarter of the total.

Because Japan's personal saving ratio is so unusual, it seems likely in China that government saving will have to continue to be substantial if a high aggregate saving rate is to be achieved. However, the Government's share of saving could probably be much lower than in the past, with greater reliance on both enterprise and household saving instead. What the precise balance among different sources of saving in China could or should be in the longer term cannot be assessed at present, since much will depend on the future course of system reform and experience in mobilizing and using enterprise and household saving (Chapter 10). But some of the possibilities are explored numerically later in this chapter, in connection with alternative projections of government expenditures and revenues.

Subsidies and Transfers

In addition to mobilizing saving, government revenues are needed, first, for public consumption (mainly education, health, defense, and public administration) and, sec-

ond, for support of household consumption through subsidies and transfers (income supplements and social relief). The Chinese Government will have to make important decisions on individual items of public consumption in the future. But for reasons discussed earlier (Chapter 1), public consumption in aggregate may not change greatly as a share of national income over the next two decades. At least the possible range of options (in terms of demands on government revenue) seems much narrower than for either government saving or subsidies and transfers.

China's Subsidies in Perspective

Large subsidies are at present the subject of widespread concern in China. But assessment of the problem is complicated by confusion over definitions, magnitudes, and economic impact. The term "subsidy" is used in China to cover various kinds of wage supplements (for everything from nonstaple foods to baths and haircuts), as well as in its two more normal senses, namely (a) government payments that reduce the prices of certain goods and services, and (b) government payments to keep inefficient enterprises in operation. Moreover, in China (as in some other countries) most subsidies are not explicit items of government expenditure, but instead reduce government revenue (by lowering state enterprise profits), which makes them hard to measure, particularly since there is uncertainty about what enterprise profits would or should otherwise have been.

Table 9.2 shows Chinese estimates of the magnitude of price subsidies and subsidies to money-losing enterprises in 1981. They totaled Y 48 billion, equivalent to about 33 percent of budget revenues and 11 percent of GDP.[4] Over half the total is food subsidies, which have become much larger in the past few years as a result of substantial increases in agricultural procurement prices with little or no increase in the retail prices of staple foods. The next largest category (21 percent of the total) is subsidies to cover the operating losses of inefficient industrial and commercial enterprises. Another substantial item (over 10 percent of the total) is the subsidy involved in keeping the rent on urban enterprise and municipal housing at only a fraction of its capital and operating costs (this apparently is paid mostly by state enterprises rather than directly by the Government).

4. Budget revenue is adjusted as explained in Annex 5 (Appendix J, Supplementary Worksheet 1). If government extrabudgetary funds were included, the share of subsidies in total government revenue would be 27 percent. GDP is measured at "producer prices" (that is, less indirect taxes plus subsidies—see Figure 9.1). This specialized national accounting usage of the term "producer prices" is confined to figures and tables in this chapter. Elsewhere in the report, the term is used to mean ex factory or farmgate prices.

With transfer payments (at present very small) added to subsidies, the total as a share of budget revenue in China is not much higher than the average for developing countries, and well below the average for industrial market economies, where transfer payments are very large (see Table 9.3). The difference between China and other developing countries would appear larger, however, if subsidies and transfers were expressed as a share of GDP, since budget revenues in China are over 30 percent of GDP, as compared with about 20 percent in the average developing country. Food subsidies, moreover, are a higher proportion of government budget expenditure in China than in all but a few developing countries (including, in the mid-1970s, Egypt, South Korea, and Sri Lanka); as a proportion of GDP they are probably higher than in any other country except Egypt.[5]

The incidence (or economic impact) of China's subsidies can be established only on specific assumptions about the situation without subsidies and may vary dramatically depending on the assumptions made. For example, China's food subsidies are often said to raise the real incomes of urban residents, but this is so only if the assumed alternative is higher retail food prices. If, by contrast, the alternative were assumed to be lower procurement prices, then the beneficiaries would be not the urban population but the rural population. An assumed alternative combination of higher retail and lower procurement prices would imply that the benefits go partly to urban, partly to rural residents. Similarly, assessment of the incidence of China's urban housing subsidy is dependent on assumptions about the level of wages without the subsidy.

Future Options for Price Subsidies

Price subsidies are not in principle a bad thing.[6] If used as negative indirect taxes in the context of market regulation, they can be useful economic levers for stimulating the production and consumption of goods and services of which there would otherwise be too little from an economic or social viewpoint. Research, training, books, and the arts are common examples in other countries. Price subsidies can also contribute to improving the distribution of living standards: food subsidies tend to accrue disproportionately to lower income groups, who spend a higher proportion of their incomes on food; children's clothing and school lunches are sometimes also subsidized for similar reasons. Price subsidies can be used to a limited degree to stabilize living standards in the face of temporary fluctuations in producer prices.

Especially in the way China now uses them, price subsidies also have some disadvantages. They can complicate fiscal planning by fluctuating unexpectedly, particularly if they arise from a commitment to keep certain prices constant (as contrasted with, say, a fixed percentage subsidy). They can also have adverse effects on economic efficiency by distorting price signals—for instance, when

Table 9.3 Subsidies and Transfers as Percentages of Government Revenue in Selected Countries

Country group	1975	1979
Industrial market economies[a]	54	56
Oil-importing developing countries[a]	30	31
India	29	36
Pakistan	19	20
Philippines	9	10
South Korea	29	34
Sri Lanka	32	26
Thailand	17	13
China[b]	..	33

Note: Data are for central government only. Capital transfers are excluded.
a. Averages weighted by 1975 GDP. Developing country average excludes China.
b. Based on a figure of Y 44.3 billion derived from Table 9.2 (the total minus Y 3.7 billion in housing subsidies paid for by enterprises), plus an estimated Y 2.0 billion of pensions and Y 1.0 million of social relief paid by the budget. Data are for 1981.
Source: International Monetary Fund, *Government Finance Statistics Yearbook* (Washington, D.C., 1982), p. 46

subsidized coal discourages the purchase of fuel-efficient stoves or when low rents cause inadequate housing maintenance. Subsidies may also be costly to administer, especially if the item in question has to be rationed.

As instruments of income redistribution, subsidies are at best crude, since they provide low prices to rich and poor alike (as contrasted with income supplements targeted at the poor, which in principle can achieve the same effect at lower cost). They may even have perverse effects: in urban China, for example, lower-paid temporary workers from the countryside and the lower-paid workers of small-town collective enterprises have less access to subsidised food and housing than higher-paid permanent state enterprise workers, and in rural China, higher grain procurement prices may have disproportionately benefited richer households, which have a greater marketable surplus, and perhaps even have harmed some poorer households, which are net purchasers of grain. As instruments for price stabilization, too, subsidies are of dubious benefit, since they encourage governments repeatedly to postpone comparatively minor price increases until the required price increases become disruptively large.

Thus although China's subsidies perhaps are not such a serious problem as is sometimes suggested, they might advantageously be reduced, modified, or replaced with

5. Jeffrey M. Davis, "The Fiscal Role of Food Subsidy Programs," *IMF Staff Papers*, vol. 24, no.1 (March 1977); Sadiq Ahmed, *Public Finance in Egypt: Its Structure and Trends*, Staff Working Paper 639 (Washington, D.C.: World Bank, 1984).

6. The advantages and disadvantages of subsidies to inefficient enterprises are discussed further in Chapters 1, 5, 7, and 8.

alternative instruments over the next few years. Food subsidies could in principle be reduced and regulated by adjusting agricultural procurement prices. This is not an attractive option, partly because it would widen the agricultural-nonagricultural income gap, but mainly because it would in principle conflict with the use of agricultural producer prices to balance supply and demand for particular agricultural products (Chapter 3). In order to enable agricultural producer prices to provide appropriate allocative signals to farmers in changing circumstances without disrupting the budget, the Government might reduce its role as a buyer and seller of agricultural products, leaving the bulk of the market to collective and individual commerce (Chapter 3). But it would also be essential to establish a rational relationship between the retail and producer prices of food and other agricultural products. This would involve restoration of normal distribution and processing margins, mainly through increases in retail prices.

At present producer prices, eliminating food subsidies would apparently require a 50–60 percent increase in the urban retail price of grain and an 80 percent increase in that of edible oil. To maintain living standards, these increases, plus those necessary to eliminate other commodity subsidies, would require urban incomes to be raised by about 25 percent on average, but perhaps by as much as 45 percent for the poorest urban households, which spend a higher proportion of their incomes on food.[7] If housing subsidies were simultaneously eliminated through rent increases, the required urban income increases would be roughly 30 percent on average and 50 percent for the poorest households.

The social problems that have sometimes followed large retail price increases in other countries seem to have occurred mainly because the price increases were used to cut real household consumption in the face of macroeconomic difficulties. In China, however, there is no need for a cut in urban household consumption (although it might be desirable for urban consumption to grow more slowly than rural consumption in order gradually to narrow the urban-rural gap). Urban households could and should thus be compensated with income increases to offset the required retail price increases—although this would mean no net improvement in the budget balance.

A major instrument of compensation would be general wage (and pension) increases for state and large urban collective workers. The earnings of individual and small urban collective workers, which are not subject to administrative regulation, could not be raised so easily, but they would tend to be pushed and pulled up by the higher wages of other workers, partly because of the need for small enterprises to attract labor, partly because of the associated increase in money spending power. Because the ratio of dependents to workers (and pensioners) varies among households, a general wage increase alone could

not accurately compensate for increased retail prices and rents, but would need to be combined with supplementary income transfers to high-dependency households. There should probably also be special supplementary interest payments on saving deposits, which would otherwise lose part of their real value, financed perhaps by a corresponding special levy on borrowers, whose loan repayment burden would otherwise decrease in real terms. (See also Chapter 10)

The specific mixture of general wage increases and supplementary income transfers chosen would depend on the relative importance attached by the Government to minimizing its outlays or revenue losses, preventing anyone's living standard from falling, and widening the wage differences between skilled and unskilled workers (for employment and incentive reasons discussed in Chapter 8). For example, equal proportionate wage increases would widen the real income differences between skilled and unskilled workers (since on average the latter tend to belong to lower-income households, which spend proportionately more on food and rent), but they would reduce living standards in low-income households unless there were wage overcompensation (wage increases that on average more than offset price increases) or larger income transfers to poor households, both of which would involve greater costs to the Government. Alternatively, at lower budgetary cost, the general wage increase could be proportionately larger for low wages than for high wages, which would maintain the purchasing power of low wages but would leave the wage differential between skilled and unskilled workers unchanged in real terms, although it could subsequently be widened gradually by faster wage increases for skilled workers (see Chapter 8).

There is room for disagreement as to whether such a major realignment of retail prices and incomes should be done in one step or more gradually. If full compensation were provided, a carefully prepared and well-explained one-step adjustment could be quite acceptable and would avoid the protracted uncertainty and delays to other necessary reforms associated with gradual adjustment. But it would also obviously increase the cost of errors in preparation (especially calculating the required increases in prices, wages, and other forms of compensation) or implementation. In any event, the Government has thus far chosen to take limited steps, such as the May 1985 increase in nonstaple food prices, which was offset by a flat-rate per capita increase in urban incomes.

---

7. These figures are rough estimates based on the urban household survey data in State Statistical Bureau, *Statistical Yearbook of China, 1983* (Hong Kong: Economic Information and Agency, 1983), and on the data in Table 9.2, assuming 75 percent of the price subsidies in categories 1–4 are for goods sold to urban residents. Urban incomes in 1981 totaled about Y 100 billion.

In the long term, once normal commercial margins have been restored, rises and falls in the producer prices of particular goods should be reflected in corresponding changes in retail prices. This would contribute to national economic efficiency by encouraging consumers to buy less of things in short supply or whose production costs are increasing and more of things in abundant supply or whose production costs are falling. Experience in other countries suggests, however, that it would be inadvisable to provide continuing automatic compensation for retail

mentioned above. Another might be extension of the social security benefits (pensions, sickness and disability payments, maternity leave) currently enjoyed by government and state enterprise employees to the rest of the nonagricultural labor force and even to part of the agricultural population. Even without this wider coverage, the Government might assume direct responsibility for providing most or all of the benefits now paid by state enterprises. Reform of the labor allocation system to increase mobility would necessitate some form of govern-

Table 9.4 Subsidies and Transfers, Alternative Projections, 1981–2000
(percent)

		2000			
Type	1981	Subsidies eliminated, low transfers (1)	Subsidies eliminated, high tranfers (2)	Intermediate subsidies, low transfers (3)	High subsidies, intermediate transfers (4)
Subsidies	10.8	0.9	0.9	4.7	8.6
Government subsidies	10.0	0.9	0.9	3.4	7.5
Food	6.0	0.0	0.0	1.8	4.5
Other consumer goods[a]	1.4	0.0	0.0	0.7	1.4
Housing	0.3	0.5	0.5	0.2	0.4
Money-losing enterprises	2.3	0.4	0.4	0.7	1.2
Enterprise housing	0.8	0.0	0.0	1.3	1.1
Transfers	1.8	3.1	12.6	3.1	7.3
Social relief	0.2	0.2	0.2	0.2	0.2
Employee benefits[b]	1.6	2.9	9.3	2.9	4.3
Paid by government	0.6	0.7	9.3	0.7	4.3
Paid by enterprises	1.0	2.2	0.0	2.2	0.0
Compensation for reduction in subsidies	—	—	2.5	—	2.2
Unemployment compensation	—	—	0.6	—	0.6
Total	12.6	4.0	13.5	7.8	15.9
Paid by government[c]	10.8	1.8	13.5	4.3	14.8
Paid by enterprises	1.8	2.2	0.0	3.5	1.1

Note: Data are percentages of GDP, at producer prices (see Figure 9.1).
a. Includes subsidies for agricultural inputs.
b. Pensions, sickness and disability payments, maternity benefits, funeral expenses, and similar benefits.
c. Possibly financed in part from mandatory contributions by employers or employees to government social insurance funds.
Source: World Bank projections.

price increases in the form of general wage or income indexation, since this tends to aggravate inflation. Even selective indexation (of low incomes, for example, or for pension funds) should be approached cautiously.

Future Options for Transfers

Over time, the share of subsidies in China's national income and government expenditure is likely to decline. But transfer payments could greatly increase over the next two decades, for a number of reasons. One is possible supplementary income payments to poor households,

ment-sponsored unemployment compensation (Chapter 8). Finally, the increase in the share of the elderly in China's total population (see Table 8.4) will mean increased pension costs, paid for at least in part by the Government.

Table 9.4 presents some illustrative projections of the cost of subsidies and transfers in the year 2000. In 1981, transfer payments were very low, consisting of government and urban (primarily state) enterprise social security expenditures for employees and government social relief payments. They amounted to less than 2 percent of GDP, with the Government and enterprises each paying about 1 percent.[8] Subsidies, in comparison, were relatively high (see Table 9.2). Overall, subsidies and transfers totaled nearly 13 percent of GDP, 11 percent covered by the Government and 2 percent paid by enterprises.

In the year 2000, at one extreme (scenario 1), subsidies might be virtually eliminated (their share in GDP cut from 11 percent to 1 percent), but social security coverage would not be expanded and no major new transfer schemes would be introduced. The share of transfers in GDP would nonetheless rise to over 3 percent, because of the increasing proportion of retirees in the government and state enterprise sectors. Subsidies and transfers together would account for only 4 percent of GDP, with less than half of this amount paid by the Government. If subsidies are eliminated, however, it is more likely that transfer payments will substantially increase their share in GDP. This is shown in scenario 2, where government-financed social security coverage is extended to the entire nonagricultural population, as well as to at least part of the agricultural population; low-income urban households are compensated for the elimination of subsidies in part through supplementary income transfers (rather than higher wages); and increased labor mobility generates a modest amount of temporary unemployment (people changing jobs and employees of failing firms laid off), necessitating a government-financed unemployment compensation system (possibly funded in part by employer contributions). Overall, government spending on subsidies and transfers would be over 13 percent of GDP, nearly all of it transfers.

In scenario 3, the Government is only moderately successful in containing subsidies, but transfer payments are kept low. Total spending on subsidies and transfers in this case would be around 8 percent of GDP, with enterprises covering nearly half of the costs. In scenario 4, at the opposite extreme from scenario 1, subsidies fall only slightly as a share of GDP while at the same time large new transfer schemes (covering the entire nonagricultural population) are introduced: subsidies and transfers total 16 percent of GDP, nearly all paid by the Government.

Much additional spending on transfers would be offset by reductions in other expenditure categories. This applies to income supplements to compensate for reductions in subsidies as well as to unemployment compensation (which at present is in effect paid by enterprises as the wages of redundant employees). Nonetheless, the larger elderly population will clearly absorb additional resources. The degree to which higher transfer payments become an additional burden on government finances also depends on financing mechanisms and the tax system. Shifting responsibility for transfer payments from state enterprises to the Government, for example, would cause increased government spending to be offset exactly by increased state enterprise profits, but it might be diffi-

cult for the Government to capture all of these profits (unless perhaps state enterprises were obliged to contribute to a Government social security fund in proportion to their wage bill or number of employees). In any event, much of the cost of extending social security protection to people outside the state sector would probably have to be borne by the Government.

Revenue Needs and Sources

Long-term government revenue needs depend on the desired levels of government-financed public consumption, subsidies and transfers, and government saving. Some illustrative projections for China in the year 2000 are shown in Table 9.5, which focuses mainly on alternative possibilities for government saving and for subsidies and transfers. At one extreme (the High scenario), the Government might account for as much as 70 percent of aggregate saving (mentioned earlier), while government subsidies and transfers might be as much as 15 percent of GDP (scenario 4 in Table 9.4). Government revenue would then have to exceed 50 percent of GDP, compared with about 40 percent at present. At the other extreme (the Low scenario), subsidies might be virtually eliminated while government transfer payments remain limited primarily to civil servants' pensions and disaster relief (scenario 1 in Table 9.4). At the same time, the Government might mobilize only 20 percent of total saving—less than half the present level, but still somewhat more than in most nonsocialist countries. Total government revenue could then be less than a quarter of GDP, as compared with 20 percent in the average developing country in 1977.

Two intermediate scenarios are used in subsequent analysis in this chapter. In the High Saving scenario, the Government accounts for 70 percent of aggregate saving (as in the High scenario), and the share of government saving in GDP rises from 15 percent in 1981 to 21 percent in 2000. Subsidies are to a considerable extent brought under control and are not replaced by new transfer programs (much as in scenario 3 in Table 9.4). As a result, government subsidies and transfers decline from 11 percent of GDP in 1981 to 5 percent in 2000. These changes roughly offset each other, so the Government occupies about the same share of the economy in 2000 as it did in 1981, but it saves more and spends less on subsidies and

8. Enterprise "transfers" exclude the many wage-like income supplements, bonuses, and "subsidies" presently paid by Chinese state enterprises to their employees. They refer only to payments of a social insurance nature, such as pensions, sick leave, and maternity benefits. (Enterprise expenditures on education and health are considered public consumption rather than transfers, though the dividing line is somewhat arbitrary—see Figure 9.1).

Table 9.5 Government Expenditures, Alternative Projections, 1981–2000
(percent)

Measure	1981[a]	2000 High	2000 Low	2000 High saving	2000 High transfers
Shares of GDP[b]					
Total uses of government revenue[c]	41	52	24	42	35
Public consumption[d]	15	16	16	16	16
Subsidies and transfers[d]	11	15	2	5	13
Saving	15	21	6	21	6
Ratio of government saving to total domestic saving	49	70	20	70	20
Shares of total government expenditures					
Public consumption	37	31	67	39	45
Subsidies and transfers	27	28	7	10	38
Saving	36	41	25	51	17

a. Data are estimates explained in Annex 5, Appendix J. GDP and saving for 2000 are from the QUADRUPLE projection discussed in Chapter 2.
b. GDP is measured at producer prices (see Figure 9.1).
c. The size of the government deficit (equal to the amount by which government-financed investment exceeds government saving) is not projected. Therefore the figures are for total uses of revenue rather than total expenditure.
d. Includes only the portion paid for by the Government; some public consumption, subsidies, and transfers are financed by enterprises (see Figure 9.1). Hence, for 1981 the underlying public consumption figure is less than that in Annex 5 (16 percent of GDP before price adjustment), and the underlying subsidy and transfer figure is Y 3.7 billion less than in Table 9.2, this difference being the estimated portion of the housing subsidy financed by enterprises.
Source: World Bank projections.

transfers. In the High Transfers scenario, government saving would be as low as in the Low case. Subsidies would be drastically reduced, but this would be more than offset by a large increase in transfer payments, reflecting the introduction of government-financed social insurance schemes (scenario 2 in Table 9.4). As a result, the share of subsidies and transfers in GDP would rise somewhat, and overall the share of the Government in GDP would fall from 41 percent to 35 percent.

China's experience during the past few years suggests that it will not necessarily be easy to achieve the revenue growth required even for the two intermediate expenditure scenarios. Budget revenue grew only about 40 percent as fast as national income in 1978–82 and grew faster in 1983 only because of a new levy on enterprise-retained profits and other extrabudgetary funds. Nonetheless, international experience does not rule out the possibility of revenue growth fast enough to achieve the High expenditure scenario (tax revenues in a sample of developing countries grew 40 percent faster than national income from 1953–55 to 1966–68),[9] although government revenues in China are already high by comparison with other developing countries. On balance, given China's political and administrative capabilities, the level of government expenditure seems unlikely to be limited simply by capacity to raise revenue. Instead, the central issue will be to weigh the economic and social benefits of higher expenditure against the various distortions and disincentives associated with higher taxation, which may be more significant in a reformed economic system than they have been in the past.

Revenue Sources

There is considerable room for choice concerning the composition of government revenue, even if total revenue requirements, the structure of the economy, and relative prices are given. Some of the issues and tradeoffs in this area are presented in Figure 9.2, which is based on the illustrative projections in Table 9.6.

Pie A in Figure 9.2 presents the situation in 1981. The Government relies overwhelmingly on levies on profits and on indirect taxes to meet revenue needs. Agricultural incomes form a large chunk of the economy but are only lightly taxed (through the stagnant agricultural tax), while wage incomes are not taxed at all. The share of indirect taxes in national income is somewhat higher than in most other developing countries.[10] The "profits" piece of the pie includes two sectors that are taxed rather differently: state and large urban collective enterprises are taxed at a rather high rate (nearly 70 percent on average), while rural collectives are lightly taxed (8 percent). Pies B–E look at different possibilities for the year 2000, based on the High Saving and High Transfers expenditure scenarios in Table 9.5, and on the macroeconomic projections introduced in Chapter 2 (QUADRUPLE for Pies B–D, BALANCE for Pie E). In all cases, structural change causes the share of wages in national income to be higher

---

9. For some countries, revenue growth was even faster. See Background Paper 4, Table 12.

10. Background Paper 4, Table 11.

Figure 9.2 Income Flows and Taxation, Alternative Projections, 1981–2000

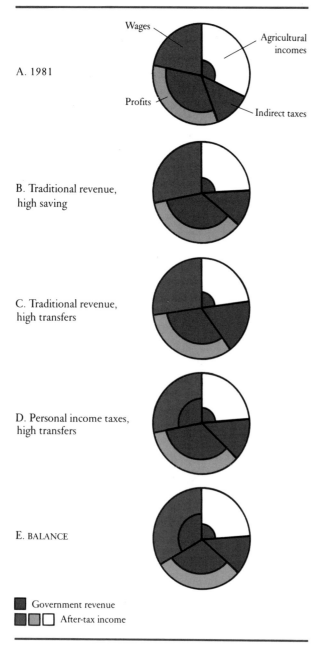

A. 1981

B. Traditional revenue, high saving

C. Traditional revenue, high transfers

D. Personal income taxes, high transfers

E. BALANCE

■ Government revenue
■■□ After-tax income

Note: Each circle represents the economy, with the main income flows shown as pieces of a fixed "pie." The colored area toward the center of each piece represents the portion of that type of income that becomes part of government revenue (through taxes and levies of various kinds.) Thus the sum of all the colored portions represents total government revenue, and the ratio of the colored area to the total area of the circle is equal to the share of government revenue in the economy. The sizes of the different pieces of the pie are determined by price and wage policies and by indirect tax rates, as well as by the structure of the economy. The share of government revenue in each piece is determined by the average tax rate on that type of income (including income, profit, and asset taxes, as well as profit and depreciation fund remittances and social insurance contributions). The piece representing indirect taxes is somewhat different from the others: in its entirety it forms part of government revenue, and the size of the piece (rather than the share of the piece taxed) is determined by the average rate of indirect taxation in the economy.
Source: Table. 9.6.

in 2000 than in 1981 and the share of agricultural incomes to be lower.

Pie B assumes that current expenditure trends and policies will broadly continue (the High Saving scenario in Table 9.5) and that the Government will continue to rely on the same revenue sources (indirect commodity taxes and enterprise profit tax). Indirect taxes remain constant as a share of GDP. The tax rate on enterprise profits remains relatively high, which means that if nonstate enterprises continue to grow more rapidly than state enterprises, profit tax rates for the former would have to be sharply increased (by 1983 the average profit tax rate for rural collective enterprises had risen to 14 percent).

Pie C is based on the High Transfers expenditure scenario (low government saving, virtual elimination of subsidies, and high government transfer payments), but on the revenue side there is continued reliance on traditional sources. Specifically, there are no new taxes on personal incomes, and indirect tax rates are increased to permit lower profit tax rates (needed because most saving must come from enterprises' after-tax profits—see below). As a result, the share of indirect taxes in GDP rises from 14 percent in 1981 to 19 percent in 2000, and the average profit tax rate falls from 68 percent to 39 percent. This would permit lower tax rates on the nonstate nonagriculture sector and more rapid growth of the sector (with the same profit tax rates as in Pie B). Given the large share of indirect taxes in national income (more than double the average in other developing countries) it would be crucial to levy such taxes in a way that minimized distortions (discussed later).

Pie D is based on the same expenditure scenario as Pie C, but on the revenue side substantial taxes on wage incomes are introduced (part of which could be social security contributions by employers or employees), and taxation of agriculture is increased (with the burden assumed to fall mainly on farmers with high incomes). This results in a tax structure in which all institutional sectors provide significant amounts of government revenue, and there is no increase in the share of indirect taxes. As in Pie C, there could be rapid growth and relatively light taxation of the nonstate nonagriculture sector.

What would happen if the structure of the Chinese economy in the year 2000 were similar to that in the BALANCE projection rather than the QUADRUPLE projection? As can be seen from Pie E (which is otherwise based on the assumptions of Pie D), the share of wages in the economy would be considerably larger and those of profits and agricultural incomes somewhat smaller. Lower saving requirements (resulting from greater efficiency) would mean a lower share of government revenue in the economy and therefore that tax rates could be reduced somewhat. In Pie E, tax rates on wages and agricultural incomes are lower, permitting a higher standard of living. Alternatively, profit tax rates or indirect

Table 9.6 Illustrative Projections for Figure 9.2
(percent)

Projection	Agricultural incomes	Wages	Profits[a]	Indirect taxes	Total[b]	Government subsidies[c]
Pie A (1981)						
Ratio to GDP	37	25	38	14	114	10
Share taxed	3	0	68	100	—	—
Revenue as share of GDP	1	0	26	14	41	—
Pie B (traditional revenue, high saving)						
Ratio to GDP	28	32	40	14	114	3
Share taxed	3	0	68	100	—	—
Revenue as share of GDP	1	0	27	14	42	—
Pie C (traditional revenue, high transfers)						
Ratio to GDP	28	32	40	19	119	1
Share taxed	3	0	39	100	—	—
Revenue as share of GDP	1	0	15	19	35	—
Pie D (personal income taxes, high transfers)						
Ratio to GDP	28	32	40	14	114	1
Share taxed	6	15	37	100	—	—
Revenue as share of GDP	2	4	15	14	35	—
Pie E (Pie D with BALANCE)						
Ratio to GDP	26	37	37	14	114	1
Share taxed	4	13	37	100	—	—
Revenue as share of GDP	1	5	14	14	34	—

Note: GDP is measured at producer prices (sum of wages, profits, and agricultural incomes).
a. Gross of depreciation and subsidies, but net of indirect taxes.
b. Equal to GDP measured at producer prices plus indirect taxes. Subtracting government subsidies from this total yields GDP at purchaser prices (see Figure 9.1).
c. Excludes enterprise housing subsidy (see Table 9.4).
Source: For 1981 (Pie A), estimates based on Chinese financial statistics. For 2000, based on the projections introduced in Chapter 2 (QUADRUPLE for Pies B–D, BALANCE for Pie E), and on the government expenditure scenarios in Table 9.5 For further details, see Annex 5, Appendix J.

tax rates could be reduced, or government spending on public or private consumption could be increased. Thus improvements in efficiency can help ease budgetary constraints.

Implications for Saving

Implicit in the revenue scenarios discussed above are different patterns of saving. Figure 9.3 (based on the numbers in Table 9.7) illustrates some of the points on alternative sources of saving raised earlier in this chapter. Specifically, it shows the implications of some of the revenue scenarios in Figure 9.2 for the composition of aggregate saving and sectoral saving rates.

Pie A1 corresponds to Pie A in Figure 9.2 showing what the situation was in 1981. Profits are highly taxed, so their share (after tax) in the economy is rather small. The Government accounts for a large proportion of total saving, while enterprises save a little over half their retained profits. Pie B1 is based on Pie B in Figure 9.2. The share of the Government in total saving rises to 70 percent (almost as high as in 1978—Table 9.1); as a result, household and enterprise saving can be relatively low. In particular, enterprises save a low proportion of their after-

tax profits compared with historical experience in China and in other countries, where the reinvestment rate from after-tax profits tends to be 50–60 percent. Enterprise saving rates of 50–60 percent in this pie would have permitted personal saving rates lower than 10 percent (or higher aggregate saving and growth rates).

Pie D1 is based on Pie D in Figure 9.2; it brings out one possible problem of less reliance on government saving to achieve a high aggregate saving rate. With the Government accounting for only 20 percent of total saving, and if households save only 10 percent of their disposable earnings, the burden on enterprises becomes very great. With income shares as in the QUADRUPLE projection, enterprises would have to save 75 percent of their after-tax profits in order for the economy as a whole to save and invest enough to meet growth targets. State enterprises in China have typically not saved as much as 75 percent of their after-tax profits in the past (the figure has been closer to 50 percent). Moreover, the nonstate sector (where a substantial share of after-tax profits needs to be distributed as dividends or bonuses) will presumably account for a considerable proportion of total profits.

One way around this difficulty is to increase enterprise

155

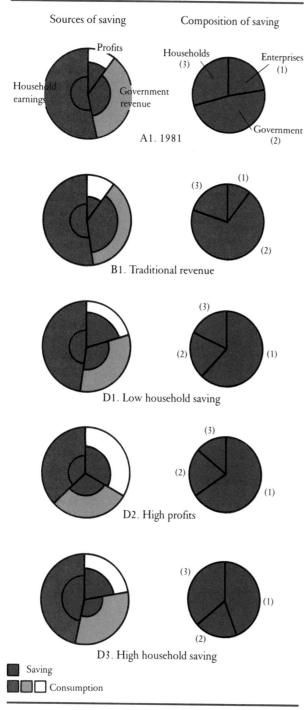

Figure 9.3 Sources and Composition of Saving, Alternative Projections, 1981–2000

Sources of saving   Composition of saving

Profits

Households
(3)   Enterprises
(1)

Household
earnings   Government
revenue

A1. 1981

Government
(2)

(3)   (1)

B1. Traditional revenue

(2)

(3)

(2)   (1)

D1. Low household saving

(3)

(2)   (1)

D2. High profits

(3)

(2)   (1)

D3. High household saving

■ Saving

■■□ Consumption

Note: Each large pie chart represents the economy as a whole, but the pieces are after-tax incomes of households and enterprises and total government revenue (not just indirect taxes). Wages and agricultural incomes are lumped together, since it is assumed that the saving behavior of these two groups is the same. The colored area toward the center of each piece of the large pies represents the part of that type of income that is saved; the sum of all those colored areas is total saving, which is the same share of national income in each of the pies. Beside each large pie is a smaller one showing the composition of saving in the economy, which can be compared directly with Table 9.1.
Source: Table 9.7.

profits to the point where the required saving rate out of after-tax profits is reduced to a realistic level (which could be accomplished through price or tax adjustments). Pie D2 illustrates this solution. The share of after-tax profits in national income is raised from 25 percent to 37 percent, while that of personal earnings is correspondingly reduced from 54 percent to 42 percent. This permits achievement of a 30 percent aggregate saving rate with a saving rate from enterprise profits of only a little over 50 percent. But the higher share of profits and the relatively low saving rate out of after-tax profits mean that a large proportion of total consumption would be financed out of profits. Some of this might be in the form of dividends or wage supplements distributed to worker-owners in collective enterprises, but large amounts might also go to high-paid workers in state enterprises, or to owners of individual enterprises (see above). This could lead to social problems.

An alternative, in many ways more attractive, solution would be higher saving rates out of personal earnings. Pie D3 shows what happens if after-tax income flows are as in Pie D1 but households save 20 percent of their disposable earnings instead of 10 percent. The required saving rate from enterprise profits is reduced to about the same level as in Pie D2, but without the undesirable consequences of an increased share of profits. Pie D3 thus somewhat resembles the situation in Japan (where a high aggregate saving rate is achieved through high personal savings).

Tax Reform

The revenue scenarios in the previous section illustrate some important choices among broad categories of taxation: indirect taxes, taxes on enterprise profits, and taxes on personal earnings. Within each of these broad categories, there are equally important choices to be made about specific tax instruments, which will play an increasing role in China's reformed economic system, both as indirect levers to influence the decisions of enterprises and consumers (see Chapter 10), and as redistributors of income.

Indirect Taxes

China now relies heavily on indirect taxes, with a highly differentiated rate structure (3–66 percent). These taxes have several advantages. Revenues generally tend to increase automatically with production, and taxes are relatively easy to collect because the number of taxpayers (primarily industrial producers and wholesale commercial units) is relatively small. Moreover, rate differentiation can be used to achieve income distribution objectives (with some reservations mentioned later), as well as to discourage the consumption of items such as cigarettes. China's indirect tax system also has its disadvantages, however. Taxation of intermediate products encourages uneconomic vertical integration and can make effective tax rates (including the taxes paid at earlier stages of production) on particular items diverge significantly from nominal tax rates. Moreover, taxation of intermediate transactions between state enterprises may not increase budget revenue.

Following reform of producer prices and restoration of normal retail commercial margins (discussed earlier), some relatively simple changes could greatly improve the industrial-commercial tax. One would be a drastic decrease in the differentiation of the rate structure. For example, there might be only three different rates for consumer goods: a low rate (possibly zero) for food; a

Table 9.7 Illustrative Projections for Figure 9.3
(percent)

Projection	Household earnings[a]	Enterprise profits	Government revenues	Total
Pie A1 (1981)				
Share of GDP	61	12	41	114
Saving rate	14[b]	54	36	—
Share of saving in GDP	9	6	15	30[c]
Share of total saving	29	22	49	100
Pie B1 (traditional)				
Share of GDP	60	12	42	114
Saving rate	10	24	51	—
Share of saving in GDP	6	3	21	30[c]
Share of total saving	20	10	70	100
Pie D1 (low household saving)				
Share of GDP	54	25	35	114
Saving rate	10	75	17	—
Share of saving in GDP	5	19	6	30[c]
Share of total saving	18	62	20	100
Pie D2 (high profits)				
Share of GDP	42	37	35	114
Saving rate	10	54	17	—
Share of saving in GDP	4	20	6	30[c]
Share of total saving	14	66	20	100
Pie D3 (high household saving)				
Share of GDP	54	25	35	114
Saving rate	20	53	17	—
Share of saving in GDP	11	13	6	30[c]
Share of total saving	36	44	20	100

Note: Income flows for nongovernment sectors are gross of depreciation, but net of all taxes and levies by the government. GDP is measured at producer prices.
a. Wages and agricultural incomes, after taxes.
b. In 1981 personal saving appears to have been unusually high, because of large stock increases in rural areas.
c. The aggregate saving rate in this table is 30 percent because GDP is measured at producer prices. With GDP measured at purchaser prices (as in the 1981 input-output table in Annex 5, and in the multisectoral model), the saving rate is 29 percent (see, for example, the discussion of QUADRUPLE in Chapter 2). The relationship between GDP at producer prices and at purchaser prices is explained in Figure 9.1.
Source: See Table 9.6.

moderate rate for most consumer goods; and a high rate for luxury goods or goods whose consumption should be discouraged. If alternative means of reducing inequality in living standards could be adopted, there might even be a single rate for all but the last category of consumer goods. In either case, the retail prices of specific goods (including the tax) would be quite closely related to producer prices, thus giving appropriate signals to consumers about relative production costs and scarcities. Intermediate goods should not be taxed; nor, perhaps, should investment goods, except to restrain investment demand or discourage uneconomic automation of production. This approach would allow continued use of tax instruments that China is familiar with, that create few economic distortions, and that generate rapid revenue growth. One problem involves taxation of commodities used both as intermediate goods and for consumption or investment, which requires either arbitrary classification or an administratively awkward system of tax exemptions for certain users.

China is already experimenting with value added taxation (VAT) for some commodities, but mainly to discourage vertical integration rather than to raise revenue. Wider use of VAT would have several advantages. Revenue from VAT tends to increase at least as fast as national income. It avoids the distortions caused by taxation of intermediate goods. VAT also can be rebated to exporters and charged on imports, which provides incentives to increase exports and economize on imports in an internationally accepted way (as with other indirect taxes—see Chapter 6), with a minimum of domestic distortions. These advantages may make VAT the most attractive indirect tax, perhaps supplemented by some commodity-specific excise or sales taxes. VAT does, however, require that the taxpayers (enterprises) keep fairly good accounts on input purchases as well as sales, perhaps making administration and compliance more costly than for the industrial-commercial tax.[11]

An advantage of all indirect taxes over direct taxes (particularly personal income taxes) is that they are more impersonal and less visible, which may make it easier to mobilize large amounts of government revenue. There is also less room for tax evasion, exemptions, and corruption. The key weakness of indirect taxes is that they are not well suited to reducing inequality in living standards (since they tax all purchasers of a given commodity, not just those who are relatively well-off). This is true even if tax rates are differentiated, but it is much more so if there is little differentiation in the rate structure (which is desirable for efficient resource allocation).

---

11. However, when VAT is calculated by the crediting method, firms purchasing goods have an incentive to make sure that suppliers pay VAT so that they can receive credit.

Profit and Asset Taxes

Taxes and levies of various kinds on enterprise profits form the other pillar of China's present tax system. Recently, a proportional profit tax was introduced to replace direct remittance of state enterprise profits to the budget. But there is a different effective tax rate for each enterprise, to offset the impact of price distortions and other factors. China has also experimented with a charge on state enterprises' fixed assets, but this was apparently abandoned after running into obstacles also associated with widely varying enterprise profitability. In other countries, taxes on enterprise profits have increased in importance during economic development and are generally regarded as an administratively convenient and economically efficient source of revenue (although it is sometimes argued that they are in fact passed on to consumers through higher prices). In China, the great variation in effective profit tax rates among state enterprises, and the fact that profit tax payments are determined largely by bargaining, make the present system highly unsatisfactory from the viewpoint of generating appropriate incentives for enterprises and ensuring steady growth of government revenue. Reform of the price system would make it possible to solve the first of these problems, but the second also requires improvements in enterprise financial discipline and a change in the relationship between state enterprises and the government organizations that now supervise them (see Chapter 10).

Once these problems are dealt with, the main issues would become the appropriate rate of profit tax and whether part of the aftertax profits of state enterprises should still be remitted to the Government (perhaps in the form of a "dividend" on the capital provided by the Government). There is an obvious tradeoff between greater incentives for enterprises from low tax rates and the need to mobilize government revenue. In this context, a charge on government-financed investment in state enterprises could both raise revenue and strengthen incentives to use capital economically. The charge could be a tax on capital assets provided by the Government through grants, or interest on (and repayment of) government loans to enterprises. A loan or asset tax system could ensure a minimum, stable return to the Government on the funds it provides for investment in profit-earning sectors of the economy. But the stability of such a charge in the face of varying enterprise revenues and costs would tend to make after-tax profits fluctuate more, complicating the financial planning of relatively independent enterprises, especially if the tax rate were high or the loan repayment period short.

Profit taxes on nonstate enterprises (rural collectives, small urban collectives, and individual businesses) are likely to be an increasingly important source of revenue in China, with the relatively rapid growth of the nonstate nonagriculture sector. They can ensure that an appropri-ate share of the surplus this sector generates is channeled to society in general. Exemptions and differential profit tax rates can also be used as economic levers to steer both nonstate and independent state enterprises in appropriate sectoral and geographical directions. In the long run, rates of taxation for state and nonstate enterprises should probably be equalized, for administrative convenience and to prevent distortions or problems in taxing mixed-ownership enterprises. But the great difference in effective profit tax rates between urban enterprises and rural collective enterprises at present (mentioned earlier) means that such equalization should proceed gradually in order to avoid large revenue losses on the one hand or excessive tax increases for nonstate enterprises on the other.

Careful attention must also be paid to the relationship between taxation of nonstate enterprises and taxation of their workers and owners. In the absence of personal income taxation (discussed below), taxation of profits encourages tax avoidance through payment of higher wages to workers, managers, or owners. However, to tax both enterprise profits and personal incomes derived from after-tax profits is a form of double taxation which can have undesirable disincentive effects if the rates are too high. This, for example, led the United Kingdom to modify its enterprise profits tax system so that distributed profits (dividends) were subject only to personal income tax, rather than, as in the United States, to both enterprise and personal income taxes. Experience in other countries also suggests the desirability of simplified taxes on small enterprises, in order to reduce collection costs and to avoid complex bookkeeping. For very small enterprises, a lump sum tax or license fee, in lieu of both profits and personal income tax, might even be sufficient.

In both state and nonstate enterprises, an excess profits tax can be used to absorb differential rents earned in activities like mining. China has already introduced a "resource" tax, which is triggered once a mining or petroleum extraction enterprise's profit rate on sales exceeds a certain threshold. These taxes can be a useful source of revenue, in principle without distorting incentives (indeed they may usefully discourage overly rapid depletion of resources). But caution is needed in setting the tax rates because of the difficulty of distinguishing accurately between differential rent and high profits due to greater efficiency or the need to compensate for high risk (most mineral exploration is unsuccessful).

Personal Income and Wage Taxation

Personal income taxes are immensely important in industrial market economies, both as a source of revenue and as a means of reducing income inequality, but they have been largely neglected by socialist countries. China has recently introduced a progressive personal income tax, aimed mainly at foreign residents. If this tax were extended to cover, say, the highest quarter of Chinese wages

158

and salaries (see Chapter 8), as well as high earnings from individual enterprises and agriculture, it could play a useful role in regulating the increases in income inequality that are likely to result from reform of the economic system. In setting tax rates, there is a difficult tradeoff between what are perceived as inequitably low rates and high rates that discourage effort and stimulate tax evasion. In other countries, the trend in recent years has been to reduce rates (which peaked at over 95 percent in some cases), while at the same time narrowing loopholes for tax avoidance and extending taxation of benefits in kind, capital gains, and personal wealth (especially when transferred between generations). Renewed attention has also been given to personal expenditure taxes (which tax consumption but not saving) as an alternative to personal income taxes.

Extending the personal income tax in China to cover the great majority of wage earners would make it a major source of revenue. The extent to which this should be done depends largely on the attractiveness (including the comparative administrative costs) and availability of alternative revenue sources, especially indirect taxes. Experience elsewhere suggests that income taxes on wages and salaries are cheap to collect, because employers can be obliged to deduct them from wages. Personal income taxes, however, probably constitute a greater disincentive to individual effort than equivalent amounts of indirect taxation. Moreover, they can be difficult to collect from individual enterprise proprietors and other self-employed people, who in some countries evade most tax.

Taxes on wages, including employers' and employees' social insurance contributions, are also an important source of government revenue in industrial market economies: in 1981, for example, social security contributions were 25 percent of all tax revenues in the United States, 39 percent in West Germany, and 44 percent in France. In China, wage taxes (discussed in Chapter 8) could be used to finance social insurance and pension schemes. But for employment and income redistribution reasons, it might be desirable to exempt low-paid workers and to levy higher rates on higher wages. In most other countries, by contrast, such taxes not only apply to all workers, but also have an upper limit such that no one pays more than a certain absolute amount, in order to reduce inequality in contributory social insurance benefits.

Taxation of Agriculture

Agricultural taxation is a difficult matter in most develop-

ing countries. Neither income taxes nor commodity taxes are very effective when the tax base is scattered and largely self-employed, and a large proportion of production is consumed in kind. Indirect taxes on the procurement of agricultural products by the commercial system, or artificially low procurement prices, coupled with high taxes (or prices) for industrial inputs into agriculture, are familiar means of extracting revenue from agriculture. But they can severely distort incentives, which has led China to reduce reliance on such instruments in recent years. Further steps in the same direction would leave Chinese agriculture subject only to the very low (on average about 2 percent) direct agricultural tax, though of course also to general indirect taxation of manufactured consumer goods and services.

It is important to distinguish between the desirable level of agricultural taxation and the choice of instruments for extracting it. So long as agricultural incomes are on average much lower than nonagricultural incomes (as seems likely for the next few decades—see Chapter 3), low direct taxation has obvious merits. But shortfalls of revenue from other sources might make heavier direct taxation of agriculture unavoidable. Moreover, progressive taxation of unusually high agricultural incomes may be desired for reasons of equity. The best instrument for this last purpose would in principle be the personal income tax, especially because it demonstrably applies the same standard of equity to agricultural and nonagricultural incomes alike. In practice, however, it could be difficult to collect such a tax on agricultural incomes—even if it was limited to a relatively small number of high-income farmers.

As a means of raising large amounts of revenue from agriculture, personal income taxation (because of its high administrative costs) is probably inferior to the present agricultural tax. The latter is in essence a land tax based on estimated income-earning potential, levied in absolute amounts that remain fixed for several years at a time. This tax, whose fixed nature provides stronger incentives to increase production in efficient ways than an income tax, could be levied at higher rates. It could also be made more flexible by expressing the tax as the product of a standard percentage rate, common to all land, and a "taxable value" peculiar to each plot of land (this is the standard form of urban property taxes in other countries). The overall tax yield could then be varied by altering the standard percentage rate, with the taxable value of particular plots subject to periodic reassessment.

10 *Development Management*

A recurring theme of all the preceding chapters is the critical importance of system reform to China's future. This is well recognized in China today. Over the past five years, far-reaching reforms introduced in rural areas have had a remarkable impact on production and income. While reforms in urban areas have been much less definitive and comprehensive, the Central Committee Decision of October 1984 indicates a firm determination to accelerate overall reform.[1] Together, the rural reforms and the October Decision constitute one of the most far-reaching attempts to improve the functioning of a socialist economic system. Moreover, this attempt is only the beginning of China's overall strategy of building "socialism with Chinese characteristics," a system "integrating the basic tenets of Marxism with actual conditions in China."

System reform in China over the next two decades will require consistent and comparable progress in three areas: (a) increasing economic dynamism and efficiency through market regulation; (b) strengthening and reforming social institutions and instruments to safeguard and further improve social welfare and equity; and (c) strengthening economic management through the coordinated use of indirect and direct controls. This final chapter, drawing partly on earlier chapters, discusses general issues in these three areas, as well as some specific issues not covered in earlier chapters. The first section discusses the role and responsibility of the state toward the individual, focusing on issues of income inequality, economic security, and basic social services. The second section reviews the relationship between the state and state-owned enterprises, as well as collective and individual enterprises, and proceeds to a discussion of investment and prices. The following section discusses the role of the state in planning and managing the economy.

The State and the Individual

In a modern society, the state generally provides a degree of economic and social security for all of its citizens. It usually also seeks to limit inequality in income distribution, and in particular to assist the poorest and least privileged. China's achievements in these areas have been most impressive and compare very favorably with those of other countries at similar levels of development. Many of these social objectives, however, are still being met through policy instruments designed when the country was much poorer and the economy and society were less stable.

Perhaps more than in any other country, social welfare and services for the urban population in China are provided by their enterprises or work units, with the state playing a limited role. Health and disability benefits are provided through a labor insurance scheme, but pensions are paid as part of current production cost and housing is usually provided by employers. Many social and distributional objectives are met by state manipulation of economic instruments. For example, wages are set relatively equal and generally at such a low level that they have to be supplemented by price subsidies on essential goods and services. Economic security is provided to urban workers through "lifetime" job guarantees. Full employment is achieved by forcing enterprises to hire more workers than they need, by restricting migration from rural areas, and sometimes by sending urban youths to rural areas. For the rural population, a subsistence level of grain is provided to the poorest households.

Although egalitarianism was a guiding principle in the past, the level of welfare or security provided has been uneven. The quality of social services and housing provided to workers in different enterprises varies substantially and in ways unrelated to the performance of the workers or the enterprises. State-owned enterprises generally provide better services and greater benefits than

---

1. Communique of the Third Plenary Session of the Twelfth Central Committee of the Chinese Communist Party, October 20, 1984. All quotations in this chapter are from this document.

collectives, while the self-employed receive few benefits. In rural areas, welfare and social services are provided mainly through the collective efforts of the local population, with limited assistance from the state, so that the quality of service varies greatly among localities and is generally much below that in urban areas.

Two important questions must be addressed: Do China's social policy instruments still meet the social and equity objectives of a modernizing society rapidly approaching middle-income levels? And are they compatible with the other changes that are taking place in the economic and social system? Unwillingness to confront the possible social consequences of economic reform has been a critical flaw in many East European attempts. The result is often an incorrect impression that reform must entail the abandonment of social concerns. This risk exists in China also, perhaps to an even greater degree than in other socialist countries, because income distribution and economic security objectives are being met in unusual ways, and particularly because social instruments are so entangled with economic instruments.

Issues of Income Disparity

It is recognized in China today that "prosperity comes unevenly in the course of economic development," and that reform will require a new way of thinking about different types of income and income inequality. An especially difficult issue in this regard may be the legitimacy and possible size of incomes from entrepreneurship. Some people in China, unfortunately, still associate entrepreneurship with all the worst aspects of pre-Liberation capitalism. Entrepreneurship, however, will be critical in achieving China's economic objectives, partly by causing markets to function more smoothly and efficiently. Entrepreneurs, for instance, buy goods at low prices in places where they are in surplus and sell them at higher prices in places where they are often urgently needed; or they produce and sell necessary goods and services initially at a high profit, thus luring others into the same activities, which increases supply and drives profits down.[2] Although their motivation is obviously to make money for themselves, they are nonetheless useful. Entrepreneurship is also essential for technical or economic innovation—the search for ways to produce something at lower cost or of higher quality and to respond to changing market conditions when there are no assurances that the search will be successful (see Chapter 7). Because entrepreneurship involves taking risks and is successful only occasionally, it will flourish only when successes are well rewarded.

In a socialist economy, income disparity resulting from private ownership of property will be relatively limited. But considerations of economic efficiency and dynamism will require that high incomes be permitted—and indeed encouraged—for successful entrepreneurs, unusually ca-

pable managers, hard-working farm households, and talented innovators in all fields. The resulting degree of income disparity might well be larger than socially desirable. But rather than distorting or suppressing economic forces, it would be preferable, to the extent possible, to deal with inequality through social policy instruments designed for this purpose. Specifically, high incomes generated by a more market-oriented economic system could be reduced to socially acceptable levels by directly taxing the incomes of the rich more than the poor (progressive income taxation), by making high-income earners contribute more to social security, or by imposing high taxes on goods and services consumed by the rich. Some options in these areas were discussed in Chapters 8 and 9.

It is essential, however, that income taxation—or other measures to reduce income disparity—should not be seen as a punitive measure against high-income earners. Indeed, continuous education of the population about the policy of the Government—and the Party—on the legitimacy of high incomes will be necessary. It would be better for the central government to set a clear policy on this issue, and to take the lead in introducing the policy instruments necessary to reduce income disparity, than to allow local communities to set their own standards—as currently seems to be happening in some places.

International experience suggests that it is better to confront the problem of high incomes directly. Faced with the dilemma of having to reward very productive or important members of their societies in the face of political pressure for equality, some countries have tried to obscure high incomes and consumption. In some countries, for instance, the wages of public officials have been kept low, but extensively supplemented through bribery and corruption. In other countries, formal incomes are low and fairly equal, but senior officials and important members of society receive special privileges such as better housing, second homes, access to special stores providing goods not available elsewhere, and sometimes even unrecorded but regular supplements to their official salaries. The benefits of such obfuscation are strictly temporary, since these practices quickly become well known, and the costs are large and long term, as they may set in motion an irreversible evolution toward a corrupt and hierarchical society.

---

2. Especially in the early stages of economic reform, reflecting the huge imbalances created by the previous rigidly administered system, entrepreneurial incomes tend to be large even in some activities that would not normally result in such high incomes. Some entrepreneurs in China are already earning annual incomes of Y 10,000, even Y 100,000, by raising chickens and selling eggs to the urban population, by opening small restaurants, or by performing badly needed household services, all of which were previously prohibited.

Social Security and Welfare

At the other end of the income spectrum, a social security program consistent with the needs of a reformed economy is urgently needed. Enterprises must function increasingly as economic entities, which will inevitably conflict with their current role as providers of many social services. Prices and wages need increasingly to reflect economic considerations and cannot be manipulated to the same extent as in the past to meet social objectives. Rapid economic change will mean accelerated growth of some enterprises but contraction and closure of others. Some skills will become obsolete, and some workers—sometimes through no fault of their own—may become at least temporarily unemployed. Thus, the absence of any organized means of supporting the unemployed and others suffering from economic change will become increasingly unacceptable. Rising expectations among the people as a consequence of economic growth will also increase pressure for the state to assume a growing and increasingly direct responsibility for social security and welfare.

Especially in the last few decades, social security programs have been introduced in all industrial countries, with the objectives of ensuring an adequate level of income for all citizens and minimizing the risk of poverty due to old age, illness, disability, unemployment, and other personal misfortune. These programs have grown rapidly, and in most Western industrial countries they now account for 15–20 percent of national income. Many, however, have evolved from a series of smaller, fragmented programs, each responding to particular social, economic, and political exigencies. Although individual programs may be quite sensible, the social security programs as a whole are not necessarily so. In some countries, for instance, complex income tax and welfare regulations have combined to produce unintended absurdities. In some West European countries, generous unemployment benefits for young people have contributed to increased unemployment by deterring them from taking arduous, dull, or low-paid jobs. Despite these and other problems, however, there is little doubt that large and steadily increasing government spending on social security, medical care, education, and other social services has contributed greatly to the reduction of inequality in industrial market economies.

A major potential advantage of social security programs is that benefits go only to those in need. By contrast, price subsidies—the most important way in which the state attempts to assist the poor in China today—benefit the rich, as well as the poor, and are therefore much more costly. Compared with price subsidies, comprehensive social security programs are of course administratively much more complex. Yet in this regard, China has considerable advantages over most other countries, particularly since it already has an institutional structure to build on. In urban areas, a household registration system, which includes detailed information about each household's situation, forms the basis for grain and other product rationing. This system could be used initially in administering social security programs. Even in remote rural areas, the former system of communes, brigades, and teams proved highly effective in reaching every household and in pursuing economic and social objectives with limited resources. Although the economic functions of these institutions were eroded by agricultural reform, they or their successors could continue to administer collective social services as well as state-run social security programs.

The major function of most social security programs is to supplement the income of households whose incomes are low either temporarily (for example, unemployed or ill workers) or permanently (for example, retired workers without other pensions). In this connection, the challenge is to provide for those in need while minimizing disincentives to work. Providing all households with a fixed income supplement (or "social dividend"), regardless of their work and other sources of income, would minimize any disincentive to work (since they would keep all other income), but would be far too costly an option for China to consider. A guarantee by the state to bring the incomes of all households up to a given level would be less costly, but would remove incentives to earn income below the guaranteed level. Concentrating income supplements on families with special characteristics (such as retired people with no other income, single-parent households, and families with many children) reduces budgetary costs and disincentives, but can increase administrative costs and is inequitable for other impoverished households. Thus all programs involve some tradeoffs among budgetary and administrative costs, disincentives, and inequities. Careful design is needed to suit a country's particular social and economic conditions and priorities.[3]

In most Western industrial countries, social security is based largely on the insurance principle—citizens contribute to a fund that then compensates them for loss of income due to old age, unemployment, illness, and so forth. The level of individual benefits sometimes depends on the size of individual contributions. The main role of

---

3. All options involve some compromise. Many economists propose that the state should establish a basic (maximum) supplement, whose amount would vary according to the size and other consumption needs of the household. The amount actually paid to an individual household would depend in some specified way on the income earned by the household, so that a household with no other source of income would receive the full basic supplement, while a household with income over a cutoff level (which would have to be higher than the amount of the basic supplement) would receive no supplement at all. This sort of scheme is sometimes referred to as a negative income tax.

the state is to administer the program, sometimes augmenting its resources with other government revenues when necessary, and to provide a "safety net" of noncontributory income supplements for those who are not covered by insurance or whose income would otherwise fall below an established minimum level. An alternative to this insurance approach, however, would be for the state to assume direct responsibility—as China has in the past—for ensuring a minimum level of economic security and to finance this from general budgetary revenues. The state-run and budget-financed scheme could then underpin additional schemes, which would use the contributory, insurance principle to provide extra benefits.

A possible scheme following this second approach, and which would also address the problem of high incomes, would be to establish a nationwide social security fund. High-income earners would be required to contribute to the fund a portion of their wages or incomes above an established level, while households with incomes below a specified minimum level would receive an income supplement. Eligibility for the supplement would extend to households afflicted by old age, unemployment, disability, and other adverse natural or economic circumstances, but not to those who simply refused to work. The costs of these income supplements—which are likely at least initially to be considerably greater than the contributions of high-income earners—would be financed largely from budget revenues. Such a scheme would minimize administrative costs, because the majority of households, which have middling incomes, would not be involved. Since high-income earners would be making a direct contribution to the relief of poverty, it might also alleviate the apparently growing resentment against them in some communities. Moreover, this kind of scheme would help to ensure that reform and policy measures introduced later (for example, allowing enterprises to dismiss workers, widening wage scales, and eliminating subsidies for food, rent, and other goods) would cause no families to fall below a socially acceptable income level.

Such a national scheme for providing a low but uniform level of income support throughout the country could be augmented by provincial and local schemes financed by local funds or contributions from participants. Groups of workers (in particular occupations or localities) could also be encouraged to save for retirement and share risks in areas such as health and disability. Especially for retirement, a minimal social security program should be seen only as an underpinning for self-financing pension schemes sponsored by local governments, employers, or other groups. (Options for organizing pension schemes have been discussed in Chapter 8).

Other countries' experience indicates that management of social security programs can often be more effective if closely linked to the provision of other social services, such as health and education. In China, for instance, it may be desirable to give the local administrators in rural areas substantial freedom in organizing the entire range of social services—including social security, pensions, health, education, and family planning—subject to some national policy guidelines. There is also a need for what may be termed "preventive welfare" (similar to preventive medicine), which involves social assistance of various kinds to improve the earning capacity of individual families. For instance, the unemployed—in addition to income support—may require retraining, help in obtaining new employment, and possibly aid in organizing for community work programs.

Thus there will be a growing need for state agencies to assist individuals in coping with the changing economic environment.[4] Institutions for this purpose will need to be developed and strengthened. One important step might be to consolidate and extend the present enterprise-based labor insurance and welfare programs into a modern state-run social security program. Because of the many complex issues involved—including administrative arrangements, financing and use of funds, determination of beneficiaries and benefit levels, and relations with the state budget and other insurance schemes—it might be desirable to create a high-level social security commission to formulate a long-term plan to be implemented in stages.

Social Security and Services in Rural Areas

A difficult issue in planning for a social security program, which affects both equity and cost, is the proportion of the population to be covered.[5] With regard to the urban population, any state-run social security program should surely cover everyone, whether employed in the state, collective, or individual sectors. To do otherwise would be inconsistent with the current objective of promoting a multiple-ownership system in the economy. Workers in township and village enterprises, as well as in collectives in small towns, should probably also be included. Over the past few years, workers in collective enterprises in some rural townships have begun to organize their own pension and social security programs. Although these initiatives should be encouraged, local governments might attempt to consolidate these fragmented efforts into

---

4. Recently, for instance, after introducing an economic responsibility system, the Capital Iron and Steel Corporation found that several thousand workers were redundant. The corporation organized these workers to form a service company and to work on environmental improvement projects, while some were retrained. Such efforts are highly commendable, and more of them will be needed. Ultimately, however, responsibility for retraining redundant workers and helping them find new jobs will have to rest mainly with the Government.

5. The possible future fiscal implications of social security schemes of varying comprehensiveness were outlined in Chapter 9.

larger programs, which would be more effective because of their larger numbers of participants.

Extension of a social security program to agricultural workers and their families would be a more difficult and complex task. In all low-income countries, as in China, the clash between the desire for equality of social welfare for all people and the limitations of administrative and financial resources has led to different treatment of the rural and urban populations. The question is whether this compromise remains necessary or desirable in China—especially because economic trends by themselves may not sufficiently narrow rural-urban income disparities (Chapters 3 and 5) and because poorer areas are likely to fall further behind other parts of the country (Chapter 5). The state may therefore need to intervene more forcefully in the social sphere to alleviate emerging inequality and potential poverty.

A rural social security program subsidized by budgetary revenues, for instance, would be an efficient means of transferring nonagricultural productivity gains to the agricultural population (Chapter 3). While the long-term target should be to have a uniform basic social security program for the whole population, an interim measure might be to combine and augment the existing subsistence grain support and Five Guarantees into a rural social security program providing needy households and communities not only with basic food, but also with a small cash income. The amount of cash income and other benefits could then be increased over time as incomes rise, with the objective of eventually merging the rural social security program with the urban program.

A disturbing aspect of recent rural reform has been the weakening of the cooperative health system in poor areas; school attendance has also been adversely affected, and in some poorer localities is now rather low (Chapters 1 and 5). These trends should be of major concern to China's planners. There is overwhelming international evidence that investment in human resources—in basic health and education—has not only been a most effective way of helping the poor, but has also contributed directly to economic growth.[6] Thus, neglect of basic education and health runs counter to the pursuit of both social equity and economic efficiency.

The state should probably finance an increased proportion of the costs of social services in poor areas, although self-reliance may remain satisfactory for well-off rural areas. Because cooperative schemes have proved effective in the past, assistance could take the form of matching grants to townships or villages below a certain average income level (that is, the state would provide an amount equal to, or some multiple of, the amount of funds collected through the cooperative system). Assistance by the state could also include assigned government health workers, subsidized training of local health workers, and priority to poor areas in state health investment. More money and effort should likewise be put into boosting school attendance (Chapter 8). China has long experience and proven capability in such matters, but action is urgently needed.

The problems of poor areas can be exacerbated by misguided concern about equality—for example, paying workers the same as in more developed areas, thereby impeding the development of poor areas (Chapter 5). But it is also necessary to guard against mistakes of the opposite kind. For instance, some localities in China are apparently making even the basic education and health systems financially independent, which is causing their scope and quality in poor areas to deteriorate further. In some of these localities, moreover, the generally sound concept of "cost recovery"—making beneficiaries pay the full cost of services—is being incorrectly extended to basic social services. These developments seem contrary to the objectives of system reform in China and need to be corrected through policy directives from the central government.

The State and Enterprises

The recent Central Committee decision has identified the task of "invigorating enterprises as the key to reforming the national economy," and acknowledges that "socialism with Chinese characteristics should, first and foremost, be able to instill vitality into the enterprise." Attention has been focused on state-owned enterprises (or more accurately, enterprises owned by the whole people); however, policy toward nonstate enterprises—collective and individual—will also be critical in China's reform of the urban economy and could indirectly contribute to reform of state enterprises.

Control and Management of State-Owned Enterprises

Over the past five years, various reforms in the management of state-owned enterprises have been introduced, mostly on an experimental and piecemeal basis. These have included: enterprises retaining a proportion of profits for workers' bonuses, collective welfare expenditures and small-scale investment; some freedom for enterprises in selling part of their output and in securing inputs; some flexibility in setting prices; and increases in managerial authority over production decisions and personnel matters. These changes, similar to reforms tried in nearly all socialist countries, have had some good results. They represent only marginal changes, however, and the fundamental problem remains of the proper relationship between the state and the enterprise.

In the past, "ownership by the whole people was taken to mean direct operation by state organs." As a result,

---

6. See, for instance, World Bank, *World Development Report 1980* (New York: Oxford University Press, 1980), Chapters 4 and 5.

"the state exercised excessive and rigid control over enterprises" and "enterprises became subordinate bodies of administrative organs." The relationship between the state organs and the enterprises was strictly hierarchical, and the former frequently interfered in enterprise operations. An important step has been taken, therefore, with the recognition in China that "ownership right can be duly separated from operating right." The direction of reform will be toward a more complex system of management, in which a multitude of state agencies, as well as the enterprise itself (both workers and managers), assume various responsibilities. Since the state retains the authority to determine the division of responsibilities among the various state organs, including enterprises, it will, of course, retain ultimate control.

Though the principle that state enterprises should have much greater autonomy than in the past is accepted, important and difficult questions remain. One is the proper degree of autonomy: should it be confined to day-to-day operating and marketing decisions, or should it extend to appointment of managers, major investment and diversification decisions, and the right to close down part or all of the enterprise? Some possible answers to this question are considered in the next section of this chapter.

Another question is how the state could or should regulate the activities of autonomous enterprises. With the exception of strategic and key enterprises (discussed below), it is impossible in a complex and rapidly changing market-regulated economy for the state to know or specify what individual enterprises should do, which may make it pointless or counterproductive for the state to attempt to direct the activities of enterprises from within. Instead, the state should primarily seek to create an external environment such that the self-interest of enterprises guides them in directions consistent with the national interest, thus making it unnecessary for managers or others within enterprises to be charged specifically with representing the interests of the state. Such an environment—whose creation is the subject of much of the rest of this chapter—involves appropriate prices, wages, and interest rates, a high degree of competition, and a well-specified legal framework, as well as the use of regulatory levers such as taxes, subsidies, and credits.

How enterprises are controlled and managed internally will largely determine what constitutes their self-interest. Even with an ideal external environment, inappropriately motivated enterprises—especially those that do not actively and continuously seek increased profits (discussed later)—may act contrary to national interests. Moreover, experience in China and other countries confirms the difficulty of devising appropriate internal management arrangements for state enterprises. The various alternatives to the past system of direct administrative control all have weaknesses as well as strengths.

Giving direct control of state-owned enterprises to their workers would promote a strong sense of economic democracy and worker participation. Japanese experience also shows the economic advantages of strong worker commitment to the well-being of the enterprise, based not just on profit-related bonuses but also on constant education and frequent consultation. But the concept of worker management suffers from the fundamental problem that state enterprises should operate for the benefit of the whole society and not only of those who work in them—a particular problem in China where state enterprise workers are already a relatively well-off group. Experience in Yugoslavia and elsewhere, including that of nationalized industries with powerful labor unions in capitalist countries, suggests that worker control could result in excessively high wages and worker benefits, inadequate labor discipline and effort, restrictions on employment (partly though excessively capital-intensive investment decisions), and indifference to profitability—net of payments to workers—beyond the minimum necessary for enterprise survival.

Experience in industrial market economies suggests that giving control of state enterprises instead simply to their managers would have important advantages, including a strong urge to expand, improve, and innovate. It also suggests, however, that completely independent enterprise managers sometimes choose a quiet life, or, more commonly, seek personal power through expansion, with insufficient attention to profitability. In socialist countries, moreover, managerial control tends to differ only slightly from worker control, since managers often find it hard to resist worker demands for greater benefits or to insist on the often unwelcome changes in work practices needed for innovation and increased efficiency. This has been the Hungarian experience. It is also already a problem in China: studies of experimentally reformed enterprises controlled mainly by their managers reveal large increases in worker benefits, but small increases in economic efficiency.

An alternative approach, common in nonsocialist countries (and now being tried in Hungary), is to give strategic decisionmaking authority in each enterprise to a board of directors. The board could contain some representatives of society at large, as well as of the workers. But to provide the necessary motivation, the board would mainly have to consist of (or represent) institutions with a strong interest in the enterprise's profits. This would be the case, for example, if the institutions were owners entitled to dispose of the enterprise's after-tax profits, either by reinvesting them in the enterprise itself or by withdrawing them for consumption or investment elsewhere. The board could then insist that the enterprise's managers behaved appropriately, partly by its authority to appoint and dismiss them, partly by linking their remuneration to profitability. The managers might in practice make most decisions, even major ones, but would be greatly influenced by their ultimate accountability to the directors.

Experience elsewhere makes it clear that merely establishing boards of directors for state enterprises is not enough. What is necessary, in addition, is that these boards should be not just profit-oriented, but also free from direct intervention by state administrative organs. However, precisely because these are state enterprises, this may be difficult to achieve. Even if an enterprise's board of directors were to consist of representatives of the Ministry of Finance or a new Ministry of State Property, rather than representatives of the relevant sectoral ministry or the government of the locality where the enterprise is situated, informal connections and pressures could effectively perpetuate direct government control of the enterprise.

A possible solution might be to spread the ownership of each state enterprise among several different institutions, each in some way representing the whole people, but with an interest mainly in the enterprise's profits rather than directly in its output, purchases, or employment. Examples of such institutions, in addition to central and local governments, are banks, pension funds, insurance companies, and other enterprises. This possible system of socialist joint stock ownership has no parallel elsewhere, but contains elements found in other countries, including extensive enterprise ownership by pension funds in most industrial market economies and by various levels of government and socially owned banks in West Germany (see Box 10.1). In China, such a system of socialist joint stock ownership could perhaps be created initially by suitable dispersion of the ownership capital of existing state enterprises. Over time, it could be reinforced by a more diversified pattern of investment finance (discussed later), with a variety of state institutions acquiring financial interests in existing and new enterprises.

Competition

The critical importance of competition in promoting efficiency and innovation is increasingly recognized in China. Competition means that "enterprises will be directly subjected in the markets to the judgment and evaluation of the masses of consumers, so that the superior will survive and the inferior be eliminated." The Party's unambiguous position on this issue is crucial, because promoting competition among state enterprises will require not only changes in policy, but also fundamental changes in the attitudes of many people.

An essential policy to promote competition is allowing free entry into all kinds of economic activities. Enterprises (both state and nonstate) should be given the right and, indeed, encouraged to enter new kinds of activities if they have the capability to do so, and to withdraw from activities that are no longer wanted by the market or where they cannot compete with more efficient enterprises. Specifically, efficient enterprises should be allowed to grow rapidly, through the use of their retained profits and other sources of finance (financial flows are discussed in a later section), in new activities as well as existing activities. They should be permitted to compete for markets, for investment funds, for land, and for foreign exchange. The objective should be to make the widest use of the superior management and entrepreneurial skills of these enterprises.

Poor performers, however, should bear the full force of market competition. They should be forced to adjust and improve, and if this is not possible, to reorganize, seek new kinds of activities, or close down if necessary. In this connection, China needs to begin formulation of laws and regulations on the treatment of enterprises, both state-owned and others, in financial difficulties. When assistance through state intervention is clearly desirable for social reasons, this is best provided through financial subsidies (including, for example, wage subsidies), so that the costs of such assistance are explicit. Assistance through restriction of entry for other enterprises' products or other means of hampering competition is much less desirable. Financial subsidies should be given for a fixed time only, so that frequent reviews can determine whether the subsidies continue to be justified.

For enterprises in financial difficulties, but for which state subsidies are not justified, explicit procedures for reorganization or closure are necessary. Most countries have bankruptcy laws, for instance, stipulating a time period during which an enterprise would be allowed to stop paying its debts while it reorganizes its finances. These laws usually include the possibility of having a court- or government-appointed administrator take over the management of the enterprise and define the rights and responsibilities of the existing board of directors, managers, and workers. They also usually specify legal procedures for closure of plants, disposition of assets, and treatment of workers and managers, which would sometimes be handled by specialized bankruptcy courts.

Any reorganization of enterprises that impedes competition should be avoided. In China recently, and frequently in the Soviet Union and Eastern Europe, enterprises have been reorganized—partly in an attempt to separate enterprise management from state administration—into large holding companies, trusts, or *centrale*. Often the holding companies are economic entities in name only, and the result is to substitute one form of bureaucratic intervention for another. Moreover, even if these companies truly function as enterprises, there is a high risk that they will quickly become monopolistic, which may be even less desirable than having enterprises controlled by administrative organs. China is fortunate that its vast size offers the possibility of domestic competition in most sectors, but steps will have to be taken to discourage local governments from imposing restrictions on internal trade and competition (Chapter 5). Improvements in transport, commerce, and communications, especially the transmission of market information, will also be needed to create a unified national market (Chapter 5). In many sectors, much greater competition from imports will be desirable, as will competition of more Chinese enterprises in world markets (Chapter 6).

Effective competition, and indeed most other aspects of reform, will also depend on expansion and improvement of China's legal system. A decentralized economy, based primarily on horizontal linkages among enterprises, with a lot of internal trade and complicated financial arrangements, cannot function properly without a comprehensive system of commercial and contract law, and the institutions and personnel (accountants and auditors, as well as lawyers) needed to implement it. Laws are also

---

Box 10.1 Dispersed Social Ownership in the Federal Republic of Germany

West Germany has a market economy dominated by private ownership of the means of production. Public enterprises (those with at least 50 percent public ownership of equity or voting rights) account for only about 10 percent of GDP. But the true extent of social ownership is much greater. Minority government ownership in enterprises is widespread; for example, the nominally private energy and industry giant VEBA is 44 percent owned by the federal government. VEBA in turn has holdings in many other firms, some of which own still other businesses. In some corporations like the Rhine-Westphalia Electrical Works (RWE), local governments exercise voting rights that are a large multiple of their nominal stock ownership.

In addition to being widespread, social ownership in West Germany is highly dispersed, among federal, state (provincial), municipal, county, and community governments and various kinds of cooperative or publicly owned banks. Multiple ownership is common, and in general public ownership does not mean close operational ties between enterprises and individual government agencies.

Social ownership is pervasive in West German banking. In 1980 five of the ten largest banks were socially owned, as were all of the next tier (eleventh to twentieth in size). Socially owned banks account for around 60 percent of the total volume of bank business. Banks have a considerable ownership stake in many firms. They also tend to have close credit ties with particular enterprises and are heavily represented on boards of directors. Most banks engage in a variety of activities; even local savings banks may lend to or own industrial enterprises, directly or through their apex institutions.

The socially owned banking sector is characterized by a diversity of forms. Urban and rural cooperative banks are permitted by law to lend 50 percent more than other banks with the same equity capital, which has enabled them to grow rapidly in recent years. Trade union–owned banks, originally established to manage the funds of trade unions, have been amalgamated into the Bank fur Gemeinwirtschaft, West Germany's ninth largest bank in 1980. The local savings banks (Sparkassen) are not "owned" by anyone in the traditional sense, but are "guaranteed" by the lowest level of government. They

have apex institutions (Landesbanken), which are sometimes owned by groups of local savings banks, sometimes partially or wholly by state governments. A long-term development bank (the Kreditanstalt fur Wiederaufbau), owned 80 percent by the federal government and 20 percent by states, plays a major role in financing government-approved projects in developing countries, in export finance, and in promoting regional development and aiding small businesses.

An example of the ownership ties that link West Germany's socially owned banking system with key sectors of the economy is the Westdeutsche Landesbank (WestLB), the largest of the regional apex institutions for savings banks and the third largest bank in the country overall. WestLB's largest shareholder is the State of North-Rhine/Westphalia (43.2 percent); the other owners are associations of savings banks in Rhineland and Westphalia-Lippe (16.7 percent each) and associations of local governments in the same two regions (11.7 percent each). WestLB is a significant shareholder in thirty-three major corporations and scores of other enterprises in such diverse fields as housing and real estate, finance, leasing, energy, engineering, mechanics and optics, construction, machinery, textiles, and computers. Some of these companies in turn own other businesses. For instance, WestLB is a 32 percent owner of Kommunale Energie Beteiligungsgesellschaft, a large energy conglomerate whose other shareholders are a number of local governments at various levels. This company in turn is a 32.6 percent owner of Vereinigte Elektrizitatswerke Westfalen, which itself has holdings in eleven other enterprises, including a mining company which is a small shareholder in Ruhrkohle, West Germany's biggest coal-mining concern (whose largest shareholder is VEBA).

Widespread social ownership in West Germany apparently does not lead to inefficiencies. This is probably due in part to the fact that government and other social entities owning enterprises generally act like ordinary stockholders, particularly in their detachment from the daily operations of firms. Moreover, the dispersed and often indirect character of social ownership and the coexistence of a large private sector mean that competitive pressures to maintain efficiency are preserved.

needed to provide for the founding and closing of enterprises as well as to regulate the economic activities of independent enterprises and individuals. In addition to providing for product and worker safety, environmental protection, and so on, legislation should prohibit—as in other countries—specified types of monopolistic, anticompetitive, or exploitative behavior. At present in China, the situation is unsatisfactorily vague, with enterprises and local officials free to place their own interpretations on general guidelines from the center, which in some cases causes unacceptable abuse, in others (probably more numerous) economically valuable activities to be regarded as illegitimate.

Motivation of Workers and Managers

Appropriate enterprise motivation should include a strong desire to increase profits. Avoidance of losses is an important aspect of this, but by itself is insufficient, since China needs enterprises that not merely pursue a passive strategy of staying out of trouble, but rather actively seek to increase production and sales of existing, improved, and new products and to cut costs of all kinds. With rational prices and competition, the best single measure of enterprise performance in this regard is usually medium-term profits (especially after deduction of the cost—depreciation and interest—of the capital employed). The desire of peasant households to—in effect—increase profits because their standard of living depends on it lies at the heart of China's recent agricultural successes. Outside agriculture, the same motivation is a natural feature of individual and family enterprises and of small enterprises owned and operated collectively, or as partnerships, by their workers. In medium-size and large enterprises, however, establishing the necessary link between profits and individual rewards is more complicated.

A distinction needs to be made between managers and workers, especially in large enterprises. Incentives for workers are mainly a question of wage policy (discussed in Chapter 8). There have been many recent attempts to introduce a production responsibility system, similar to that in agriculture, for individuals and units within enterprises. Progress has apparently been limited, partly because managers are not yet sufficiently motivated to pay workers by results and partly because many workers—as in other countries—resist this, but also because it takes time and experimentation to devise incentive payment schemes that fit the varying circumstances of individual enterprises. It will probably be necessary to allow each enterprise to establish its own payment-by-results system for workers, based on qualitative and quantitative evaluation of performance, in accordance with its particular conditions but in line with general principles established by the Government.

The extent to which an enterprise's total wage bill (including all bonuses and benefits) should be linked to profit is a more difficult issue. Some large enterprises in capitalist countries have profit-sharing schemes for workers, because they believe this to be good for incentives and morale. But most do not, mainly on the grounds that variations in profitability over time are not much influenced by worker behavior, as opposed to management decisions and external conditions. This would be true also of most state enterprises in China, with the added complication that profit-sharing schemes, whether introduced by individual enterprises or uniformly prescribed by government regulation, could undermine macroeconomic wage control (Chapter 8). In the longer term, if state enterprises were controlled by boards of directors interested in increasing profitability, administrative control of wage bills might cease to be necessary, and enterprises could be allowed to introduce profit-sharing schemes where they felt this to be conducive to efficiency. But for the time being, the disadvantages of linking the remuneration of workers directly to profits may well outweigh the advantages.

Managers—the staff responsible for major decisions on production, engineering, sales, and other activities—should be held accountable, much more than the workers, for the enterprise's performance, both in the long and short run. Entrepreneurship is also part of the enterprise management function, and the criteria against which managers should be judged and rewarded should include the enterprise's ability to respond to market demands, to seek ways of producing goods at lower cost and of higher quality, and more generally to innovate and introduce technological changes. A large proportion of managers' incomes, and decisions concerning their promotion or dismissal, should thus depend on enterprise profitability. In China, this will require a broader view of the responsibilities of enterprise management and a willingness to reward superior managers appropriately.

Obviously price reforms, including appropriate charges for use of valuable assets (such as capital, skilled labor, natural resources, and urban land), are needed in order to make profitability an economically rational or socially defensible basis for managerial remuneration. Moreover, no schemes for linking individual or group pay to enterprise performance will work properly without substantial improvements in financial accounting and auditing. At present in China, there is apparently little discipline in accounting, and enterprises are able to ignore state regulations by, for instance, recording bonuses as collective welfare expenditures. Accurate accounts, subject to thorough, compulsory, and independent audits, with severe penalties for noncompliance, will be essential if China is to establish a workable, efficient, and honest system of independent enterprises.

Management of Strategic and Key Enterprises

State enterprises in China cover a vast range of activities, from power stations and railways to neighborhood restaurants, and come in many sizes, from huge industrial complexes such as Anshan Steel employing several hundred thousand workers, to small retail stores employing a few persons. It would be impractical to try to manage all these enterprises in the same way. A more realistic approach might be to identify various categories of enterprises for which particular principles of state control and management would apply.

Some enterprises will surely remain under the direct supervision or control of state administrative organs, for instance defense-related industries, as well as basic public services such as electric power and rail transport. And in sectors where the economically optimal scale of operation is so large that enterprises naturally became regional or national monopolies, direct state regulation may also be necessary. But even in these *strategic enterprises*, managers should be given increased authority, and incentive systems established to reward and penalize according to agreed performance criteria and evaluation procedures. In this regard, the experience of some East European countries (most notably East Germany), as well as some nonsocialist countries, in evaluating managers of noncompetitive enterprises may be useful. In France, for instance, many state-owned enterprises are managed on the basis of formal three- to five-year contracts between the government and the enterprise, which set out a number of performance targets for the enterprise and the obligations of the government regarding financial support and policies affecting enterprise performance. These contracts also distinguish between normal operational objectives and any specific social objectives that the enterprise is expected to meet.[7]

The state may also wish to exercise direct control over selected *key enterprises*, including those exploiting energy and other mineral resources on a large scale, very large enterprises in other sectors, and some enterprises in priority subsectors. Particular machine tool enterprises, for instance, might be selected for state-directed technical transformation in order to compete in international markets, or pilot plants in electronics could pioneer the use of advanced technology.

Such selective intervention has been successfully pursued even in countries where governments do not normally play a direct role in industrial development. France and Japan, for instance, have been particularly successful in selective interventions in specific industries and enterprises, especially because they have insisted on increased efficiency and technological progress (by contrast, many countries have nationalized declining or inefficient industries, but have seldom succeeded in making them economically viable). Competition, from both domestic and foreign firms, is thus vital for key enterprises. Subsidies may be justified when these enterprises are still in an infant stage, but only for a fixed period.

The proportion of state enterprises designated as strategic or key, and hence subject to direct government regulation, should perhaps be larger in the early stages of reform, when distorted incentives, bottlenecks, and uncertainties are more serious, and when mandatory production planning and materials allocation still play an important role. But as other aspects of urban economic reform proceed, such directly regulated enterprises could become a small (albeit very significant) minority, with independent enterprises constituting the overwhelming bulk of the state sector.

Diversification of the Ownership System

Reform of state enterprise management is the central element of urban reform, but by itself is likely to be insufficient. Many types of economic activities cannot be efficiently undertaken by state enterprises, however managed. Even in socialist economies dominated by public ownership, collective and individual enterprises can play an important and irreplaceable role as discriminating purchasers, as efficient suppliers of inputs, and as competitors to the state sector. Dynamic nonstate enterprises can thus both assist and put pressure on state enterprises to improve efficiency and upgrade technology. Perhaps as important as the recognition of the need to reform and invigorate state enterprises, therefore, is the position taken in the recent Party decision that "the initiative of the state, the collective and the individual should all be encouraged. We must work to develop diversified economic forms and various methods of management."

Evidence from many countries, socialist as well as nonsocialist, illustrates the kinds of nonagricultural activities that are difficult to organize in state enterprises (or even large corporations in capitalist economies). They include personal services (restaurants, repairs), much retailing and wholesaling, small-scale construction and transport, high-quality consumer goods, specialized services to industry (technical consulting, research and development), and small-order parts and components not suitable for assembly line production. In the course of economic development, moreover, demand for activities provided by small-scale enterprises normally increases just as fast as demand for the products of large-scale industry, partly because of increasing specialization in material production, but also because services (such as preparing meals, making clothes, repairs) hitherto organized within the household become parts of the exchange economy, and because there is a growing need for business services to lubricate the increasingly complex economy (for example, communications, information services, consulting, financial services).

---

7. For other examples, see World Bank, *World Development Report 1983*, Chapter 8.

Thus, in industrial countries such as Japan and the United States, small-scale enterprises account for a large share of national output, partly as subcontractors to large corporations, and are also important sources of innovation (Chapter 7).

Even when collective and individual enterprises have been restricted, as in many socialist countries, such activities have nonetheless flourished, but have become part of a "second economy." An estimate for Yugoslavia for 1973–77 was that about 30 percent of services and repairs were performed illegally. In the Soviet Union during the 1970s, in addition to large earnings by private housing repairmen, using supplies and materials of questionable legality, new urban housing construction earned black market builders an estimated 1 billion rubles per year. Because the output and services of the second economy are in great demand, official restrictions have not only been rather ineffectual, but have also had unfortunate side effects. The Soviet Union, Yugoslavia, and Hungary have all found that making individual activity illegal results in a tremendous amount of illegality, bribery, and corruption, waste of working hours, and theft of state property. Potential tax revenue is lost, control over relative earnings is weakened, and respect for the system of economic management and regulation is undermined.

Promotion of collective and individual enterprises in socialist countries requires above all the removal of restrictions on their activities and of discrimination against their owners and workers. There is usually a vast store of initiative that can be tapped once restrictions are removed. Despite the recent Party decision, however, it will take time for the population generally to view employment in nonstate enterprises as comparable to state employment, because of the long history of discrimination against small collectives and individual activities, and people will need to be convinced that the new policy will remain in force.

An important step would be to provide equal access to social services and welfare benefits for workers and entrepreneurs in the nonstate sector. They should also be given access to credit from banks and other financial institutions. Large collectives may continue to be taxed on the same basis as state enterprises, but taxation of smaller collectives and individual enterprises should be simple to minimize bookkeeping requirements (Chapter 9). Access to materials and premises is also crucial: collective and individual enterprises are seriously handicapped by the present allocation system and would benefit from its relaxation or replacement by market regulation, especially for key materials.

Most important will be a set of simple, unambiguous, and stable regulations on the establishment and operation of these types of enterprises. Such regulations, backed up by legal arrangements for enforcement and appeal, would, among other things, protect small enterprises from financial extortion by misguided or corrupt officials at lower levels—a problem common in other countries, of which examples are now emerging in China. Regulations that remain in force for many years are also essential to persuade nonagricultural entrepreneurs, like farmers, to take a long-term view and invest in their businesses, rather than aiming at quick profits for immediate consumption (Chapter 9).

Some state enterprises in small-scale industries and repair and service activities might be contracted to groups of workers who would then manage them as collectives (as is currently being considered in China) or simply sold to collectives or individuals. The latter option may be especially relevant for state enterprises suffering persistent losses (which would otherwise be closed down), but also for highly successful parts of some enterprises, which might be spun off as specialized small-scale enterprises. Chapter 7 gives the example of a machinery-producing workshop within a bicycle enterprise, which in most other countries would be spun off as a specialized company to further develop its capability. Similarly, the research or engineering departments of some enterprises might be spun off as consulting companies, which could then serve more enterprises.

Small collectives share with individual enterprises the major advantage of an extremely close link between the enterprise's financial performance, both short and long term, and the personal rewards of its workers—who in most cases will also be the owners. This advantage is lost in large collectives (such as those in urban China, which are managed much as state enterprises) and more generally in all collectives whose workers do not share heavily in their ownership. An interesting exception to this generalization has been China's commune and brigade enterprises. Although these enterprises are owned by the entire township or village and not by their managers or workers, the latter all come from the township, whose population is highly immobile. There is therefore a much greater feeling of solidarity and a stronger incentive to develop and expand these enterprises and, most important, to create employment opportunities for relatives still working in agriculture. Experience in other countries, including France, Spain, and the United States, confirms that enterprises owned by communities work particularly well when the community is stable and well integrated, especially in remote areas.

But there are few examples in the world of success with genuine large and medium-scale collectives (where the workers are the owners), especially in manufacturing. Most successful collectives are small or in nonindustrial lines of activity, especially commerce and distribution (where they are often consumer or producer, rather than worker, cooperatives). The problem seems to be in retaining a strong sense of ownership beyond a certain size; the few successful examples of larger-scale industrial collectives (for example, Mondragon in Spain) have developed elaborate procedures regarding contributions and withdrawals of capital. The advantages and disadvantages of the different forms of collective enterprises will thus require continuous review in the course of reform.

Incentives to increase efficiency and innovate are obviously strong in enterprises owned and managed by individuals or families. The issues in China are the maximum acceptable scale of these enterprises (and related questions such as the number of workers they can employ) and the acceptable share of these enterprises in overall economic activity. To prohibit the growth of individual enterprises beyond a certain size, or to restrict their numbers, would stifle a potentially dynamic force within the economy. An alternative might be to require individually owned enterprises to sell majority ownership to the state, or other socialist institutions (such as state enterprises or banks) once they exceed a certain size. The minority owners could continue managing the enterprises, perhaps supervised by a board of directors representing all owners. For this approach to work well, without discouraging promising small enterprises from expanding, the sale of ownership rights to the state would of course have to be at a fair price—diminishing the control of the individual, but not confiscating his wealth. In other countries, many successful small businesses are voluntarily sold after a few years to larger firms.

Socialism with Chinese characteristics is envisaged by the Party to include "a cooperative relationship between state, collective and individual enterprises." The next two decades—and beyond—will be a period of continuous and experimental search for the mix of ownership and management systems that would best serve China's economic, social, and political objectives. What seems certain is that there will be a variety of types of enterprises, each suited to certain sorts of activities. Diversified ownership arrangements are already emerging even within the state sector, with enterprises being established by other enterprises, with provincial and local governments cooperating to found new enterprises, and with joint ventures between state and collective enterprises and between Chinese state enterprises and foreign private enterprises.

Investment and Price Reform

A central element of system reform is to expand the role of market regulation. An important component of this effort is, of course, the reform of enterprise management discussed in the preceding section. Other components, including changes in the labor allocation, wage, and tax systems, stronger incentives for technological change and dissemination, and reform of internal and external trade, have been discussed in earlier chapters. This section discusses two additional issues—investment decisions and financing, and price reform.

Investment Decisions and Financing

In infrastructure, education, health, and defense, the Government will want to retain direct control over the bulk of investment decisions. Similarly, in agriculture, it will want to control investment in infrastructure such as irrigation and land development, though most other investment will probably be undertaken by households and collectives. In industry, however, an issue that needs to be considered is the extent to which investment decisions should be made at the enterprise level.

An argument for investment decisions by enterprises is that a degree of responsibility over the *future* of the enterprise, in addition to responsibility for current production decisions, would give enterprise managers more meaningful responsibility for the enterprise. Enterprise performance depends, after all, not only on current management decisions, but also on investment decisions made in the past. Enterprises, and their managers, cannot be held accountable for current performance if investment decisions were made by state administrative organs.

Enterprise responsibility for investment decisions is also often necessary to improve the efficiency of investment. All investment decisions involve risk, and a certain proportion of failures—and unexpected successes—is inevitable with any decisionmaking system. But, as with production, managers of enterprises should have a much better understanding than state administrative organs of the benefits and costs of available investment opportunities. This advantage of decentralized investment decisionmaking is enhanced during intensive growth (Chapters 1 and 7), which requires continuous reassessment of the existing structure of production, as well as a continuous search for ways of lowering costs and improving quality.

Moreover, higher-level administrative officials, however intelligent and conscientious, have no financial stake in the success or failure of the projects they are deciding on. By contrast, decisionmakers at the enterprise level—the owners in small businesses, managers appointed and supervised by boards representing the owners in larger concerns—have or can be given a substantial direct personal financial interest in the enterprise. Experience—positive and negative—both in China and elsewhere suggests that personal financial involvement in the outcome of an investment decision can be a very effective way of encouraging bold and innovative thinking combined with thorough analysis, hard-headed calculation, and the avoidance of waste. This is true not only of the expansion or renovation of existing enterprises, but also of the establishment of new enterprises.

Finally, delegating more responsibility for investment decisions to independent enterprises could help in striking a better overall balance between infrastructural and other investment. Economic efficiency in China, as in other socialist countries, has suffered from a "medium-sighted" bias in favor of directly productive industrial investment, which in practice still remains strong, especially among local governments. This bias might be reduced if government at all levels had less of a role in organizing and financing such investment and could thus concentrate more on infrastructural investment. In particular, making enterprises independent and giving them more investment responsibility could oblige local governments—as in other countries—to improve infrastructure in order to attract industrial investment.

Many socialist countries, including China in recent years, have permitted state enterprises to retain a part of their profits for specified categories of investment. This has had some good results, but has also encountered serious problems. In China, irrationality of prices, shortcomings of the material supply system, and protection of local industries have led enterprises and local governments to make some investment decisions that are highly undesirable from the national perspective. There has been overinvestment in sectors with high administered prices, underinvestment in vital but unprofitable sectors such as energy and transport, and continued proliferation of uneconomically small and low-quality projects aimed at increasing local self-sufficiency in materials or equipment (Chapter 5).

Another problem has been inappropriate motivation of enterprises and their managers (discussed in the previous section). State enterprises have much to gain from expansion of fixed assets and production—increased bonuses for staff and workers, more resources for collective welfare, and the enhanced prestige and power that come with larger size. The negative consequences of misguided investments are also much attenuated by subsidies and other forms of assistance from state organs. This leads to ''investment hunger,'' as in other socialist countries, with enterprises competing for investment resources even when the potential economic returns are low or negative. The resultant tension between central planners seeking to control the level of investment and the hungry enterprises frequently results in sharp investment cycles. Even in China, where the authority of enterprises over investment has been very restricted, this tension nonetheless exists between central and local authorities (including the rural collective sector), with similar investment cycles.

In Hungary and Yugoslavia, which have experimented more than any other socialist countries with decentralized investment decisionmaking, this has not improved investment efficiency also because of the limited mobility of investment funds. Highly profitable enterprises tend to be efficient and dynamic and should therefore be allowed more investment resources—but not necessarily for investment in their existing activities. They should also consider investment opportunities elsewhere in the economy, evaluating these against opportunities for either new activities or expansion of existing activities within their present fields. Only in this way could investment resources flow to the uses offering the highest economic returns. In Yugoslavia and Hungary, not only is the flow of investment funds among enterprises limited, but enterprises are constrained in their ability to enter new lines of activity. As a consequence, enterprises have often made investment decisions that might be sensible from their own perspective, but inefficient from the national perspective. Since each enterprise's own resources are limited, there has also been a bias toward projects below the economically optimal scale. Delegation of investment decisions to enterprises thus has to proceed in parallel with reforms of the price system and other aspects of enterprise management, and with increased mobility of investment funds.

ALTERNATIVE CHANNELS OF INVESTMENT FLOWS. In the traditional socialist system, mobility of savings is largely vertical. Savings are mobilized by the state budget through profit remittance, taxation, and other fiscal instruments and then allocated according to the plan either through the budget as grants or through state-run banks as credits. In addition, there is some compartmentalized reinvestment of savings generated within particular sectors and localities. In a reformed socialist economic system, the relative importance of different institutional sources of saving could be quite different (Chapter 9), as could be the ways in which saving is channeled into investment. Vertical flows and compartmentalized reinvestment, although they would remain important, should be increasingly supplemented and replaced with horizontal flows.

First, enterprises could be allowed and encouraged, as mentioned earlier, to enter new kinds of activities, financing such new activities with credits or other external funds as well as internal resources (more profitable enterprises tend to have better access to both internal and external finance). This would not only create flows of investment funds (as well as other resources such as management skills, labor, and capital equipment) to new activities or sectors where they could be more usefully employed (even though they remained within the enterprise), but would also greatly increase competition in the economy.

Second, horizontal flows of investment resources could be achieved through direct investment between economic units. Enterprises could be permitted to invest in other enterprises, establish new enterprises, or participate in joint ventures with other enterprises, local governments, collectives, or even foreign companies. Such horizontal flows and cooperation are already emerging in China, in many different forms, mostly from lower-level initiatives, but with the Government's encouragement and support. (Ensuring the supply of key materials has apparently been a major motive—for instance, investment in Shanxi coal mines by industrial enterprises in energy-deficient Jiangsu.)

These forms of direct investment between economic units should be encouraged and, with further reforms in other aspects of the economic system, will be increasingly guided by economic criteria. But these horizontal flows can offer only a limited channel for investment resource mobility. They are comparable to bilateral trade (bartering) for commodities, since they involve the direct exchange of resources between suppliers and potential users. For more efficient and possibly larger flows of investment resources, horizontal flows through financial institutions functioning as intermediaries between the suppliers and users of resources will also be necessary.

One function of financial institutions would be to mobilize investment funds from individuals, collectives, state enterprises, and local governments, by accepting deposits and by issuing financial instruments such as bonds (either by themselves or on behalf of the users of capital). They would have to offer an interest rate (or other return) that reflected the scarcity of investment funds in the economy. In this way, enterprises with internal funds available would be made aware of the potential returns to investment opportunities elsewhere in the economy and would be able to choose rationally between direct investment (internal or in another enterprise) and indirect investment (by depositing the funds with financial institutions).

The funds raised by these institutions would be made available to potential investors, particularly enterprises of all kinds. The funds could be provided as loans, with fixed rates of interest and repayment periods. At least some financial institutions, however, should be able to provide ownership capital, partly because many worthwhile projects are too risky to be financed largely by loans, partly because directly sharing in the risks and benefits would motivate financial institutions to give more assistance in project design and implementation. In this case, the financial institution would be an investor itself, much as local governments, bureaus, state enterprises, and collectives now participate in joint investment projects.

These institutions would thus be similar to commercial banks, investment trusts, development finance companies, and other intermediaries in capitalist countries, but with the difference that they would be dealing with flows of funds that were to a large extent socially owned—by government organs, state enterprises and other state institutions, or collectives. They would, however, also be fundamentally different from existing banks in socialist countries, which primarily implement planned vertical flows. These institutions would in effect create a socialist market for investment funds.

Whether capital is provided as loans or equity, the relationship between the financial institution and the enterprise that receives the capital (or that was founded by the financial institution, either alone or in cooperation with other institutions) should be economic, rather than

administrative. In addition to financial support, the financial intermediaries could also—as in other countries—provide technical assistance in financial management and information in areas such as technology and marketing. Indeed, the activities of such institutions as highly motivated gatherers and disseminators of economically relevant information would be just as important as the financial flows themselves.

Diverse organizational forms and a multiplicity of overlapping and competing institutions would be highly desirable (see Box 10.1 on variegated social ownership in West German banking). If only a single financial institution existed, or several that had mutually exclusive areas of responsibility, they would tend to become monopolistic, bureaucratic instruments of particular levels (or agencies) of government. In China, which has begun to diversify its financial system since 1979, there could be many different forms of financial institutions—banks, credit cooperatives, investment trusts, insurance and pension funds, and so on. In rural areas, for instance, some of the economic institutions of the former communes and brigades, which still exist following the reorganization of local government administration, could be transformed into financial institutions. Such township banks or investment companies could mobilize investment resources from collective enterprises to establish new enterprises, help existing enterprises expand and modernize, and support agricultural development. However, the operations of financial institutions should not be geographically restricted. The experience of Yugoslavia confirms that regional banks tend to impede rather than facilitate flows of investment resources between regions and thus contribute to regional autarky.

State intervention in the management of financial institutions, and specifically in their allocation of funds, is a more complex issue. There is obviously a need for state regulation. A major function of financial institutions is to reduce risk for both savers and borrowers and thus increase incentives to save and invest efficiently. Government regulations and intervention are required largely to reduce the risk to savers, through deposit insurance schemes, restrictions on the scope of various institutions' operations and the types of assets held, requirements on full disclosure of information, and monitoring the performance and viability of these institutions. Since the activities of the financial sector may have a substantial impact on the overall level of economic activity and prices, the Government clearly also has to intervene in financial markets in order to regulate the overall supply of money and credit (see Box 10.2). All this would require broadening and strengthening the functions of the People's Bank, which is to become a specialized central bank.

The appropriate degree of government intervention in credit allocation and interest rates is more controversial. Excessive intervention obviously risks turning financial

Reform of China's system of economic management will greatly increase the importance of monetary control. When most goods are administratively allocated, the availability of money and credit to pay for them is of secondary importance, and monetary policy plays a passive, accommodating role. Moreover, when most enterprises are administrative organs, whose economic survival is guaranteed, it is futile to attempt to restrain their spending through monetary and credit restrictions. In Eastern Europe, for example, state enterprises respond to a tight credit policy by refusing to pay their bills on time, generating involuntary trade credit that cascades throughout the economy as firms settle accounts outside the banking system and formal or informal separate clearing mechanisms emerge. This creates great difficulties for the banking system, and sooner or later the authorities feel compelled to return to a relatively easy credit policy.

By contrast, in a market-regulated economy, with financially independent enterprises, the supply of money and credit crucially affects the overall level of (monetary or nominal) demand for goods and services, and hence, especially in the medium term, the general price level. For this reason, and particularly since the inflationary surge of the 1970s, the governments of market-regulated economies have attached increasing importance to monetary control. In China, both the need to control money and credit and the existence of a connection between fiscal policy and monetary policy are well understood. But a separate central bank was established only in 1984, and recent experience of unexpectedly rapid credit expansion suggests that there may be scope for improved techniques and instruments of monetary control.

In other countries, one pillar of monetary control is the imposition of minimum reserve ratios on individual banks, which require them to keep at least a certain proportion of their assets in the form of cash and deposits with the central bank. This puts an upper limit on the "money multiplier"—the relationship between the stock of "high-powered money" (cash plus deposits at the central bank) and the total stock of money, including all bank deposits, which is several times larger. The second pillar of monetary control is central bank regulation of the stock of high-powered money, most commonly through purchases and sales of government bonds ("open-market operations") and varying the terms of central bank lending to commercial banks (the "discount window").

Monetary control of a market-regulated economy is by no means easy. Opinions differ as to whether the main object of control should be money (variously defined), credit, or interest rates. The size of the money multiplier may fluctuate unpredictably, for example, if banks keep more than the required amount of reserves. Changes in the money supply likewise do not cause precisely predictable changes in the overall level of demand for goods and services, which in turn do not have precisely predictable effects on the price level (or the real volume of economic activity). None of this vitiates either the need for, or the feasibility of, strict medium-term monetary control. But the short-term causes and consequences of changes in monetary magnitudes may be too complex and uncertain to permit exclusive reliance on any simple or automatic formula for monetary control.

---

institutions into state organs, impeding improvements in the efficiency of investment, without necessarily increasing effective central control. In Yugoslavia, after the 1965 reform, for example, the government kept the interest rate (after allowing for inflation) at a level much below that necessary to balance the supply of and demand for investment funds, and hence the investment hunger of enterprises and local governments persisted, requiring frequent administrative intervention by state organs in the financial system and causing continued cyclical investment fluctuations.

During periods of rapid growth in Japan and South Korea, in contrast, their governments played a major role in the allocation of credit to specific sectors and enterprises. Since in both countries' credit accounts for an unusually large proportion of enterprise investment funds, this gave their governments a lot of control over the allocation of investment, although much of this con-

trol was exerted indirectly, by offering low interest rates and favorable repayment terms to particular activities of private enterprises. Unlike those in Yugoslavia, these enterprises were highly motivated to increase profits over the medium term and were made conscious of the true economic value of their subsidized credits by informal parallel financial markets, which among other things "recycled" some of the subsidized funds at much higher interest rates. Moreover, as their economies have developed further, both Japan and South Korea have given greater independence to their financial systems.

EVOLUTIONARY CHOICE. For China, continued experimentation and exploration in the area of investment decisionmaking and financing will be necessary, especially because the experience of other countries provides no precedent for a socialist financial market. The exact shares and relative importance of alternative forms of investment allocation and financing should be allowed to evolve with the lessons of experience and the development of institutions.

Savings mobilized through the state budget would at a minimum continue to finance large amounts of investment in infrastructure, energy, and the social sectors. In addition, part of budgetary savings could be channeled through financial institutions to enterprises to finance other investment. The government would also indirectly regulate the level and content of the growing share of total investment undertaken directly by enterprises and households.

Financial intermediaries would mobilize an increasing share of savings, tapping the potential for household saving, as well as funds from enterprises with limited internal investment opportunities. These institutions would also play an increasing role in investment decisionmaking, through their evaluation of investment proposals by borrowing enterprises and through their own direct investment.

Enterprises would not only make an increasing proportion of investment decisions, but would also generate an increasing share of savings from their retained profits, supplemented (largely at their discretion) by loans or equity capital from other institutions. The speed with which enterprise-level investment should increase in importance depends on the speed with which it is possible to establish, first, linkages between the personal interests of managers and the outcome of investment decisions, and, second, economically rational prices, interest rates, and other signals that reflect relative costs in the economy.

While many of the vertical and horizontal flows of investment funds would be in the form of credits, some would be in the form of equity capital. The latter would include flows between enterprises (both state and nonstate), between financial intermediaries and enterprises, and from households to enterprises, either directly or through financial intermediaries such as pension funds. Diversified flows of funds would therefore be both consequence and cause of a diversified pattern of enterprise ownership.

Price Reform

It is recognized in China that "rational prices constitute an important condition for ensuring a dynamic and stable economy, and reform of the price system is the critical element of the entire program of system reform." This is because the decentralized decisions of independent, profit-oriented enterprises would otherwise often be inefficient for the whole economy. Yet price reform is complex and difficult, partly because prices have up to now been used largely for other purposes, including income redistribution and government revenue raising. Moreover, deficiencies in other aspects of the system themselves constitute obstacles to price reform—including lack of competition, inadequate motivation to hold down costs, and investment hunger, all of which contribute to chronic shortages of many commodities.

One ingredient of reform should thus be to minimize the nonallocative role of prices, through greater reliance on taxes, transfer payments, and other instruments discussed earlier to achieve social and fiscal objectives. Prices could then be used mainly to signal relative costs, needs, and scarcities to enterprises and households, guiding their production, expenditure, and investment decisions in economically appropriate directions. To accomplish this, as the Government recognizes, the price-setting system must itself be changed to give market supply and demand forces a greater role. Administered changes in prices set by the state are also needed, especially in the near term. Several aspects of price reform were discussed in earlier chapters, including more flexible pricing of agricultural products (Chapter 3), altering the prices of various sources of energy (Chapter 4), restoring the link between producer and retail prices of essential consumer goods (Chapter 9), adjustment of prices that influence the spatial location of economic activities, especially transport tariffs and land use charges (Chapter 5), and stronger connections between domestic and world prices (Chapter 6). This section concentrates on some general issues relating to adjustment of energy and raw material prices and to the reduction of administrative price control.

ADJUSTMENTS OF ENERGY AND RAW MATERIAL PRICES. The most obviously distorted of all China's producer prices are the state-set prices of energy and some raw materials—far below opportunity costs[8] in domestic and world markets. But the sheer magnitude of these distortions makes them hard to correct: to introduce the required price adjustments at one stroke would involve dramatic changes in the financial circumstances of many enterprises and institutions; yet to make them in small steps would undesirably prolong the period of adjustment, particularly because these key prices directly and indirectly influence almost all other prices, which are themselves in need of other sorts of adjustments. Whether in one administrative step, or in a number of announced steps, or through rapid transformation of the present two-tier pricing system into a unified market pricing system, major adjustments of energy and raw material prices seem urgently needed. Postponement of these adjustments over the past few years has led to the extension of ad hoc state interventions in other areas, including

---

8. Opportunity cost is the value of other economic possibilities created or forgone by producing or consuming a specific commodity. For goods that can be traded, consideration of opportunity costs should include markets abroad as well as in China.

enterprise-specific subsidies and "adjustment" taxes and retroactive and frequent changes in tax rates. Hungarian experience confirms that interventions of this kind tend to negate the benefits (and slow the futher progress) of socialist system reform.

Possible adverse effects on state revenues are one of the concerns that have inhibited the government from increasing energy and raw material prices. In principle, of course, since state enterprises constitute the great bulk of both producers and users of these commodities, price adjustments should mainly simply redistribute an unchanged aggregate amount of profit and tax among state enterprises. Even so, this could alter budget revenues unless there were simultaneous adjustment of the varying rates of profit tax on individual enterprises. Moreover, given China's weak accounting and auditing, enterprises whose profits increased as a result of these price adjustments might report less of a rise than they should, while others might exaggerate their additional costs. (Following recent increases in coal prices, some coal mines even claimed that their profits went down because of unauthorized increases in input prices!) Such leakages would make enterprises better off at the expense of the state: if there were tight control of worker remuneration and benefits, this would mainly increase the proportion of investment funds in the hands of enterprises—a consequence that would be less worrisome once prices more accurately reflected relative costs.

The possible ripple effects of large energy and raw material price increases on the prices of other goods are another source of concern in China. But many of these ripple effects should be welcome: higher energy prices, for example, cannot and should not be fully absorbed in energy-using enterprises, but should be partly passed on in the form of higher prices for energy-intensive products, whose use needs to be discouraged in order to improve the overall energy efficiency of the economy. Moreover, increases in the prices of energy and energy-intensive products would not necessarily raise the general price level, since they would soak up purchasing power and hence tend to reduce the demand for, and prices of, other products.

The state might nonetheless wish to manage the ripple effects caused by major adjustments of energy and raw material prices. For "strategic" and "key" enterprises (discussed earlier), a unified program for the adjustment of product prices, costs, and taxes could be worked out in some detail by controlling administrative organs, including the Price Bureau and the Ministry of Finance. In other areas, where competition is still minimal, enterprises might be required to pass on only a specified proportion (larger in sectors with lower profitability, and vice versa) of their increased costs in higher average product prices. They could be allowed greater latitude in varying the relative prices of individual products (both to reflect

differing energy intensities and to eliminate other current irrationalities in the relation of prices to production cost and product quality). Enterprises operating in more competitive areas could be given greater flexibility in varying their output prices, since competition and market pressure would work against excessive price increases.

MARKET PRICING. Despite their potential usefulness in correcting accumulated distortions, there is increasing recognition in China that administrative price adjustments—which tend to lack the flexibility, complexity, and precision needed in a modern economy—are only part of price reform. More critical is to give market demand and supply a greater role in price determination. There has been progress in this direction over the past few years: the prices of many minor items, and of some transactions in more major items, are already determined by market forces. Major progress has, however, been impeded by the fear that, because there are chronic shortages of many goods, price decontrol might lead to a sudden acceleration of inflation.

In a properly functioning economy, excess demand in one sector would imply excess supply in others, and such imbalances would be corrected through relative price changes induced by market forces. Generalized excess demand and price inflation would in principle arise only if there were macroeconomic mismanagement—for example, budget deficits financed by money creation or excessive expansion of bank credit. The solution to such problems would thus lie not in price control, but in more restrictive macroeconomic policies.

Experience in China and elsewhere strongly suggests, however, that there are more deep-rooted causes of generalized excess demand in most socialist economies. These include the inefficiency and rigidity of centralized material allocation and production planning, the lack of concern among enterprise managers about cost and profitability, the absence of competition, and the "investment hunger" of enterprises and local governments (discussed later). The "seller's markets" that prevail for most commodities in such economies thus cannot be eliminated simply through tight fiscal and monetary policies.

The fact that chronic shortage appears to be a universal and permanent feature of the traditional system of socialist economic management suggests, however, that reform itself would create the necessary preconditions for price decontrol. This view is supported by China's experience in the past few years, especially in agriculture, where relaxation of direct controls has turned long-standing shortages into abundance. The same could happen in other sectors with the implementation of reforms in enterprise management, commerce, competition, and so on. Increases in specific prices could eliminate shortages by stimulating supply and reducing demand. These price increases, moreover, would tend to reduce purchasing power over (and hence the prices) of other goods, provided that the Government did not give compensating tax reductions or subsidies and more generally kept strict control of the budget balance and the availability of money and credit.

Implementation of the other reforms necessary to eliminate chronic shortages will take time, however, as will some of the required demand and supply responses in nonagricultural sectors. Smooth adjustment could also be impeded by downward inflexibility of some prices and of wages. In addition, China lacks experience of indirect macroeconomic management through fiscal and monetary policy, which would become much more important in a reformed economic system (see Box 10.2). Even countries with much greater experience in this regard still suffer from rising prices (although rapid inflation has almost invariably been the result of political irresponsibility, especially unwillingness to restrain consumption or investment to the limits set by production and external borrowing capacity). For these reasons, price decontrol probably has to be gradual though steady.

PRICE DECONTROL OF PRODUCER GOODS. The Government's strategy is to reduce administrative control of the prices of materials, machinery, and equipment in parallel with the gradual dismantling of annual production planning and allocation. This has already happened to a significant degree: the number of goods subject to production planning and allocation has declined. And for many goods, only a part of total output remains allocated, at a fixed price, to meet requirements for high-priority production. Enterprises acquire their remaining requirements at the prevailing market price. This two-tier pricing arrangement has substantial advantages over the former system, but also gives rise to certain problems, including inequities among using enterprises and the complexities involved in determining and regularly adjusting the state allocations. It should thus probably be only a transitional means of reforming the price and material allocation systems. One option would be to move the administered price of each commodity, say, halfway toward the market price in each time period (the length of the period being determined by progress in other aspects of reform mentioned above), so that the two prices eventually converge. Another option—which could be combined with the first—would be to gradually reduce the share of output subject to allocation and administered prices until all transactions were at market prices.

DECONTROL OF CONSUMER PRICES. Though the prices of many minor items now float freely, the Government is especially hesitant about decontrolling the prices of other—essential or major—consumer goods. The immense inflation before Liberation has not been forgotten, and even slow inflation is regarded as unacceptable be-

cause of the costs it might inflict on certain—especially poorer—groups. There is also fear that initial moderate price increases might be greatly magnified by panic buying, especially because household bank deposits are now very large (at the end of 1984 they equaled 36 percent of the year's retail sales).

The experience of other countries suggests that these apprehensions are not without foundation, but can easily be exaggerated. Most increases in the prices of particular consumer goods will be offset by decreases in the prices of other consumer goods, provided that fiscal and monetary policies are prudent. Even if it is not possible to keep the consumer price level absolutely stable, most people are apparently adaptable enough to live easily with moderate inflation, especially if their incomes are increasing steadily in real terms. And although general indexation of incomes is not to be recommended (Chapter 9), the living standards of some vulnerable groups can be protected by indexation, as well as by allowing and encouraging greater household ownership of real assets such as housing.

Indeed, an early major increase in the extent of home ownership in urban areas could serve several related objectives. It could be accomplished by offering most state- or enterprise-owned residences for sale to their occupants, while at the same time announcing a schedule for substantial increases in their presently hugely subsidized rents. Though these rent increases should be compensated by wage and other income increases (Chapter 9), they would nonetheless give people an incentive to make use of their savings to purchase their homes, probably at a somewhat concessional price. This would lead to better maintenance of housing. It would provide many people with an asset that in other countries has proved an excellent hedge against inflation. And it would enable the state to absorb a large fraction of urban household bank deposits. (Toward this last objective, especially in rural areas where most housing is already privately owned, the Government might also encourage lump-sum contributions to pension funds—as mentioned earlier and in Chapter 8).

Economic Planning

An implication of the preceding discussion is that the state should reduce its direct involvement in many economic areas, including production, commerce, prices, and employment. This would release resources, financial and human, for much needed increases in state activity in other areas of economic and social importance. Moreover, it will continue to be the primary responsibility of the state to guide the country's overall development. This will, however, require a broader and fundamentally different concept of planning than in the past.

New Approach to Planning

Direct control over economic activities has been the single most important feature of China's past management system. Three main instruments may be distinguished: physical planning of production, centralized allocation of materials, and budgetary grants for fixed investment. Together, these instruments constituted a system for managing the economy mainly by controlling supply. What was not controlled was not planned in any meaningful way. The central plan for coal production and allocation, for instance, did not include output from coal mines controlled by provincial authorities; provincial plans for coal did not include output from mines belonging to rural communes and brigades. Similarly, provincial investment plans did not take account of investment projects financed either by the central government or by collective enterprises. In fact, often the absence of control implied the absence not only of planning, but also of knowledge: provincial authorities had little knowledge of where output from centrally controlled enterprises was allocated or of the overall level and content of investment activities in the province. It is this notion that direct control equals planning that causes some in China to fear that a reduction of direct control must mean the erosion of planning.

Planning in a meaningful sense must extend beyond activities under direct state control, and indeed in a reformed system a large part of the planning effort will involve measures of an indirect nature. Reforms that have already been introduced, as well as possible further changes discussed in earlier sections, will mean that farmers and enterprises have greater latitude to make their own supply decisions and to use various market channels for their sales. Central control over investment allocation could also be reduced. There will thus be a far greater number of decisionmakers, each with some control over a part of national resources. Planning will accordingly and increasingly have to involve determination of the economic environment within which relatively independent economic agents—farmers, enterprises, financial institutions—operate.

This raises the question of whether greater reliance on indirect controls would reduce the Government's ability to manage the economy. In this regard, it seems important to recognize that—as discussed above—direct controls are inevitably limited in scope, while indirect controls generally influence the whole economy. An additional drawback of direct, as compared with indirect, control is that it must be shared among vertically distinguished sectors, or horizontally divided localities, or some compromise between the two, which leads—as is well known in China—to autarkic tendencies and segmentation of the economic management effort. On balance, then, indirect controls appear potentially at least as effective as direct controls in economic management and almost certainly more efficient.

A second and closely related question concerns the extent to which a different mix of direct and indirect

controls will lead to more uncertainty. The number of economic decisionmakers is, after all, greatly increased, and their objectives are not mutually consistent, nor necessarily in harmony with the Government's objectives. Much will thus depend on the clarity and stability of medium-term policies, which constitute the core of the development plan; the better these are enunciated, the less the uncertainty surrounding decisionmakers or other economic agents, and the less the chances of their decisions having a destabilizing effect. Even so, indirect control involves a relationship between instruments and objectives that can never be precise, since it depends on the responses of a multitude of individual decisionmakers, including farmers, enterprises, collectives, and consumers. It is impossible to predict their behavior with complete accuracy, and therefore the instruments used will never be exactly what is needed to achieve particular objectives; the residual is a source of uncertainty that defies policy intervention. This shortcoming of indirect control may be no greater than some of the shortcomings of the traditional system of direct control. But especially in the early stages of reform, when the coordinated use of indirect instruments of control is still a new concept, planning and policy will need a high degree of flexibility and responsiveness.

Of major importance to the new concept of planning is the newly established view in China that planning and markets can coexist and develop harmoniously. Although the potential for clashes between direct and indirect controls should not be forgotten, and although the governments of other countries differ widely in their attitudes toward markets and planning, international experience tends to support the present Chinese view. Planning has been used to a differing extent between countries and over time, and it is not easy to generalize about its efficacy, especially since actual developments cannot be directly attributed to the extent or quality of planning. But where market mechanisms were neglected or not taken sufficiently into account, planning was usually less effective and national priorities became distorted, often with inefficient use of scarce resources. Conversely, there is considerable evidence that planning can be strengthened if it is exercised in a way that allows market forces to reinforce rather than oppose it.

Mutually consistent roles for plan and market imply that planning must be based on managing demand as well as supply. This is essentially because it is the growing level and evolving structure of demand, reflecting the rising prosperity of the society, that should mainly drive the changing composition of supply. In a large part of the economy, planning is thus mainly a matter of the state's managing and guiding changing demand, with supply responding through the decentralized decisions of peasant households and enterprises. Mandatory planning of supply, involving directives from planners or other state administrative organs, will still be essential in developing infrastructure and in regulating part or all of the production and use of certain commodities. For a large and growing proportion of economic activities, however, plan objectives should be realized through guidance, including manipulation of taxes and credits to influence the relative profitability of different sorts of production and investment.

ANNUAL PLANNING. The nature of annual planning in the future depends on what happens to the material allocation system. Without centralized material allocation, annual physical planning of production loses much of its meaning. China has already reduced, and is continuing to reduce, the scope of mandatory production targets and material allocation. The question is now whether they could be abandoned altogether in the near future, weighing the possible benefits of retaining the present system against its costs, including the incentives it creates for local governments at all levels, as well as enterprises, to invest for self-sufficiency and assured supply. The experience of Hungary, which abandoned directive production planning in a single step in 1968, strongly suggests that such a change would not disrupt or destabilize the economy—though, of course, Hungary is a far smaller country than China. But it would cause annual plans to become mainly the step-wise implementation of the medium-term plan. This should be closely linked to the budget cycle.

Annual planning and budgeting in a mainly indirectly controlled economy also involves regulating the overall pace and stability of growth through fiscal, monetary, and exchange rate policies (rather than—as in the past—through direct intervention in production, investment, prices, and foreign trade). Among other things, maintenance of short-term macroeconomic stability involves the manipulation of taxes, government expenditures, money and credit (see Box 10.2), and the exchange rate to offset temporary fluctuations in economic activity of domestic or external origin.

The experience of other countries shows that such indirect macroeconomic management is not easy, although China is fortunate in being a large and diverse economy, with a relatively small foreign trade sector. But experience elsewhere has also provided much useful information concerning the coordinated use of fiscal, monetary, and related policies, which have been perhaps the main subject of theoretical and empirical research among Western economists during the past half century. China could benefit from this body of information and experience, possibly in part through contact with organizations such as the International Monetary Fund.

POLICY PLANNING. The planning of economic policies is the central element in a planning system that places limited reliance on direct controls. It attempts to use available instruments in ways that influence the decisions of market participants, bringing these into line with the objectives of medium- and long-term development. Economic policies need to form a coherent and internally consistent package rather than to be formulated individually. The translation of development objectives into a set of policies that directly and indirectly guide the development process thus requires considerable coordination within the government—more than now exists in China. Governments are not monolithic, and the interpretation of general development objectives in terms of responsibilities and actions may differ among ministries and between central and lower-level government organizations. While it is essential for each agency to look at its own responsibilities in the wider context of national development, it is equally essential for one government agency to have the analytical capability to develop comprehensive policy scenarios and to present these as the basis for policy decisions by all the agencies concerned.

Policies cannot be expected to achieve the desired impact immediately, and policy planning must have a medium-term (three- to five-year) horizon. Moreover, any set of policies agreed for the medium term will require phased implementation and may need to be adjusted in light of changing economic circumstances and assessments of effectiveness. Examples abound in China and abroad of economic policies that were appropriate and effective for several years, but lost their usefulness as the economic structure gradually shifted. These same policies have frequently ended up as stumbling blocks for policy reform. Particularly in countries expecting rapid structural and technological change, as in China over the next few decades, an argument can be made for the promulgation of policies for strictly limited periods, at the end of which they expire unless explicitly renewed.

In preceding chapters, the need for policy planning has been discussed in several contexts: guiding price trends and ensuring price stability for agricultural products; leading the technological transformation of industry; correcting distorted energy prices; decreasing the rural-urban income gap; changing and extending the social security system; assisting poor and backward localities; and using foreign trade to promote economic efficiency. These are issues that cannot be dealt with through short-term actions or with a single policy instrument. Also, the effects of the necessary policies are pervasive and their macroeconomic consequences difficult to assess. There are moreover alternative ways of addressing these issues, each with its own costs and benefits. Comprehensive analysis of alternative scenarios is needed, on which decisions can be based, but the institutional capability for doing this does not yet seem to exist in China.

The medium-term plan is thus the core of the entire planning system, serving as the vehicle for policy adjustment and change, and as the instrument to forge the consensus needed about those policies between all the agencies concerned. And it is medium-term policy planning that should become the main responsibility of the State Planning Commission, or of some other high-level organ without specific responsibility for implementing any particular set of policies. This in turn will require development and strengthening of the statistical and analytical capability to evaluate and study the current situation, to offer comprehensive programs of policies to address specific issues, including time phasing for implementing the programs, and to monitor program implementation.

PROVINCIAL PLANNING. The division of responsibility between central and local governments is a difficult issue that cannot be resolved quickly. It appears consistent with the direction of reform that the central government would increasingly concentrate on policy planning while planning of much infrastructure development and most social services would take place at lower levels.

Indeed, the consideration being given in China to delegating major responsibility for planning to provincial governments, or perhaps even to municipal authorities, which would also have responsibility for surrounding rural areas, seems to fit quite well with the new approach to planning suggested above. Provincial governments should be able to monitor and project the growth of production, the creation of new employment opportunities, and the generation of incomes within provincial boundaries. Their proximity to lower-level authorities and markets should allow them to identify problem areas and remedies quickly. Moreover, provinces are large enough to be able to remove bottlenecks by reallocating resources, to promote promising investments, and to ensure a fair distribution of the benefits from growth within their boundaries.

Over the next two decades, interprovincial trade will rapidly gain in importance, overcoming past autarkic tendencies. Thus the national economy will be more integrated, but the central government will correspondingly need to promote more consistency among the various provincial production and investment plans. The Government will also need to monitor and regulate the levels of saving and investment in different provinces and flows of investment funds among provinces—especially between those with widely differing income levels. These flows will partly involve transfers through the central budget, but the Government may also wish to participate in investments across provincial boundaries and to influence flows through the banking system.

LONG-TERM PLANNING. Although the medium-term plan can function as the core of all other planning activities, it may not provide a sufficient framework for all

planning efforts. Particularly in sectors where long lead times are required for new investments, or where a long-term technological strategy is essential, there is a need for a longer perspective, say, fifteen to twenty-five years. Planning for these sectors will require the framework of a longer-term view—not necessarily very precise or detailed—of the whole economy. The sector plans are unlikely to be fully consistent with the overall long-term framework; some may be subject to a significant margin of error or present alternative scenarios. The essence of long-term planning is, rather, to anticipate possible basic problems, so that timely policy adjustments can avoid otherwise insuperable bottlenecks or imbalances.

France and Japan, for example, were selective in choosing the sectors for planning; their objective was to make these sectors more efficient and enable them to face international competition. Both countries emphasized consultation with the enterprises in the industries concerned and the need for a consensus. France's planning agency was not sufficiently highly placed in the government to have powers of direct enforcement, but merely tried persuasion, backed by investment subsidies. In Japan, the leading role was assumed by the Ministry of International Trade and Industry, which could back up its strong views about the course and character of industrialization with resources and policy instruments, but still relied mainly on consensus and allowed dissenting views. (Japanese experience in strategic planning of technological development was discussed in Chapter 7. Comparable South Korean experience in electronics is described in Box 7.3.)

Sector plans should not be limited to targets for output, efficiency, and profitability, but should also address such issues as changing the organization of production; the number, size, and location of enterprises in the sector; and therefore the closure, merger, or expansion of existing production facilities and the establishment of new ones. They should also address the creation or strengthening of research capability and the training of skilled staff. Ministries responsible for formulating plans and consulting with enterprises about their implementation must be well informed on the state of technology in their sector, both in China and abroad, and capable of disseminating this knowledge. Thus the role of sectoral ministries in China could change greatly, yet remain of critical importance to the task of development management.

Tools for Planning

The quality of planning depends not only on the way it is organized, but also on the quality and relevance of information received. Adequate analytical capability is needed to handle inflows and outflows of information.

INFORMATION SYSTEMS. The quality and timeliness of decisionmaking depends on the information available to decisionmakers. At present in China, both vertical and horizontal information flows are inadequate for sound policy planning. The process of aggregating data before passing them to the next highest level of government precludes analysis of more detailed data at higher levels, even for the main economic indicators, as well as different aggregations of data. Another problem is that data are passed up through vertical channels, but not adequately distributed horizontally. Thus, a provincial planning commission may not be aware of the production, employment, or investment data that state enterprises under central control are reporting to their ministry.

For proper planning and delegation to lower levels, further work is needed to manage existing and new data flows in ways that provide meaningful information. Comprehensive tabulations need to be designed to meet the particular requirements of each level of government for data on production and consumption, financial flows, interprovincial and external trade, and investment expenditures. Most important, users—economic researchers, policy analysts, planners—should have a major voice in deciding what types of data are collected and should have access to the primary data base.

In a decentralized economy, the behavior of the numerous economic agents controlling resources needs to be understood when designing economic policies. This requires collection and analysis of data on the behavior of economic agents—a field of statistical activity barely touched in China. The most obvious gap concerns consumer behavior, in different parts of the country and at different income levels, in response to changes in incomes and prices. Although household budget data are collected, they are not processed in ways that allow much economic analysis. Similarly, on the production side, little is known about the supply response to prices and other market forces, whether in the agricultural or the nonagricultural sectors.

ANALYTICAL TOOLS. The range of analytical devices for planning includes both the very simple and the very sophisticated, as well as both specific and comprehensive tools. In many countries, planners use quantitative models for policy analysis. Only a few countries have, however, constructed models for medium-term planning; even fewer have succeeded in putting these models to timely and effective use. The task is far from easy, requiring the allocation of scarce talent, well in advance of the planning process, to a demanding and even risky undertaking.

Models also have to be designed with specific objectives in mind. A set of specifically focused, but not exactly mutually consistent, models is usually more helpful for policy purposes than a large multipurpose model. For example, the multisectoral model described in Chapter 2 is useful mainly to analyze the long-term effects of changes in the level and composition of final demand (consumption, investment, and external trade) on production, investment, and employment. It is not suited either to analyzing most problems of specific sectors (it was supplemented with more detailed agriculture and energy projections), or to investigating some other macroeconomic issues, such as urban-rural income distribution or government revenue-raising (which Chapters 5 and 9 addressed with simpler projections).

Constructing models for these and other purposes, and maintaining approximate consistency among them, could be made easier if the various kinds of data collected in China were based on an overall accounting framework such as a social accounting matrix. Many statistics are collected for administrative purposes, and their coverage is limited by administrative needs and spheres of control. Economic analysis, in contrast, requires data by sectors, commodities, or economic activities, irrespective of the agencies involved in their production, trade, or use. Social accounting could provide the necessary integrating framework and thus assist policy analysis and planning.

The potential contribution of economic modeling, or other sophisticated analytical tools, should not be exaggerated. The effectiveness of all tools depends not so much on their technical complexity, but on how they are used. The quality of economic planning in China will thus depend largely on the common sense and good judgment of planners, on improved economic training (not only for planners, but also for decisionmakers throughout the economy), and on wider dissemination and discussion of economic and social information.

Overview

Coordinated changes are required in many aspects of China's economic and social system. One set of changes involves increasing the dynamism and efficiency of the economy through greater autonomy for peasant households and enterprises, more lively competition, and promotion of collectives and individual enterprises to complement the state sector. International experience, as well as experience in China over the past few years, makes clear the need for coordination among the various elements of this economic reform. To be efficient, for instance, enterprises must be motivated to increase their profits and to respond to demand; they must be given independence and freedom of maneuver; they must be faced with economically rational prices; and they must be subjected to competition. None of these elements is individually easy to establish, and the absence of any one of them reduces or nullifies the benefits of the others: for example, appropriate motivation produces bad investment decisions if prices are irrational and exploitation of customers in the absence of competition.

An enlarged role for markets and competition, though it will undoubtedly improve efficiency and accelerate technological progress, could potentially also have undesirable economic and social consequences, including unemployment, unacceptably low (and high) wages, bankruptcy of enterprises and dismissal of workers, and the poor and the backward being left further behind in the development process. Increasingly, there will thus be tensions between concern for greater efficiency and dynamism, and concern about fairness and about the very poor. These tensions could become especially great in China, not only because its socialist ideology emphasizes fairness and poverty alleviation, but also because many of China's current social institutions and instruments are ill-suited to deal with the emerging problems of a reformed economy. Reform in China must therefore include strengthening policies and institutions to address social and equity concerns, and especially to help the poor.

Reform in China must also involve strengthening the state's ability to direct the future course of economic and social development, combining more limited use of direct controls with much expanded use of indirect controls. The range of instruments available to the Government will need to be selectively used in a consistent, purposeful, and effective manner. Many of these instruments will need to be designed to influence decisionmakers throughout the economy, rather than to confine or prescribe the behavior of specific economic units.

On each of these fronts, there are promising ways forward, but also problems and hard choices to be faced. In addition, it is hard to overstate the importance and difficulty of striking a correct balance among the three. Very few countries have combined state and market regulation in such a way as to produce rapid and efficient growth, and fewer still have also managed to avoid intolerable poverty among substantial segments of their populations. On the contrary, there are far more countries in which unhappy combinations of plan, market, and social institutions have produced neither rapid growth, nor efficiency, nor poverty reduction.

There is thus a vital need to guard against losing the strengths of the existing system—its capacity to mobilize resources, as well as to help the poor—in the course of overcoming its weaknesses. This will surely not deter China—in the past, a successful pioneer in many areas—from moving ahead. But it argues for a gradual advance, with experimentation and evaluation at each step, even though a one-stroke change would in principle involve fewer internal inconsistencies. Experience in Eastern Europe also suggests the importance of moving steadily and of trying to avoid ill-judged steps in the direction of market regulation that subsequently have to be reversed or administratively tampered with, thus creating needless uncertainty. Indeed, quite apart from the immense size of China and the need to avoid major mistakes, the type of reform envisaged by China's leaders requires a new way of thinking, and a new pattern of behavior, from economic decisionmakers at all levels that can come only gradually.

Not all the steps need be small, though. In some cases, despite the greater risk of error, it may be best to introduce substantial packages of simultaneous reforms. Nor need progress be slow. What has been accomplished in China's rural areas in the past few years has provided not only an example, but also an excellent opportunity and indeed a vital need for complementary and similarly rapid progress in the urban economy. Though in many ways more complicated and troublesome than rural reform, urban economic reform probably has the advantage of not needing to be so uniform. Other countries—notably France and Japan in recent decades—have successfully applied different management methods in different sectors and enterprises, and China should be able to do the same, while constantly seeking to refine and improve the mixture.

In system reform, and in the many other areas covered by this report, both the potential for progress and the problems involved are so large, and there is so much that is without historical precedent, that an even-handed and credible conclusion may be impossible. At a minimum, though, China's long-term development objectives seem attainable in principle, and if recent experience is any guide, there is a good chance that they will be attained in practice.

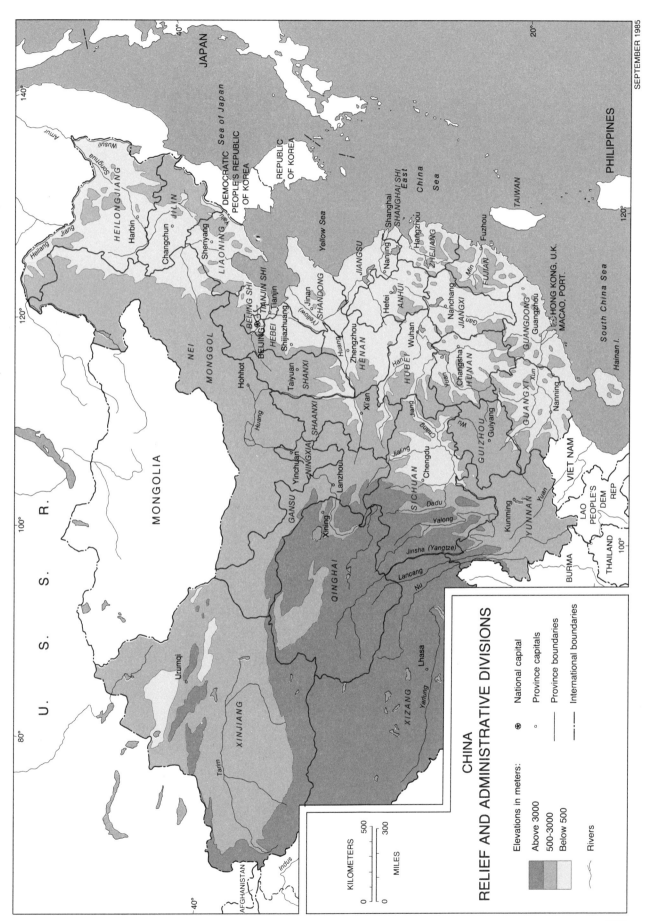

CHINA
RELIEF AND ADMINISTRATIVE DIVISIONS

Elevations in meters:
⊛ National capital
○ Province capitals
— Province boundaries
—··— International boundaries

Above 3000
500-3000
Below 500

〜 Rivers

KILOMETERS
0 300 500

MILES
0

SEPTEMBER 1985

183

The most recent World Bank publications are described in the annual spring and fall lists. The latest edition is available free of charge from Publications Sales Unit, Department B, The World Bank, Washington, D.C. 20433, U.S.A.